Rethinking the Foundations of Modern Political Thought

Quentin Skinner's classic study of *The Foundations of Modern Political Thought* was published by Cambridge in 1978. This was the first of a series of outstanding publications that have changed forever the way the history of political thought is taught and practised. *Rethinking the Foundations of Modern Political Thought* looks afresh at the impact of the original work, asks why it still matters and considers a number of significant agendas that it still inspires. A distinguished international team of contributors has been assembled, including many of the leading intellectual historians writing today, and the result is an unusually powerful and cohesive contribution to the history of ideas, of interest to large numbers of students of early modern history and political thought. In conclusion, Quentin Skinner replies to each chapter and presents his own thoughts on the latest trends and the future direction of the history of political thought.

ANNABEL BRETT is Senior Lecturer in History at the University of Cambridge and a Fellow of Gonville and Caius College. Her previous publications include *Liberty, Right and Nature: Individual Rights in Later Scholastic Thought* (Cambridge, 1997).

JAMES TULLY is the Distinguished Professor of Political Science, Law, Indigenous Governance and Philosophy at the University of Victoria. His previous publications include *An Approach to Political Philosophy* (Cambridge, 1993) and *Strange Multiplicity* (Cambridge, 1995).

HOLLY HAMILTON-BLEAKLEY earned a BA in Economics from Wellesley College, and an MPhil and PhD in intellectual history and political thought from the University of Cambridge. She has published several articles on late medieval moral and political philosophy, and is currently working on a monograph on medieval and early modern conceptions of moral science.

T0345446

Rethinking the Foundations of Modern Political Thought

Edited by

Annabel Brett and James Tully with
Holly Hamilton-Bleakley

CAMBRIDGE
UNIVERSITY PRESS

CAMBRIDGE
UNIVERSITY PRESS

University Printing House, Cambridge CB2 8BS, United Kingdom

Published in the United States of America by Cambridge University Press, New York

Cambridge University Press is part of the University of Cambridge.

It furthers the University's mission by disseminating knowledge in the pursuit of
education, learning and research at the highest international levels of excellence.

www.cambridge.org
Information on this title: www.cambridge.org/9780521615037

© Cambridge University Press 2006

First published 2006

A catalogue record for this publication is available from the British Library

ISBN 978-0-521-84979-1 Hardback
ISBN 978-0-521-61503-7 Paperback

Contents

Contributors

DAVID ARMITAGE is Professor of History at Harvard University.

WARREN BOUTCHER is Reader in Renaissance Studies at Queen Mary, University of London.

ANNABEL S. BRETT is Senior Lecturer in History at the University of Cambridge and a Fellow of Gonville and Caius College.

CATHY CURTIS is a Lecturer in Political Theory at the University of New South Wales.

MARTIN VAN GELDEREN holds the Chair of European History at the European University Institute, Florence.

MARCO GEUNA is Associate Professor of the History of Political Thought at the University of Milan.

MARK GOLDIE is Senior Lecturer in History at the University of Cambridge and a Fellow of Churchill College.

HOLLY HAMILTON-BLEAKLEY is an independent scholar.

KINCH HOEKSTRA is Fellow in Ancient and Modern Philosophy and Senior Tutor at Balliol College, Oxford.

HARRO HÖPFL is Reader in the Department of Accounting, Finance and Management at the University of Essex, and was previously Senior Lecturer in Political Theory at Lancaster University.

J. G. A. POCOCK is Harry C. Black Emeritus Professor of History at The Johns Hopkins University.

QUENTIN SKINNER is the Regius Professor of Modern History at the University of Cambridge.

RICHARD TUCK is the Frank G. Thomson Professor of Government at Harvard University.

JAMES TULLY is the Distinguished Professor of Political Science, Law, Indigenous Governance and Philosophy at the University of Victoria.

Preface

James Tully and Annabel Brett

The present volume has its beginnings in a conference of the same title held at Gonville and Caius College, Cambridge, in 2003 – the twenty-fifth anniversary of the publication of *The Foundations of Modern Political Thought*. We would like to start by thanking everyone involved in making that event a success. To Holly Hamilton-Bleakley we owe both the original idea for the conference and an enormous amount of the work involved in organising it. Aysha Pollnitz and Jacqueline Rose helped us out with exemplary efficiency and cheerfulness. But our greatest thanks are, of course, due to our speakers, whose uniformly excellent papers and comments made for such a memorable and stimulating intellectual occasion. We can only regret that for reasons of space we were not able to include all their contributions in this volume, and we would like to express our gratitude in particular to David Colclough, Tim Hochstrasser, Kari Palonen and Joan Pau Rubies for their part in the proceedings. We would like to express our special gratitude to John Salmon, whom we remember for his generous help with the project and outstanding contribution to the history of European thought.

There are several reasons why, twenty-five years on, Quentin Skinner's *Foundations* presented an apt subject for the kind of rethinking we wanted to encourage. It was in many ways an act of rethinking itself. One of Skinner's stated aims in the preface to that volume was simply to write 'a more up-to-date survey' of the transition from medieval to early-modern political thought, taking into account the new research and approaches which had evolved since what he viewed as the last such attempt, Pierre Mesnard's *L'essor de la philosophie politique au XVIe siècle* of 1936. The episodes, figures and categories he deployed bear the distinctive mark of a prior tradition of analysis, going back to the work of his Cambridge predecessor John Neville Figgis at the beginning of the twentieth century. But his ambitions for the two volumes did not rest solely with integrating new research into an inherited analytical framework. As his Preface goes on to make plain, he wanted to rethink this material in such a way as to demonstrate two major new ideas of his own: one, that the story of this transition is the story of the genesis of the modern concept of the state; two, that to write this story means writing not, in the first instance, about the 'great texts' of the Western canon, but about the normative vocabularies or ideologies that constituted the political discourse of the time. Only within these vocabularies, Skinner famously postulated, do the great texts find their intentionality and their sense; only in this context can continuity, change and transition be located.

In this sense, Skinner's book looked both backward, towards a by-then classic tradition of writing, and forward, towards a new vision of what the history of political thought could look like. The success of his Janus-faced *Foundations* is as remarkable as it is well known. Skinner effectively reconfigured the field of late-medieval and early-modern political thought, and a subsequent generation of scholars has gone to work within its outlines, inspired by his map and his method. Nonetheless, as they have done so, they have inevitably pushed at some of the boundaries he set out, questioning, refining or expanding both the substantive analyses and their methodological premises. Indeed, Skinner himself has to some extent done the very same thing. In the spirit of the original, the aim of the conference and of this volume was both to look back at these developments and assess their significance, and at the same time, more importantly, to look forward to where these new developments point us now at the beginning of the twenty-first century.

The Foundations of Modern Political Thought was not a book about method in itself, but it was one that self-consciously aimed to exemplify a method. Accordingly, the first two chapters of this book devote themselves, by way of introduction, to that theme. Mark Goldie situates *Foundations* within the intellectual context of Cambridge in the 1970s, while Holly Hamilton-Bleakley views the work from the perspective of Skinner's methodological dialogue with Collingwood, Wittgenstein and Austin. The following four chapters centre largely on volume I of *Foundations* and are concerned with two themes to which Skinner has continued to devote a great deal of attention: Renaissance civic humanism and liberty. John Pocock goes back to the book's founding moment to characterise its original dialectical intentions and critically to assess some of the directions Skinner's work on these themes has taken since. Marco Geuna begins by examining the reconstruction, in *Foundations*, of an Italian pre-humanist rhetorical culture, and goes on to consider its implications for Skinner's later work on Machiavelli and on the 'neo-Roman' idea of liberty in *Liberty before Liberalism*. Warren Boutcher looks at the period through a different lens, questioning the possibility, within Renaissance print culture, of recovering the intentions of authors and hence the moment of historical agency on which Skinner's method ultimately turns. Finally, Cathy Curtis takes an author who looms large in Skinner's story of Renaissance political thought, Thomas More, re-examining the nature of his republicanism and questioning the explanatory power of 'neo-Roman' terminology in relation to his work.

The next three chapters take up the major themes of the second volume of *Foundations*, Skinner's original and powerful reinterpretations of scholastic political thought in the Counter-Reformation and Calvinist resistance theories. Harro Höpfl questions the historical propriety of some of Skinner's categories and, to some extent, the whole notion of a 'scholastic political thought' as such. Annabel Brett considers the place of the scholastics within the story of an emerging concept of the state, asking how far it changes our picture of both to include their reflection on non-European peoples. Martin van Gelderen resituates Skinner's work on resistance theories with a new examination of the contrast between Calvinist and Lutheran discourse, extending the analysis to seventeenth-century Protestant theories of resistance up to Locke, as Skinner himself had intimated in *Foundations*.

Pursuing this same direction, chs. 10–12 deal with Thomas Hobbes and the modern concept of the state, around which *Foundations* was ultimately orientated. Richard Tuck and Kinch Hoekstra debate the question of whether or not Hobbes is a democratic theorist, a question which, as they show, involves considering at a very deep level his understanding of the nature and function of the state. By contrast, David Armitage looks beyond the territorial state to question Hobbes's place in the theory of international relations and its history. Finally, Quentin Skinner offers his own reflections both on *Foundations* itself and on the chapters, replying to some of their strongest claims, clarifying some of his own, and offering new and characteristically enlightening thoughts on these controversial and important topics.

In the process of editing this volume we have incurred further debts which it is a pleasure to acknowledge here. We would like to thank Richard Fisher of Cambridge University Press for his continuing encouragement and support. We would also like to thank Conor Donaldson, Mike Simpson and our copy-editor Hilary Scannell for coping admirably and patiently with the minutiae of the editing process. We are also grateful to the Pierre Trudeau Foundation of Canada and to Gonville and Caius College, Cambridge, for their support. But we must end with our warmest appreciation and gratitude to Quentin Skinner for everything he has done in connection with this project, and for his continuing intellectual and personal inspiration to us and to so many others of his students and colleagues.

Part I

Introduction

1   The context of *The Foundations*

Mark Goldie

I

Quentin Skinner's early work was devoted as much to questions of method as to substantive historical exposition. Indeed, he became known to far wider audiences through his methodological essays than through those in his first field of research, the political thought of the English Revolution.[1] His most cited article, 'Meaning and Understanding in the History of Ideas', published in 1969, was strikingly polemical in the anathemas it pronounced upon the practices of his colleagues.[2] Accordingly, when *The Foundations of Modern Political Thought* appeared in 1978, its reviewers were as much concerned to assess the book in relation to its author's methodological injunctions as to judge its contribution to its historical topic. *Foundations* was, among much else, a heroic hostage to fortune, and there was no little *Schadenfreude* among those reviewers who claimed it had failed its author's own tests.

In this essay I revisit some aspects of Skinner's approach to intellectual history, taking note of early reactions to *Foundations*. My aims are threefold. First, I explore some of the impediments, within the historical profession in the 1960s, which Skinner believed stood in the way of the study of intellectual history. Second, I consider a specific criticism of *Foundations*, that it was overly committed to a teleological account of the emergence of the modern theory of the sovereign state. Third, interwoven throughout, I stress the extent to which Skinner's work was indebted to the German social theorist Max Weber. In this discussion it should be kept in mind that a principal context for *Foundations* lay in the practice of history in Britain in the 1960s, for the book's origins lay in lectures which Skinner first delivered in Cambridge in 1965.

For their comments on an earlier draft of this essay I am indebted to Holly Hamilton-Bleakley, Clare Jackson, Jacqueline Rose and Sylvana Tomaselli.

Short reviews of *Foundations* are cited by author and journal title only.
[1] Many of Skinner's essays are now collected, in revised form, in Quentin Skinner, *Visions of Politics*, 3 vols. (Cambridge: Cambridge University Press, 2002). His principal early essay on the seventeenth century was 'History and Ideology in the English Revolution', *Historical Journal* 8 (1965), pp. 151–78, repr. in Skinner, *Visions*, III.
[2] Quentin Skinner, *History and Theory* 8 (1969), pp. 3–53; repr. in Skinner, *Visions*, I.

What has, quite properly, dominated discussion of Skinner's methodology is his indebtedness to the philosophy of language enunciated by R. G. Collingwood, J. L. Austin and the later Wittgenstein, and it is to this topic that Holly Hamilton-Bleakley's companion chapter in the present volume is devoted. Less readily noticed is the rather different source of inspiration in Max Weber, who casts long shadows over *Foundations*, and whose *Economy and Society* is the first work cited in it, just ahead of a compliment to Collingwood.[3] The widespread revival of interest in Weber in the 1960s was instrumental in the effort to remove the barriers that stood in the way of the refurbishment of intellectual history. By the early 1970s Skinner was addressing closely theories of action and explanation as conceived within the Weberian tradition of theoretical sociology.[4] This interest was enhanced when he became a member of the Institute for Advanced Study at Princeton in 1974, for in such social scientists as Clifford Geertz he encountered a tradition of hostility to positivism which could be traced to Weber's concept of *verstehen*, a concept which placed at the heart of the understanding of social action individual agents' own subjective meanings.

In the middle decades of the twentieth century a strong version of positivism was implicit, and sometimes explicit, in the work of a broad swathe of British historians, especially those who studied 'high' politics, and who indeed tended to regard 'high' politics as the essence of their discipline. Skinner's critique of his fellow practitioners within intellectual history is well known – 'Meaning and Understanding in the History of Ideas' is chiefly addressed to them – but his indictment of the 'high' political historians, who deprecated intellectual history altogether, deserves notice. He devoted essays to dissecting the assumptions of two of the doyens of the British historical profession, Lewis Namier and Geoffrey Elton. His critique of Namier appeared in 1974 in a *Festschrift* for his Cambridge colleague J. H. Plumb.[5] Plumb had, in *The Growth of Political Stability in England, 1675–1725* (1967), declared his own liberation from Namier's strictures, and thereby opened a route to reinstating the history of political thought in the era of the first English political parties.

[3] Quentin Skinner, *The Foundations of Modern Political Thought*, 2 vols. (Cambridge: Cambridge University Press, 1978), I, p. x. Max Weber, *Economy and Society: an Outline of Interpretive Sociology*, eds. Guenther Roth and Claus Wittich, 2 vols. (Berkeley: University of California Press, 1978). The Weberian element in Skinner's work is well brought out in Kari Palonen, *Quentin Skinner: History, Politics, Rhetoric* (Cambridge: Polity Press, 2003).

[4] Quentin Skinner, '"Social Meaning" and the Explanation of Social Action', in Peter Laslett, W. G. Runciman and Quentin Skinner (eds.), *Philosophy, Politics, and Society*, 4th series (Oxford: Blackwell, 1972), repr. in Skinner, *Visions*, I; Quentin Skinner, 'Some Problems in the Analysis of Political Thought and Action', *Political Theory* 2 (1974), pp. 277–303; repr. in Skinner, *Visions*, I.

[5] Quentin Skinner, 'The Principles and Practices of Opposition: the Case of Bolingbroke versus Walpole', in Neil McKendrick (ed.), *Historical Perspectives: Studies in English Political Thought and Society* (London: Europa, 1974), pp. 93–128, repr. in Skinner, *Visions*, III.

Skinner's withering criticism of Elton, the senior professor in his own university, did not appear until much later, in 1997. He pointed to Elton's 'cult of the fact', his narrow veneration of political history, his insistence that intellectual history was 'removed from real life' and the striking lopsidedness of his views about what kinds of history were 'hard' and 'real'.[6]

Namier and Elton were historians of whom it might almost be said that their guiding principle was the rejection of historical agents' own accounts of what they were doing. Namier regarded ideology, the exposition of normative ideas about social and political life, as pathological, a systematic distortion of how things really were. For him, the historian was an unmasker of ideology, who lays bare the material foundations of political action. The fault of intellectual historians was that they were naive enough to take seriously the utterances of historical agents. The arguments which princes, courtiers, statesmen and intellectuals put forth were so much sophistical self-justification, incidental to the dynamics of power and to the 'real' motives and interests of the actors. Ideologies were, in Namier's memorable term, mere 'flapdoodle'.[7] They were, to use more technical jargon, 'epiphenomenal'. The latter term was familiarly used by Marxists, and this points to the paradox that conservative practitioners of 'high' politics shared a fundamental assumption with Marxists, that what was argued and published by people in the past was not the vital material of history. Historians of ideas accordingly belonged, in Elton's words, in the 'scullery' of the historical profession and not in the 'drawing room'.[8]

Namierite and Eltonian canons of historical rectitude had two consequences for ordinary practice in historical research and writing. By their lights, manuscript archives were privileged above printed sources. Typically, the correspondence of politicians should assume precedence over the treatises, tracts and sermons of their times. A properly professional historian went to the Public Record Office and the county record office and not to the rare books library. While it was impossible to evade the obvious thought that nearly all historical work depended on studying the utterances of past agents, it was held that utterances in private correspondence were less compromised than those in public speech. Public speech was characteristically described as 'propaganda', and hence judged to be inherently distorted. Any historian who inhabited only the milieu of rhetorical affect and public persuasion was fundamentally debilitated. It was an argument which entailed a view about the authenticity of private utterance, as if private speech were exempt from 'ideology'.

---

[6] Quentin Skinner, 'The Practice of History and the Cult of the Fact', *Visions*, I, pp. 8–26, originally published in *Transactions of the Royal Historical Society* 7 (1997), pp. 301–16.

[7] L. B. Namier, *England in the Age of the American Revolution* (London: Macmillan, 1930), p. 95. For his general reflections on method see *Personalities and Power* (London: Macmillan, 1955).

[8] G. R. Elton, *Return to Essentials* (Cambridge: Cambridge University Press, 1991), p. 12; quoted in Skinner, 'The Practice of History and the Cult of the Fact', p. 14.

A second consequence for practice is found in the prose of much historical writing at mid-century. Historians provided analyses of events and motives, of causes and consequences, but tended to think it irrelevant or distracting to allow us to listen to the voices of the actors. They did not often quote the words of the people about whom they wrote. Virtually every development since the 1960s, whether it be the invitation to 'empathy' or the close relationship now existing between history and literature, has taught us to be better attuned to the languages of the past. While Namier and Elton worried about the corrupting effects of the betrothal of history to the social sciences, they scarcely imagined that their approach to history would turn out to be far more seriously challenged by the betrothal of history to literature. It is neither sociology, nor even hermeneutic philosophy, that has had greatest impact on how historians write, but rather literature. Historians of all kinds now think far more carefully about voice, genre, rhetoric and metaphor. They take it to be important to heed the self-descriptions of historical agents, and in turn to understand the public languages within which self-descriptions were embedded. While Skinner has warned against the more flaccid aspects of 'empathy', and has insisted that historians can have explanatory ambitions beyond redescription of how the world looked to past agents, none the less a fundamental ambition of *Foundations* was to be perspectival, to allow the reader a sense of how past actors understood and articulated their actions and intentions and, more particularly, how they justified themselves rhetorically in speaking to their contemporaries. 'Seeing things their way' is the simple injunction in the title of Skinner's recent introduction to his collected methodological essays.[9]

Skinner's 1974 essay against Namier focused on the era of Sir Robert Walpole, the third and fourth decades of the eighteenth century. He used his examination of Viscount Bolingbroke's celebrated political and literary assault on the Whig prime minister as a case study of his theorem that understanding ideology is a necessary part of explaining historical action. He conceded, with the Namierites, that it was not necessary to take the sincerity and putative elevated motives of the Bolingbrokeans at face value. Skinner is suspicious of historians' resort to categories of 'sincerity' and 'insincerity'. Sincerity is not something which can be established. We understand actors from the outside, by discerning what they publicly perform. Yet, on the other hand, against the Namierites, he denied that it was feasible to dismiss Bolingbroke's ideas as *ex post facto* rationalisations disguising material motives. Rather, Bolingbroke's appeal to traditional Whig ideals served to legitimate an otherwise seditious

---

[9] Skinner, *Visions*, I, ch. 1. On the uses and limits of 'interpretative charity' see ibid., I, ch. 3; and Quentin Skinner, 'The Rise of, Challenge to, and Prospects for a Collingwoodian Approach to the History of Political Thought', in Dario Castiglione and Iain Hampsher-Monk (eds.), *The History of Political Thought in National Context* (Cambridge: Cambridge University Press, 2001), pp. 175–88, at pp. 185–6.

programme of political opposition by aligning it with conventionally accept-able canons of patriotic rectitude. Bolingbroke's political programme was only possible in so far as it was rendered justifiable in the court of public discourse. Political action is predicated upon public legitimation.

Skinner's essay had a Weberian cast. While Weber did not flinch from the thought that relationships between human beings are relations of power, and that power is ultimately grounded in coercion, none the less power is rarely naked. In most societies, people are persuaded that the demands placed upon them are legitimate. This throws the weight of social explanation away from the exercise of force to the production of legitimacy. Weber provided an antidote to the Marxist tendency – and to all parallel tendencies on the political right – to dismiss the sphere of ideology as epiphenomenal to the material motors of history. Weber argued that ideologies function as enablers. Political agents are enabled to proceed if, and only if, they are successful at publicly construing their ambitions in terms which their audiences recognise as legitimate by the standards of their normative beliefs about what is honourable, virtuous, godly or patriotic. This shifts attention from specifying the interests which agents have to specifying the values which communities hold and the ways in which those values are transmuted by the discursively proficient. Political revolutions depend on conceptual revolutions. They involve a kind of legerdemain, in which the political innovator achieves a transformation while trailing the colours of conventional beliefs. Normative languages are the force-field within which ideologists function, and those languages may be deeply constraining of what is practically possible, or liberating for those skilled in reshaping the conventions.

Foundations was grounded in this set of assumptions. In the preface, for example, speaking of the humanist norm of 'honour', Skinner wrote:

Anyone who is anxious to have his behaviour recognised as that of a man of honour will find himself restricted to the performance of only a certain range of actions. Thus the problem facing an agent who wishes to legitimate what he is doing at the same time as gaining what he wants cannot simply be the instrumental problem of tailoring his normative language in order to fit his projects. It must in part be the problem of tailoring his projects in order to fit the available normative language.[10]

Throughout *Foundations*, the verb 'legitimate' and its cognates were perva-sive. The twelfth century, Skinner remarked, saw 'the formation of an ideology designed to legitimate the most aggressive of the Papacy's claims to rule'. The Huguenots set out to 'legitimate the first full-scale revolution within a modern European state'. Pierre du Moulin helped to 'legitimate the rule of absolute monarchy in France'.[11] Theorists were seen to be doing ideological work on behalf of some specified cause. They were said to meet 'pressing ideological

---

[10] Skinner, *Foundations*, I, pp. 12–13.   [11] Ibid., I, p. 14; II, pp. 241, 264.

needs', to perform 'ideological services' or to provide 'an armoury of ideological weapons'.[12] Ideas enabled action, but action was constrained by what could successfully be achieved in the work of legitimation. Not least of the consequences of this approach was that the world of ideas, construed as the production of legitimacy, was no longer disjoined from the history of 'actions' and 'interests'. Deeds are predicated upon the possibilities and constraints which words offer.

Max Weber exemplified his concept of legitimation in his classic study of *The Protestant Ethic and the Spirit of Capitalism* (1904). Here he countered the Marxist analysis which traced the genealogy of capitalism in the economic dynamics of the decline of feudalism. He suggested that capitalism owed its triumph to the ability of its early proponents to legitimate it in relation to prevailing religious values. On this argument, the Protestant ethic, with its godly injunctions to industriousness, its puritanical distaste for luxurious display and its preference for indefinitely deferred gratification, proved peculiarly suitable for sustaining commercial enterprise. To understand the emergence of capitalism it was necessary therefore to understand not only economics but also theology. In the early 1970s Skinner intended to write a major revaluation of the Weber thesis through an investigation of the transmutations of early-modern godly vocabulary as it came to be applied to the values of commercial society. How was it, for example, that commendations entailed in the notion of living in accordance with God's 'providence' came to be applied to 'provident' forms of conduct in the worldly lives of industrious and parsimonious capitalists? The project was abandoned, but elements of it surface in his writings.[13] It was a project which brought together Weber's concept of legitimation and the lexical preoccupations of linguistic philosophy, a fusion which has lain at the heart of Skinner's procedure.[14]

The emphasis on the history of ideologies in *Foundations* had a consequence for the way in which 'classic' authors and texts were treated. From the outset Skinner had been sceptical of the canonising of the classics. His 1969 essay, 'Meaning and Understanding', was originally entitled 'The Unimportance of the Great Texts in the History of Political Thought'.[15] The demotion of the classic texts was in part an entailment of the concept of legitimation. Theorists cannot be understood 'on their own terms', as engaging in unmediated intellectual activity, but in terms of the way they operate within prevailing conventions. Even at its most innovatory, political theory is necessarily conventional. Skinner's account of Thomas More, to take one instance, was woven into a collective account of Erasmus, Starkey, Elyot and Budé, for it was necessary to

---

[12] Skinner, *Foundations*, I, pp. 6, 11; II, p. 310.   [13] See the items cited in n. 4 above.
[14] See Palonen, *Skinner*, p. 53.
[15] P. Koikkalainen and S. Syrjämäki, 'On Encountering the Past: an Interview with Quentin Skinner', *Finnish Yearbook of Political Thought* 6 (2002), pp. 34–63, at p. 35.

investigate a wide body of texts in order to establish the moral norms embedded in the ordinary language of debate. The study of ideologies required the investigation of genres, schools, traditions and shared beliefs rather than singular texts. The range of hitherto hidden authors recovered in *Foundations* was remarkable, from Azo to Zasius and Accolti to Zabarella. It was a striking feature of the book that no chapter heading contained a person's name. Rather, chapters had such titles as 'The Florentine Renaissance' or 'The Duty to Resist'. This elementary fact about the book's plan liberated it from the litany of pedestalled classics that structured most textbooks: Machiavelli, More, Bodin, Hobbes, Locke. *Foundations* was, as one reviewer remarked, 'collectivist' history of political thought.[16] For those reviewers who were attached to a more heroic conception of political philosophy, Skinner's book was demeaning to philosophy. It flattened the distinction between, in Michael Oakeshott's words, genuine 'philosophical reflection' and the 'forensic' jousting of pamphleteers engaged in 'mere justification'. Judith Shklar likewise wished Skinner had distinguished more strongly the 'continuously interesting political theorists from those who only concern us as part of the general scenery'.[17]

Foundations implicitly posed large questions about canonicity and about the genres that should fall within the purview of the 'history of political thought'. *Foundations* based itself primarily, and more or less traditionally, on treatises and tracts which addressed politics as a distinctive field of human activity and moral difficulty. At the same time, it drew attention to less familiar sources. It encompassed works by theologians, diplomats, lawyers and educationists, together with advice books, panegyrics, city chronicles, annotations in the Geneva Bible and plays by Shakespeare and John Bale.[18] As Shklar remarked, once the canon is broadened there is unavoidable slippage towards highly unstable territory as regards genre.[19] In the decades since *Foundations* was published, generic expansiveness has become much more comprehensive. Skinner's intimations, for example, of the importance of the history of curricula are carried forward more fully, not least in his own study of the context of Hobbes's civil science.[20] He also argued, in an essay of 1987, for a major enlargement of genre in his account of the political theory of the frescoes in the Palazzo Pubblico

---

16 C. Trinkaus, *American Historical Review* 85 (1980), p. 79n.

17 Michael Oakeshott, *Historical Journal* 23 (1980), pp. 450–1; Judith Shklar, *Political Theory* 7 (1979), p. 551n. I have dwelt thus far on positivist deprecations of intellectual history: some critics, however, within intellectual history, have found Skinner's own position to be prejudicial to the proper autonomy of the history of thought.

18 For the two last see Skinner, *Foundations*, II, pp. 99, 222.

19 She wrote that, for Skinner, the political theorist is 'seen as the necessary partner of the historians, jurists, theologians, and poets of his age. For reasons not altogether clear, scientists, metaphysicians, deviant and mystically inclined religious seers, and dabblers in magic are not included': *Political Theory* 7 (1979), p. 551.

20 Quentin Skinner, *Reason and Rhetoric in the Philosophy of Hobbes* (Cambridge: Cambridge University Press, 1996).

in Siena.[21] Generic expansiveness is, *inter alia*, the product of the impact of literary 'new historicism', which has brought to the attention of historians of political thought the poetry and drama of the past. By the 1990s some of the humanist and republican themes essayed in *Foundations* were being explored in work on, for instance, Sir Philip Sidney's *Arcadia* and the poetry of the English Civil War.[22] A signal instance of this advent is the study of the Boling-brokean assault on Walpole. The three decades since Skinner's essay of 1974 on this topic saw a remarkably fertile range of research, much of it by literary scholars. The topic now involves consideration of the novels of Jonathan Swift, the poetry of Alexander Pope and James Thomson, the plays of John Gay and Henry Brooke, the cartoons of Hogarth and the oratorios of Handel.[23] Generic expansiveness has eroded the orthodox boundaries of 'the history of political thought', and, a quarter-century after *Foundations*, it is less clear whether the subject survives other than as subsumed into intellectual history more generally, and in turn into cultural history.

The emphasis in *Foundations* on ideologies rather than 'classic' authors has latterly carried with it further hazards in the practice of the discipline. As the 'linguistic turn' across the whole of the humanities made its impact, and as Marxism retreated, the term 'ideology', which was conspicuous by its presence in *Foundations*, gave way to the ubiquity of the preferred terms 'language' and, above all, 'discourse'. Postmodern doubt about authorial agency, and emphasis upon the reception of texts, has had the effect of rendering the world of ideas less the production of authors than the common, unowned, vernacular of their time. Ambient 'discourses' are apt to replace individual authors and texts. Iron-ically, the result can be a variety of intellectual history which is rather like the old history of ideas which Skinner had set out to castigate, in which Platonic ideas float free of authors and historical contingencies. Biancamaria Fontana has recently complained, apropos a collection of essays on early-modern republicanism, of

surreal battlefields, where languages and vocabularies, jargons and paradigms joust strenuously against each other, like the empty armours of non-existent knights in Italo Calvino's *Our Ancestors*. The result is little different from the struggle of opposing 'isms' in the old (pre-Cambridge-method) textbooks of the history of political thought.[24]

---

[21] Quentin Skinner, 'Ambrogio Lorenzetti: the Artist as Political Philosopher', *Proceedings of the British Academy* 72 (1987), pp. 1–56; repr. in Skinner, *Visions*, II.

[22] Blair Worden, *The Sound of Virtue: Philip Sidney's Arcadia and Elizabethan Politics* (New Haven: Yale University Press 1996); David Norbrook, *Writing the English Republic: Poetry, Rhetoric, and Politics, 1627–1660* (Cambridge: Cambridge University Press, 1999).

[23] For a survey see Mark Goldie, 'The English System of Liberty', in Mark Goldie and Robert Wokler (eds.), *The Cambridge History of Eighteenth-Century Political Thought* (Cambridge: Cambridge University Press, 2006), pp. 70–4.

[24] Biancamaria Fontana, 'In the Gardens of the Republic', *Times Literary Supplement*, 11 July 2003, reviewing Martin van Gelderen and Quentin Skinner (eds.), *Republicanism: a Shared European Heritage*, 2 vols. (Cambridge: Cambridge University Press, 2002).

This tendency is further enhanced by the methodological injunction, which John Pocock was especially keen to insist upon, that political languages are not to be confused with political doctrines, still less with particular programmes or policies.[25] The effect can be to speak of this or that 'discourse' as a web of words not of any agent's making. The result can be slack practice in which the historian is exonerated from the spadework of excavating exact circumstance and the context of authorial engagement. Ideas are not, as the late Richard Ashcraft remarked in praise of the method of *Foundations*, 'a cloud bank moving through the stratosphere'.[26]

II

A central purpose of *Foundations* was to elucidate the emergence of the modern concept of the state. Skinner defined the state in explicitly Weberian terms as 'the sole source of law and legitimate force within its own territory'.[27] Within the body of the book his definitions tended more toward the juridical, for he accented the emergence of the idea of legal sovereignty, and turned to the glossators of Roman law to find its earliest expressions, notably in Bartolus of Saxoferrato.[28] In this respect the book constructed an arch from Bartolus to Bodin, from the fourteenth-century jurist who responded to the overweening claims of the emperor to the sixteenth-century jurist who reshaped the idea of sovereignty in the circumstances of the French Wars of Religion. The framing of the *Foundations* as a search for origins prompted the most persistent complaint by reviewers, that it tended towards the teleological. John Salmon remarked on the 'tension between two of the professed aims of the book, between the exemplification of a newly prescribed historicist method in the history of ideas and the somewhat Whiggish intent to illuminate the process by which the modern concept of the state came to be formed'.[29] Oakeshott, engaging in a piece of *tu quoque*, asked,

is it not 'unhistorical', anachronistic, to think of [the concept of the state] as a construction erected on 'foundations' laid by Marsiglio, Bartolus, Machiavelli, Beza, etc.? These writers were not laying foundations; they were casuistical moralists and lawyers fumbling for circumstantial arguments to support their clients.[30]

Similar criticism has resurfaced more recently. James Alexander has suggested that while John Pocock's *Machiavellian Moment* (1975) might be called

25 J. G. A. Pocock, *Politics, Language, and Time* (New York: Macmillan, 1971).

26 Richard Ashcraft, *Journal of the History of Philosophy* 19 (1981), p. 390.

27 Skinner, *Foundations*, I, p. x; cf. II, pp. 351–3.

28 Skinner, *Foundations*, I, pp. 9–10, and *passim*.

29 John Salmon, *History of European Ideas* 4 (1983), p. 331. Cf. D. Boucher, *Political Theory* 8 (1980), pp. 406–8; W. J. Bouwsma, *Catholic Historical Review* 67 (1981), pp. 84–5; K. R. Massingham, *Politics* 16 (1981), pp. 124–9.

30 Michael Oakeshott, *Historical Journal* 23 (1980), p. 452.

Jacobite intellectual history, because it charted a concept, civic republicanism, that has been eclipsed by modernity, *Foundations* was, by contrast, Whig intellectual history, because it traced how modern political life came to be equipped with its most persistent and potent concept, sovereignty.[31] It is this aspect of *Foundations* about which Skinner is today himself apologetic. In 2002 he confessed that he was:

wrong . . . in using a metaphor that virtually commits one to writing teleologically. My own book is far too much concerned with the origins of our present world when I ought to have been trying to represent the world I was examining in its own terms as far as possible. But the trouble with writing early-modern European history is that, although their world and our world are vastly different from each other, our world nevertheless somehow emerged out of theirs, so that there's a very natural temptation to write about origins, foundations, evolutions, developments. But it's not a temptation to which I would ever think of yielding in these post-modern days.[32]

While *Foundations* is vulnerable on this score, it is misleading to suppose that the book exemplified the 'modernisation' thesis that pervaded so much historical work during and beyond the 1960s. Exponents of that thesis almost invariably looked to the early-modern period as defining a sharp disjuncture between the 'medieval' or 'traditional' and the 'modern'. Conventional political science had invested a great deal in the notion that the 'birth of modernity' lay in the concept of the state that emerged between Machiavelli and Hobbes, and much undergraduate pedagogy still rests on this assumption. By contrast, one of the achievements of *Foundations* was its break with the conventional chronological boundary that typically defined the 'birth of the modern'. Much of the book is about the middle ages, a fact somewhat obscured by the first volume having the title *The Renaissance*. Its first date is 1085. What was startling was the decisive shift in the historical centre of gravity from the orthodox – Machiavelli, Bodin, Hobbes – to the unexpected – Bartolus, Marsilius, Dante.

There is much in *Foundations* about adaptations of Roman law and classical rhetoric. None the less, the exploration of the middle ages, and the construction of the second volume around Luther, Calvin and the Counter-Reformation, unavoidably entailed an encounter with theology. *Foundations* is, arguably, truest to its historicist brief in taking political theology seriously. This is somewhat in tension with Skinner's occasional programmatic remarks, redolent of the 'modernisation' thesis, about the birth of the secular.[33] It is also at odds with his insistence on the pervasive presence of a pagan, Ciceronian stream within

---

[31] James Alexander, 'An Essay on Historical, Philosophical, and Theological Attitudes to Modern Political Thought', *History of Political Thought* 25 (2004), pp. 116–48, at pp. 137–8.
[32] Koikkalainen and Syrjämäki, 'On Encountering the Past', p. 53. Cf. Palonen, *Skinner*, pp. 71–2.
[33] Skinner, *Foundations*, e.g. II, pp. 339, 347, 358.

European thought.[34] And it is further at odds with his personal predilections, which are hostile to Christianity.[35] Even so, the turn towards Christian political theology and the middle ages remains fundamental to the book, and it carried with it significant consequences. The book's character was in part the result of a further engagement with Weber's Protestant ethic thesis, yet this time Skinner definitely rejected it, breaking the link between Protestantism and modernity. In turning to the Catholic middle ages he drew upon a quite different historical tradition, German also and contemporaneous with Weber, a tradition associated especially with Otto Gierke and, in England, with John Neville Figgis. It was a tradition of historical understanding which, as will be noted in closing, was closely tied to the earliest roots of the study of the history of political thought within Skinner's own university.

The backward shift in chronology was a surprising outcome to the author himself. Skinner originally intended to write a single volume on early-modern political thought conforming to the orthodox chronology. This is signalled in the title of his earliest Cambridge lectures of 1965, 'History of Political Thought, 1500–1800'. In the early 1970s he continued to lecture on the period from the Renaissance to the Enlightenment. In the event, *Foundations* covered *c*.1200–1600 and not 1500–1800. The book stops somewhat abruptly around 1600, and the truncation is a matter of great regret for historians of the later period. My own notes from Skinner's lectures include his survey of the ideological context of Montesquieu's *Spirit of the Laws*. Had that been included in his book, another arch would thereby have been completed, concerning the ideological uses of historical scholarship. The rival 'Romanist' and 'Germanist' theses about the origins of the French polity, which Hotman and Bodin debated during the Wars of Religion and which feature in the second volume of *Foundations*, resurfaced in the contest between the *thèse royale* and *thèse nobiliaire* waged between Dubos, Boulainvilliers and Montesquieu. In *Foundations*, the most visible archaeological remains of Skinner's original chronology are his regular references to Locke as a culminating point of the story. His remarks on Locke form ellipses that carry the account from the Huguenot theory of revolution, lying within the boundary of *Foundations*, to the *Two Treatises of Government*, lying a century beyond it. In this respect, *Foundations* provided corroboration for a book Skinner especially esteemed, John Dunn's *The Political Thought of John Locke* (1969), a corroboration of the contention that it makes better historical sense to see Locke as the inheritor of 'radical Calvinist politics' than as the 'first modern liberal'.[36]

---

[34] Skinner, *Foundations*, I, ch. 2. The theme is yet stronger in later work: *Visions*, II, *passim*.

[35] Quentin Skinner, 'Who are "We"?: Ambiguities of the Modern Self', *Inquiry* 34 (1991), pp. 133–53 (on Charles Taylor).

[36] Skinner, *Foundations*, II, pp. 147n., 239; cf. pp. 328, 338–9, 347. For similar ellipses between Bodin, Filmer and Bossuet, see II, pp. 114, 301.

Foundations, however, entered a crucial caveat. 'Radical Calvinist politics' turned out not to be definitively Calvinist after all. Each of the two volumes of *Foundations* rested on a dramatic predating. The first volume challenged Hans Baron's Florentine crisis of the early fifteenth century, and started the story of the Renaissance much earlier.[37] More pertinent here is that the second volume contradicted Michael Walzer's thesis, in *The Revolution of the Saints* (1966), that the theory of political revolution, which reached its fruition in the Scottish and English parliaments' rebellions against Charles I (and, in turn, in Locke's *Two Treatises*), originated in distinctive aspects of Protestant theology. Modern revolutions were, in Walzer's view, the child of Calvinism, and their ur-texts were those of the Huguenots, Beza, Hotman and the anonymous author of the *Vindiciae contra Tyrannos*. His contention was that the Protestant worldview was midwife to modernity, in the form of political individualism and revolution. Walzer was by no means alone in arguing thus. The association of 'Puritanism and Revolution' was deeply embedded in the Weberian-tinged Marxism of Christopher Hill, whose many books dominated reading lists in the 1960s and 1970s.[38]

Despite being initially attracted by Walzer's thesis, Skinner came to regard it as mistaken. Not only were the lineaments of Calvinist theory to be found among Lutheran defenders of the German princes in the 1530s, but also, more strikingly, its distinctive ingredients could be traced beyond Protestantism to Catholic theologians. These included the neo-Thomists of the 'second scholastic', Vitoria, Molina, Soto, Suárez and Mariana, and the Parisian teachers of the turn of the sixteenth century, John Mair (or Major) and Jacques Almain. The latter were, in turn, heirs to arguments developed in the fourteenth and early fifteenth centuries by William of Ockham and Jean Gerson.[39] Links between Catholics and Protestants were personal as well as ideological. Signally, the great Scottish Calvinist proponent of the doctrine of resistance to tyrants, George Buchanan, had been a pupil of Mair.[40] Gerson, Almain and Mair were conciliarists, exponents of the view that supreme authority in the Catholic church lay with the General Council of the church, and that accordingly the church was a constitutional and not an absolute monarchy. It was a doctrine which had legitimated the dramatic deposition of three popes at the Council of Constance in 1414. Hence, in late medieval Catholic ecclesiology could be found a powerful theory of constitutionalism and resistance.

---

[37] Hans Baron, *The Crisis of the Early Italian Renaissance*, 2 vols. (Princeton: Princeton University Press, 1955); Skinner, *Foundations*, I, p. 69 and *passim*.

[38] Notably *Puritanism and Revolution* (London: Secker and Warburg, 1958); *Society and Puritanism in Pre-Revolutionary England* (London: Secker and Warburg, 1964); and *Intellectual Origins of the English Revolution* (Oxford: Clarendon Press, 1965).

[39] Skinner, *Foundations*, II, pp. 114ff, 135ff.   [40] Ibid., pp. 44, 340.

Skinner judged that 'the main foundations of the Calvinist theory of revolution were in fact constructed entirely by their Catholic adversaries'. He noted that, consequently, his account was 'at odds with the sort of Weberian analysis of Calvinism as a revolutionary ideology which has recently come to be so widely accepted'.[41] He rejected the notion of Calvinist radicalism radiating downwards 'to the political thought of modern times', carrying with it a set of 'modernising' political tendencies.[42] By demonstrating the Catholic and medieval roots of theories of constitutionalism and resistance, Skinner dismissed a cardinal tenet of the modernisation thesis held by liberals and Marxists alike, that early-modern Protestantism was the midwife of modern political thought. It was, Skinner concluded, 'a mistake . . . to think of the development of this modern "liberal" theory of constitutionalism essentially as an achievement of the seventeenth century'. Indeed, 'the radical Saints of the seventeenth century [did not] hesitate to make use of the dialectical weapons which had thus been fashioned for them by their papist enemies'.[43]

As this last remark hints, there are, oddly enough, parallels between Skinner's argument in *Foundations* and histories of political thought written by Royalists and Tories in Restoration and post-Restoration England. Writing in reaction against the ruination wrought by the civil wars and regicide, these writers sought to demonstrate that the Parliamentarians and Whigs inherited their 'king-killing' doctrines from the papists. They dwelt, it is true, not upon Catholic conciliarist constitutionalism, but rather on a different Catholic doctrine, no less dangerous to kingly authority, the doctrine of the papal 'deposing power'. In their formidable erudition they revealed a deep familiarity with a wide range of medieval and sixteenth-century Catholic authors. One such polemicist, Mary Astell, writing in 1704, pronounced that, in whatever its guises, 'the deposing doctrine . . . is . . . rank popery'. She proceeded to reveal the origins of the 'poison of rebellious principles' and the doctrine of the 'mutual compact between king and people' in the works of Bellarmine, Mariana, Molina, Soto and Suárez, and in turn in 'John Major, a Scotchman, and Buchanan's master'.[44] Skinner invoked precisely the tradition within which Astell wrote, for he cited the Civil War Royalist John Maxwell, whose contention was that it was a mistake to find the roots of revolution only in the Calvinists, in Knox

---

[41] Ibid., pp. 321–2.

[42] Ibid., p. 322, quoting Hans Baron, 'Calvinist Republicanism and its Historical Roots', *Church History* 8 (1939), pp. 30–42, at pp. 31, 41.

[43] Skinner, *Foundations*, II, pp. 347–8. A brief footnote (another of Skinner's ellipses) dismissed C. B. Macpherson's influential *The Political Theory of Possessive Individualism* (Oxford: Oxford University Press, 1962), and thus the entire Marxian agenda for the seventeenth-century revolutions (p. 347).

[44] Mary Astell, 'An Impartial Enquiry into the Causes of Rebellion and Civil War', in *Political Writings*, ed. Patricia Springborg (Cambridge: Cambridge University Press, 1996), pp. 152–9.

and Buchanan, for the rebels against King Charles I 'borrowed their first main tenet of the Sorbonnists', and particularly from William of Ockham and Jacques Almain.[45]

It is worth observing at this point that it continues to be a surprise to some modern readers that Catholic theology produced radical political outcomes. It has been a surprise to Protestant and secular minds alike ever since nineteenth-century Catholics, in flight from the French Revolution, transformed Catholicism into a fortress against liberalism and socialism. And indeed a surprise ever since seventeenth-century Catholics, in appalled reaction against the assassination of Henri IV by the monk Ravaillac, turned Catholicism into a bastion of monarchical absolutism. Bossuet, around 1700, and De Maistre, around 1800, decisively separated modern Catholic political thought from the 'king-killing doctrine' of 'the Sorbonnists' and Mariana. The Catholicism of the post-French Revolution era in turn reinforced in the Protestant liberal, and socialist, mind of nineteenth- and twentieth-century Europe an instinctive association between the Reformation, revolution, liberty and modernity. This was not least for Weber himself, who wrote under the shadow of Bismarck's *Kulturkampf*, in a Germany where the contrast between northern Protestant progressivism and southern Catholic reaction seemed palpable.[46] It was similarly the case for historians like Christopher Hill, who belonged to the generation whose leftism was forged in the face of Franco's Catholic fascism: the Protestant and often Nonconformist or Methodist ethic within English Marxism has been noticed by its historians.[47] By contrast, to insist, historically, as Skinner did, upon the phenomenon of Catholic political radicalism marked Skinner's sharpest deviation from Weberian models in *Foundations*.[48] His move was strongly anti-Whig, hostile, that is, to an orthodox teleology about modernity and liberty. Herbert Butterfield, in his classic indictment of the *Whig Interpretation of History* (1931), rightly dwelt on the Protestant character of the Whig mindset. One is tempted to say that Skinner recovered the Catholic political tradition in order to dispose of Protestant theories of liberal modernity. He did so not of

---

[45] John Maxwell, *Sacro-Sancta Regum Maiestas* (1644); Skinner, *Foundations*, II, p. 123. A better-known Royalist who pursued the same theme was Sir Robert Filmer, in the opening pages of *Patriarcha* (*Patriarcha and Other Writings*, ed. Johann P. Sommerville (Cambridge: Cambridge University Press, 1991)).

[46] Anthony Giddens, *Politics and Sociology in the Thought of Max Weber* (London: Macmillan, 1972); Norman Stone, 'The Religious Background to Max Weber', in W. J. Sheils (ed.), *Persecution and Toleration* (Oxford: Blackwell, 1984), pp. 393–407.

[47] Raphael Samuel, 'British Marxist Historians, 1880–1980', *New Left Review* 120 (1980), pp. 21–96.

[48] A parallel development over the past thirty years has been the recovery of what would once have been regarded as an oxymoron, the Catholic Enlightenment. For a survey, see Dale Van Kley, 'Piety and Politics in the Century of Lights', in Goldie and Wokler (eds.), *The Cambridge History of Eighteenth-Century Political Thought*, pp. 110–46.

course in order to recommend Catholicism, but rather to clear the ground for a quite different route into the history of concepts of liberty, a subject upon which so much of his more recent work has dwelt.[49]

In making his move into the terrain of late-medieval Catholic political theology, Skinner returned to an older historiographical tradition which had identified just such a line of development from Catholic conciliarism to Calvinist constitutionalism. It was a minority tradition, yet one which produced some of the earliest works to emerge in the history of political thought as an organised university discipline. In *Political Thought from Gerson to Grotius* (1907), John Neville Figgis had written that the decree which Gerson had penned for the Council of Constance was 'probably the most revolutionary official document in the history of the world', for it prefigured the arguments of early-modern revolutionaries.[50] Figgis's claim is echoed in the useful historical catchphrase, 'the road from Constance to 1688'.[51] A number of reviewers of *Foundations* were struck by its resemblance to Figgis's book and to a body of work written about the same time. 'There is nothing here', wrote Keith Thomas, 'which Otto Gierke or John Neville Figgis or A. J. Carlyle or J. W. Allen would not have recognised.'[52]

Figgis was one of the earliest teachers of history in Cambridge after the founding of the undergraduate course in 1873. The parallel between Skinner and Figgis points to a key aspect of the context of *Foundations*, namely that, for all the scepticism about intellectual history exuded by Geoffrey Elton in the Cambridge of the 1960s, the Cambridge history school had, from the outset, allotted a privileged place to the history of political thought. The subject was at first compulsory in the degree course, a fact owing largely to Sir John Seeley's influence in the creation of the course. Seeley provided one prospectus for the emerging faculty of history, oriented towards providing a school of statesmanship, within which the understanding of political theories and institutions in historical perspective was central. It was a position defended in often quarrelsome contention against those who held the Rankean view that the history course should be a professional apprenticeship in archival research. True to its

---

[49] Quentin Skinner, *Liberty before Liberalism* (Cambridge: Cambridge University Press, 1998).

[50] J. N. Figgis, *Studies of Political Thought from Gerson to Grotius, 1414–1625* (Bristol: Thoemmes, 1998), p. 63.

[51] Francis Oakley, 'On the Road from Constance to 1688', *Journal of British Studies* 2 (1962), pp. 1–31. See also Brian Tierney, *Religion, Law, and the Growth of Constitutional Thought, 1150–1650* (Cambridge: Cambridge University Press, 1982); and cf. Skinner, *Foundations*, II, p. 123. Oakley's many works on conciliarism themselves stand within the tradition they describe, for they seek to vindicate a liberal Catholic's dislike of contemporary papal monarchy. See, most recently, Francis Oakley, *The Conciliarist Tradition: Constitutionalism in the Catholic Church, 1300–1870* (Oxford: Oxford University Press, 2004).

[52] Keith Thomas, *New York Review of Books*, 17 May 1979, p. 27; cf. Denys Hay, *Journal of Ecclesiastical History* 31 (1980), pp. 223–6; S. T. Holmes, *American Political Science Review* 73 (1979), pp. 1133–5.

Rankean roots, the latter camp took its cue from a conception of *Realpolitik* in which the evidence of the chancelleries was the essence of history. Elton was heir to that tradition, just as Skinner inherited that of Seeley. Seeley's version had gained renewed impetus with the creation of a chair in political science within the history faculty in 1928, the chair to which Skinner was elected in 1979, following the publication of *Foundations*.[53]

If Ranke was godfather to one historical tradition within Cambridge, the Figgisians were no less Germanic in their chosen inspiration, for behind Figgis and Seeley lay Gierke, whose *Deutsche Genossenschaftsrecht* (1868) remains unsurpassed.[54] Gierke told a medieval story, of a Catholic political theology in which Roman law was incorporated into canon law. That system of law gave rise to a conception of corporate bodies as plenary legal entities, having authority independent of, and superior to, any individual person. Such corporate bodies, whether councils, cities or parliaments, came thereby to possess the ideological means with which to challenge the authority of popes, emperors and princes alike.

Skinner's thesis in *Foundations*, by virtue of its decisive investigation of Catholic political theology, entailed its author keeping unexpected historiographical company. Figgis, who eventually withdrew to a monastery, was a high Anglican at odds with the sovereign state of his day. There was an element of nostalgia in his dismay at the shape of modernity and he leaned toward a kind of communitarian medievalism.[55] This of course could hardly be further removed from Skinner's political preferences. What the two men shared was a general conviction that the history of political thought was central to the historical enterprise, and a particular conviction that there were reasons to doubt the prevailing political doctrines. By writing intellectual history, Skinner has

[53] For the early history of the Cambridge history school see Stefan Collini, 'A Place in the Syllabus: Political Science at Cambridge', in S. Collini, D. Winch and J. Burrow (eds.), *That Noble Science of Politics: a Study in Nineteenth-Century Intellectual History* (Cambridge: Cambridge University Press, 1983); Stefan Collini, 'Disciplines, Canons, and Publics: the History of "The History of Political Thought" in Comparative Perspective', and Robert Wokler, 'The Professoriate of Political Thought in England since 1914', both in Castiglione and Hampsher-Monk (eds.), *History of Political Thought in National Context*; and Mark Goldie, 'J. N. Figgis and the History of Political Thought in Cambridge', in Richard Mason (ed.), *Cambridge Minds* (Cambridge: Cambridge University Press, 1994).

[54] English editions: Otto von Gierke, *Political Theories of the Middle Ages*, trans. F. W. Maitland (Cambridge: Cambridge University Press, 1900); and Otto von Gierke, *Natural Law and the Theory of Society, 1500–1800*, trans. E. Barker (Cambridge: Cambridge University Press, 1934).

[55] Figgis's politics and that of his contemporaries in the early decades of the twentieth century ('the political theory of pluralism') have recently attracted extensive attention. See Paul Hirst (ed.), *The Pluralist Theory of the State* (London: Routledge, 1993); Julia Stapleton, *Englishness and the Study of Politics: the Social and Political Thought of Ernest Barker* (Cambridge: Cambridge University Press, 1994); David Runciman, *Pluralism and the Personality of the State* (Cambridge: Cambridge University Press, 1997).

argued, we come to see the often parochial contingencies that gave rise to our presiding and apparently permanent doctrines. He has written that:

we are prone to fall under the spell of our own intellectual heritage . . . [for] it is easy to become bewitched into believing that the ways of thinking . . . bequeathed to us by the mainstream of our intellectual traditions must be *the* ways of thinking about them. Given this situation, one of the contributions that historians can make is to offer us a kind of exorcism.[56]

---

[56] Skinner, *Visions*, I, p. 6; cf. Skinner, *Liberty before Liberalism*, pp. 116–17.

2   Linguistic philosophy and *The Foundations*

Holly Hamilton-Bleakley

In this essay I will seek to provide an introduction to the philosophical ideas behind the methodology which Quentin Skinner practised in *The Foundations of Modern Political Thought*. I will do this through an analysis of the ways in which Skinner drew on the work of R. G. Collingwood, Ludwig Wittgenstein and J. L. Austin to develop two concepts which are at the heart of his early work on method: context and agency.

These concepts pervade Skinner's work and have presented themselves at times as a pair related through an inherent tension, where an emphasis upon one leads to an escape from the other.[1] Yet Skinner's early work on method emphasised the agency of the author, precisely because it emphasised the context in which he wrote, or so I will argue here. The 'canonist' method of studying the history of political philosophy which prevailed when Skinner started his work demoted authorial agency in several ways, largely because it ignored the wider social, intellectual and linguistic context out of which a text arose, and Skinner's advancement of his own method against this approach showed him to be deeply concerned to recover this agency. I will discuss two ways in which this recovery was accomplished: first, by showing that the meaning of a text was bound up with the way the author was intentionally using particular conventions of language to either affirm or change prevailing normative concepts of her time and, second, by revealing the author as a political practitioner through an insistence upon the direct relationship between political thought and political action. I will conclude by discussing how, although Skinner has expressed unease with the concept of agency in his assertions that he principally studies 'languages' rather than individual contributions to those languages,[2] his own practice of intellectual history shows him to be chiefly interested in the activity of individuals challenging conventional political languages – an activity which

---

I am very grateful to Jim Tully and Mark Goldie for helpful comments on an earlier draft of this essay.
[1] See for instance the discussion in Quentin Skinner, 'Interpretation and the Understanding of Speech Acts', in *Visions of Politics*, 3 vols. (Cambridge: Cambridge University Press, 2002), I: *Regarding Method*, pp. 103–27, at 117–19.
[2] Ibid., p. 118.

he not only emphasises through his methodology, but also practises himself with his methodology.

The canonist approach as it was practised in the early 1960s was, according to Skinner, characterised by the view that there was a canon of classic texts in the history of philosophy, which contained "'timeless elements'', in the form of "universal ideas", even a "dateless wisdom" with "universal application"'.[3] Thus, these texts remained perennially relevant and could therefore be read in order to address our contemporary political concerns.[4] Indeed, they must be read to address our problems, for their relevance to our concerns justified their study.[5]

This approach demoted the agency of the author of the text in several ways, but for reasons of space I shall mention only one: it encouraged a kind of isolation of certain ideas or doctrines from the authors who generated them. This tendency could take the form of A. O. Lovejoy's 'unit-ideas' approach,[6] or find expression in the more common injunction to study only the 'problems' of political philosophy rather than the theorists who articulated them.[7] However, this bifurcation of the author from her utterances could also be found in a more subtle way in the general methodology of the canonists. This methodology was founded on the assumption that an author's position concerning a particular doctrine was sufficiently understood by focusing on what that author had said concerning that doctrine. The key to the meaning of an author's utterances was to be found within the utterance itself, because the utterance was understood through an understanding of 'the sense in which [the author was] using words'.[8]

---

[3] Quentin Skinner, 'Meaning and Understanding in the History of Ideas', in James Tully (ed.), *Meaning and Context: Quentin Skinner and his Critics* (Princeton: Princeton University Press, 1988), pp. 29–67, at p. 30.

[4] Ibid., p. 30. For a restatement of Skinner's characterisation of the canonist approach, see P. Koikkalainen and S. Syrjämäki, 'On Encountering the Past: an Interview with Quentin Skinner', in *Finnish Yearbook of Political Thought* 6 (2002), pp. 34–63, at p. 38.

[5] See for instance the argument in A. Hacker, '*Capital* and Carbuncles: the "Great Books" Reappraised', *American Political Science Review* 48 (1954), pp. 775–86, at pp. 784 and 786.

[6] A. O. Lovejoy, *The Great Chain of Being: a Study in the History of an Idea* (Cambridge, Mass.: Harvard University Press, 1970), pp. 3–23, esp. 15.

[7] For an example of this injunction see Hacker, '*Capital* and Carbuncles', p. 786.

[8] J. Plamenatz, *Man and Society*, 2 vols. (London: Longmans, Green & Co., 1963), I, p. ix. Here Plamenatz makes a classic case for the textualist method employed by the canonists: 'Those who say that to understand a theory we must understand the conditions in which it was produced sometimes put their case too strongly. They speak as if, to understand what a man is saying, we must know why he is saying it. But this is not true. We need to understand only the sense in which he is using words. To understand Hobbes, we need not know what his purpose was in writing *Leviathan* or how he felt about the rival claims of Royalists and Parliamentarians; but we do need to know what he understood by such words as law, right, liberty, covenant, and obligation. And though it is true that even Hobbes, so 'rare' at definitions, does not always use a word in the sense which he defines, we are more likely to get the sense in which he does use it by a close study of his argument than by looking at the condition of England or at political controversies in his day.'

The consideration of the wider context of why the utterance was issued need not be considered.[9] In this 'textualist' method, authors themselves need not be considered in the meaning of their utterances; divorced from why it was issued, the utterance becomes removed from its author.

Skinner asserted that this separation of what was said from why it was said led to the writing of a history of philosophy which was 'nonsense'.[10] He proposed a new methodology which would lead to a genuinely historical history of philosophy, at the centre of which was the re-uniting of an utterance with, first, its author, by identifying what an author 'meant' by his utterance with authorial intention and, second, the context within which it was uttered, by emphasising the need to discover intentions through the conventions within which they are expressed. Thus, the new methodology was nothing less than a philosophy about meaning, where 'meaning' is interpreted as what an author meant by what he said in his text.[11]

The first casualty in Skinner's theory of meaning was the canonist assumption that the great texts of political philosophy all addressed in some way a set of perennial questions, and could therefore be used to address our current political problems. He drew on the work of Collingwood to assert instead that any text must be seen as being written in response to particular questions or problems at a particular time.[12] Collingwood had put forward the notion of a 'logic of question and answer',[13] in which he argued that in order to understand what a man means by what he has said, one must know not only what he has said, but 'also what the question was to which the thing he has said or written was meant as an answer'.[14] The logic of question and answer was meant as a refutation of propositional logic, the main characteristic of which Collingwood saw to be the assignation of the properties of truth and falsehood to free-standing propositions.[15] Instead, 'truth . . . was something that belonged not to any single proposition, nor even . . . to a complex of propositions taken together; but to a complex consisting of questions and answers'.[16]

---

[9] Plamenatz, *Man and Society*, p. ix. See previous footnote.

[10] See for instance Skinner, 'Meaning and Understanding', pp. 47–50.

[11] Thus, whenever the word 'meaning' is used in this essay, it will refer to what the author meant by issuing a particular utterance, unless otherwise noted (it should be noted that this is one definition which Skinner himself gave of 'meaning' in his essay 'Motives, Intentions and the Interpretations of Texts', pp. 68–78, at p. 70). I am aware that there are many different senses of 'meaning' of a text, and that Skinner has noted these distinctions. However, as I interpret Skinner, to be concerned with what an author meant by saying what he said in his text leads to a better understanding of philosophical texts than when we are not so concerned with it. In this way, he gives priority to this kind of meaning of a text. Indeed, not to be concerned with what an author meant by what he said in his text leads to a 'nonsensical' reading of philosophy.

[12] Skinner, 'Meaning and Understanding', pp. 56 and 64–5.

[13] R. G. Collingwood, *An Autobiography* (Oxford: Oxford University Press, 1939), pp. 36–7.

[14] Ibid., p. 31.   [15] Ibid., pp. 34 and 36.   [16] Ibid., p. 37.

In appropriating this idea, Skinner came to assert that what an author means by what he says in his text is bound up with identifying the questions to which the text is an answer, the context of argument in which it is meant as an intervention.[17] He further innovated within Collingwood's logic of question and answer by asserting that not only was a text meant as an answer to a question, but that this concept could be translated into identifying the text as a response to a specific political problem. In this way, Skinner moved the text away from the largely dialectical context of Collingwood's and later Gadamer's 'question and answers', and located it within a more practical framework.[18] Thus, the text is not timeless, but as particular and contingent as the problems it answers.[19]

This notion of context thrust his concept of the author to the forefront of his methodology, for if a text is written as a response to a particular, contingent problem, what becomes important in understanding it is not just the text itself, but also what the author, as agent, is doing in writing it. In this way, the notions of context and agency cannot be disentangled in Skinner's methodology, where 'context' requires a recovery of the particular problems to which the text is an answer, and 'agency' asserts that authors are actors because in their texts they are responding to particular situations and particular other texts.[20]

It will be clear by now that Collingwood's insights were useful in attacking not only the canonists' notion of timeless audiences, but also their textualist method, as Collingwood's description of propositional logic was not unlike the textualist assertion that the meaning of an utterance is contained within the utterance itself.[21] Skinner saw in the textualists what Collingwood had seen in the adherents to propositional logic: they both failed to recognise that the meaning of an utterance is not sufficiently understood through the definitions of

---

[17] See for instance Skinner, 'Meaning and Understanding', pp. 56–8. For a more recent, and more elaborate, discussion of this point see Quentin Skinner, 'The Rise of, Challenge to, and Prospects for a Collingwoodian Approach to the History of Political Thought', in Dario Castiglione and Iain Hampsher-Monk (eds.) *The History of Political Thought in National Context* (Cambridge: Cambridge University Press, 2001), pp. 175–88. See also the concise treatment in Skinner, 'Interpretation', pp. 114–16.

[18] See Hans-Georg Gadamer, *Truth and Method*, 2nd rev. edn (London: Continuum, 2004), pp. 363–71, for his discussion of the logic of question and answer.

[19] The word 'problem' here should not be understood in the Kantian sense as an abstract concept which stands outside history, but rather, on the contrary, as a particular problem that comes about in historically situated political life. For a critique of Kantian problems through an affirmation of the logic of question and answer, see Gadamer, *Truth and Method*, pp. 368–70.

[20] It is, to a great degree, this Collingwoodian notion of agency, of connecting what an author may be responding to – and thus what his intentions are – in writing his text with its meaning, that has been criticised in the work of postmodernists, with the claim that authorial intentions are irrecoverable, or unimportant because texts have a public meaning that need not refer to the intentions of their authors. See the discussion in Skinner, 'A Collingwoodian Approach', esp. pp. 177–81. The notion of intention and its relation to agency in Skinner's work is discussed below.

[21] See Collingwood, *An Autobiography*, p. 31.

the words of that utterance.[22] Rather, what Skinner saw as more important for discerning the meaning of a word was the way it was being used by the author within a wider linguistic context, particular to the time and place of the author, of which the text was a product. Thus, in order to restore the historical context of the text, Skinner worked out his own philosophy about meaning around the notion of the meaning of a word as its use. In this, Skinner drew heavily upon Wittgenstein's later philosophy, most notably his *Philosophical Investigations*.

In *Philosophical Investigations* Wittgenstein had put forward a notion of language as a 'multiplicity of tools'.[23] Just as a tool could be used in a variety of ways, Wittgenstein asserted that there was a countless variety of different 'kinds' of words and sentences, by which he meant 'countless different kinds of use' of words and sentences.[24] Because we can, and do, use words in many different ways, Wittgenstein argued that we simply cannot think of words as merely 'names of objects'.[25] In this he was arguing against the traditional view in the philosophy of language, where the meaning of a word was identified with an object of some kind which it was meant to signify, and the function of a sentence was therefore thought to be one of making a statement, describing a state of affairs.[26] Wittgenstein, however, saw the meaning of a word as 'its use in the language'.[27] The different uses to which we can put words and sentences can all be thought of as different 'language games',[28] and our language as a whole consists of a collection of language games. Indeed, language in general is likened to a game, where a game is an activity that is governed loosely by rules, in the sense that as games are played the players seek at times to alter the rules, or make them up as the game progresses.[29] Thus, the meanings of words are not fixed, but can change depending upon the rules of the particular language game in which they are being used. Furthermore, particular language games are in a state of flux themselves, in that the rules in any language game are continually being altered by the players.[30]

Through building his own philosophy of meaning upon Wittgenstein's notion of the meaning of a word being largely determined by its usage within a particular language game, Skinner was able to argue against the textualist method of the canonists which sought to understand a philosopher's ideas solely through studying what that philosopher said about them. Because our language is nothing more than a collection of language games, any idea, when it appears, is appearing within the context of a particular language game being played at a

---

[22] See Skinner, 'Meaning and Understanding', p. 55.
[23] Ludwig Wittgenstein, *Philosophical Investigations*, trans. G. E. M. Anscombe (Oxford: Oxford University Press, 1968), para. 23. See also paras. 11–14.
[24] Ibid., para. 23.   [25] Ibid., para. 27.
[26] P. M. S. Hacker, *Wittgenstein's Place in Twentieth-Century Analytic Philosophy* (Oxford: Oxford University Press, 1996), pp. 125–6.
[27] Wittgenstein, *Philosophical Investigations*, para. 43.
[28] Ibid., para. 23.   [29] Ibid., para. 83.   [30] Ibid., para. 82.

particular time. Therefore, in order to understand its meaning, the conventions of the language game within which it is being used must be understood.[31] However, since the meaning of a word is equated with the way it is being used, an essential part of understanding its meaning is to be aware that there are different usages to which the word could have been put, and therefore that there are a range of meanings which the word could have sustained at any one time.[32] Thus the recovery of meaning requires that one discern the range of language games available to the author when he was writing. Only when this range of uses has been determined does the significance of the author's choice of words become apparent. In this way, what an author *means* when he discusses a particular concept cannot be determined solely by what he *says* about it; one must also understand how the author is using the words he employs to discuss the concept, which can only be determined within the context of other possible usages of those words.

Indeed, it is this distinction between what an author said, and what he meant by what he said, that seemed to drive the development of Skinner's philosophy about meaning. In emphasising this distinction, he turned to the work of J. L. Austin. Like Wittgenstein, Austin was interested in the idea that words and sentences could be used to perform functions in addition to naming and describing. In *How To Do Things With Words*, Austin put forward, and explored, the notion of a 'performative utterance', which he defined as an utterance which, when it is issued, constitutes the 'performing of an action', over and above 'just saying something'.[33] Austin thought of 'saying something' as 'the utterance of certain noises, the utterance of certain words in a certain construction, and the utterance of them with a certain "meaning"', where the 'meaning' of the utterance was the 'sense and reference' of the words.[34] Austin named this act of saying something the 'locutionary act' and argued that the performance of a locutionary act was 'also and *eo ipso* to perform an illocutionary act'.[35] The illocutionary act performed is determined by the way in which the locution is used, such as to ask a question, give a warning, issue a threat, make a criticism, posit agreement, offer a defence, give information, offer assurance, issue an order, etc.[36] To determine the illocutionary act performed is to discern what Austin called the 'force' of the words used, how the words 'ought to have been taken', or the speaker's 'point'.[37] Thus a linguistic act is to be assessed not only by the sense and reference of the words used, but also by what illocutionary act the speaker is performing in uttering these words – that is, what he is doing *in* saying those words.[38]

Skinner sought to graft his distinction between what a speaker said and what he meant by what he said on to Austin's distinction between a locutionary

---

[31] Skinner, 'Meaning and Understanding', pp. 63–4.   [32] Ibid., pp. 55–6.
[33] J. L. Austin, *How to Do Things with Words* (Oxford: Oxford University Press, 1962), p. 132.
[34] Ibid., p. 94.   [35] Ibid., p. 97.   [36] Ibid., p. 98.   [37] Ibid., p. 99.   [38] Ibid., p. 99.

act and an illocutionary act. As a result, he argued that in order to determine what a speaker meant by what he said, we need to determine what that speaker was doing in saying what he said. That is, the illocutionary act with which an utterance was performed needs to be understood in order to understand the meaning of that utterance.[39]

Perhaps the most important way, for our purposes here, in which Skinner used Austin's notion of the illocutionary act was to build upon it a theory of speaker intentionality, for Skinner's concept of authorial agency is essentially his concept of authorial intention.[40] For Austin, when we gain 'uptake' of the illocutionary force of an utterance, we understand what the agent was doing in saying that utterance – that is, we understand whether he was warning his audience, informing them, ordering them, trying to persuade them, etc. For Skinner, understanding the illocutionary force of an utterance is equivalent not only to understanding what an agent is doing in issuing that utterance, it is also equivalent to understanding 'that agent's primary intentions *in* issuing that particular utterance'.[41] It is crucial to note here that Skinner is interested in the agent's intentions *in* issuing a particular utterance, not the agent's intentions *to* issue a particular utterance. To focus on this particular notion of the agent's 'intention in' saying something is to recognise the illocutionary act which the agent intentionally performs in uttering a statement. That is, when performing an illocutionary act, the agent must intend to say a certain utterance with a particular force or meaning, and intend to have that utterance understood by his audience in the way that it was meant.[42] There is, therefore, the 'closest possible connection' between an agent's intentions *in* writing something, and the 'meaning of what he writes'.[43]

The key to understanding the meaning of a text, then, is to recover, as much as possible, the agent's intentions in writing that text.[44] Although this recovery is fraught with difficulty,[45] Skinner maintained that the only way it could be done was by focusing on the linguistic and social conventions particular to the agent.[46] Indeed, in the performance of an illocutionary act, conventions are crucial for the speaker in making his intentions understood, and for the audience

---

[39] Skinner, 'Motives, intentions and interpretation', p. 76.
[40] Tarlton noticed this in his critical summary of Skinner's notion of intention. See C. D. Tarlton, 'Historicity, Meaning and Revisionism in the Study of Political Thought', *History and Theory* 12 (1973), pp. 307–28, at 324.
[41] Skinner, 'Motives, Intentions and Interpretation', p. 74, my italics.
[42] Skinner, 'Interpretation and the Understanding of Speech Acts', p. 105.
[43] Skinner, 'Motives, Intentions and Interpretation', p. 75.
[44] Ibid., p. 77, and see also Skinner, 'Some Problems in the Analysis of Political Thought and Action', pp. 97–118, at 105.
[45] For a discussion of some of these difficulties, and Skinner's response to them, see Skinner, 'A Collingwoodian Approach'.
[46] For Skinner's two 'rules' on recovering intentions, see 'Motives, Intentions, and Interpretation', pp. 77–8; see also 'Some Problems in the Analysis of Political Thought', pp. 94–5.

in understanding the speaker's intentions.[47] It is only through conventions that we can understand a certain utterance to be intended as an act of warning, an act of ordering, an act of criticism, etc.[48] Thus, if an agent wants his intentions in speaking, and therefore his meaning, to be understood by his audience, he must conform his communication to the linguistic and social conventions of the day.

This concept of how agents are bound in important ways by convention in their acts of communication is in many respects at the heart of Skinner's methodology as he practised it in *Foundations*, and indeed how he has developed it since. Furthermore, it is a concept fundamental to both the notions of context and of agency in Skinner's work. Concerning the notion of context, let us recall Collingwood's logic of question and answer, which Skinner translated into a notion of context as a set of particular problems to which a text was written as a response. We can now see how Skinner further augmented Collingwoodian context with a detailed theory about the meaning of an utterance and therefore of texts. For context includes not only identifying the problem or texts to which an agent can be seen as responding with his own work, but also identifying the linguistic and social conventions within which the author must operate in order to make his response. And, just as agency is emphasised in the first way that we noted Skinner adopt the Collingwoodian notion of context, because the author is doing something as he responds with his text to a particular problem, so agency also comes to the fore with the notion of context as convention.[49] For this notion of context enables us to identify *what* the author is doing in responding to a particular problem.

Specifically, we need to identify what an agent is doing with the concepts available to him in responding.[50] He has a certain amount of linguistic, and therefore conceptual, resources at his disposal to respond to these problems. Which ones has he chosen to use? Is he singling out certain concepts in his argument and ignoring others? Which concepts does his argument serve to reinforce, and which ones does it reject or criticise?[51] His agency is evident in that the meaning of his argument cannot be understood unless these sorts of intended illocutionary acts are discerned. And this can only be done through gaining an understanding of the conventions surrounding political discourse

---

[47] Skinner, 'Motives, Intentions and Interpretations', p. 77.

[48] Quentin Skinner, 'Conventions and the Understanding of Speech Acts', *The Philosophical Quarterly* 20 (1970), pp. 118–38, at pp. 131–3.

[49] Tarlton, however, saw Skinner's connection between intentions and the conventions within which they are expressed as a move by Skinner to 'abandon' intentions 'in favour of conventions', thereby dissolving the agent into his linguistic context. See Tarlton, 'Historicity, Meaning and Revisionism', p. 325.

[50] Quentin Skinner, *The Foundations of Modern Political Thought*, 2 vols. (Cambridge: Cambridge University Press 1978), I, pp. xiii–xiv.

[51] Ibid., p. xiii.

at that particular time. For, as we have seen, it is only by discovering the range of meanings which a concept can sustain, which is dictated by prevailing conventions, that an audience can determine the significance of the use of the concept by the speaker.

Although the agency of the author is emphasised simply through locating the meaning of an author's argument in his illocutionary intentions, it is, for Skinner, more closely associated with the author who uses the concepts available to him through convention in new and innovating ways. Convention constrains an agent to an important extent in what he can and cannot do with these concepts, and it is when authors are merely 're-iterating, underpinning and defending commonplace insights' that they 'readily come to seem the mere precipitates of their contexts'.[52] Yet Skinner's adaptation of Wittgenstein's notion of language games meant that he saw room for revision within any set of conventions. It is precisely by recognising the limits of convention that one can observe how an author manipulates certain concepts in order to push past those limits, and therefore to move political discourse in another direction.[53] Thus the agency of the author is magnified as the focus comes to rest on what the 'innovating' author is doing in his text with these conventional concepts, for what he is doing will be nothing less than an attempt to either bring about, or ward off, conceptual change.[54]

There is another, closely related way in which linguistic conventions serve to reinforce the mutual presence of context and agency in the methodology of *Foundations*, which stems from Skinner's hallmark concern to connect political principles with political practice. I should like briefly to review Skinner's notion of the relationship between theory and practice, and then discuss the way this relationship highlights the importance of context and augments the role of agency in his methodology.

Precisely because linguistic convention acts as a constraint on the way a society discusses its political problems it also constrains the way individuals in that society act upon those problems. Especially, according to Skinner, it is the way that a society employs language to evaluate the actions of its members

---

[52] Skinner, 'Interpretation and the Understanding of Speech Acts', p. 118.

[53] Skinner, 'Some Problems with the Analysis of Political Thought', pp. 105–6; see also p. 107, where Skinner gives a strong statement about authorial agency by asserting that we must go beyond 'the language or the traditions themselves' and focus 'on the range of things which can in principle be done with them and to them at any given time'.

[54] The manipulation of conventional concepts to bring about conceptual change has remained a central feature of Skinner's work and is of course essentially connected to his notion of legitimation, which is discussed below. I have chosen to discuss legitimation after discussing the conceptual change which takes place through novel linguistic usage to keep conceptually separate two essentially related functions which agents perform in a text of political thought: (1) bringing about conceptual change, and (2) altering constraints on action through that conceptual change. For a citation of works which contain general discussions of conceptual change and legitimation see below, n. 67.

that will have the most significant of effects upon those actions.[55] In order to advance this claim, Skinner employed conceptual resources from Max Weber, and from the philosophy of language inspired by the work of Austin.[56] From Weber, Skinner borrowed the idea of the legitimation of an action, using it to emphasise the distinction – but close connection – between an agent's desire to perform a particular action, and his desire to show that action to be legitimate.[57] To explain how this legitimation takes place, Skinner turned to recent developments in the theory of speech acts, borrowing the notion that there exists a special group of terms 'which performs an evaluative as well as descriptive function in the language'.[58] That is, there is a group of terms which are used to describe actions or states of affairs; but to employ them as descriptions is also to perform the speech act of evaluating those actions or states of affairs. This group of terms is very wide ranging, but examples would be words such as courageous, honest, treacherous, disloyal, democracy, justice, etc.[59] Skinner sought to associate closely the evaluative function of these terms with his notion of an illocutionary act, arguing that when an agent uses these terms, which Skinner called 'evaluative-descriptive', he also performs certain illocutionary acts, such as showing, expressing or inviting approval or disapproval of 'the actions or states of affairs which he uses them to describe'.[60] Thus, an agent uses these terms with the intention of either legitimating or repudiating a particular action.

Therefore, because of the evaluative character of this set of terms, any agent who wishes to legitimate his own actions to others in his society must in some way draw upon them to describe his behaviour.[61] This desire to legitimate one's actions, however, carries with it important constraints on those actions, precisely because the legitimation must be done through these normative terms.[62] Like any linguistic resource, the ways in which these normative terms are used are governed by conventions which enable a shared understanding between an agent and the others in his society. In specifying the various limits on the usages of these terms, convention specifies the various limits on the range of actions which can be described under them.[63] Thus, only a certain range of actions can be considered legitimate under any particular normative vocabulary.[64] And this means that any agent is bound in an important way by that vocabulary, in the

---

[55] Skinner, 'Some Problems with the Analysis of Political Thought', p. 111.
[56] See the discussion, ibid., pp. 111–16.
[57] As Mark Goldie discusses in this volume, pp. 7–8.
[58] Skinner, 'Some Problems with the Analysis of Political Thought', p. 111.   [59] Ibid., p. 112.
[60] Ibid., p. 111.   [61] Ibid., p. 112; see also Skinner, *Foundations*, p. xii.
[62] Skinner, *Foundations*, pp. xii–xiii.
[63] See Skinner, 'Some Problems with the Analysis of Political Thought', p. 112, and Skinner, *Foundations*, p. xii.
[64] Skinner, 'Language and Social Change', pp. 132–3, and Skinner, *Foundations*, p. xii; see also Skinner, 'Some Problems with the Analysis of Political Thought', p. 117, for his assertion about the application of constraints of convention even in the face of those who wish to push past those constraints (see also the discussion below concerning the 'innovating ideologist').

sense that he must conform his actions so that they 'fit the available normative language'.[65]

In this way there are crucial links between political theory and political practice, for the political theory of any given time is comprised of a normative vocabulary, and understanding the conventions of this vocabulary will enable one to discover the range of behaviour available to political actors at that time.

However, if the context of normative vocabularies enables one to understand how individuals are constrained in their actions, and therefore offers one explanation of those actions, it also enables one to emphasise the agency of those individuals who attempt to revise normative vocabularies. Although Skinner's insistence upon the relationship between theory and practice was meant in large part as a repudiation of historians who asserted that political actions could not be explained through normative principles,[66] much of his work deriving from this insistence both before and after *Foundations* has been driven by the idea that changes in a normative vocabulary will result in an alteration of the boundaries constraining social and political behaviour.[67] Thus, a crucial figure in Skinner's philosophy has been that of the 'innovating ideologist' – the individual who, as Goldie explains, in an attempt to legitimate an otherwise untoward action, manipulates certain normative terms by using them to describe an action which does not meet the criteria for the conventional use of those terms.[68] His intentions are not only to bring about conceptual change, but to do it expressly for the purpose of changing the constraints on action.

We have seen how the text in political theory is a *locus* of general conceptual change.[69] However, because the language of political theory is fundamentally a normative language, the text is, first and foremost, a *locus* of normative conceptual change – it is a place where the author manipulates and redefines normative terms. But although, as we have seen, the agency of the author becomes clear when we consider what he is doing with these normative terms, the scope of his agency is augmented when it is considered that this conceptual innovation

---

[65] Skinner, *Foundations*, p. xiii.

[66] See for example Skinner, 'Some Problems with the Analysis of Political Thought', pp. 107–11, and 116–17, as well as a concise statement in Skinner, *Foundations*, pp. xi–xii.

[67] This theme is explored in pieces such as Skinner, 'Language and Social Change', pp. 119–32, and Quentin Skinner, 'The Idea of a Cultural Lexicon', in *Visions*, I, pp. 158–72. In general, of course, this theme is behind his work on legitimation, much of which occurs in Skinner, 'Some Problems with the Analysis of Political Thought' and is further explored in Quentin Skinner, 'Moral Principles and Social Change', in *Visions*, I, pp. 145–57. A restatement of the importance of studying conceptual change and its inevitable effects on social change is given in Quentin Skinner, 'Retrospect: Studying Rhetorical and Conceptual Change', in *Visions*, I, pp. 175–87.

[68] See Goldie, p. 7, above. For Skinner's discussion of how this manipulation takes place, see 'Some Problems with the Analysis of Political Thought', pp. 112–16.

[69] Of course, many texts of political thought are the *locus* of conceptual stability, not conceptual change, and those are the texts which set the normative context. I am grateful to Mark Goldie for prompting me to point this out.

is intended to have, and will have, profound consequences for future politi-cal *action*. Indeed, the direct link between conceptual change and social and political behaviour emphasises the agency of the author because it illuminates political theorising as a political action. When an author uses language in her text with the intention of bringing about changes in social and political behaviour, this use of language is, in itself, a political action. Thus, the distinction between theory and practice is revealed to be one of great complexity and overlap, where the author is a political actor, with her text as the *locus* of her actions.

I have tried to show how Skinner's methodology in *Foundations* is not only a methodology about ideological context, but also about agency within, and against, that context. Agency is emphasised through Skinner's assertion that the meaning of a text must be found in the author's intentions, thereby enabling us to see the text as a political action. Context accompanies this emphasis as an author's intentions, and therefore actions, can only be understood through a consideration of the wider linguistic conventions of the time, reminding us that the text was aimed at a specific historical audience. Both concepts work together in our quest to understand the meaning and significance of a text, leading us through a humbling process of exegesis that enables us to see that the text was not written for us, and therefore should not be asked to solve our contemporary problems.[70]

It is true that recently Skinner has argued that in his methodology agency has a secondary role in the study of normative vocabularies – describing his work as leaving the author in 'extremely poor health'.[71] Yet, when this assertion is taken in conjunction with a consideration of the way that Skinner himself practises his methodology, one perceives an element of ambiguity.[72] For Skinner's practice of his method demonstrates the high value which he places on agency, not only because he tends to focus on theorists who intentionally act as catalysts for

---

[70] Skinner's memorable phrase comes to mind: 'We must learn to do our thinking for ourselves' in his 'Meaning and Understanding' p. 66.

[71] Skinner, 'Interpretation and the Understanding of Speech Acts', p. 118.

[72] Indeed, this ambiguity is found not only in the way Skinner practises his method, but also in the way he interprets it. For instance, in the same volume in which he describes the author in his work as a patient in 'extremely poor health', Skinner also argues that a 'moral' to be drawn from his work is that 'agency deserves after all to be privileged over structure in social explanation. Language, like other forms of social power, is of course a constraint, and it shapes us all . . . however, language is also a resource, and we can use it to shape our world. There is thus a sense in which the following chapters, far from reflecting a depoliticised stance, may be said to culminate in a political plea. The plea is to recognise that the pen is the mighty sword. We are of course embedded in practices and constrained by them. But those practices owe their dominance in part to the power of our normative language to hold them in place, and it is always open to us to employ the resources of our language to undermine as well as to underpin those practises. We may be freer than we sometimes suppose.' (Skinner, 'Introduction', in *Visions*, I, pp. 1–7, at p. 7.) Despite this ambiguity, however, I argue below that the emphasis of Skinner's work must fall on agency, because his practice of his methodology is a striking revelation of his own agency.

the mutation of their ideologies, but also, and especially, because he himself engages in this activity with his methodology.

Indeed, if we view Skinner's work in the light of his own methodology, we can ask ourselves what his intentions are in writing about alternative normative vocabularies. For the effect of writing about these vocabularies is to encourage the reader to scrutinise his own normative language and its limits in the light of past alternatives. In other words, although the practice of studying past political thought as a series of normative vocabularies ruthlessly requires us to keep it fenced off from the present, the effect of this methodology, paradoxically, is nothing less than an encouragement of conceptual change, here and now.

So, what is Skinner doing in recovering past ideologies? It seems that in his recent work Skinner has posed this same question himself, asserting in *Liberty before Liberalism* that historians must be prepared to ask themselves 'what is supposed to be the *point*' of their studies.[73] That Skinner equates the 'point' of an utterance with its speaker's intention signals that when he speaks of the 'point' of his study of intellectual history, he is speaking of his own agency as a historian. He answers that what he is doing in practising intellectual history is 'acting as a kind of archaeologist, bringing buried intellectual treasure back to the surface, dusting it down and enabling us to reconsider what we think of it'.[74] This archaeology, however, is not without a purpose for the present world, for the reconsideration that it encourages will enable us to 'stand back from and perhaps even to reappraise some of our current assumptions and beliefs'.[75] Skinner's assertion is thus that his intention in his work is to provide his readers 'with information relevant to the making of judgements about their current values . . .'[76] He concludes strikingly by casting his project in a Nietzschean light, declaring that the purpose of his archaeology is to leave his readers to 'ruminate'.[77]

The use of the term 'ruminate' reveals the significance of what Skinner is doing with his methodology, for it shows that he identifies in his practice of intellectual history an element critical towards current values which is similar to Nietzsche's approach. In this way, it brings prominently into relief his agency *vis-à-vis* his context. For instance, in *Liberty before Liberalism*, rather than 're-iterating, underpinning and defending commonplace insights', Skinner moves away from the current liberal mindset to challenge the conventional political language of liberty. In this work, Isaiah Berlin is the conventional thinker – the theorist subsumed in the prevailing language who fails to step outside the hegemonic definition of negative liberty.[78] Skinner sees the prevailing convention and acts against it, using his practice of intellectual history to respond to Berlin, intentionally intervening in the current debate on liberty.

---

[73] Quentin Skinner, *Liberty before Liberalism* (Cambridge: Cambridge University Press, 1998), p. 108.
[74] Ibid., p. 112.   [75] Ibid.   [76] Ibid., p. 118.   [77] Ibid.   [78] Ibid., pp. 113–16.

Thus, Skinner's practice of intellectual history is itself an activity of countering prevailing conventions, with profound consequences for both thought and action. The reappraisal of our current beliefs which his method naturally produces results in a shifting of the conventional boundaries upon the usages of certain terms in our normative vocabulary. Indeed, in the case of *Foundations*, its readers come away with altered understandings of terms such as virtue, liberty, state, and right, just to name a few. This altering of political language calls into question the constraints upon our behaviour. In short, Skinner's invitation to 'ruminate' upon his intellectual artefacts is an announcement of the potential potent effects of his work upon his readers in their capacity as political actors. Thus, even when Skinner practises intellectual history, it can never remain wholly in the past.

Part II

Rethinking the foundations

3   Foundations and moments

J. G. A. Pocock

I

Context is king; but the present writer, to his embarrassment, cannot consider *The Foundations of Modern Political Thought* apart from a context formed by his own historical memory, in which he plays a large and autobiographical part. I shall elaborate on these memories, in the hope of offering a commentary on Quentin Skinner's work shaped by that work's relations with my own.

I can claim to have been present at the creation, not of *Foundations* alone but of the enterprise of which Skinner has become the leader. I date its birth about 1949, when Peter Laslett's edition of Filmer's *Patriarcha*[1] pioneered the enterprise of finding out exactly when, and for what, a work of political theory was (a) written, (b) published, (c) answered. Laslett separated by nearly half a century the moment when *Patriarcha* was written (the 1630s) from the moment when it was published; he radically separated intention from effect, and focused attention on what was intended, and what actually happened, when Filmer's works were republished, by agents we are still thinking about, in 1679–80. What Laslett then did had two sets of consequences. In his own work it led to the revolutionary discovery that Locke's *Treatises of Government* were written about 1680, with intentions and therefore meanings necessarily unlike those he had when he published them in 1689.[2] In mine – I must inject myself here as an actor in the story – it led my researches into the work of Robert Brady to the discovery that the republication of Filmer led to two concurrent debates in different idioms (I began calling them 'languages') of political argument: one concerned with the origins and rights of government – the classic field and definition of 'political thought' – the other with the historic origins and vicissitudes of government in England.[3] The pursuit of contexts now became the pursuit of languages as well as of moments. Locke, it emerged, had taken

---

[1] Robert Filmer, *Patriarcha and Other Political Works of Sir Robert Filmer*, ed. Peter Laslett (Oxford: Basil Blackwell, 1949).

[2] John Locke, *Two Treatises of Government*, ed. Peter Laslett (Cambridge: Cambridge University Press, 1988 [1960]).

[3] J. G. A. Pocock, *The Ancient Constitution and the Feudal Law: a Study of English Historical Thought in the Seventeenth Century* (Cambridge: Cambridge University Press, 1957).

part in the first debate, but hardly in the second. His friend James Tyrrell had endeavoured to act in both, and it is a comment on the discipline we practise, rather than on his intellectual stature, that it has been fifty years since the time I am recounting before a monograph on Tyrrell has at last appeared.[4] For me, as for Skinner, the point of importance has been that the study of the contexts in which political speech acts have been performed can entail, and even become, the study of the diverse languages, ways of thinking and views of the world in which they have been conducted. It is a question whether 'political thought', 'political theory' and 'political philosophy' can be studied in ways which reduce to a single narrative the history in which they have interacted.

The Laslettian moment, as I will call it, lasted through the later 1950s, when *Philosophy, Politics and Society* – a series initiated and edited by Laslett, whose contents were so rigorously analytical as to leave little room for historical reconstruction – aroused in me the thought that if there were so many ways of validating a statement, each of these ways might have a history of its own and exist in history. I made a first attempt to elaborate a Laslettian methodology for the history of political thought in 1962,[5] when Laslett's work on Locke was mainly done and his interests were about to take a new turn. I published further methodological essays between 1968 and 1987;[6] these do not invite the same intensity of analytical attention that has been paid to Skinner's writings of the like kind, though I dare say that comparison would reveal both similarities and dissimilarities between the ways in which we attempt to reconstitute the performance of speech acts constituting political discourse in history. I am more interested in comparing the historical narratives we have constructed than

---

[4] Julia Rudolph, *Revolution by Degrees: James Tyrrell and Whig Political Thought in the Late Seventeenth Century* (New York: Palgrave Macmillan, 2002).

[5] J. G. A. Pocock, 'The History of Political Thought: a Methodological Enquiry', in Peter Laslett and W. G. Runciman (eds.), *Philosophy, Politics and Society*, Second Series (Oxford: Basil Blackwell, 1962).

[6] J. G. A. Pocock, 'Time, Institutions and Action: an Essay on Traditions and their Understanding', in Preston King and B. C. Parekh (eds.), *Politics and Experience: Essays Presented to Michael Oakeshott* (Cambridge: Cambridge University Press, 1968), pp. 209–38; J. G. A. Pocock, *Politics, Language and Time: Essays in Political Thought and History* (New York: Atheneum, 1971, now published by University of Chicago Press); J. G. A. Pocock, 'Verbalising a Political Act: towards a Politics of Language', *Political Theory* 1 (1973), pp. 3–17; J. G. A. Pocock, 'Political Ideas as Historical Events: Political Philosophers as Historical Actors', in Melvin Richter (ed.), *Political Theory and Political Education* (Princeton: Princeton University Press, 1980), pp. 139–58; J. G. A. Pocock, 'The Reconstruction of Discourse: towards the Historiography of Political Thought', *Modern Language Notes* 96 (1981), pp. 959–80; J. G. A. Pocock, *Virtue, Commerce and History: Essays on Political Thought and History, Chiefly in the Eighteenth Century* (Cambridge: Cambridge University Press, 1985); J. G. A. Pocock, 'The Concept of a Language and the *métier d'historien*: Some Considerations on Practice', in Anthony Pagden (ed.), *The Languages of Political Theory in Early Modern Europe* (Cambridge: Cambridge University Press, 1987), pp. 19–40; J. G. A. Pocock, 'Texts as Events: Reflections on the History of Political Thought', in Kevin Sharpe and Steven N. Zwicker (eds.), *Politics of Discourse: the Literature and History of Seventeenth-Century England* (Los Angeles: University of California Press, 1987), pp. 21–34.

in comparing their methodological structures. By 1964 Skinner's essays, both metahistorical and historical, had begun to appear and had laid the foundations of an alliance between us, and with others, that nothing seems likely to shake.

II

A moment of secondary creation; readers of Tolkien will know that this is the real danger point. *The Foundations of Modern Political Thought* appeared in 1978, and the circumstance I cannot refrain from mentioning is that *The Machiavellian Moment: Florentine Political Thought and the Atlantic Republican Tradition* had appeared from Princeton three years earlier. It is a further contextualisation and complication that in 2003, the year in which the silver jubilee of *Foundations* was celebrated at the conference that gave rise to the present volume, *The Machiavellian Moment* was reissued with an afterword dealing with its reception and afterlife;[7] and in the same year I published *The First Decline and Fall*,[8] a survey through the centuries of the idea that the Roman empire and its decline were alike consequences of the fall of the republic, which might well have been subtitled 'Gibbon's Machiavellian Moment'. These volumes, in turn, appeared close on the heels of Skinner's three-volume *Visions of Politics*, and there is a complex if somewhat elephantine round-dance that encourages me to comment on what Skinner has been doing in the light of what I have been doing myself.

It was, of course, Skinner who suggested the first part of my 1975 title – nobody but myself should bear responsibility for the second – but the meaning of 'the Machiavellian moment' has developed beyond what he may have had in mind. It does not mean only 'the moment when Machiavelli performed his speech acts and effected their consequences (including those he could not have intended)', or 'the moment at which it is possible to say that Machiavelli's intentions assumed the shape they had' (there are of course two moments implicit in the latter formulation). These are Skinnerian moments and I certainly intended to isolate and describe them; but there is a further level of meaning to 'the Machiavellian moment' which it might be less plausible to say that Skinner meant to intimate to me. The phrase came – in the course of writing the book of which it is the title – to denote two moments of transitoriness which Machiavelli perceived, lived in and explored in his writings: the moment at which some form of government – e.g. the regime set up by Cosimo de' Medici in the early fifteenth century – was seen to be fragile and a republic both possible

---

[7] J. G. A. Pocock, *The Machiavellian Moment: Florentine Political Thought and the Atlantic Republican Tradition: with a New Afterword by the Author* (Princeton: Princeton University Press, 2003).
[8] J. G. A. Pocock, *Barbarism and Religion*, vol. III: *The First Decline and Fall* (Cambridge: Cambridge University Press, 2003).

and necessary; and the moment at which the republic in its turn encountered problems within or without its own nature with which it could not cope. Short of some millennial future, I came to argue, the republic attempted so perfect an equilibrium among the components of a necessarily imperfect human nature that it must be thought of as deliberately incurring its own mortality; the Christian Augustine knew this, and so did the pagan Machiavelli.

There is, then, an element of historicism about my volume of 1975 – scarcely congenial though the word may be to one like myself whose thinking was shaped in the era of Karl Popper; the republic, and by implication the society, is perceived in its historicity. It is possible, though it should be attempted only with caution, to link this with the proposition that the thrust of Skinner's strategy of contextualisation is to return the text, and the speech acts implied in writing it, to the language context existing at a particular time, and to construct the author's intentions as they were shaped at that time; whereas *The Machiavellian Moment* and the works growing out of it have directly addressed the question of what happens when a language of discourse persists and is redeployed in a historical situation, or context, other than that in which it was deployed previously. My book attempts to narrate how Machiavelli's texts, and the implication of his language, were employed by some and attacked by others, first in seventeenth-century England and then in eighteenth-century England and America. That is not attempted in, and may be precluded by, the structure of *The Foundations of Modern Political Thought*, though we come closer to it as we pass from the second to the third volume of *Visions of Politics* almost a quarter-century later.

Foundations consists of two volumes, entitled *The Renaissance* and *The Age of Reformation*. The first is focused on the politics of Italian humanism and the Italian city-states; it deals with the principle that the life of a citizen in a republic is natural and necessary to men (not to women), with Machiavelli's recension of this idea, and with the consequences of the downfall of the republics in the *cinquecento*. The second is discontinuous with the first, being centrally concerned with a problem the republics never faced: that of the circumstances, if any, in which the subject is entitled to resist the ruler in the name of religious truth. There is no need of a narrative showing how the problems of the first volume came to be replaced by those of the second, since it is unlikely that such a process can ever be located. *Foundations* concludes, however, with a statement[9] that seems to imply a future development and a narrative: that 'the foundations of modern political thought' were laid when (a) the subject of political thought came to be predominantly 'the state', (b) 'the state' came to be the subject of a kind of thought to be termed 'philosophy'. How far these propositions have determined the course of Skinner's work since 1978 may be

---

[9] Quentin Skinner, *The Foundations of Modern Political Thought*, 2 vols. (Cambridge: Cambridge University Press, 1978), II, 'Conclusion', *passim*; especially p. 358, concluding the whole work.

debated; it is certain, however, that they are not addressed – and I see no reason why they should have been – in *The Machiavellian Moment* or any of my work since 1975.

This is not a disagreement between us. I was not offering a generalised history of political thought, and shared what might be considered Skinner's doubts as to whether there could be such a thing. I was not much concerned with the moment at which political thought became 'modern', or with the 'foundations' of whatever entitled it to be so regarded; and I do not suggest here that his work should be treated as attempting to solve such questions. I have not engaged – nor, I think, has he – with the pursuit of 'modernity', though I have noted several historical moments at which the term 'modern' was employed in changing senses. In Skinner's work, however, I see the second and third volumes of *Visions of Politics* as displaying a structure not unlike that of *Foundations*, which may furnish both a narrated process and some points arguable between him and me.

The second volume of *Visions* resembles the first of *Foundations* in that it consists of essays on republican and civic thinking before and during the time of Machiavelli. The third consists of essays about Thomas Hobbes, and may be thought of as going beyond the themes of *Foundations'* second volume to a time when 'the state' was being called into existence to solve the devastating problems of religious resistance and civil war. It is clear, moreover, that Hobbes knew the language which depicted citizens as living in republics to assert their civil, military and moral virtue, and that he altogether repudiated it; and it is possible to suppose that he intended to counter the image and ideal of the citizen with that of the subject, who had evoked the state to protect him and owed it unqualified obedience. There might be found here a broadly conceived narrative, in which one ideal confronted another and the confrontation had outcomes; but it remains a question whether we are following a process of change or simply moving to another part of the forest.

This question is entangled in others. In the first volume of *Foundations* Skinner proposed an important modification of something Hans Baron had said, and I had not abandoned, about the origin and originality of Italian republican ideas of civic liberty. Baron – so challenging a proponent of 'civic humanism' that it is still thought worth while to devote an entire volume to criticism of him and all associated with him[10] – was in his own way a Laslettian contextualiser; he had argued, in great bibliographic detail, that Florentine humanists turned from medieval imperialism to 'modern' (as he thought of it) republicanism under the stress of a single historical experience, the Viscontian war of 1400–2. I had not adopted this thesis – I recall, though I cannot now document, receiving

---

[10] James Hankins (ed.), *Renaissance Civic Humanism: Reappraisals and Reflections* (Cambridge: Cambridge University Press, 2000).

a letter from Professor Baron in which he expressed regret that I had not seen fit to endorse it – but I had accepted the argument that there were Florentines who carried the idea of active citizenship to lengths that made it part of 'the Machiavellian moment'. I hold to this position, though it may be worth recording that I do not see these assertions as constituting a birth of the 'modern' or its 'foundations'. There are too many problems attached to a concept of the 'modern' as resting upon a rebirth of the 'ancient'; and the notion of 'modernity' exercises a hold on the scholarly mind that I find shapeless and would like to see de- and reconstructed.[11]

I had also argued strongly that the idea of active citizenship rested on Aristotelian foundations. This has been much misunderstood, and I may have misled readers through failure to foresee this. Clearly, a fully 'Aristotelian' or 'scholastic' training was not conducive to 'civic humanism' and might underwrite the king as readily as the republic; I might have made it clearer that when I wrote 'Aristotelian' I did not have the whole body of his philosophy in mind. But I had found in the *Politics* the most satisfying theory of the active citizen I had, or have, encountered: that in which he (she had yet to be included) is an equal, ruling over equals and so ruled by them, taking decisions which extend to the shape and character of the *polis* or *res publica*, and finding in the exercise and enjoyment of this equality a freedom and authority necessary to the nature of the human being. I continue to employ this image of the citizen in the criticism of my own world as well as in the reconstitution of worlds past, and I am clearly at the danger point where the heuristic or the prescriptive may become, or be confounded with, the historical; but having found this concept in the *Politics*, a text as well known to Florentine humanists as any other, I thought myself safe in employing it in the interpretation of their thinking and believed I had some evidence of its presence in their texts.

What Skinner proposed in the first volume of *Foundations* was to move the entire formulation – or as we should now say 'invention' – of active citizenship back from the *quattrocento* where Baron had placed it, to the *trecento* or even before, in the crisis of Hohenstaufen disintegration and Guelf predominance which humanists and historians came to treat as cardinal. This entailed moving it from Aristotelian terms to Ciceronian, from Greek to Latin, and from philosophy to rhetoric, and uncovering a language of citizenship employed by *dictatores* at large, by Brunetto Latini, Tolomeo da Lucca, possibly St Thomas himself, and developed in pictorial form by Ambrogio Lorenzetti in the frescoes of good and bad government at Siena of which Skinner has written in such fullness. This massive shift – is it a paradigm shift? – from a Greek to a Roman vocabulary has been of enormous value, clarifying and enriching our understanding of the

---

[11] J. G. A. Pocock, 'Foundations of Modernity in Early Modern Historical Thinking', forthcoming in *Intellectual History Review* 19 (2007).

history of the civic. Yet when we explore its intimations for what Baron or I had been attempting to say, we find ourselves in terrain where Skinner is not the only actor – as he never thought he was – and intentions additional to his have to be taken into account.

III

Isaiah Berlin's *Two Concepts of Liberty* had been published in 1958; his *The Originality of Machiavelli* by 1972.[12] The former initiated the debate over 'positive' and 'negative' concepts of liberty which is still going on, and has claimed Skinner's attention, through his inaugural lecture on *Liberty before Liberalism* to his Isaiah Berlin lecture of 2001. This has been a normative and analytical debate – which concept makes better linguistic sense? which concept is on the whole to be preferred? – and though Skinner and I have both been attentive to it in our historical writings, and have probably given indications of our respective normative preferences, it is certainly not the case that either of us has been writing history as a contribution to the debate. Nevertheless, the two concepts are of substantive as well as heuristic value in the writing of history, since both have from time to time been articulated and set in opposition. It was Charles I on the scaffold who declared that the liberty of the people consisted in their freedom under law, not in their having a voice in their own government. In the historical enquiry which Skinner and I have been pursuing, the 'republican' concept of active citizenship – particularly in the Aristotelian form in which I have sought to express it – articulates at a high level the 'positive' concept of liberty; it is the freedom *to* speak, *to* act, *to* associate, *to* enter upon relations with one's equals, *to* take decisions, *to* affirm what one's city and one's self shall be; to be – in short – the political creature it is said one is, and ought to be, by nature. It is less a freedom to do than to be; less an assertion of right than an exercise of virtue. At another extreme, the individual presupposed by Hobbes, who accepts the sovereign's actions as his own that he may be free from the fear of death, has carried negative liberty about as far as it is possible to go, and may be intelligible to the philosopher when he can no longer be represented by the rhetorician.

To pass from Machiavelli to Hobbes is to pass from *Visions II* to *Visions III*, not from *Foundations I* to *Foundations II*; Skinner's engagement with Hobbes may belong chiefly to the period after 1978. Yet the presence of Berlin and the two concepts has long been apparent to me – though I cannot now remember when I first noticed it – when I consider the proposal in *Foundations I* to move the origins of the ideal of citizenship from the *quattrocento* to the *duecento* and

---

[12] For the latter, see Myron P. Gilmore (ed.), *Studies on Machiavelli* (Florence: Sansoni, 1972), pp. 149–206.

from Aristotle to Cicero. This is not a perception of Skinner's intentions, but of the climate in which we were both writing. I was aware – and I still am – of a deep-seated reluctance to accept the humanist concept of citizenship and its equation of virtue with autonomy and activity as an independent and enduring voice in the human conversation about politics. There are several reasons for this; a preference for Berlin's negative liberty over his positive is only one of them. The history of political thought – an academic sub-discipline – has from the beginning, and for good reasons, been conceived as an interplay between the languages of philosophy, theology and jurisprudence, and the intensely rhetorical, historical and Roman language of republican citizenship does not fit easily into this framework. There has been a tendency to rework the history of civic thought so that it conforms to the prevailing paradigm, and since a strong element in the latter has been the language of jurisprudence, which presupposes a subject who has rights and a sovereign who makes law, there has been an inbuilt bias in favour of a negative concept of liberty. In most criticism directed against Baron, against myself, and against Skinner in so far as he is seen as making use of us, I think I detect an impulse not to rewrite the history of civic humanism, but to write it out of history as far as possible.

Skinner of course does not share this impulse, though I am a little suspicious when he seems to suggest replacing 'republican' by 'neo-Roman', on the grounds that the latter seems to appeal to Roman law rather than to Roman virtue and to Caesar rather than to the republic. The proposal in *Foundations* to ground citizenship in medieval Ciceronianism, however, long predates the invention of the neo-Roman and was aimed mainly against Baron's contention that active republicanism was born suddenly and traumatically in 1400–2. In *The First Decline and Fall* I have returned to this enquiry, and have been led to suggest that the civic virtues praised in 1250–1350 were not incompatible with a *translatio imperii*, in the sense that they could survive the republic, to flourish and become Christian under the good emperors. Turning to Leonardo Bruni, however, I find it unequivocally asserted that the liberty which sustained virtue, and the empire which virtue sustained, began to collapse and decay with the first Caesars, who deprived the Romans of the liberty of the republic.[13] Here is something much more like the dramatic breach with medieval imperialism and papalism which Baron affirmed, though I have not followed him in seeking to identify its moment or its causes.

I have not done so because I am pursuing the continuous if intermittent history of a theme in Western historiography which is also a theme in political thought: the theme of *libertas et imperium*, seen as inseparable and yet incompatible. Only the liberty obtained by expulsion of the kings, says Sallust, enabled the Romans to build up an empire; the extent of that empire, says Tacitus, made

---

[13] Pocock, *The First Decline and Fall*, ch. 8.

a return to monarchy necessary; the consequent loss of liberty, say Bruni and Machiavelli, destroyed both virtue and empire. There takes shape a historiography in which empire is seen as corrupting both the republic and the principate; and the consequence for political theory and philosophy is that liberty is exercised in history and is self-problematising. It is hard to be free and rule ourselves without ruling others who are not free; a problematic by no means archaic in the year 2003. In this way the Machiavellian moment becomes an enduring constituent of Euro-American political thought, a theme still pursued in *The First Decline and Fall*.

IV

If the 'Machiavellian' scenario survives and persists – as I contend it does far into the eighteenth century – it is fair for me to ask how it will stand in relation to any scenario that may appear in Skinner's further work. I am writing at a moment when his work is big with a future whose argument is not yet disclosed, and it would be a waste of good trees to fill pages with speculations about that future, or ask him to anticipate intentions he is in process of carrying out; one does not really know one's intentions until one sees them declared and put in practice. Nevertheless, this volume stands at a moment of commemoration which is also one of anticipation, and since he is certainly about to do something other than what I have done, it may be suggestive to employ *The Machiavellian Moment* in asking what that something is going to be.

I have suggested that neither the two volumes of *Foundations* nor the second and third volumes of *Visions* supply us with a covering narrative or macro-narrative. Let me say at once that there is no reason why they should have done so, or why they should be any the worse if they do not. It is possible that Skinner's historical intelligence is focused on the synchronic, the detailed reconstruction of language situations as they exist at a given time, whereas mine leans to the diachronic, the study of what happens when languages change or texts migrate from one historical situation to another. If this is so, there comes a point when our intentions diverge and neither offers more than an incidental criticism of the other. It is none the less true that to have, or not to have, a given set of intentions has consequences, and that it is legitimate on these grounds to enquire whether his work may in future entail a covering narrative, and whether that will – as there is no reason why it must – resemble that of *The Machiavellian Moment*.

I have contended that *Foundations I* and *II* do not supply a covering narrative, for the reason that there is no process or series in which writers can be seen moving from the language of Renaissance citizenship to the language of Reformation resistance; these are simply two different stories, told in the order of time. The situation is somewhat different when we turn to *Visions II* and *III*, since Hobbes knew about Machiavelli and found him problematic in his world. That is to say, concepts and arguments from the thought-world of classical and humanist literature – Ciceronian, Plutarchan, Machiavellian and Tacitist – had, somewhat surprisingly, made their way into the thought-world and rhetorical armoury of Stuart England; and Hobbes considered their presence there harmful and set out to refute and expel them. It would therefore be possible to construct a narrative in which humanist language about citizenship and its virtues collided with a Hobbesian language about right, law and sovereign will, and the latter, probably more deeply entrenched in England, won what looks like a series of victories, which however did not (as we shall see) expel the former from the English conceptual vocabulary.

To construct this narrative would have a further interesting effect. The Italian citizen affirming his virtue and the English subject defending his rights may without much distortion be made to stand for the 'positive' and 'negative' poles of Isaiah Berlin's 'two concepts of liberty', and these concepts, or phenomena not unlike them, may be found operative in the narrative of history as well as in the schematisations of philosophy. It might be said that Skinner's *Reason and Rhetoric in the Philosophy of Hobbes* is a sophisticated and brilliant exploration of the intimations of their presence in conflict there. Such a narrative, however, would be multi-dimensional and have a tangled plot. The text of *Leviathan* is extremely rich and many threads, with accompanying narratives, run through it; Hobbes's antipathy to the rhetoric of civic action and civic virtue is not more than one, though an extremely interesting one, of them. There are other narratives with other starting points. Skinner's recent publication indicates one such: his *A Third Concept of Liberty*, which carries on the enterprise, evident even before *Liberty before Liberalism*, of seeking a way of defining liberty, valid both as philosophical concept and as historical phenomenon, identical with neither Berlin's 'positive' nor his 'negative' liberty. This third concept may be defined, very tersely, as the proposition that one is free only if one's will is not dependent on that of another. In his Isaiah Berlin lecture under this title, Skinner both explores this concept in the spirit of the analytical philosopher, which is one of the things he is, and gives evidence for the presence of language suggesting it in the history of the English Civil War, arriving at a moment when 'an apoplectic Hobbes picked up his pen' to answer it.

I have certain reservations about the third concept of liberty. Philosophically, the condition of having no master, to which it very often amounts, seems to me oddly incomplete when set beside the Aristotelian definition of liberty as equality, mentioned earlier. Equality is more than the mere absence of inequality; it may denote an actual and positive relationship, a friendship or fraternity (gender-free equivalent wanted) between equals which is to be enjoyed for its own sake and, when converted into decision, becomes a necessary way of asserting one's humanity. To have no master, and so to be neither slave nor villein, is a means or prerequisite of equality, not the end for which one has it; so that when put forward as an alternative to the positive freedom of the citizen, it begins to look like a diminution of the latter. Historically, it seems that this definition of freedom could be situated in a number of linguistic contexts having meaning to the minds of the seventeenth century, so that one would need to know in what particular context it was being situated before one knew what particular speech act was being performed. In the historical material Skinner puts before us, the condition of having no master seems to become the liberty one has under law, which defines one's properties and rights and makes one the equal of others who are, like oneself, *legales homines* and neither serfs nor villeins. Whether this concept of liberty is termed 'neo-Roman' seems to depend on whether the civil or the common law is thought of as providing the definition.

I am inclined, then, to suspect a certain indeterminacy in this definition of liberty, especially when it is used to denote a form of argument continuously involved in history. I do not doubt that the argument that to be deprived of recourse to law is to be reduced to slavery is regularly to be found in history, from the English Civil War to the War of the American Revolution, or that it is one of several arguments (not all reducible to it) which Hobbes set out to answer. But – while waiting for the text of Skinner's Ford lectures to instruct me, as they surely will – I suspect that there were other arguments going on – some to be found answered in *Leviathan* and others not – and consequently a number of narratives to be recounted, especially if, in Skinner's company or without it, we journey past Hobbes into the very different world after 1688.

V

Here I resume a narrative of my own which does undertake that journey. It may be recalled that I selected for my pivotal figure of the English Revolution not Thomas Hobbes but James Harrington.[14] While we know what Harrington thought of Hobbes we do not seem to know what Hobbes thought of Harrington; but we do know that if the two differed radically as to the meaning of *libertas* on the towers of Lucca, they were agreed, though for opposite purposes, that the first bishops did not owe their office to supernatural grace conferred by the hands of apostles. I proposed that Harrington constructed a 'Machiavellian meditation on feudalism', in which the decay of feudal tenures restored, for the first time in a millennium and a half, the prospect that free armed proprietors might act as citizens and display that governing virtue which made them the

[14] Pocock, *The Machiavellian Moment*, ch. 11; James Harrington, *The Political Works of James Harrington*, ed. J. G. A. Pocock (Cambridge: Cambridge University Press, 1977); J. G. A. Pocock (ed.), *Harrington: Oceana and a System of Politics* (Cambridge: Cambridge University Press, 1992).

images of God. I regard it as evidence of the deep division in the twentieth-century scholarly mind opened by Berlin's *Two Concepts of Liberty* that I have been beset by critics bent on proving that Harrington was not a civic humanist in some sense or other, or therefore at all. It also seems no accident that Richard Tuck brought his *Government and Philosophy* to an end in 1651, the year of *Leviathan*, and did not go on five years to the date of *Oceana*. Harrington was not a philosopher as Tuck uses the term, and cannot be brought within a history of political thought controlled by the concept of philosophy. The multiplicity of paradigms remains the issue.

In reply to those who criticised my interpretation of Harrington, I have replied, secondarily, that his philosophy, if he had one, contained a strong admixture of Platonism; primarily, that he constructed a history of arms, property, liberty and virtue, running from ancient times to his own and intended to culminate in a rebirth of the capacity for republican self-government.[15] This was an achievement scarcely attempted before his time, and injected historical narrative into political argument on a scale not previously known. Within half a century, however, it was being attacked, with the intention of replacing it, by a counter-narrative in which the need to bear arms and act in one's own government was overtaken and relegated to a past both classic and barbaric, by the capacity, or rather the opportunity, to enter into the relationships of a commercial society, in which one was defended by professionals one paid and governed by representatives one elected. There ensued an almost revolutionary pervasion – if not a takeover – of political thought by a new language of commerce, manners and politeness,[16] whose transforming effects have been the theme of most writers on eighteenth-century discourse, and of all my own writings since (and including) the second half of *The Machiavellian Moment*. This is a sequence into which Skinner's historical pursuits have not yet led him, and it is possible to wonder whether they will.

There was debate in the eighteenth century for, but significantly also against, this transformation of both politics and history. Those who assailed it commonly looked back to a Roman or Gothic past, in which the individual retained his virtue through his direct participation in the exercise of arms and politics; those who defended it were able to depict 'virtue' as feudal and barbaric, but found it harder to supply commercial man with a personality replacing the unity he had lost. There arose, a century before Benjamin Constant, a debate between 'ancient' and 'modern liberty', having much in common with Berlin's 'positive' and 'negative', but situated within a pessimist historicism that depicted a unified personality as looking back to the savage, the civilised personality as looking forward to corruption and disintegration. Its representative among modern

---

[15] Pocock, *The Machiavellian Moment*, pp. 567–9.

[16] J. G. A. Pocock, 'Virtues, Rights and Manners: a Model for Historians of Political Thought', in Pocock, *Virtue, Commerce and History*, pp. 37–50.

philosophers has been not Berlin but Hannah Arendt, arguing that in the eighteenth century the political was overtaken by the social, and the study of action superseded by that of behaviour.[17]

I am tempted to develop this narrative into a critique of postmodernism, as completing the disintegration of the self in a commodified society whose beginnings I see detected three centuries ago. The points of substance for the present essay, however, are first, that its pursuit has supplied me with a narrative, and even a narrative of the transformation of narrative itself; second, that in pursuing it I have been able to relate the modification of political thought by the operation, and perhaps the changing roles, of modes of discourse other than the philosophy, theology and jurisprudence canonically supposed to constitute it throughout its history. My perception fifty-five years ago that the Filmerian controversy was conducted in the language of history as well as philosophy was enlarged and enhanced by the discovery of civic humanism and then of political economy; and in all this I owe enormous debts to two scholars, Peter Laslett and Quentin Skinner. In speculating on Skinner's further work, therefore, I ask myself the following questions. Will he find a narrative – does he need one at all? – in which the subject matter and governing procedures of political thought are transformed by the injection of new languages? I have been led away – at no time unwillingly – from the study of philosophy and the state towards that of historiography and civil society (themselves new and innovative concepts). Does he still pursue the dictum at the end of *Foundations*, that 'modern' political thought consists in the former mode of study? If so, his definition of 'modernity' will probably differ from any I use, but I would rather be emancipated from defining it at all. I much doubt if he will allow himself to be dominated or constrained by his language of 1978, but I cannot predict with what governing concepts he will study the history of political thought down to Hobbes and possibly beyond. It will be worth waiting to find out.

---

[17] Hannah Arendt, *The Human Condition* (Chicago: University of Chicago Press, 1958), ch. 6.

4 Skinner, pre-humanist rhetorical culture and Machiavelli

Marco Geuna

It has been suggested that *The Foundations of Modern Political Thought* is actually 'a thesis book, highly polemical and with a profiled perspective of its own'.[1] In what follows I would like to take this suggestion seriously and consider some of the interpretative choices and historiographical theses developed in that book. In particular, I will examine Quentin Skinner's theses on pre-humanist rhetorical culture and on the origins of humanism, and I will analyse his interpretation of Machiavelli and of the intellectual contexts necessary for an understanding of the Florentine Secretary. I will then show how these theses provide the basis for Skinner's historical and philosophical work of the 1980s, from the essays on Machiavelli and Lorenzetti to the essays on the ideal of political liberty. Lastly, I will discuss briefly some of his latest texts, from *Liberty before Liberalism* to *Visions of Politics*, and argue that Skinner has remained attached to the substance of his original historiographical theses, while widening the scope of his research and of his argument, and making some significant changes in the terminology in which they were couched. I will emphasise that Skinner's later work marks a shift in emphasis, but does not substantially modify his earlier presentation of modern political thought, of its conflicting vocabularies and its opposing traditions.

I

According to Skinner, if we want to understand the foundations or the origins of modern political thought we must return to the twelfth century. The opening chapter of *Foundations* takes the reader back to the *comuni*, the Italian city-republics and their experience of self-government: their practice of electing magistrates (first the *consoli* and then the *podestà*) and *consigli*. Skinner is convinced that in the rhetorical, juridical and philosophical reflections which emerged from those experiences lay some of the roots of modern political thought. In so doing, Skinner is making a precise historiographical choice. He

[1] Kari Palonen, *Quentin Skinner: History, Politics, Rhetoric* (Cambridge: Polity Press, 2003), p. 91.

is strongly opposing the theses of Hans Baron, according to whom the origins of humanism, and ultimately of modern political thought, were to be located at the beginning of the *quattrocento*, in the period of the Florentine opposition to the expansionistic designs of Giangaleazzo Visconti. In *The Crisis of the Early Italian Renaissance*, Baron had argued that prior to that moment and prior to the writings of 'civic humanists' like Salutati and Bruni, no republican ideology defending the special virtues of republican civic life had been produced. Furthermore, Baron claimed that prior to this cleavage the majority of political thinkers adhered to the medieval idea of 'imperial monarchy' and that before the early fifteenth century it was impossible to find a positive re-evaluation of the moral and political ideas of Cicero and a developed 'Republican interpretation of Roman history'.[2]

In many passages of the first chapters of *Foundations* Skinner challenges the chronology and the historiographical theses of Baron,[3] later taken up by many historians, ranging from Ronald Witt and George Holmes to John Pocock. Against Baron, Skinner takes as a starting point the studies of Paul Oskar Kristeller on Renaissance thought.[4] Already in the 1950s and 1960s, Kristeller had shown the importance of constructing a specific and precise concept of humanism. He had argued, in fact, that within Renaissance thought it was possible to distinguish a variety of strains: the classic, the scholastic and the specifically humanist strain. He considered the humanists, the scholars who pursued the *studia humanitatis*, as the heirs of those teachers of rhetoric of the previous centuries, of the masters of the *ars dictaminis*. Skinner further develops the hypotheses of Kristeller[5] and, taking up some observations of Charles Davis and Jerrold Seigel, outlines an interpretation which is a radical alternative to the one originally put forward by Hans Baron.

Thus the first part of *Foundations*, devoted to 'The origins of the Renaissance', opens onto a discussion of the 'ideal of liberty' that emerges from the experience of the *comuni*, in their opposition to both the papacy and the empire. This ideal centred on the vindication of the independence of the cities and in the assertion of the value of republican self-government. Skinner reconstructs the conceptual strands of this ideal of liberty and the languages through which it was formulated. Two distinct traditions of thought make this defence of the

---

[2] Hans Baron, *The Crisis of the Early Italian Renaissance*, 2nd edn (Princeton: Princeton University Press, 1966), pp. 49, 58, 64, 160, 444–6.

[3] Quentin Skinner, *The Foundations of Modern Political Thought*, 2 vols. (Cambridge: Cambridge University Press, 1978), I, pp. 27, 54, 70–1, 77, 79, 82, 102.

[4] P. O. Kristeller, *Studies in Renaissance Thought and Letters* (Rome: Edizioni di Storia e Letteratura, 1956); P. O. Kristeller, *Renaissance Thought: the Classic, Scholastic and Humanistic Strains* (New York: Harper & Row, 1961).

[5] Skinner refers to his debt in many passages: *Foundations*, I, pp. xxiii–xxiv, 71–2, 102–5. He will also acknowledge it in subsequent writings. See e.g. Quentin Skinner, *Visions of Politics*, 3 vols. (Cambridge: Cambridge University Press, 2002), II, p. 92n.

political experience of the city-republics possible: the tradition of rhetoric, developed in the teaching of the *ars dictaminis* in the universities of Bologna and of the other cities of the *Regnum Italicum*, and the scholastic tradition of Aristotelian derivation, that finds one of its highest points in Marsilius' *Defensor pacis*.

Skinner does, in fact, devote a chapter to the theme 'Scholasticism and liberty' in which he reconstructs the reception of Aristotle's *Politics* in the last decades of the thirteenth century and presents the thought of Remigio de' Girolami and Tolomeo da Lucca, as well as the philosophical and juridical theories of Marsilius of Padua and Bartolus of Sassoferrato. But his most important contribution is certainly to be found in the preceding chapter devoted to 'Rhetoric and Liberty'. This chapter takes into consideration a series of writings, some by unknown or lesser-known authors, in order to show the political significance of texts which until then had only been considered from the perspective of the history of rhetoric or for their literary value. Having clarified the basic principles of the traditional teaching of rhetoric in Bologna, from the *Praecepta dictaminum* of Adalberto Samaritano to the *Rhetorica novissima* of Boncompagno da Signa – principles to be followed in the composition of official letters and other public documents – Skinner concentrates on the development of the *ars dictaminis* in the second half of the twelfth century and the first half of the thirteenth century. Taking as a starting point the studies of Hélène Wieruszowski, he shows how epistolography turned its attention increasingly to practical-political problems and how the *ars dictaminis* became increasingly paired up with the *ars arengandi*, the art of pronouncing official political speeches, as borne out by the texts of Guido Faba. Above all, Skinner emphasises how these transformations of the *ars dictaminis* led to the emergence, already in the first half of the thirteenth century, of two new literary genres: the city chronicles, a completely new form of civic historiography, and the advice-books for the *podestà* and for the magistrates of the city. While we can attribute to the first genre works by Boncompagno da Signa and by Rolandino da Padova, to the second genre we can attribute the anonymous *Oculus pastoralis*, conventionally dated at 1222, and the *Liber de Regimine Civitatum*, written between 1240 and 1250 by Giovanni da Viterbo. Following on the tracks of Kristeller, Skinner traces the transformations of the *ars dictaminis* in Italy determined by the reception of the French innovations in the teaching of rhetoric, according to which rhetoric should not be taught simply in terms of rules, but also through the study and imitation of classical authors. Having shown that for the Orléans school the teaching of rhetoric was essentially based on the *De inventione* of Cicero and on the pseudo-Ciceronian *Rhetorica ad Herennium*, Skinner centres his attention on the contributions by Brunetto Latini and Giovanni di Bonandrea, and on the ample space they gave in their writings to Cicero, through the reception of the French innovations. Skinner unhesitatingly locates 'the emergence of

Humanism' in these further developments in the understanding and teaching of rhetoric, in the idea of the necessary study and imitation of classical authors.

Having outlined these developments diachronically, Skinner concentrates synchronically on clarifying the political outcomes of this overall rhetorical culture and reconstructs the 'structure' of this pre-humanist 'ideology'. He underlines that many of its authors adopt and defend the ideal of *libertas*: they argue in favour of the independence of cities and the superiority of republican self-government, opposing it to the 'tyranny' of the *signori*. They reflect on the causes of the crisis of republican liberty, on the reasons for the emergence of the *signori*. They find these causes in the formation of factions, which weaken and threaten civic concord, and in the increase of riches, in the search for private profit, which undermines the attention to the common good and to the public virtues. These authors claim that in order to avoid the crisis of republican orders one must encourage and fortify the *virtù* of the people and of the magistrates: they repropose the classical typology of cardinal virtues, matching them with long lists of vices, from avarice to cupidity, from cruelty to fraud, that need to be avoided.

In order to find a defence of republican liberty, therefore, it is not necessary to wait for the first civic humanists of the early *quattrocento*; we can find it in the rhetorical culture of the thirteenth and fourteenth centuries, in texts such as *Oculus pastoralis* or the writings of Giovanni da Viterbo, Brunetto Latini and Albertino Mussato. While in the past many scholars focused their studies on the Aristotelian roots of scholasticism, and on the continuities between scholasticism and the humanist culture of the *quattrocento*, Skinner's originality lies, first of all, in having shown the existence of a rhetorical culture which, prior to the rediscovery of Aristotle, and basing itself on Roman sources (above all, Cicero and Sallust), already produced a political ideology that was capable of legitimating and defending the political experience of the city-republics. I would like to point out that Skinner's thesis has two components: the political culture with roots in the tradition of rhetoric developed 'before the rediscovery of Aristotle', and it was structured by reference to and use of 'Roman sources'. Furthermore, I would like to emphasise that in recovering this rhetorical literature, in incorporating it in the history of political thought, Skinner is consistent with his methodological assumptions, which he also illustrated in the preface to *Foundations*. In particular, he adheres to the methodological assumption of not being biased to the high points of philosophical-political reflection, the so-called 'classic texts', but rather paying equal attention to minor authors, to the anonymous texts that emerge from political practice,[6] which constitute the

---

[6] Skinner, *Foundations*, I, pp. x–xi and 77 on the need to examine also 'diplomatic negotiations, city chronicles and other forms of political propaganda dating back at least as far as the middle of the thirteenth century'.

ideological structure of a given historical moment and that offer the context which allows the classic texts themselves to be interpreted adequately.

Skinner's thesis, as a matter of fact, is not simply that the pre-humanist rhetorical culture developed prior to the recovery of Aristotelian moral and political philosophy and on the basis of Roman sources, but also that this culture survived the advent of Aristotelianism without major changes. The discovery of a rhetorical culture, and of its persistence and continuity in time, allows Skinner to put into question some consolidated historiographical theses. First of all, it allows him to criticise the theses proposed by John Pocock and Walter Ullmann that attribute a crucial role to the recovery and diffusion of Aristotle's *Politics* and *Nicomachean Ethics* in the 'rebirth of the citizen' and, more generally, in the formation of a true republican ideology.[7] Against those who see the decisive turning point in the recovery of these Aristotelian texts and assert a continuity between the culture of scholasticism and that of humanism, between Marsilius and Machiavelli, Skinner underlines that in doing so one devalues the role played by the rhetorical reflections on politics and history in the advent of humanism.

His reconstruction of the rhetorical culture which developed in the city-republics between the thirteenth and fourteenth centuries has been received with great attention by the scientific community and has led to further research by a variety of historians from diverse cultural backgrounds, ranging from Cary Nederman and Anthony Black in the English-speaking world, to Enrico Artifoni in Italy.[8]

At this point it is clear that the recovery of pre-humanist rhetorical culture, and its roots in Roman historical and political thought, proves to be of long-lasting importance to Skinner, granting him a different view of the political culture of the Renaissance. While Eugenio Garin had emphasised above all the Platonic roots of much political-philosophical thought in the Renaissance, and Pocock and Ullmann had emphasised the role played by the recovery of Aristotle, Skinner insists on the importance of the philosophical thought of Cicero and Seneca, and the historical thought of Sallust and Livy, for

---

[7] Skinner refers to J. G. A. Pocock, *The Machiavellian Moment: Florentine Political Thought and the Atlantic Republican Tradition* (Princeton: Princeton University Press, 1975); and W. Ullmann, *A Short History of the Papacy in the Middle Ages* (London: Methuen, 1972). Cf. *Foundations*, I, pp. 49, 82, 102.

[8] See C. J. Nederman, 'Nature, Sin and the Origins of Society: the Ciceronian Tradition in Medieval Political Thought', *Journal of the History of Ideas* 49 (1988), pp. 3–26; C. J. Nederman, 'The Union of Wisdom and Eloquence before the Renaissance: the Ciceronian Orator in Medieval Thought', *Journal of Medieval History* 18 (1992), pp. 75–95; A. Black, *Political Thought in Europe, 1250–1450* (Cambridge: Cambridge University Press, 1992); E. Artifoni, 'Sull'eloquenza politica nel Duecento italiano', *Quaderni medievali* 35 (1993), pp. 57–78; E. Artifoni, 'Retorica e organizzazione del linguaggio politico nel Duecento italiano', in P. Cammarosano (ed.), *Le forme della propaganda politica nel Due e nel Trecento* (Rome: École française de Rome, 1994), pp. 157–82.

pre-humanists like Brunetto Latini and Albertino Mussato, for humanists of the early *quattrocento* like Leonardo Bruni, and for late humanists like Machiavelli. In his opinion, Rome, not Athens, Roman thought rather than Greek thought, was more important and had a greater impact on the political thought of the Renaissance.

Skinner argues, therefore, that there is a continuity between the rhetorical elaborations of the thirteenth and fourteenth centuries, the 'civic humanist' thought of a Leonardo Bruni and a Poggio Bracciolini, and the historical and political reflections of late humanists such as Machiavelli and Guicciardini. Such continuity is not only based on shared values and ideals, above all that of the excellence of republican government, and on the analyses of the causes of the crisis of republican orders and of the remedies for this crisis, but also on a shared resort to the same literary genres. In fact, Skinner finds continuity between the advice-books for the *podestà*, such as the *De Regimine Civitatum* of Giovanni da Viterbo, the texts of the *specula principum* tradition of the *quattrocento* from Patrizi to Pontano, and Machiavelli's arguments in the central chapters of *The Prince*. It is time, then, to consider Skinner's interpretation of the Florentine Secretary.

II

In his book on Machiavelli, published in 1981, Skinner presents the Florentine Secretary as 'an exponent of a distinctive humanist tradition of classical republicanism'.[9] But already in *Foundations* he reads Machiavelli's thought, and his republicanism, within the context of the *longue durée* of the humanist tradition: from the pre-humanist writings of the *dictatores*, to the texts of the civil humanists of the early *quattrocento*, to the works of the late humanists such as Guicciardini and Giannotti. These are the three diverse but deeply interrelated contexts to which Skinner constantly brings back Machiavelli's theses in order to establish which of them simply repropose shared assumptions and which constitute radical innovations.

Machiavelli's thought is dealt with in two separate chapters, 'The Age of Princes' and 'The Survival of Republican Values'. In the first chapter attention is, of course, given to *The Prince*, while in the second it is given to the *Discourses on Livy*. Not even in Machiavelli's case, then, does Skinner think it worthwhile to give a unitary treatment of an author. He prefers to keep faith with his initial methodological assumptions and continue to illustrate ideologies and traditions

---

[9] Quentin Skinner, *Machiavelli* (Oxford: Oxford University Press, 1981), p. v. On Skinner's interpretation of Machiavelli, among recent studies: M. Senellart, 'Républicanisme, bien commun et liberté individuelle. Le modèle machiavélien selon Quentin Skinner', *Revue d'éthique et de théologie morale*, *'Le Supplément'*, 193 (1995), pp. 27–64; R. Talamo, 'Quentin Skinner interprete di Machiavelli', *CroceVia* 3 (1997), pp. 80–101.

of thought rather than analyse individual authors.[10] Thus he offers two separate treatments of the two great works of the Florentine Secretary, discussing each one in relation to the cultural and ideological contexts that in his opinion are most significant and revealing.

In this way Skinner can, to some extent, sidestep the delicate problem of the relation between Machiavelli's two central works. It can be pointed out that, after all, Skinner basically accepts the chronological hypothesis and the overall interpretation developed by Baron in his famous article of 1961 'Machiavelli: the Republican Citizen and the Author of the Prince'[11]. Baron, insisting on the difference between the two works, argued that Machiavelli wrote *The Prince* first, in the second half of 1513, and only later composed the *Discourses*, which in Baron's view required the acquisition of a culture profoundly different from that possessed by Machiavelli up to that moment. In so doing, Baron was challenging the hypothesis, first formulated by Chabod and then taken up by many other interpreters, including Gennaro Sasso, according to which at least the first eighteen chapters of the *Discourses* had been written before *The Prince*. This hypothesis implied that the philosophical presuppositions of the two works were identical and that Machiavelli's culture was unitary and had not substantially changed from one work to the other.[12] Although Skinner dutifully reminds the readers that 'the dating of the *Discourses* remains a subject of learned debate' he finds that 'Baron's general argument seems plausible'.[13] The idea of an intellectual development in Machiavelli between *The Prince* and the *Discourses* seems acceptable to him and appears to underlie his choice of commenting on the two works in two distinct chapters.

It is worth noting that already in his 'Meaning and Understanding' of 1969 Skinner criticised the 'mythology' of coherence that leads interpreters into the fallacy of claiming to resolve antinomies and contradictions present in different texts by the same author, or even in one and the same text. In that context, he gave as one of the examples the differences between *The Prince* and the *Discourses*. Against the attempt to build a general and unitary scheme that explains away all differences, Skinner argued that the historian must not limit himself to 'anything

[10] Cf. Skinner, *Foundations*, I, pp. x–xi. On the limitations which Skinner's method poses for any extended treatment of individual authors, see Quentin Skinner, 'A Reply to my Critics', in James Tully (ed.), *Meaning and Context: Quentin Skinner and his Critics* (Cambridge: Polity Press, 1988), pp. 231–288, at pp. 276–7; Skinner, *Visions*, I, pp. 117–18.

[11] Hans Baron, 'Machiavelli: the Republican Citizen and the Author of the Prince', *The English Historical Review* 76 (1961), pp. 217–53. On Baron's interpretation, see the recent article by John M. Najemy, 'Baron's Machiavelli and the Renaissance Republicanism', *American Historical Review* 113 (1996), pp. 119–29.

[12] Gennaro Sasso has repeatedly contested Baron's hypothesis that the writing of the *Discourses* required a culture which radically differed from that needed for writing *The Prince*. Among his later contributions see G. Sasso, *Niccolò Machiavelli*, 2 vols. (Bologna: Il Mulino, 1993), I, pp. 330 and 350–6.

[13] Skinner, *Foundations*, I, p. 154.

so straightforward as an attempt to indicate the nature of the developments and divergences from *The Prince* to the later *Discourses*', and referred in a footnote to Baron's essay.[14]

In *Foundations*, the theses of *The Prince* are inserted into several contexts. One such context is the tradition of advice-books for the *podestà* and other magistrates; the other context, closer to Machiavelli, is the literature of *specula principum* developed in the second half of the *quattrocento*, to which Francesco Patrizi, Bartolomeo Sacchi and Giovanni Pontano, among others, contributed. For Skinner, only if we keep in mind these contexts will we be able fully to understand Machiavelli's critique of humanist values, the originality and even the 'revolutionary' character of his theses. Skinner asserts unhesitatingly that *The Prince* 'succeeded in making a contribution to the genre of advice-books for princes which at the same time revolutionised the genre itself'.[15]

Machiavelli shares with the authors of *specula principum* some of their values and ideals, which they, in turn, inherited from the 'civil humanists' of the early *quattrocento*. The prince is presented as an individual who seeks honour, glory and fame. As the highest incarnation of the *vir virtutis*, the prince opposes himself to the malign character of Fortuna and avoids for the most part the ruin caused by her constitutive instability. To this end, the prince must fully possess and practise all the virtues: for the humanists these virtues were the Christian virtues together with the four cardinal virtues, variously listed by ancient moral philosophers. But already at this point, on the question of how to understand virtue, Machiavelli's systematic dissent appeared. On the one hand, 'the format, the presuppositions and many of the central arguments of *The Prince* make it a recognisable contribution to a well-established tradition of later quattrocento political thought'. On the other hand, as soon as Machiavelli begins to redescribe the *virtù* of the prince, one clearly sees that he intended 'to question or even to ridicule' some of the shared values of the authors of the *specula principum* and, more generally, 'he was in fact concerned to challenge and repudiate his own humanist heritage'.[16]

First of all, Skinner shows that Machiavelli distances himself most from the humanist culture when he attributes a decisive role to sheer force and violence in politics, when he insists on the importance of good arms and not only of good laws to 'maintain the state', in short, when he recognises a constitutive relation between war and politics. Secondly, Skinner elegantly demonstrates how the central chapters of *The Prince*, chs. XV to XVIII, are to be understood as an intentional subversion of the humanist conceptualisation of virtue, which often

---

[14] Quentin Skinner, 'Meaning and Understanding in the History of Ideas', *History and Theory* 8 (1969), pp. 3–53, at 20; later in Tully, *Meaning and Context*, pp. 29–67, at 42.
[15] Skinner, *Foundations*, I, p. 118.   [16] Ibid., p. 129.

found its models in Cicero's *De officiis* and in Seneca's *De clementia*.[17] Once again Skinner follows and exemplifies his methodological assumptions, which had been influenced by his reading of Wittgenstein's *Philosophical Investigations* and Austin's *How to do Things with Words*.[18] Assuming that in language we can distinguish the dimension of meaning from the dimension of linguistic action, Skinner constantly asks what the authors are doing when they write such and such texts, what kind of linguistic action they are accomplishing. In the case of Machiavelli and the central chapters of *The Prince* the answer is univocal: the Florentine Secretary was subverting some of the basic values of the humanist tradition.[19]

Machiavelli and the authors of *specula principum* fully agree 'about the nature of the goals which princes ought to pursue', but they radically differ with regard to the means, to 'the methods they took to be appropriate for the attainment of these ends'.[20] Skinner can therefore take an unambiguous stand on a long-running interpretative controversy. He distances himself from Croce's thesis according to which in these chapters of *The Prince* and in his overall political philosophy Machiavelli asserts the autonomy of politics with regard to ethics. Skinner is aware that many other interpreters have taken up this thesis in the twentieth century, first of all Chabod. But he has no doubts that Machiavelli does not propose 'a view of politics as divorced from morality'; he is convinced that Machiavelli opposes to the imperatives of Stoic and Christian ethics the imperatives of a different form of ethics, the imperatives of a 'political morality'.[21] Skinner reformulates in this way the suggestive thesis of

---

[17] In subsequent writings, Skinner will present Machiavelli's discussions of liberality and clemency, in chs. 16 and 17 of *The Prince*, as paradigmatic examples of 'rhetorical redescription', of 'paradiastolic redescription'. See Quentin Skinner, *Reason and Rhetoric in the Philosophy of Hobbes* (Cambridge: Cambridge University Press, 1996), pp. 170–1; Skinner, *Visions*, I, pp. 184–5.

[18] On Skinner's methodological reflections, see James Tully, 'The Pen is a Mighty Sword: Quentin Skinner's Analysis of Politics', in Tully, *Meaning and Context*, pp. 7–25. Among the many subsequent contributions to this debate, for a useful comparison between Skinner's approach and other approaches to the history of political languages and concepts, see: M. Richter, *The History of Political and Social Concepts* (Oxford: Oxford University Press, 1995) and Kari Palonen, *Die Entzauberung der Begriffe. Das Umschreiben der politischen Begriffe bei Quentin Skinner und Reinhart Koselleck* (Münster: Lit Verlag, 2004), which include comprehensive bibliographies. See also Iain Hampsher-Monk, 'The History of Political Thought and the Political History of Thought', in Dario Castiglione and Iain Hampsher-Monk (eds.), *The History of Political Thought in National Context* (Cambridge: Cambridge University Press, 2001), pp. 159–74.

[19] In later writings, Skinner argues that Machiavelli continued to consider important three of the cardinal virtues (courage, temperance, prudence) and dismissed only the fourth, the virtue of justice. Cf. Quentin Skinner, 'The Idea of Negative Liberty: Philosophical and Historical Perspectives' in R. Rorty, J. B. Schneewind and Quentin Skinner (eds.), *Philosophy in History* (Cambridge: Cambridge University Press, 1984) pp. 193–221, at 214–16; Skinner, *Visions*, II, pp. 207–9.

[20] Skinner, *Foundations*, I, p. 134.

[21] Ibid., p. 183. Skinner uses this expression in the title of one of his essays: 'Machiavelli's Political Morality', *European Review* 6 (1998), pp. 321–5.

the originality of Machiavelli proposed by Isaiah Berlin and writes that 'the essential contrast is rather between two different moralities – two rival and incompatible accounts of what ought ultimately to be done'.[22]

With this claim, Skinner also takes a stand against the interpretation of Machiavelli offered by Leo Strauss in the 1950s. According to Strauss the doctrines presented in *The Prince* and in the *Discourses* are ultimately 'immoral and irreligious' and, more generally, the Florentine Secretary needs to be considered not only as a thinker who subverts classical political philosophy, but as a veritable 'teacher of evil'.[23] Skinner sees in these assertions the last echo of the stereotype of 'the murderous Machiavelli' found in Shakespeare's plays and of the condemnations of Machiavelli to be found in Christian political writings, such as Innocent Gentillet's *Anti-Machiavel*.

In his reading of the *Discourses*, Skinner employs a strategy of interpretation analogous to that used in the reading of *The Prince*. He first lists the assumptions which Machiavelli shares with previous humanists, and then he points out the theses in which Machiavelli was original, the aspects in which he distances himself from shared beliefs. In order to understand the theses of the *Discourses*, Skinner looks closely at two contexts: the republican thought of the civic humanists of Bruni's generation and the 'revival of Florentine Republicanism' which took place in the early sixteenth century, and whose main actors were Machiavelli's contemporaries such as Francesco Guicciardini or Donato Giannotti. The *Discourses*, as a free commentary on the work of Livy and simultaneously as a theoretical work on politics, do not fit easily into any literary genre. The attempts to compare them with the *Rerum memorandarum libri* of Petrarca and to the *Miscellaneorum centuria prima* of Poliziano are not convincing.[24] Therefore, in relating the *Discourses* to humanist culture, Skinner understandably begins by showing the values and the ideals shared by both sides. The first value that Machiavelli shares with the other Florentine humanists is political liberty. Also for Machiavelli, liberty means, first and foremost, independence, independence from external aggression, and republican self-government, that form of self-government which guarantees against tyranny. Skinner stresses the central role of political freedom in the *Discourses* and claims that 'Machiavelli's preoccupation with political liberty provides him with his basic theme in all

---

22 Skinner, *Foundations*, I, p. 135. See Isaiah Berlin, 'The Originality of Machiavelli', in M. P. Gilmore (ed.), *Studies on Machiavelli* (Florence: Sansoni, 1972), pp. 147–206.

23 L. Strauss, *Thoughts on Machiavelli* (Glencoe: The Free Press, 1958). For a critique of Skinner's interpretation from a Straussian point of view, see N. Tarcov, 'Quentin Skinner's Method and Machiavelli's Prince', in Tully, *Meaning and Context*, pp. 194–203. On Strauss's interpretation of Machiavelli, the latest analyses include G. Sfez, *Leo Strauss, lecteur de Machiavel. La modernité du mal* (Paris: Ellipses, 2003).

24 Cf. C. Dionisotti, *Machiavelli letterato*, in Gilmore, *Studies on Machiavelli*, pp. 109–43, at 134–5, later in C. Dionisotti, *Machiavellerie. Storia e fortuna di Machiavelli* (Turin: Einaudi, 1980), pp. 226–66, at 258–9; Sasso, *Niccolò Machiavelli*, I, pp. 492–3.

three books of the *Discourses*'.[25] Machiavelli shares with the other humanists also the thesis that a mixed type of republican rule represents the best form of government. But he prefers a *governo largo*, a government that gives adequate voice to the *popolo*, and distances himself from the admiration granted to the *governo stretto* of Venice, which was widespread among Florentines with aristocratic sympathies, ranging from Bernardo Rucellai to Francesco Guicciardini.

These remarks on Machiavelli's basic choices already reveal Skinner's clear historiographical standpoint. He openly rejects the reading of Machiavelli as a 'value-free' political scientist, purely interested in dispassionately classifying various forms of government. The thesis had been put forward in the 1940s by Ernst Cassirer in *The Myth of the State*, and subsequently also by French scholars such as Augustin Renaudet and by Italian historians such as Luigi Russo and Nicola Matteucci. Skinner rightly emphasises that Machiavelli is a 'partisan' writer: he reminds readers of Machiavelli's basic choice in favour of republican governments, his normative stance, one might say. For Skinner, 'by background and conviction Machiavelli was basically a Republican'.[26]

The Machiavelli of the *Discourses* is presented as a 'philosopher of liberty'.[27] Liberty, in fact, is considered by Skinner as the 'basic value' of the *Discourses*, while security is seen as the key value of *The Prince*.[28] Skinner wants to find a point of equilibrium and reconcile two requirements: that of giving an account of the differences between the two works and that of indicating their shared conceptual framework. In order to avoid slipping into the 'mythology of coherence' he insists, following Baron, on the differences. But in order to remain faithful to the texts, he cannot avoid pointing out the common conceptual threads. Skinner suggests that in order to account for the differences one has to look at the values that inspire the works, more than to the different forms of government, principality and republic, which each work apparently praises. He points out, on various occasions, that Machiavelli's discourse on the respective merits of principality and republic is never abstract, but takes into account the historical-political conditions in which these forms need to be realised. Principality is a form of government which is recommended in a precise historical situation: in *The Prince* as in the *Discourses* Machiavelli suggests that in a condition of advanced political corruption it will always be necessary to resort to a government of a single person in order to bring the city, or the state, out of its corruption and restore civil life.[29]

With the humanists, as we have seen, Machiavelli shares the assumption that political liberty is the basic value and, in general, shares the preference for republican governments. Skinner points out other common assumptions: the

---

[25] Skinner, *Foundations*, I, p. 158.   [26] Ibid., p. 153.
[27] 'The philosopher of liberty' is the title of the chapter devoted to the *Discourses* of his book on Machiavelli; see Skinner, *Machiavelli*, p. 48.
[28] Skinner, *Foundations*, I, pp. 156–7.   [29] Ibid., pp. 124 and 159.

condemnation of the resort to mercenary forces and the belief in the superiority of militias; the preoccupation with corruption and the analysis of the different ways in which it grows in a republic. On this last point, it is interesting to note that Skinner emphasises Machiavelli's concern with the growth of individual wealth, with the striving for personal gain at the expense of the striving for the common good. Skinner shows how this concern brings Machiavelli closer to many writers of the pre-humanist rhetorical tradition, from Latini to Compagni and Mussato, who took up the analyses of Sallust for whom the search for profit could weaken public virtues, and the growth of personal wealth could lead to factions in the city. Skinner also points out that this concern was not shared by the humanists of the early *quattrocento*, for they believed that personal wealth was compatible with the pursuit of virtue and could have positive consequences on the overall life of the city-republic. On these, as on other themes, Skinner elegantly shows the continuities and discontinuities of Machiavelli with respect to the beliefs of earlier humanists.

On two basic issues, however, Machiavelli decisively parts company with the theses of all generations of humanists. The first issue is the judgement on the tumults and the civic discords that marked the history of the Roman Republic; the second is the judgement on the compatibility of political *virtù* with Christian virtues. According to Skinner, the positive view that Machiavelli has of the dissensions which 'made that republic free and powerful', voiced in ch. 4, book I of the *Discourses*, not only breaks with the Venetian paradigm, as John Pocock has already pointed out, but also constitutes a radical break with respect to 'Florentine political thought' as a whole, and more generally with humanist thought in its entirety, which followed Cicero and Sallust in their praise of concord. Asking implicitly 'what was Machiavelli doing when he defended that thesis in the *Discourses*?', Skinner answers that Machiavelli was questioning one of the most basic premises of the previous three hundred years of political thinking, namely the premise that civil discord should be banned because it leads to the most nefarious factions. This premise was not only shared by the humanist rhetorical tradition but also by those thinkers who made use of the scholastic framework, from Remigio de' Girolami to Dante.

When we come to Skinner's discussion of these aspects of Machiavelli's thought, we find, perhaps, a deliberate historiographical silence on his part. Skinner never mentions Claude Lefort's interpretation in *Foundations*. In *Le travail de l'oeuvre. Machiavel*, Lefort stressed the importance of conflicts in the thought of the Florentine Secretary, but he often resorted to a Marxist language, talking of *lutte de classes*,[30] rather than the clash between *umori*, as Machiavelli

[30] C. Lefort, *Le travail de l'œuvre. Machiavel* (Paris: Gallimard, 1972), pp. 474–531. On Lefort's interpretation, see P. Manent, 'Vers l'œuvre et le monde. Le Machiavel de Claude Lefort', in C. Habib and C. Mouchard (eds.), *La démocratie à l'œuvre. Autour de Claude Lefort* (Paris: Editions Esprit, 1993), pp. 169–90.

does. Skinner, for his part, insists on the fact that Machiavelli breaks with the tradition that gave preference to the value of *homonoia*, of *concordia*, but he does not go as far as offering an overall interpretation of the role of disunions, of tumults, in Machiavelli's thought. He tries to avoid, most of all, readings that, in his opinion, are anachronistic, constructed as they are from categories that belong to other conceptual frameworks.

The other radical point of departure in relation to the humanist tradition is Machiavelli's presentation of the character of *virtù*. The virtue which is singled out in the *Discourses* is no longer the virtue of the individual, of the prince, but is rather the virtue of the citizen body: 'a more collective view of *virtù*' emerges in this work.[31] Machiavelli presents *virtù* as the necessary quality for the survival of a free republic and for its attainment of greatness. His emphasis is on the constitutive relation between *virtù* and political freedom. But Machiavelli also presents *virtù* in terms that are very different from the Christian virtues and the cardinal virtues praised by the humanists. If '*virtù* is the key to political success', then it is *virtù* itself that requires citizens to place freedom and security of the republic above all other considerations: the hierarchy of Christian values and the hierarchy of humanist virtues are radically subverted. Skinner concludes that 'for all the many differences between *The Prince* and the *Discourses*, the underlying political morality of the two books is thus the same'.[32] In this 'political morality' the traditional requirements of justice, conveyed both by classical Stoic ethics and Christian ethics, become secondary. What comes to the foreground is the value of *mantenere lo stato* (preserving the state) to use the expression of *The Prince*, or the value of guaranteeing *la salute della patria* ('the health of the commonwealth'), to use the expression of the *Discourses*. Skinner can thus effectively discuss a veritable historiographical *topos*: the different relation between politics and justice that Machiavelli and Erasmus place at the centre of their political works, written at nearly the same time.

If these are the main lines of the interpretation proposed in *Foundations*, we may wonder if this kind of presentation, which analyses Machiavelli's individual works in different chapters, may understate the importance of some aspects of Machiavelli's thought. I would like to mention at least one of them: Machiavelli's reflections on time and politics, on history and politics.[33] Obviously Skinner mentions the relation between *virtù* and *fortuna*, as well as Machiavelli's attention to the dynamics of corruption, and he points out that it is precisely in the treatment of corruption in the *Discourses* that Machiavelli envisages a special role for the principality. But Skinner neglects other important themes: the relevance of *occasione* (opportunity) in politics; the problem of

---

[31] Skinner, *Foundations*, I, p. 176.   [32] Ibid., p. 183.

[33] This issue was instead crucial in Pocock's reading in *The Machiavellian Moment*. For a recent interpretation of these themes with a philosophical approach, see M. E. Vatter, *Between Form and Event: Machiavelli's Theory of Political Freedom* (Dordrecht: Kluwer, 2000).

riscontro con i tempi (matching the times) which change constantly; the question of the *ritorno ai principii* (return to beginnings), for example. He cannot therefore ask whether these concepts offer a precise and original vision of the relation between time and politics, between history and politics. Skinner limits himself to mentioning Machiavelli's famous reformulation of Polybian cyclical theory in the second chapter of the first book of the *Discourses* and presents it as a sign of Machiavelli's acceptance of an 'ultimately fatalistic view'.[34] But perhaps this observation is out of place. Perhaps it is inevitable that some aspects of a thinker as rich and complicated as Machiavelli had to be left on the sidelines, in the context of a history mainly devoted to the reconstruction of wide ideological frameworks and traditions of political thought.

III

The Foundations of Modern Political Thought can be considered as the starting point of much of Skinner's historical and philosophical work of the subsequent twenty-five years. With regard to the historical work, Skinner deepens and widens his analysis of the pre-humanist rhetorical literature in a series of stimulating essays written during the 1980s. Suffice to cite two of them: 'Ambrogio Lorenzetti: The artist as a Political Philosopher' of 1986 and 'Machiavelli's *Discorsi* and the Pre-humanist Origins of Republican Ideas' of 1990. While in *Foundations* the fresco of the *buon governo* was mentioned only in a footnote and, following the well-known thesis of Nicolai Rubinstein, its interpretation was referred back to an Aristotelian conceptual context, in the new study Skinner proposes a completely different interpretation of the Sienese frescoes. He claims that in order to understand the allegories of Ambrogio Lorenzetti, and in particular to identify the mysterious regal figure that dominates the middle section of the fresco, we do not have to look at the Aristotelian culture, at scholastic political philosophy, but precisely to the pre-humanist rhetorical culture so dear to him.[35] Thus Skinner has the opportunity to further develop the reconstruction of pre-humanist culture which he had put forward in 1978. For example, he refers to more instances of the literary genre of advice books for the *podestà*, such as the *De regimine et sapientia potestatis* of Orfino da Lodi, and to the *Florilegia* and the moral treatises of Roman inspiration that transmitted the doctrines of Seneca and Cicero. He then examines closely how

---

[34] Skinner, *Foundations*, I, p. 187.
[35] Quentin Skinner, 'Ambrogio Lorenzetti: the Artist as Political Philosopher', *Proceedings of the British Academy* 72 (1986), 1–56. Skinner's interpretation of Lorenzetti is discussed by, among others, M. M. Donato, 'Testo, contesto, immagini politiche nel tardo Medioevo. Esempi toscani', *Annali dell'Istituto storico italogermanico in Trento* 19 (1993), pp. 305–55; N. Rubinstein, 'Le allegorie di Ambrogio Lorenzetti nella Sala della Pace e il pensiero politico del suo tempo', *Rivista Storica Italiana*, 120 (1997), pp. 781–99.

pre-humanist writers formulated the key notions of peace, concord, common good and justice.

In the second essay, Skinner considers another theme developed by pre-humanist authors: the way in which they present greatness – 'greatness of standing, greatness of power, greatness of wealth'– as one of the ends, perhaps the main one, that city-republics ought to pursue. After identifying the source of this claim in Sallust's *Bellum Catilinae* and *Bellum Jugurthinum*, he analyses the relations between greatness, peace and concord found in these pre-humanist authors. Skinner then examines some aspects of Machiavelli's republicanism in order to show how in essence it does not diverge radically from the pre-humanist republican standpoint. Skinner obviously mentions the points of disagreement openly stated by Machiavelli, first of all his attack on the ideal of *concordia ordinum*, but he prefers to emphasise 'the many continuities' and concludes that 'Machiavelli not only presents a wholehearted defence of traditional republican values; he also presents that defence in a wholeheartedly traditional way'.[36]

Skinner also has the opportunity to further develop the interpretative framework proposed in *Foundations* by examining not only pre-humanist writers, but also another tradition of thought which preceded the recovery of Aristotle's *Politics*, namely, the juridical tradition of the Glossators. In particular, in his contribution to the *Cambridge History of Renaissance Philosophy*, of 1988, he examines the figure of Azo and his interpretation of the concepts of *iurisdictio* and *merum imperium* which prepared the way for the recognition of the sovereignty of all communities that were *de facto* independent.[37] Skinner's intention is in any case clear: to emphasise that prior to the recovery of Aristotle's *Politics* there were at least two languages of politics, two traditions of political thought, that elaborate a defence of the independence of the cities (and of other political communities formally under the jurisdiction of the emperor) and that bring arguments in favour of the institutions of self-government. It is not surprising that in these essays Skinner continues his polemic against those authors who attribute a decisive role to the recovery of the political vocabulary of Aristotle. As targets of his critique, in addition to John Pocock and Walter Ullmann, he now lists Nicolai Rubinstein.[38]

But Skinner, throughout the 1980s, devotes more attention to the philosophical side of his research: he focuses on a rigorous analysis of the concept of

---

[36] Quentin Skinner, 'Machiavelli's *Discorsi* and the Pre-Humanist Origins of Republican Ideas', in G. Bock, Quentin Skinner and M. Viroli (eds.), *Machiavelli and Republicanism* (Cambridge: Cambridge University Press, 1990), pp. 121–141, at pp. 135 and 141.

[37] Quentin Skinner, 'Political Philosophy', in C. B. Schmitt (ed.), *The Cambridge History of Renaissance Philosophy* (Cambridge: Cambridge University Press, 1988), pp. 389–452, at pp. 389–95.

[38] Skinner, 'Ambrogio Lorenzetti', p. 56n.; Skinner, 'Machiavelli's *Discorsi*', p. 121n. Cf. Skinner, *Visions*, II, pp. 12–13, 91–2.

liberty and on a historical reconstruction of the different families or traditions of thought which have variously conceptualised liberty. In so doing, Skinner subverts and fruitfully complicates the terms of the discussion, which until then had opposed family theories of negative liberty, essentially derivative from Hobbes, to one or more families of theories of positive liberty. Skinner, in fact, draws upon his long-standing historical excavations and he seeks to clarify the way in which Machiavelli and other republican thinkers conceptualise liberty. Skinner believes that Machiavelli and the republican thinkers develop a specific conception of negative liberty of great interest and coherence, which deserves to be taken seriously by contemporary political philosophy. His efforts in the last two decades have been devoted to clarifying this conception of freedom in all its aspects, examining a series of conceptual problems related to it: first and foremost, the concept of constraint which it implies and then the relation between freedom and equality.

Skinner's theses on liberty were presented for the first time in an essay of 1983, 'Machiavelli and the Maintenance of Liberty', which analysed the Florentine Secretary's approach to individual and collective liberty. These theses were then put forward in a wider historical and conceptual framework in a series of essays, which included 'The Idea of Negative Liberty: Philosophical and Historical Perspectives' (1984), 'The Paradoxes of Political Liberty' (1986), and 'The Republican Ideal of Political Liberty' (1990).[39] With these wide-ranging essays, Skinner is intervening in quite distinct debates: first, the long-standing discussion on the concept of liberty in English analytical philosophy, a discussion we are used to tracing back to Isaiah Berlin's famous essay. Skinner demonstrates a very precise knowledge of all the facets and subtleties of that debate on the existence of two basic ways of conceptualising liberty, and more generally of the existence of two families of theories of liberty. Masterfully treating the arguments of Oppenheim, the critiques posed by MacCallum to Berlin's dichotomy, as well as the discussion of MacCallum's own triadic interpretation of freedom brought forward by Baldwin and others, Skinner shows the one-sidedness and naivety of analytical philosophers in their reading of the classics of political philosophy, in particular of Hobbes.

[39] See Quentin Skinner, 'Machiavelli on the Maintenance of Liberty', *Politics* 18 (1983), pp. 3–15; Quentin Skinner, 'The Idea of Negative Liberty: Philosophical and Historical Perspectives', in Rorty et al., *Philosophy in History*, pp. 193–221; Quentin Skinner, 'The Paradoxes of Political Liberty', in *The Tanner Lectures on Human Values* 7 (1986), pp. 225–50; Quentin Skinner, 'Il concetto inglese di libertà', *Filosofia politica* 3 (1989), pp. 77–102; Quentin Skinner, 'The Republican Ideal of Political Liberty', in Bock et al., *Machiavelli and Republicanism*, pp. 293–309. See also Quentin Skinner, 'On Justice, the Common Good and the Priority of Liberty', in C. Mouffe (ed.), *Dimensions of Radical Democracy* (London: Verso, 1992), pp. 211–24; Quentin Skinner, 'Two Concepts of Citizenship', *Tijdschrift voor Filosofie* 55 (1993), pp. 403–19. For a contextualisation and interpretation of these essays, see Palonen, *Quentin Skinner*, pp. 95–132.

With these essays, Skinner is intervening in another political-theoretical debate of those years: the debate between liberals and communitarians.[40] Skinner avoids entering into the juxtapositions and dualisms generated by this debate in order to subvert the very terms of the debate. The opposition between the liberal theorists of negative liberty and the neo-Aristotelian defenders of positive liberty is, in his opinion, a false opposition. While Skinner takes seriously the attack of neo-Aristotelians against the impoverishment of political language caused by liberal theories, with their insistence on individual rights and negative liberty, he cannot accept their metaphysically-laden answers to the crisis of the present. There is in fact more than one family of theories of negative liberty. There is the liberal family, with its noble genealogy from Bentham to Constant, from Mill to Berlin. But there is also the republican family, from Machiavelli to Harrington, from Milton to Sidney, which adopts and develops another negative conception of liberty.

In so doing, Skinner was joining another debate, the more strictly historical debate on the nature and specificity of the republican tradition. He was putting forward an interpretation of republicanism which was radically opposed to the one advanced by Pocock, which at the time was paradigmatic.[41] It is well known that *The Machiavellian Moment* rests on two central theses: the idea of the continuity between Aristotelianism and republicanism, and the presentation of the republican tradition as preceding, and as an alternative to, the liberal tradition. Pocock claimed that the key ideas of the republican tradition were derived from classical authors: first of all, Aristotle and Polybius. In particular, Pocock presented the citizen theorised by modern republican thinkers as the reincarnation of the Aristotelian *zoon politikon*. He explicitly challenged the reconstructions of modern political thought proposed by liberals, Marxists and Straussians, all of whom considered it as the univocal assertion of liberalism, from Hobbes and Locke onwards. In Pocock's opinion, instead, modern political thought was to a large extent permeated by a republican language, and by its conceptualisations; liberal ideology, built on the categories of the tradition of natural law, needed a lot of time and effort to supplant republican language, if it ever did. It is worth noting that many critics of Rawls's theory of justice, thinkers soon labelled communitarians, such as Michael Sandel and Charles Taylor, took up Pocock's theses in philosophical and political debates. And this is not at all surprising because Pocock's republicanism offered them a conception of the individual and of political society that could be easily used

---

[40] For an introduction to this debate, see S. Mulhall and A. Swift, *Liberals and Communitarians*, 2nd edn (Oxford: Blackwell, 1996).

[41] For an introduction to the debate on republicanism in the 1970s and 1980s, one may still refer usefully to D. T. Rodgers, 'Republicanism: the Career of a Concept', *The Journal of American History* 79 (1992), pp. 11–38.

in the polemic against Rawls and in general against liberalism. The theoretical *continuum* between Aristotelianism, republicanism and communitarianism was thus already established by the end of the 1970s.

But in fact Skinner was rejecting this theoretical continuity. From a historiographical point of view, as we have seen, he stresses that the language of the modern republican tradition was derived from Roman philosophical and historical sources. In this way, he breaks, or reduces the importance of, the continuity between Aristotelianism and republicanism emphasised by Pocock. From a strictly interpretative point of view, opposing the claims by MacIntyre and other communitarians according to which the philosophical choice today is between liberal individualism and some version of Aristotelianism, Skinner tries to define an autonomous identity for republicanism, avoiding the embraces of old and new Aristotelians. In his opinion, republicanism is not a form of Aristotelian politics. To demonstrate this point, he examines the *Discourses* of Machiavelli to show that the Florentine Secretary, as well as his republican followers, do not make use of many of the typically Aristotelian premises: the human being is not considered to be an *animal politicum et sociale*, to employ the Thomistic formula, but is rather a being exposed to 'corruption', tending to disregard his duties towards the community. Furthermore, in the *res publica* individuals pursue different ends; we cannot assume the necessary existence of ends shared by all. The freedom theorised by republicans is not positive liberty, but a specific form of negative liberty: the individual participates in the affairs of his *res publica* not because this is his natural destination, but in order to prevent the government from degenerating into a hateful tyranny, which endangers his security and private property. Political participation is not an ultimate end, but a means or an intermediate end.[42]

Skinner gives theoretical autonomy to republicanism by freeing it from the metaphysical assumptions present in the teleology of Aristotelian politics, and reconfigures republicanism as a third way[43] between liberal individualism and Aristotelian communitarianism. A reformulation of the republican theory of

---

[42] Republicanism, as defined by Skinner in these essays, has been labelled by some of his interpreters as an 'instrumental republicanism'. Cf. Alan Patten, 'The Republican Critique of Liberalism', *British Journal of Political Science* 26 (1996), pp. 25–44, at p. 26. See also the remarks by Burtt and Spitz: S. Burtt, 'The Politics of Virtue Today: a Critique and a Proposal', *American Political Science Review* 87 (1993), pp. 360–8 (in which Burtt distinguishes between an 'Aristotelian politics of virtue' and an 'instrumental politics of virtue') and J.-F. Spitz, *La liberté politique. Essai de généalogie conceptuelle* (Paris: PUF, 1995), p. 172 (with reference to Skinner's interpretation, Spitz talks of an 'instrumentalisation de la vertu et de l'auto-gouvernement').

[43] See J.-F. Spitz, 'Le républicanisme, une troisième voie entre libéralisme et communautarisme?', *Le Banquet* 2 (1995), pp. 215–38. Skinner's essays are presented as a contribution to the debate between liberals and communitarians in M. Edling and U. Mörkenstam, 'Quentin Skinner: from Historian of Ideas to Political Scientist', *Scandinavian Political Studies* 18 (1995), pp. 119–32; and in A. Berten, P. Da Silveira and H. Pourtois, 'Introduction générale', in A. Berten, P. Da Silveira and H. Pourtois (eds.), *Libéraux et communautariens* (Paris: PUF, 1997), pp. 1–19.

liberty, in his opinion, would make possible an interesting and innovative theory of citizenship. He is aware that 'we have no realistic prospect of taking active control of the political process in any modern democracy', but he is convinced that 'there are many areas of public life . . . where increased public participation might well serve to improve the accountability of our *soi disant* representatives'.[44]

The interpretation of republicanism offered by Skinner has quickly become influential.[45] Historians and theorists were increasingly aware that in the scholarly community radically different interpretations of republicanism confronted each other. If for many years the term coined by Hans Baron, 'civic humanism', and the term 'classical republicanism' preferred by Felix Gilbert, were often used as synonyms, from the 1990s onwards they have been more frequently used to denote radically different conceptual frameworks. Among political philosophers, John Rawls was the one who underlined the interpretative differences. In *Political Liberalism* he used the term 'classical republicanism' to refer to an interpretation of republicanism *à la* Skinner, and he used the term 'civic humanism' to denote a 'form of Aristotelianism' and an interpretation of republican themes *à la* Pocock. Rawls added furthermore that there was no substantial incompatibility between classical republicanism so understood and his political liberalism, whereas there was a 'fundamental opposition' between his theory and civic humanism.[46]

At this point, two observations of a general nature concerning these essays on liberty are necessary. The first is that while in *Foundations* Skinner stressed that two traditions of political thought had provided legitimacy to the institutions of self-government in the city-republics, the scholastic tradition of Aristotelian derivation and the humanist tradition developed from the teaching of rhetoric, in the later essays on freedom his attention is exclusively devoted to the humanist tradition and to its formulation of republican concepts and ideals. Skinner puts at the centre of his attention, as we have seen, the 'classical republican tradition' and clarifies the theory of political freedom that lies at the heart of this tradition. From this point onwards, one of his objectives has been to clarify the conceptual

---

[44] Skinner, *The Republican Ideal*, pp. 308–9.

[45] Philip Pettit was one of the first scholars to systematically examine and endorse Skinner's interpretation. See e.g. P. Pettit 'The Freedom of the City: a Republican Ideal', in A. Hamlin and P. Pettit (eds.), *The Good Polity* (Oxford: Blackwell, 1989), pp. 141–67; P. Pettit, 'Liberalism and Republicanism', *Australian Journal of Political Science* 28 (1993), pp. 162–89; P. Pettit, 'Negative Liberty, Liberal and Republican', *European Journal of Philosophy* 1 (1993), pp. 15–38; P. Pettit, *Republicanism: a Theory of Freedom and Government* (Oxford: Clarendon Press, 1997).

[46] J. Rawls, *Political Liberalism* (New York: Columbia University Press, 1993), pp. 205–6. Rawls had already proposed a similar distinction in 'The Priority of Right and Ideas of the Good', *Philosophy and Public Affairs* 17 (1988), pp. 151–76.

structure of modern republicanism, starting from the key value of freedom, but also taking into consideration other concepts and values linked to it.[47]

The second point is that in his historical as well as in his philosophical essays of the 1980s, Skinner presents Hobbes as the thinker who radically opposes the assumptions central to the republican tradition. Hobbes not only elaborates a concept of freedom as absence of 'externall impediments of motion' which is opposed to the concept of freedom at the heart of republicanism, but, more generally, he proposes a political theory that represents a radical alternative, at all levels, to republican political theorising since it is based on concepts such as individual rights and contract, representation and artificial person. At the end of his contribution to the *Cambridge History of Renaissance Philosophy* Skinner writes:

The humanist ideal of virtuous public service was increasingly challenged and eventually supplanted by a more individualistic and contractarian style of political reasoning, the style perfected by Thomas Hobbes in *Leviathan* . . . Hobbes decisively repudiated the distinctive ideals of Renaissance political theory, burying them and writing their epitaph in the same breath.[48]

This opposition between Hobbes, and political theories based on individual rights, on the one hand, and Machiavelli and republican theories centred on *virtù* and public service, on the other, will recur constantly in his subsequent writings.

IV

Liberty before Liberalism registers some interesting terminological changes and significant conceptual elucidations. Whereas in the essays of the 1980s Skinner strove to reconstruct the conceptual profile of the republican tradition, placing at the centre of his attention the thought of Machiavelli, in *Liberty before Liberalism* the historiographical focus shifts to the English theories of the seventeenth century. In order to find out how republican thinkers conceptualised freedom, Skinner analyses the thought of well-known figures such as John Milton, James Harrington, Algernon Sidney, and examines less-known authors such as Marchamont Nedham, John Hall and Francis Osborne. His starting point is the fact that these thinkers held widely differing opinions on the institutional framework for their ideal commonwealth. While some of them argue for a mixed

---

[47] This interest led him to edit, and contribute to, collective works such as Bock et al., *Machiavelli and Republicanism*; D. Armitage, A. Himy and Quentin Skinner (eds.), *Milton and Republicanism* (Cambridge: Cambridge University Press, 1995); M. van Gelderen and Quentin Skinner (eds.), *Republicanism: a Shared European Heritage*, 2 vols. (Cambridge: Cambridge University Press, 2002).

[48] Skinner, 'Political Philosophy', p. 452.

form of government in which the monarch still plays an important political role, others are convinced that only a political community governed by a freely elected parliament and executive, without a monarch, can be properly called a republic. Keeping in mind the shared understanding between these authors of the concept of freedom, rather than the differences in institutional frameworks, Skinner prefers to refer to their thought with the new term of 'the neo-Roman theory of freedom', and employs 'republicanism' only in reference to those anti-monarchical authors who deny any political role to the monarch.

According to Skinner, the conception of freedom developed by neo-Roman political thinkers is a negative conception. Freedom is defined negatively, as the absence of constraint. The problem is how to interpret the idea of constraint. For neo-Roman thinkers constraint is not only caused by interference but also by dependence in all of its forms. The antonym of freedom is therefore a complex one: interference and/or dependence. Taking up a point raised by Philip Pettit, Skinner examines once again what distinguishes the neo-Roman conception of freedom from that proposed by Hobbes and subsequently by liberal thinkers. If in the essays on freedom of the 1980s he claimed that the difference between republicans and liberals did not turn on the meaning of freedom, but only on the means necessary to the preservation of freedom, in *Liberty before Liberalism* he argues that their disagreement is not only about the means to guarantee freedom, but also on the meaning of freedom itself.[49] The neo-Roman thinkers hold 'a view according to which our freedom should be seen not merely as a predicate of our actions but as an existential condition in contrast with that of servitude'.[50]

In order to clarify the concepts of freedom, constraint and dependence, Skinner returns once again to the sources of seventeenth-century thinkers. He acknowledges their debt to Machiavelli, but is convinced that also in their case, as for Machiavelli himself, the crucial sources are Roman ones. The label 'neo-Roman' has been chosen with good reason. When the English theorists conceptualise freedom, and especially when they define freedom as the opposite of slavery, they are following closely the Roman historians and moralists, from Sallust to Tacitus, Cicero to Seneca. Skinner rightly points out that behind the conceptions of these historians and moralists lay the Roman legal tradition. To that end he proposes to look at the *Digest* of Justinian, as the place where this tradition is best condensed, to understand the definition of freedom and of its antonyms.

---

[49] Quentin Skinner, *Liberty before Liberalism* (Cambridge: Cambridge University Press, 1998), p. 70. For an interesting analysis of this book, cf. Kari Palonen, 'Liberty is too precious a concept to be left to the liberals', *Finnish Yearbook of Political Thought* 2 (1998), pp. 243–60. See also M. Geuna, 'La libertà esigente di Quentin Skinner', in Quentin Skinner, *La libertà prima del liberalismo* (Turin: Einaudi, 2001), pp. vii–xli.

[50] This is argued in a subsequent article, to summarise the interpretation put forward in *Liberty before Liberalism*: cf. Skinner, *Visions*, I, p. 178.

The historiographical thesis of the Roman origins of the republican tradition put forward in *Foundations* is thus reaffirmed and reinforced in *Liberty before Liberalism*. While previously Skinner had pointed out, against the claim of a continuity between Aristotelian thought and republican tradition, the role played by Roman historiography and moral and political thought, in this work he brings out the crucial role played by Roman legal conceptualisations in the formulation of the most important concept in the political lexicon of Western modernity, that of freedom. We can say that the later work constitutes an interesting development of his more general thesis.[51]

The work on the conceptual history of freedom in the 1980s and 1990s, the opposition between neo-Roman theories and Hobbesian theories, the analysis of the different ways of understanding constraint and the meaning of freedom, has led Skinner to emphasise the existence of rival and opposing political theories. But this feature, in fact, was already present in *Foundations*. That book was divided into two volumes: the first analysed the pre-humanist and humanist theories of civic virtue and republican self-government, the second examined the formation of absolutist theories and the emergence of rival theories of natural rights. The focus was therefore on the existence of alternative traditions of political thought, on the clash between rival ideologies and political languages. We should also mention the other investigation in conceptual history[52] which Skinner has carried out in the last two decades, devoted to the emergence of the idea of the state as an artificial person. This research, which had been foreshadowed in the pages of *Foundations*, has led him to conclude that the idea of the state as an artificial person endowed with sovereignty was fully worked out only by Hobbes and was completely alien to the thinkers of the republican or neo-Roman tradition, both before and after Hobbes.[53] So also on this aspect we find opposed conceptualisations and rival ideologies.

It comes as no surprise that Skinner emphasises this point in the preface to his last work in 2002, a collection of his studies on method, on Renaissance virtues, and on Hobbes and civil science. We may note, in passing, that the title of his work is *Visions of Politics* and not 'Visions of the State'. Only one of the traditions that are studied therein, the one that finds its paradigmatic formulation

---

[51] The thesis of the Roman origins of the modern republican tradition has been put forward and reformulated by many scholars. See e.g. M. N. S. Sellers, *American Republicanism: Roman Ideology in the United States Constitution* (London: Macmillan, 1994); M. N. S. Sellers, *The Sacred Fire of Liberty: Republicanism, Liberalism and the Law* (London: Macmillan, 1998).

[52] Skinner himself presents his essays on liberty and the state as attempted 'conceptual histories'; cf. Skinner, *Visions*, I, p. 178.

[53] Quentin Skinner, 'The State', in T. Ball, J. Farr and R. L. Hanson (eds.), *Political Innovation and Conceptual Change* (Cambridge: Cambridge University Press, 1989), pp. 90–131; Quentin Skinner, 'Hobbes and the Purely Artificial Person of the State', *The Journal of Political Philosophy* 7 (1999), pp. 1–29. See Skinner, *Visions*, II, pp. 368–413, III, pp. 177–208. For a use of this 'conceptual history' of the state, see e.g. R. Geuss, *History and Illusion in Politics* (Cambridge: Cambridge University Press, 2001), pp. 47–52.

in Hobbes, gives centre stage to the concept of the state. Skinner recognises that one way to speak about politics, the one centred on the state, has become hegemonic starting from the seventeenth century, but he also emphasises how it was constantly challenged by other ways of thinking about politics and common life.

From *Foundations*, through *Liberty before Liberalism*, to *Visions of Politics* Skinner may be considered the historian of rival political theories, of opposing traditions of political thought. He is a historian who has repeatedly stressed the need to recover the 'lost treasures' of our past, the political conceptions and the languages that have been defeated and sidelined, the interpretations of common values that have been covered over by the 'hegemonical accounts' of the 'mainstream of our intellectual traditions'. We may refer here to the concluding pages of *Liberty before Liberalism*.[54] We may also refer to the final lines of the preface to *Visions of Politics*, in which Skinner, referring to the Renaissance republican theories analysed in the second volume and to the political philosophy of Hobbes examined in the third, claims to have studied and compared 'two contrasting views we have inherited in the modern West about the nature of our common life'. To which he pointedly adds: 'One speaks of sovereignty as a property of the people, the other sees it as the possession of the state. One gives centrality to the figure of the virtuous citizen, the other to the sovereign as a representative of the state. One assigns priority to the duties of citizens, the other to their rights.'[55] These are not only historical oppositions but also theoretical alternatives for the present.

But it is not surprising that radical alternatives and profound oppositions characterise the heavens of political philosophy. For Skinner, at bottom, the space of politics is a terrain of conflicts, and political theories participate in these conflicts. Political theories and political ideologies take part in these conflicts by constantly legitimating and delegitimating the political actors on the ground. Wittgenstein teaches us that 'words are deeds'. Skinner has never ceased applying this lesson to political theory.

---

[54] Skinner, *Liberty before Liberalism*, pp. 116–20.   [55] Skinner, *Visions*, II, p. xi.

5   Unoriginal authors: how to do things with texts in the Renaissance

Warren Boutcher

The first volume of *The Foundations of Modern Political Thought* offered a new account of the relationship between rhetorical resources and political moments. Quentin Skinner balanced attention to the normative traditions of political language with attention to the new force they acquire at critical times. The first part of this chapter argues that the balance had a specific controversial origin. In the late 1960s and early 1970s, Hans Baron's thesis that the political crisis of the early Florentine *quattrocento* had been the catalyst for a new humanism came into conflict with Paul Oskar Kristeller's restatement of the continuities between medieval and Renaissance, ecclesiastical and lay traditions of rhetoric and thought.[1] Skinner took the academic community beyond these encamped positions with his historical account of the instrumentality of political rhetoric. One always had to ask what a given 'author' was doing in his particular moment, how he was exploiting handed-on rhetorical resources to build a position on a current issue or crisis.

The second half of this chapter aims to reconsider Skinner's model in the light of subsequent advances in textual studies. It uses works from the second half of the sixteenth century (Philip Sidney's *Arcadia* and *A Letter to Queen Elizabeth*, Etienne de la Boétie's *De la servitude volontaire* and Montaigne's *Essais*), a period when the circulation and publication of manuscript and printed texts coexisted in a hazardous and censorious environment. For Skinner shares one important methodological assumption with more traditional scholars of political thought like Baron. Historical interpretations of what an author thought or said must rest, yes, on a sound textual basis. It is important to know exactly what the author intended to say and when he or she intended to say it. But, it is assumed, this does not mean that the *culture* of textual production and circulation need be a principal or ever-present concern of the intellectual historian.

---

[1] The controversy centred on an exchange between Baron and Jerrold Seigel, who used Kristeller's work to counter Baron's thesis about 'civic humanism'. See J. E. Seigel, '"Civic Humanism or Ciceronian Rhetoric?" The Culture of Petrarch and Bruni', *Past and Present* 34 (1966), pp. 3–48; Hans Baron, 'Leonardo Bruni: "Professional Rhetorician" or "Civic Humanist"?', *Past and Present* 36 (1967), pp. 21–37.

I believe it should be, and that limiting the role of textual criticism to the search for a 'sound textual basis' and an authoritative date sidelines some of the core issues in early modern intellectual history. It may be that the 'media' in the modern sense did not yet exist to monopolise the communication of political discourse, but there are still questions to ask about the role of textual media in the shaping of political experience. How did the physical forms and cultural modes of circulation of the textual instruments of political discussion – and of knowledge about their origins and uses – condition the agency of actors?

If anything, the assumption to which I referred in the paragraph before last is more obvious in Skinner's than in Baron's work. For good reasons, Skinner wants to get away from the image of the moral or political thinker handling perennial themes in contemplative isolation. So he re-imagines the agent of discourse (the 'author') as one who acts by speaking in a given context or conversation. The author is equivalent to the live speaker of a crafted oration in a forum or parliament – hence the successful application of Skinner's methods to actual political speech-making.

But when we talk about political rhetoric in the Renaissance – especially the northern Renaissance – we are not normally referring to live speech acts, to oratory. We are referring to rhetoric which circulates in the form of manuscript and printed texts and engages in debate and controversy with and by means of other such circulating texts. Furthermore, knowledge about the background and uses of these texts circulates alongside them in written or oral form. It is subject to uncertainty and manipulation. I shall clarify these points in relation to La Boétie's *De la servitude volontaire* and an example of an oration that becomes a circulating manuscript letter between two versions of Sidney's *Arcadia*.

If the field of action is textual rather than oral or (as in the fictional example taken below from Sidney's *New Arcadia*) a mixture of both, then our approach needs to take that consistently into account. The expectation that the evidence should normally lead back to an original and transparent situation in which a single author-speaker acts upon a particular audience for clear purposes may be inappropriate. Even where there is such transparency, might it not be artificially contrived, something that has to be actively put in place? Might it not be in producers' interests to leave clues leading us back to this 'original' context so that we will not – from their point of view – misinterpret or misuse the work? If we follow those clues too innocently are we not in danger of missing the struggle about 'context' that occurs at the time of a work's first composition, publication and circulation? And finally, does the agent of discourse, the author whose circumstances and objectives determine meanings, always have to be identified with the 'original' writer of a published work? The answer I offer on this last point is that the agents whose doings interest us can also be unoriginal authors: the readers, the copiers, the recommenders of texts.

Take a text on moral or political themes composed between 1300 and 1600, even one Skinner does not address. *The Foundations of Modern Political Thought* will give you a very good idea what questions you need to ask about its context. This is the true measure of a book which, more than any other, heralded a much needed paradigm shift in the history of ideas. There were past precedents and contemporary parallels for what was being done, but they were confined to particular fields. In 1965 Felix Gilbert had related the works of Machiavelli and Guicciardini to the topical arguments accompanying the vicissitudes of Florentine political history after 1494. Donald Kelley, Skinner's colleague at the Institute of Advanced Study, published a book three years after *Foundations* placing the Huguenot classics in the context of the development of reformed ideologies.[2] But *Foundations* did more than both books put together. It provided an account of the 'social and intellectual matrix' of three centuries of political thought.[3] It carefully balanced internal against external explanations of the history of political thought.[4]

In volume I's discussion of 'liberty, rhetoric and Renaissance humanism' the balance in question had a specific origin. Skinner brought intellectual temperance to the controversy that had broken out in the previous decade between disciples of Hans Baron's and of Paul Oskar Kristeller's divergent approaches to these topics. The roots of the controversy lay in the interwar crisis of the German and Italian humanities, and in the intellectual migration to the United States before and during the Second World War.[5] Baron used textual criticism to date crucial early works of Leonardo Bruni to the period immediately after the Florentine crisis of 1402 (when Milan seemed about to attack). He argued that these works revealed the effects of a revolution in moral and political thought caused by the crisis. From Kristeller's perspective, on the other hand, they were continuous with a whole tradition of manuscript rhetorical works going back two centuries.[6]

What might *Foundations* be said to be doing in the context of this controversy? The book has recently been credited by James Hankins – a one-time research assistant to Kristeller – with subjecting Hans Baron's thesis to 'a searching critique'. Skinner, according to Hankins, showed that 'many of the ideas Baron

[2] Felix Gilbert, *Machiavelli and Guicciardini: Politics and History in Sixteenth-Century Florence* (Princeton: Princeton University Press, 1965); Donald R. Kelley, *The Beginning of Ideology: Consciousness and Society in the French Reformation* (Cambridge: Cambridge University Press, 1981).

[3] Quentin Skinner, *The Foundations of Modern Political Thought*, 2 vols. (Cambridge: Cambridge University Press, 1978), I, p. x.

[4] See especially ibid., I, pp. 102–3.

[5] Warren Boutcher, 'The Making of the Humane Philosopher: Paul Oskar Kristeller and Twentieth-Century Intellectual History', in John Monfasani (ed.), *Kristeller Reconsidered: Essays on his Life and Scholarship* (New York: Italica Press, 2006), pp. 39–70.

[6] Skinner, *Foundations*, I, pp. 70–3.

credited to the 'civic humanists' had a long prehistory in medieval scholastic and rhetorical traditions'. This is certainly true. Skinner showed that by the end of the thirteenth century the Italian protagonists of republican liberty were already drawing on existing scholastic and rhetorical traditions. They needed ideological weapons 'to conceptualise and defend the special value of their political experience' in the context of the rise of the *signori*.[7]

Baron had underestimated the extent to which early *quattrocento* humanists were professional rhetoricians whose social roles and literary activities had a long history. The medieval teachers of the *ars dictaminis* had begun two centuries before to illustrate the rhetorical rules with less remote and fanciful examples than thitherto. The new, more topical examples of political advice giving had 'more obvious value and relevance for their pupils in their personal lives or careers'. At the same time, the teachers supplemented their usual lists of model letters with lists of exemplary orations. Once the study of rhetoric 'came to embody so much incidental political content' it was a short step from 'giving an exposition of the *ars dictaminis* to offering direct commentary on civic affairs'. Rhetorical instructors began to look like natural political advisers. There were knock-on effects in historiography and advice-books. The centre-piece of Boncompagno da Signa's account of *The Siege of Ancona* (*c*.1201–2) is a speech in praise of liberty delivered by an elderly citizen at the moment when the emperor's emissaries are offering a deal for surrender.[8]

What was new, then, in the humanist style of teaching imported from France in the later *duecento*, was the displacement of the rather dry and technical examples that the *dictatores* had made up for all these purposes. In came classical letters, poems and orations to illustrate the rhetorical rules in action. It followed that the classical poets, orators and historians became models of good rhetorical style, 'serious literary figures worthy of study and imitation in their own right'.[9] At the same time, the humanists consolidated the public political profile gained by the *dictatores*. The sciences of speaking and of self-government were yoked still more conspicuously together. It is in this context, as the city-republics confronted the rapid advance of the *signori*, that a systematic rhetorical defence of liberty and praise of virtue emerged a century before the work of Baron's civic humanists.[10]

The point I want to make about this argument is that it is at least as much a critique of Kristeller's – or Kristeller's disciples' – as it is of Baron's approach. Both scholars had missed the pragmatic contexts of rhetoric. Kristeller's revisionist insistence that 'humanism' amounted not to a civic or any other form of philosophy but to a new, more classically literate way of teaching rhetoric

---

[7] James Hankins, 'Introduction', in James Hankins (ed.), *Renaissance Civic Humanism: Reappraisals and Reflections* (Cambridge: Cambridge University Press, 2000), pp. 1–13, at 5; Skinner, *Foundations*, I, p. 27.
[8] Skinner, *Foundations*, I, pp. 30–3.   [9] Ibid., I, pp. 35–7, at 37.   [10] Ibid., pp. 40–1, 44–5.

(and, of course, of glossing newly recovered classical texts) had one unfortunate consequence for intellectual historiography.[11] It directed too many scholars to focus exclusively on the pedagogical history of Latinate literary style, on the history of the manuals' treatments of *elocutio* and the tropes from Antiquity to the Renaissance.[12] Skinner's point was that right through from the pre-humanist *dictatores*, those who started choosing more topical examples, to the fifteenth- and sixteenth-century humanists who drew on classical models, one had to look not only at the rules, the programme but at the force and the incidental political content of the examples chosen.

Scholars of translation – to use an example of my own – who study Cicero's *De optimo genere oratorum* in the context of Renaissance rhetorical literature invariably forget its fifteenth- and sixteenth-century publishing context.[13] It often appeared in extract or in full alongside a Latin translation (usually Leonardo Bruni's) of the two Greek orations it had originally been designed by Cicero to accompany: Demosthenes' *On the Crown* and Aeschines' *Against Ctesiphon*.[14] Demosthenes had won an argument on a particular occasion against a noted opponent whose reputation was destroyed by the encounter. The debating issue had been a technical one but it had had broad ramifications for the public understanding of the Athenian struggle for political liberty. So, *pace* Kristeller, rhetoric could be a matter of ceremonial elegance or literary exercise, yes, and no, its practitioners did not share a common philosophy of man or politics. But its most important paradigms, its key instances, were interventions at crucial junctures of a particular type. They were junctures at which princes' and people's powers and liberties were pragmatically or deliberatively at stake, as in the case of the speech in *The Siege of Ancona*.

This crucial advance in the understanding of the history of rhetoric lay at the heart of *Foundations'* account of early modern intellectual history. The paradigms of Renaissance discourse were shown to be fundamentally pragmatic and instrumentalist. They were also oral, deriving as they did from classical oratory. They were geared to doing things with verbal instruments on particular occasions to specific ends. Later, I want to ask how the intellectual historian should re-introduce the fact that the instruments actually used in practice were of course predominantly textual not oral.

---

[11] See especially Paul Oskar Kristeller, 'Humanism and Scholasticism in the Italian Renaissance', *Byzantion: International Journal of Byzantine Studies*, American Series III, 17 (1944–5), pp. 346–74, reprinted in his *Studies in Renaissance Thought and Letters* (Rome: Edizioni di Storia e Letteratura, 1956) and in *Renaissance Thought: the Classic, Scholastic, and Humanistic Strains* (New York: Harper & Row, 1961).

[12] As in, for example, Brian Vickers, *In Defence of Rhetoric* (Oxford: Clarendon Press, 1988).

[13] This is true of the major study in the field: Glyn P. Norton, *The Ideology and Language of Translation in Renaissance France and their Humanist Antecedents* (Geneva: Droz, 1984).

[14] See, for example, the editions of Cicero's works published in 4 vols. at Milan in 1498 (British Library IC.26894) and in Basel in 1534 (British Library 11396.l.1).

For now, let us return to *Foundations* I, ch. 4, 'The Italian Renaissance', where Skinner begins by acknowledging Kristeller and by delivering the critique of Baron that follows on from the exposition of the preceding chapters.[15] On the one hand, Baron had failed to appreciate the origins of the civic humanists' themes in the literature of the city-republics of medieval Italy. On the other hand, he had not understood the 'nature of the links between the Florentine writers of the early quattrocento and the wider movement of Petrarchan humanism' as it followed on from the culture of the medieval *dictatores*.[16] Skinner's exposition of the latter allows him to bring out the centrality of the concept of *virtus* and its struggles with *fortuna*, and to explain the fact that Renaissance political treatises devote so much space to instituting the 'right process of education' for leaders and citizens.[17]

But towards the end of the chapter we find an equally searching critique of Kristeller's 'influential account of the evolution of Renaissance culture'.[18] For Skinner insists that whatever the merits of his philological and chronological arguments about Bruni's early works and his thesis about the year 1402 as the threshold between medieval and Renaissance eras, Baron still has a point that Kristeller does not tackle. It is true that the civic humanists' arguments derived from earlier scholastic and pre-humanist writings. But 'we still need to ask why it happened that these particular arguments were revived in one particular generation – and with such particular intensity – at the beginning of the fifteenth century'.[19] This is not, of course, the way Baron had phrased the question. He had asked about the circumstances of the moral and intellectual conversion of an individual humanist (Leonardo Bruni) to modern political allegiances and modern ways of thinking.

After *Foundations*, Skinner's new way of phrasing the question became routine in early modern historiography. As applied specifically to the study of *quattrocento* humanism it is still being asked and answered twenty years later by one of the most important contemporary critics of the whole debate between Baron's and Kristeller's disciples, John M. Najemy. Najemy's approach itself descends directly from the history of normative vocabularies and their use offered in *Foundations*. He writes a history of ideologies as 'powerful stories that organize experiences, aspirations, fears, and memories into more or less coherent accounts of how the world is perceived to be and how it ought to be – but usually *not* how it actually is'.[20] So the early *quattrocento* language of civic humanism was a 'normative discourse' regenerated, Najemy argues, not so much by the threat from Milan, as by the transformation of domestic politics from the 1380s on. Civic humanism's real antagonist was less the duke of

---

[15] Skinner, *Foundations*, I, pp. 69–71, 71n.   [16] Ibid., p. 71.
[17] Ibid., p. 88.   [18] Ibid., p. 102.   [19] Ibid., p. 103.
[20] John M. Najemy, 'Civic Humanism and Florentine Politics', in Hankins, *Renaissance Civic Humanism*, pp. 75–104, at p. 80.

Milan than the 'popular, guild republicanism' that had periodically surfaced to challenge the hegemony of the élite in the thirteenth and fourteenth centuries.[21] The answer may have changed, then, but the question is still the one first posed in *The Foundations of Modern Political Thought*.

I claimed earlier that *Foundations* would give you a good idea what questions had to be asked about the context of any text on moral or political themes composed between 1300 and 1600. I registered one qualification right at the outset: the missing question of how knowledge – both at the time and now – about the circumstances of transmission of texts can affect their possible meanings in ways that are open to manipulation. Let me both back up my earlier statement and introduce the question of manuscript and print circulation by taking a text Skinner does not address but that another scholar indebted to his approach does. On the one hand, I argue below, an approach such as Blair Worden's to the political contextualisation of Sidney's *Arcadia* relies on the groundwork and the questions established by *Foundations*.[22] On the other hand, questions about textual transmission continue to be preliminary or marginal in Worden's work. Worden is of course aware of the differences between the various versions of the *Arcadia* and of the difficulties presented by its textual bibliography. But the transmission of texts and of knowledge about texts is not an integral part of the story he has to tell. Whereas it *is* an integral part of the story that Sidney has to tell when he revises his prose fiction.

At the beginning of the earliest extant draft of Philip Sidney's *Arcadia*, the *Old Arcadia* completed *c*.1581, the counsellor Philanax addresses an oration to his prince, Basilius. The omniscient narrator of the story tells us that Basilius, inspired by vanity and curiosity, has consulted the Delphic oracle about his and his family's future. The oracle's cryptic reply seems to tell him that all in one year his eldest daughter shall be stolen by a prince and his younger by a rustic, that he shall commit adultery with his own wife, and that a foreign state shall sit in his throne. In understandable panic, he discloses his predicament only to his faithful friend and counsellor Philanax. He does this not – the narrator tells us – because he is open to advice, but because he wants his own fancies confirmed. For he has already decided to avoid confronting the cruel menaces of fortune head on; he will take refuge in a 'solitary place' with his family, handing his eldest daughter over to what he thinks is an honest herdsman, and keeping his youngest daughter under his own close supervision. As to the government of his country and the manning of the frontiers against foreign invasion, he will leave that to deputies headed by Philanax himself.[23]

[21] Najemy, 'Civic Humanism', p. 81.

[22] Blair Worden, *The Sound of Virtue: Philip Sidney's 'Arcadia' and Elizabethan Politics* (New Haven: Yale University Press, 1996).

[23] Philip Sidney, *The Countess of Pembroke's Arcadia (The Old Arcadia)*, ed. Jean Robertson (Oxford: Clarendon Press, 1973), pp. 4–6.

For 'fashion's sake', then, Basilius asks Philanax for his counsel. Philanax starts by saying that he 'should in better season and to better purpose have spoken' had he been asked before Basilius went to Delphos. He nevertheless goes on to deliver what *Foundations* tell us is an entirely conventional set of humanist counsels. As for Basilius' desire for knowledge from the oracle, wisdom and virtue are the only destinies appointed to man to follow. They make a man see so direct a way of proceeding 'as prosperity must necessarily ensue'. Besides, standing or falling with virtue, a man is never in evil case. And in heavenly matters, prayer and reverence must oust vain curiosity. As for Basilius' plan to retire from government, what justification could there be for this? For thirty years, out of the good constitution of the state and a wise providence, obedient subjects have not lacked justice, while neighbours have found the prince 'so hurtlessly strong that they thought it better to rest in your friendship than make new trial of your enmity'. Why, then, should he seek new courses, deprive himself of governing his dukedom out of fear? He should instead arm himself with courage against the oracle, be in his subjects' eyes, let them see the benefits of his justice daily more and more, live and die like a prince.[24]

Philanax then applies the same arguments to the question of the government of the princesses' education. Hitherto, this has been fitly to restrain them from evil, while giving their minds virtuous delights, and 'not grieving them for want of well ruled liberty'. But now, in has come suspicion, 'the most venemous gall to virtue'. After elaborating this theme and lamenting the elevation of a clown to the post of royal guardian, Philanax concludes by beseeching Basilius to face the assays of fortune, 'to stand wholly upon your own virtue' as the surest way of maintaining 'you in that you are', i.e. in his state. But Basilius, already wedded to his opinion, is not listening. It seems that the virtuous constitution of the state, established by former prince-lawgivers and the 'well bringing up of the people', is to fall because this prince is to abnegate the struggle between *virtù* and *fortuna*.[25]

Sidney's *Arcadia* sits squarely within the humanist rhetorical tradition described by Skinner. It is studded with set-piece eclogues and oratorical speeches like that of Philanax. As a humanist romance, it bears the hallmarks of rhetorical pedagogy and was quickly incorporated into the teaching repertoire of Elizabethan vernacular humanists.[26] But *Foundations* also enables us to trace the tradition of Philanax's conventional arguments very precisely. Italian Renaissance authors of princely advice-books and theorists of republican liberty had both used the concept of *virtù* to denote 'those qualities which guarantee success in political life', whatever the assaults of *fortuna*.[27] Virtue

---

[24] Sidney, *The Countess of Pembroke's Arcadia (The Old Arcadia)*, pp. 6–8.
[25] Ibid., p. 9.   [26] Ibid., pp. xxx–xxxiii.   [27] Skinner, *Foundations*, I, p. 177.

was conventionally broken down into its constituent cardinal virtues, including wisdom and justice.[28] Philanax's oration is, though, more specifically redolent of these themes as received by the northern humanists of the first half of the sixteenth century and 'assimilated into their own very different range of experiences'. The Italian obsession with *libertas* has gone, replaced by the problem of counselling princes moved by tyrannical passions.[29] Northern humanist discussions of these topics, Skinner tells us, as well as placing greater emphasis on piety, conventionally culminated 'in a denunciation of what Milton was to call a "fugitive and cloistered virtue"'.[30] This is exactly how Philanax's oration indeed culminates.

So what was Sidney doing? He was reviving the traditional arguments of the humanist counsellors and tutors to his father's generation. But again, the further question *Foundations* has bequeathed to us – and to Blair Worden in his book *The Sound of Virtue* in particular – is why Sidney is reviving these arguments in this fictional form at a specific political moment around 1580? If we look, as *Foundations'* introduction suggests, at some of the 'more ephemeral contemporary contributions to social and political thought' we quickly find Sidney's *A Letter to Queen Elizabeth* about the Alençon courtship. In the letter Sidney describes the proposed marriage to the French king's brother as a 'refuge' procured by 'fears'. Why would the Queen even contemplate such a hazardous change in her calm 'estate'?[31]

Questions still remain. It does not follow from this – as Blair Worden seems on occasions to argue – that the author of the *Old Arcadia* is just elaborating the letter on Protestant virtue to the queen in a different form.[32] The evidence suggests that copies of *A Letter* circulated widely in manuscript, like the *Old Arcadia*, but to a different audience. By design, the *Old Arcadia* circulated among Sidney and his sisters' family friends, not among his seniors and betters. The work, it might be argued, was written for this kind of distinct and controlled circulation and not for 'common' consumption – even though Fulke Greville claimed it had met this fate by 1586. Whereas *A Letter* was in a sense authored by Sidney's seniors and betters in order that it be freely and widely copied for propagandistic purposes. It formed part of a campaign by the earl of Leicester and his supporters against the French marriage. It did for a noble and court audience what John Stubbs's printed 1579 tract *The discoverie of a gaping gulf* did for a more popular audience.[33]

---

[28] Ibid., p. 126.   [29] Ibid., pp. 200, 217.   [30] Ibid., p. 218.

[31] Philip Sidney, *Miscellaneous Prose*, ed. Katherine Duncan-Jones and Jan van Dorsten (Oxford: Clarendon Press, 1973), pp. 46–7.

[32] Worden, *The Sound of Virtue*, pp. 127–41, 195–96.

[33] H. R. Woudhuysen, *Sir Philip Sidney and the Circulation of Manuscripts 1558–1640* (Oxford: Clarendon Press, 1996), pp. 100, 151–2, 301, 421. See Alan Stewart's shrewd commentary on *A Letter* and its circumstances in *Philip Sidney: a Double Life* (London: Chatto & Windus, 2000), pp. 218–21.

Commenting upon *A Letter* to Sidney himself Languet says he is glad it 'has come to the knowledge of so many persons'. But he also reminds Sidney that he was 'ordered to write' as he did 'by those whom you were bound to obey' (his father Sir Henry Sidney's politically Protestant allies) so that he could not be blamed for putting forward freely what he thought good for his country.[34] If Philip was commissioned to write this letter by powerful sponsors to whom he was bound by his father's authority, in what sense did he see himself as its 'author'? Was Languet hinting that Sidney should guard against the exposure that came with the court public's knowledge of his authorship of the letter by letting it be known more widely that he had been ordered to write it? Is Philanax, in fact, not a figure for Philip Sidney but for Sir Henry and his powerful patrons speaking through Philip? We noted, above, that the oration/letter contains arguments associated specifically with Sidney's father's generation. Is it so clear that the relationship between the Philanax episode at the beginning of the *Old Arcadia* and *A Letter* is a matter of two equivalent political speech acts? The relationship may indeed signify to a readership that the author of the widely circulated manuscript letter is also the author of the manuscript prose romance. But it may also serve to differentiate the two texts and the kinds of authorship and circulation with which they are to be associated.

We begin to get a glimpse here of circumstances that bear on the interpretation of both the *Arcadia* and *A Letter*, and of the relationship between them. But they are of a different order from those habitually considered as primary contexts in *Foundations* and in Blair Worden's study alike. I refer, again, to the circumstances and forms in which texts, and knowledge about the background to texts, are circulated at the time of their first transmission.

Sidney draws our attention quite explicitly to these circumstances. The *Old Arcadia* was not printed until hundreds of years later. But Philip also worked on a revision, the so-called *New Arcadia*, which was published by Fulke Greville in 1590. In this version the original story is broken up and embedded in a much more complex narrative. The context of Philanax's oration changes in a very interesting manner. The oration becomes a circulating manuscript letter. Sidney has made the circumstances in which Philanax's speech circulates part of the story, as though he is reflecting on the early transmission of his own letter addressed to Elizabeth.

The *New Arcadia* begins with Pyrocles' and Musidorus' shipwreck. Musidorus makes it ashore but witnesses the taking of the heroic Pyrocles by pirates. 'Shall virtue become a slave to those that be slave to viciousness?' he exclaims. Some shepherds then introduce Musidorus to an Arcadian gentleman, Kalender, of whom it is said that no news stirs but it comes to his ears.[35]

---

[34] Sidney, *Miscellaneous Prose*, p. 33.
[35] Philip Sidney, *The Countess of Pembroke's Arcadia (The New Arcadia)*, ed. Victor Skretkowicz (Oxford: Clarendon Press, 1987), p. 9.

Having seen, in the gallery of Kalender's summer house, a royal family portrait that rather curiously lacks the elder princess, Musidorus is puzzled. Kalender promises to discover unto him not only that knowledge he has in common with others, but knowledge which 'by extraordinary means is delivered unto me'. It is then Kalender who begins to tell Musidorus the story that is told by the omniscient narrator directly to the reader at the beginning of the *Old Arcadia*.[36]

It turns out that the *un*common knowledge he possesses about the reasons for Basilius' mysterious retirement is derived from the copy of a letter that has fallen into his hands. His son Clitophon had been a gentleman of the privy chamber and had taken a copy of a letter that the prince had laid in a window after reading, 'presuming nobody durst look in his writings'. Clitophon had plenty of time not only to read but also to copy the letter. Kalender tells Musidorus that he blamed his son for the curiosity that made him break his duty 'in such a kind whereby kings' secrets are subject to be revealed'. Since it was done, though, Kalender was 'content to take so much profit, as to know it'.[37]

Before Kalender reads the letter – which for his good liking he has carried about him ever since – he tells Musidorus the background. The background amounts to the virtuous character of the author, Philanax himself, and whatever Kalender can deduce about the circumstances from the text. He gathers that the Prince has 'written unto him his determination . . . upon some oracle' he has received at Delphos. He then reads the text, which is very close to the text of the oration in the *Old Arcadia*. He says afterwards that he does not know what the oracle said, and gathers from the text that Philanax did not know either. He deduces from what he calls 'this experience', i.e. the text of the letter and the ongoing uncertainty of the political situation, that Basilius 'hath rather heard then followed the wise . . . counsel of Philanax'. The prince has lost the stern of his government, 'strange bruits are received for current' among the people, 'the prince himself hath hidden his head'. Kalender apologises to Musidorus for his long discourse. Perhaps old men, he admits, are particularly keen to eternise themselves not only by children but 'by speeches and writings recommended to the memory of hearers and readers'. He assures Musidorus, however, that he has not revealed these matters so freely to any but him, in whom he already sees so much to love and trust.[38]

Here, then, is a fictionalised account of the circumstances in which speeches and writings might be recommended to the memories of hearers and readers in English Renaissance culture. Do Kalender's act of recommendation and its context have a place, though, in Skinner's historiography of moral and political thought? Or is there only a place for the act of the original letter-writer? The letter is addressed to a prince who does not hear its contents, and reaches its readership by means of copies taken 'accidentally' at court. Kalender is an

---

[36] Ibid., pp. 15–16.   [37] Ibid., p. 20.   [38] Ibid., pp. 20–23.

agent of political discourse, but not in Skinner's sense of an author who is doing something by means of a published work he has composed. He serves as a kind of clearing-house for both common news and uncommon manuscripts. He recommends the letter to the memory of Musidorus, and reads it to him, filling in the context as best he can.

Crucially, however, there are aspects of the context to which Kalender is not privy. He does not have the letter written by the prince to Philanax and he does not know the original cause of both letters: the contents of the oracle. The 'secret' letter ultimately serves not to persuade the prince of anything, but to begin to link together a network of like-minded writers, recommenders and hearers. The point of the letter, indeed, becomes the fact that the prince has heard but not heeded its wise counsel. To reduce it to a speech act or to Philanax's intention in writing, to ignore the experience Kalender brings to the text and passes on with it, is to miss the meaning of the text in context. As it circulates, it becomes an index of the friendship, of the shared political experience of noblemen who would preserve the understanding of true virtue and wisdom in times of tyranny, rebellion and slavery. We shall see that a similar meaning attaches to a real text in circulation in mid-sixteenth-century France.

I am suggesting that questions about the transmission of texts can be material to their interpretation as documents of moral and political thought in ways comprehended neither by Skinner's model nor by traditional reception studies. I use the fictional example in part because these kinds of circumstances are notoriously hard to track and document in the archives. But I shall now move on to a historical example that lacks the satisfying shape and outcome of Sidney's fictional story about a letter's transmission. This is the example of northern humanist Étienne de la Boétie's discourse *De la servitude volontaire*, or, if you prefer, *Contr'un*. It will lead us naturally into a discussion of Montaigne's *Essais*, a work originally intended to have played host to an edition of La Boétie's discourse. The *Essais* might be said to originate not so much in the ruminative silence of the tower-library on Montaigne's estate, as in the author's role as a recommender of La Boétie's and his father's works.

La Boétie's discourse is neither an oration nor a letter. But, as a rhetorical piece addressed to a particular individual, it has affinities with both. It is an extreme, possibly unique example, but it does raise pertinent general questions about what exactly makes a 'classic' political text; questions, also, about the confidence with which we skirt round the complexities of the transmission of texts and assign them confidently for interpretation to an 'original' authorial context. At the same time it still offers a concrete example of the cultural process at the heart of *Foundations*' account of intellectual history: the process whereby a particular, shared political experience comes to be conceptualised by means of more or less 'traditional' argumentative resources recirculated from other contexts.

La Boétie's *De la servitude volontaire* is an important document in Montaigne studies. But why has it not become a classic in its own right? Why is it not a 'Cambridge text in the history of political thought'? Skinner famously specifies in the introduction to *Foundations* that his approach to classic texts 'enables us to characterise what their authors were doing in writing them'.[39] Is the answer, then, that a classic political text, like a rhetorician's model oration, has to be recommended to us with a clear story – which *De la servitude volontaire* does not have – about its contextual origins, a story captured in a definitive sixteenth-century or modern printed edition of a manuscript? If so, the complication is that what Skinner calls 'the context in and for which' an author was writing was often a matter of uncertainty, dispute, manipulation at the time.[40] In the case of La Boétie's discourse, we can isolate neither its original textual state nor its original context of composition, nor even its original title, from the various copies, comments and circumstances of its early *fortuna*.[41] Just as Kalender was uncertain about the exact occasion of Philanax's letter, so even Montaigne may not have known for sure what the 'original' occasion of La Boétie's work was.

La Boétie died in 1563. Manuscript copies of the discourse were certainly circulating among networks of gentlemen and humanists before then. Montaigne says that when he first saw La Boétie's 'essay against tyrants in honour of freedom' it had 'long circulated among men of discretion – not without great and well-merited esteem'.[42] But we only have hard evidence of the text as it was transmitted, copied, 'recommended' and refuted by others long after it was composed. The majority date from the period after 1570.[43] The nature of the evidence that survives is clearest in what has traditionally been taken to be the most authoritative manuscript. I refer to the famous collector Henri de Mesme's copy, now in the Bibliothèque de France. For De Mesme's transcription of the text is immediately followed by his own notes refuting La Boétie's arguments.[44]

De Mesme copied it, that is, as a text needing refutation at a particular moment. Although these notes are in themselves highly interesting for the history of political thought, I do not wish to describe them here. The point I am making is that we always catch this text in the act of transmission, not as an authorial speech act that reverberates only in one original context. I do not

[39] Skinner, *Foundations*, I, p. xiii.   [40] Ibid., p. 61.

[41] This has become particularly clear in the latest contribution to the scholarship. See J.-E. Girot, 'Une version inconnue du *Discours de la Servitude Volontaire* de La Boétie', *Bibliothèque d'Humanisme et Renaissance* 53 (2001), pp. 551–65.

[42] Montaigne, *The Complete Essays*, trans. M. A. Screech (Harmondsworth: Penguin, 1991), p. 206.

[43] See Étienne de la Boétie, *De la servitude volontaire ou Contr'un*, ed. Malcolm Smith (Geneva: Droz, 1987), pp. 22–6; Roger Trinquet, 'Montaigne et la divulgation du Contr'un', *Revue d'Histoire littéraire de la France* 64 (1964), pp. 1–12.

[44] Étienne de la Boétie, *De la servitude volontaire ou Contr'un*, ed. Nadia Gontarbert (Paris: Gallimard, 1993), pp. 196–211.

think this makes Skinner's approach inapplicable – quite the contrary – but I do think his question needs modifying. It is not always about what the author is doing, at least in the conventional sense of that term.

More important still than the fact that we do not have a stable authorial text or genealogy of copies is the fact that we do have more than one Kalender figure recommending the text to us with contextualising stories about its circumstances of composition. And the stories conflict. De Thou tells us that it was composed as an immediate response to the Guyenne revolt of 1548 against *la gabelle*, the hated royal salt tax imposed under Henri II.[45] Montaigne tells us that 'this subject was treated by him in his childhood purely as an exercise' though he does not doubt that La Boétie believed what he wrote, for 'if he had had the choice he would rather have been born in Venice than in Sarlat'.[46] Both of these stories are taken seriously by editors and inform some of the divergent interpretations offered by critics.

By contrast, modern editors are positively embarrassed about the story told by Agrippa d'Aubigné. According to him the discourse was written in a fit of irritation after a royal guard, pestered by La Boétie to grant access to the Louvre's ballroom, dropped his halberd deliberately on the author's foot. D'Aubigné claims La Boétie went running through the Louvre crying for justice but was laughed at by the grandees that heard him.[47] Modern scholars add further stories. One has recently insisted that we pay more attention to La Boétie's embedded dedications to Guillaume de Lur-Longa. He has tied the text to the moment when La Boétie succeeded Lur-Longa as *conseiller* at the Bordeaux *parlement*. He has read it in this local political gift context as an encouragement to members of the *parlement* of Paris at a moment when it was in conflict with the crown.[48] But it should be noted that at least one of the manuscript copies lacks one of the addresses to Lur-Longa.[49]

Few could deny that the power of *De la servitude volontaire's* argument and the force of its language ought to have made it a political classic. I cannot summarise the discourse in any detail here. With declamatory brilliance, La Boétie denounces the exercise of absolute power by a single man, without control or moderation, at the expense of a whole community. But it is not – I should specify in current circumstances – about a tyrant's oppression of a non-consenting people by terror. La Boétie argues that monarchical tyranny can only come about with the tacit accord of the people, who subject themselves

---

[45] La Boétie, *De la servitude volontaire*, ed. Smith, p. 8.
[46] Montaigne, *Essays*, pp. 218–19.
[47] La Boétie, *De la servitude volontaire*, ed. Smith, p. 11.
[48] See G. Demerson, 'Les exempla dans le *Discours de la Servitude Volontaire*: une rhétorique datée?', in M. Tétel (ed.), *Etienne de La Boétie. Sage révolutionnaire et poète périgourdin*, Actes du Colloque International, Duke University, 26–28 mars 1999, *Colloques, Congrès et Conférences sur la Renaissance Européenne* 30 (Paris: Honoré Champion, 2004), pp. 195–224.
[49] Girot, 'Une version inconnue', p. 563.

voluntarily to a single man. The situation is intolerable, and goes against nature, which makes each individual man free. It can only pertain in a degenerate society, for since the whole of society is a pyramid culminating in the tyrant and his entourage at its summit, social relationships at all levels down to the bottom are corrupted. La Boétie's work is a classically powerful discourse.

And so it appeared to its first readers. When the exiled Florentine humanist Jacopo Corbinelli encountered a copy of the text in an unidentified Parisian library, possibly Henri de Mesme's or Claude Dupuy's, he wrote to his friend Vincenzo Pinelli in Padua in November 1570 as follows:

I would like to have a copy of a writing that I have seen in the most elegant French de voluntaria servitute that Brutus himself could not have said better. I read it and it is learned and deep but dangerous for these times.[50]

A copy did find its way to Pinelli though it is not certain whether it was provided in the event by Corbinelli or not.[51] Paolo Carta has recently excavated the circumstances behind Corbinelli's remarks and his desire for a copy of a discourse whose author and origins appear to have been unknown to him. In the context of Florentine politics, Corbinelli was an anti-Medicean republican. His projects in exile included a plan for a French edition of Giannotti's *Republica fiorentina*, a text that heralded the coming of a 'new Brutus [*nuovo Bruto*]' to Florence. Writing to Pinelli at Padua in the Venetian republic, Corbinelli inserts his reading of La Boétie into the construction of a cultural platform for the hoped-for return of republicanism to Florence. At the same time, Corbinelli is a supporter and servant of Catherine de Medici. In the entirely different context of French politics, he reads the text as one that at that particular moment, in the hands of the wrong readers, the hands of the growing Huguenot 'resistance', could be very dangerous for the Valois monarchy.[52]

In an address to the reader, dated August 1570, but published in the slim 1571 edition of some of La Boétie's works, Montaigne says something very similar in the course of explaining why he cannot print *De la servitude volontaire*. In this address and in other dedicatory letters he describes what difficulties he has had collecting enough texts of enough weight to represent his friend's genius. La Boétie had spread his works around in manuscript copies without any care for their fortunes. But even though Montaigne had found a copy of this and another

---

[50] 'Vorrei poter haver copia d'una scritt[ura] che io ho visto in franzese elegantiss[mo], De voluntaria servitute, che Bruto stesso non harebbe detto meglio. Io l'ho letta et è cosa dotta et recondita ma per questi tempi pericolosa' (J. Corbinelli to V. Pinelli, 4 November 1570, Pinelli collection, B. 9, fol. 131, Biblioteca Ambrosiana Milan). I use the transcription given by N. Panichi, *Plutarchus Redivivus? La Boétie e i suoi interpreti* (Naples: Vivarium, 1999), p. 21.

[51] Girot, 'Une version inconnue', 565.

[52] P. Carta, 'Les exilés italiens et l'anti-machiavélisme français au XVIe siècle', in P. Carta and L. De Los Santos (eds.) *La République en exile (XVe–XVIe siècles)* (Lyons: ENS-Editions, 2002), pp. 93–117. I am grateful to Professor Carta for sending me a copy of his chapter.

discourse he could not publish them as their manner was 'too delicate and dainty' for them to be abandoned to the gross and heavy air of such an unpleasant season.[53] But *De la servitude volontaire* did of course reach the gross and heavy air. In 1574 a large section of La Boétie's discourse was pirated and inserted without acknowledgement into the mouth of a pro-revolutionary *politique* in one of the printed dialogues of the famous *Reveille-Matin*, or 'alarm-call' to revolutionary Protestants. The work was published again in Simon Goulart's cleverly propagandistic, pro-'resistance' collection of *Mémoires* of the reign of Charles IX in 1578, and in another, separate Huguenot edition published at Rheims (1577).[54]

Meanwhile, Montaigne had been planning to embed this delicate discourse at the heart of book I of the *Essais*, to surround it with a prophylactic commentary that would allow it to be released into the common air. But 'having discovered', as he says, 'that this work of his has since been published to an evil end by those who seek to disturb and change the state of our national polity without worrying if they will make it better, and that they have set it among works of their own kidney', he decided not to publish it in the *Essais* after all.[55]

I am arguing that La Boétie's is a text which does have a precise historical 'moment' to illumine its meanings. But if we continue to ask what the author is doing with his arguments at that moment then we must understand the author to be a group of readers, copiers and editors, including Montaigne himself. For a decade between 1570 and 1580 *De la servitude volontaire* (or whichever title we ascribe to it) provided seasonal arguments for liberty and against tyranny. It could serve to express the liberty-loving sentiments of anti-Huguenot supporters of the French monarchy, including those who backed republicanism in Florence and Venice, while also being self-evidently applicable, and therefore – from one perspective – dangerous in the context of the growing body of anti-Valois, revolutionary Huguenot propaganda. The problem that Montaigne faced and failed to solve was how La Boétie's discourse could be circulated in print in such a way as to fix its definitive context as the former, rather than the latter. He was meant to be Kalender to La Boétie's Philanax. But controlled, 'contextualised' circulation of texts in the sixteenth century was a much messier, more uncertain and more hazardous enterprise than either Sidney's fiction or much modern scholarship suggests.

By the mid-sixteenth century the textual fortunes of virtuous and free speech and the potentially vicious curiosity of readers and copiers were as much a matter of active concern to producers of discourse as the intellectual definition of the

---

[53] Étienne de la Boétie, *Œuvres complètes*, ed. Louis Desgraves, 2 vols. (Bordeaux: William Blake, 1991), I, p. 149.

[54] Panichi, *Plutarchus Redivivus?*, pp. 21–9; La Boétie, *De la servitude volontaire*, ed. Gontarbert, pp. 245–7.

[55] Montaigne, *Essays*, p. 218.

vices and virtues and their relationship to political liberty and the chances of fortune. I think this applies to Montaigne, and that his concern derives specifically from his bitter experience with the fortunes of his great friend La Boétie's texts. For when we describe what Montaigne is doing in the *Essais* we should take into account that the author figures in the first edition as a 'recommender' of others' texts. We have seen that the first volume was centrally to have included an edition of La Boétie's praise of liberty. The largest essay in the second volume, likewise, apologises for a fifteenth-century text that had been recommended to Pierre Eyquem (Montaigne's father) by a humanist, Pierre Bunel. Montaigne translated the text, Raymond Sebond's *Natural Theology*, as a filial duty and published it eleven years before the first edition of the *Essais*.

The point here, again, is that Sebond's intention is less important than Bunel's. Bunel's intention – an intention co-opted by Montaigne's father – had been to provide a textual prophylactic against the spread of licentiously critical reasoning occasioned by the Lutheran protest against the established church. Sebond's text was indeed held by Montaigne's betters and patrons to be a useful instrument in preserving true Catholic piety at this time. This despite the fact that the Roman church – the protagonist most interested in this case in the original author's intentions – was highly suspicious of Sebond's prologue (which was eventually placed on the Index of Prohibited Books). The problem was that the *Natural Theology* was in many ways a 'weak' book designed for readers with relatively little formal learning, readers such as Pierre Eyquem and the ladies at court.[56] It looked flimsy and inadequate when put up alongside other works being produced by court theologians and philosophers. It needed protection and support from its patron (Pierre) were it to serve the purpose intended by Pierre's learned guest, and vicariously by Pierre himself. In his father's name, Michel brings in some heavy-duty argumentative resources from Sextus Empiricus to provide this protection and meet this purpose. The new wrapping changes the nature of the gift – it now undermines rather than rebuilds the foundations of man's rational knowledge – but it serves the same purpose. More important than Sebond's original intention is what Pierre – co-opting his humanist client's idea – intended to do with the text, and Montaigne, I would argue, is faithful to this intention. We can understand Pierre as the author here, if we want, but only if the agency of both his intellectual servant and his son is somehow comprehended.

Behind the *Essais*, then, are two highly complex stories about the transmission of others' texts. Montaigne's attempts in his first edition to recommend

---

[56] Ibid., pp. 490–91 (from II.12, 'An Apology for Raymond Sebond'); E. Limbrick, 'Métamorphose d'un philosophe en théologien', in Claude Blum (ed.), *Montaigne, 'Apologie de Raimond Sebond'. De la 'Theologia' à la 'Théologie'* (Paris: Honoré Champion, 1990), pp. 229–46, at pp. 234–8; F. Rigolot, 'D'une Théologie "pour les dames" à une Apologie "per le donne"', in ibid., pp. 261–90.

these texts dovetail with his increasingly elaborate attempts in the same and subsequent editions to recommend his own. In describing what Montaigne is doing in the *Essais* it is certainly helpful to refer in the spirit of Skinner to an act of free speech before an audience of friends and familiars. But one must also refer to a carefully deliberated and manipulated act of publication. The traditional story of a book composed in isolation in a library-tower without a thought for printers, publishers and readers outside the family should not be taken too much at face value. For Montaigne sets out to shape a clear story about the contextual origins of his works so as to shape the ethos of their reception. The context in and for which he was writing is a crucial part of his subject matter, subject matter that he shapes with a definite purpose.

For the story Montaigne tells about his own book is a solution to a problem in specific social and cultural circumstances. The problem is how safely to communicate freely formed critical opinions as one's own in an age of print piracy and violent controversy, an age in which criticism of authorities is used to perpetuate civil and religious war. The fate of La Boétie's manuscript *De la servitude volontaire* dramatised the problem only too clearly for him as he prepared the first edition of the work that was to have accompanied it into print. The standard instrument for solving this problem was the familiar or dedicatory letter. Works could be accompanied by a carefully confected set of dedicatory letters – as in the case of Montaigne's editions of La Boétie. Or the works could consist of a collected volume of familiar letters to friends.

Since the Reformation, the theory had been that one could publish free judgements on ticklish matters in the safe and controlled environment of a letter to a friend. Even in Erasmus's case the theory had not worked out that well in practice. However much he tried to control the circulation of his familiar letters, to circumscribe their political force, the letters 'turned out all-too-easily to escape his authorial control'. Erasmus's own semi-fictionalised efforts were overtaken by devastatingly effective and polemical publications of entirely counterfeit correspondence.[57]

From one perspective, Montaigne's particular solution to the problem is to tell the story of a wise man's live ethical experiment in frankness and openness, the fortunate success of which he observes and comments upon in later editions of the text.[58] As the work, after first publication, finds far-flung and trusting readers, and as Montaigne, who is consubstantial with his book, travels and networks, encountering people who – despite his candour – receive him

---

[57] Lisa Jardine, 'Before Clarissa: Erasmus, "Letters of Obscure Men", and Epistolary Fictions', in T. Van Houdt, J. Papy, G. Tournoy and C. Matheeussen (eds.), *Self-Presentation and Social Identification: the Rhetoric and Pragmatics of Letter Writing in Early Modern Times. Proceedings of the International Colloquium Leuven-Brussels, 24–28 May 2000*, Supplementa Humanistica Lovaniensia 18 (Leuven: Brill, 2002), pp. 385–403, at pp. 400–3.

[58] See especially Montaigne, *Essays*, pp. 1201–5.

well, both are emboldened to be more openly themselves, to speak more freely and experimentally on a variety of potentially controversial topics. In other words, the ethical self-experimentation has demonstratively positive outcomes. Montaigne on his estate and on his travels, the book both locally and internationally, does manage to survive unscathed in such a dangerous season and to make friends. He has brought his true and natural self in all (or almost all) its nakedness out into private social life and it has been welcomed, not censored, requisitioned or killed.

As this already makes clear, the solution to which I refer is also a strategy for the publication of a uniquely free but unrevolutionary and uncontroversial book. The strategy has intellectual, literary and commercial aspects. For a start, Montaigne does not, like La Boétie, disperse himself in miscellaneous manuscript works given to friends and family on various occasions, works which are then recopied by others for potentially illegitimate uses. Nor does he, like Sidney, remain a manuscript author but seek to exercise more control over his works by various means. He collects himself in a printed book. And it is himself. For he does not choose a subject that controls him, that limits his freedom of intellectual movement. He does not choose a subject, such as contemporary events, that, given his natural *liberté*, would lead him to publish unlawful and punishable judgements. He finds a core subject of which he is the undisputed master but about which he is free to talk (i.e. himself).[59]

He abandons the standard generic choice. He does not confect letters to friends with whom he is no more than acquainted but to whom he would become publicly obliged for the maintenance of his reputation. He does not, in other words, use the tired fiction of a printed collection of familiar letters to friends. He collects himself in a new genre of *essais*.[60] He tries to control the distribution and use of the *Essais* by means of their format and content, as though the work were a single manuscript circulated only to friends who know the author and accept his good faith. Instead of writing new works he takes advantage of the *privilège* system to keep control of his one work by periodically preparing expanded editions.[61] By various rhetorical means he directs the work to the private spaces of his readers' households, where it will have no role in bitter public controversies. At the same time, again, the text becomes bolder and freer

---

[59] Ibid., p. 120.

[60] See ibid., pp. 279, 282–3. It is not just that Montaigne's letters failed to survive the ravages of time. Contemporaries noted that Montaigne did not play the epistolary game. Catherine Magnien quotes a near contemporary of Montaigne's, Ogier, speculating that the conspicuous lack of letters to friends left by Montaigne could have been due to his distance from worthy correspondents, or to his choosiness in friendship. See Catherine Magnien, 'Etienne Pasquier "familier" de Montaigne?', *Montaigne Studies* 13 (2001), pp. 277–313, at p. 300.

[61] See George Hoffmann's classic article, 'The Montaigne Monopoly: Revising Montaigne's *Essais* under France's Privilege System', *Publications of the Modern Language Association* 108 (2) (1993), pp. 308–19.

as it goes, from one edition to another, the more confident the author becomes about his reception. This, at any rate, is the story Montaigne tells about himself and his book. The intellectual historian, of course, should not take it at face value. But that is another story.

Since the publication of *Foundations* we have become more aware of the cultural and physical conditions informing textual production and consumption in the early-modern period. This means that we now have some supplementary questions to ask of early-modern texts of moral and political thought. We must question traditional stories about the circumstances of composition of texts, interrogate producers' strategies for controlling and circumscribing their interpretation, and consider whether the 'author' whose doings interest us is not sometimes the reader, the copier, the 'recommender' of others' works. These are, though, only supplementary questions. The foundational questions are still firmly in place.

6   'The Best State of the Commonwealth': Thomas More and Quentin Skinner

Cathy Curtis

As many commentators and critics have acknowledged and vigorously applauded, Quentin Skinner has continuously rethought and revised his methodology, and the fundamental categories and descriptions in his scholarship.[1] His very recent and magisterial three-volume collection of new and revised essays, entitled *Visions of Politics*, brings into focus this development over the twenty-five years since the publication of *The Foundations of Modern Political Thought*. Exemplifying the contextualist approach which is now associated with the Cambridge school of history, *Foundations* concerned itself with the process by which the modern conception of the state – 'its nature, powers, and right to command obedience' – came to be formed from the late thirteenth century to the end of the sixteenth century.[2] The political theory of the northern Renaissance was shown to be 'an extension and consolidation' of a range of arguments which arose in *quattrocento* Italy, although subject to a critical re-evaluation.[3] Early-modern England received particular attention in this respect. The impact of *Foundations* has been profound; through the close and meticulous textual analysis of a myriad of well-known and lesser-known writers in their intellectual context, Skinner drew a typology which has guided countless scholars and students of the period.

A decade after *Foundations* a fresh emphasis had emerged in Skinner's 1988 essay, 'Political philosophy'. One of Thomas More's chief preoccupations in *Utopia*, it was said, was to restate a crucial tenet of classical republicanism:

I am indebted to David Colclough and the participants of the conference 'Rethinking the Foundations' for their comments and criticisms. Conal Condren, Andrew Fitzmaurice and Jean Pretorius responded to earlier drafts. The editors, Annabel Brett and James Tully, helped me sharpen and clarify my arguments. My greatest thanks are due to Quentin Skinner for his generosity as a scholar and teacher, which extended to discussions concerning this paper.

[1] James Tully (ed.), *Meaning and Context: Quentin Skinner and his Critics* (Cambridge: Cambridge University Press, 1988); Quentin Skinner, *Visions of Politics*, 3 vols. (Cambridge: Cambridge University Press, 2002), I: *Regarding Method*.

[2] Quentin Skinner, *The Foundations of Modern Political Thought*, 2 vols. (Cambridge: Cambridge University Press, 1978) I, p. ix.

[3] Ibid., p. 244.

'that the noblest way of life is one of virtuous public service'.[4] The essay concluded that, as the contrasts between scholastic and humanist principles were considered more deeply in the course of the sixteenth century, 'the humanist ideal of virtuous public service was increasingly challenged and eventually supplanted by a more individual and contractarian style of political reasoning, the style perfected by Thomas Hobbes in *Leviathan*'. Political liberty was now calibrated according to the extent of individual rights, and 'this new tradition found the humanist attempt to connect liberty with virtue and public service at best paradoxical and at worst a sinister misunderstanding of the concepts involved'.[5]

And more than a decade later, *Visions of Politics* now compares these 'two contrasting views we have inherited in the modern West about the nature of our common life'; the neo-Roman theory of freedom and self-government on one side, and 'the modern theory of the state as the bearer of uncontrollable sovereignty' on the other.[6] The reconciliation of 'these divergent perspectives', it is said, 'remains a central problem in contemporary political life'; Skinner's hope is that his 'excavation' of the history of these 'rival theories' will 'contribute something of more than purely historical interest to these current debates'.[7] And certainly it is the values of the neo-Roman vision of politics that Skinner believes have been neglected and misconstrued by its scholastic critics and their modern Gothic counterparts, such as John Rawls and Robert Nozick.

It was in his *Liberty before Liberalism* of 1998, developed from his Inaugural Lecture as Regius Professor of Modern History in the University of Cambridge, that Skinner adopted the terminology of neo-Roman rather than republican theory of liberty for the first time, arguing that it allowed the inclusion of those writers who did not strictly oppose the institution of monarchy, but rather may even have preferred that an element of monarchy be part of a mixed constitution.[8] In a trenchant review of *Liberty before Liberalism*, Blair Worden considered that certainly

in the English-speaking world there existed, at least from the early seventeenth century, a loose but enduring vocabulary which connected liberty not, or not only, with individual rights but with particular forms of government (sometimes republican, sometimes mixed-monarchical).

But the challenge facing Skinner, he argued, was 'to establish more fully the relationship of seventeenth century English thought of the Civil War and Interregnum to classical and Italian thinking about the free state, and

---

[4] C. B. Schmitt and Quentin Skinner, 'Political Philosophy', in *Cambridge History of Renaissance Philosophy* (Cambridge: Cambridge University Press, 1988), p. 451.
[5] Schmitt and Skinner, 'Political Philosophy', pp. 451–2.
[6] Skinner, *Visions*, II, p. 9.   [7] Ibid., p. xi.
[8] Quentin Skinner, *Liberty before Liberalism* (Cambridge: Cambridge University Press, 1998), p. 11n., 54n., 55n.

to demonstrate the place within the English tradition of the "neo-Roman" conception of liberty' – if indeed that terminology offers any discriminatory advantages.[9] Worden was also disconcerted by 'a tension between the claims of historical-mindedness and those of present-mindedness' in *Liberty before Liberalism*; that is, between the recovery of the past for its own sake by the historian of political thought, and historicism which serves to recover former political values which might function as alternatives to present practice, or at least be commended as having a present pertinence.[10] It should be said at the outset, however, that *Liberty before Liberalism* was never intended to present the definitive study of the discrediting of neo-Roman theory and the success of classical liberalism. Skinner is now embarked on a full-length work of that history which extends into the eighteenth century.[11]

The following is a limited and specific intervention into the debate now in process about the direction and implications of Skinner's agonistic archaeology of political philosophy – even if Skinner's *Visions of Politics* has now offered a partial reply to Worden. I first wish to consider Skinner's interpretation of Thomas More's *Utopia* and the best state of the commonwealth in his account of the rise of the modern concept of the state and the lost vision of neo-Roman liberty.[12] I then would like to suggest points of extension and divergence in my

---

[9] Blair Worden, 'Factory of the Revolution', *London Review of Books*, 5 February 1998, pp. 13–15, at 15. On Skinner's refiguration of the concept of negative liberty, see Quentin Skinner, 'The Idea of Negative Liberty: Machiavellian and Modern Perspectives', *Visions*, II, ch. 7; Quentin Skinner, 'The Republican Ideal of Political Liberty', in Gisela Bock, Quentin Skinner and Maurizio Viroli (eds.), *Machiavelli and Republicanism* (Cambridge: Cambridge University Press, 1990), pp. 293–309; Quentin Skinner, 'Machiavelli on Virtù and the Maintenance of Liberty', *Visions*, II, pp. 160–85; Paul Rahe, 'Situating Machiavelli', in James Hankins (ed.), *Renaissance Civic Humanism: Reappraisals and Reflections* (Cambridge: Cambridge University Press, 2000), pp. 270–308. Like Worden, Rahe also questions the usefulness of the terminology of neo-Roman theory. Other challenges and comments come from Graham Maddox, 'The Limits of Neo-roman Liberty', *History of Political Thought* 23 (2002), pp. 418–31; William Walker, '*Paradise Lost* and the Forms of Government', *History of Political Thought* 22 (2001), pp. 270–91; Jonathan Scott, *England's Troubles* (Cambridge: Cambridge University Press, 2000); Conal Condren, 'Liberty of Office and its Defence in Seventeenth-Century Political Argument', *History of Political Thought* 17 (1997), pp. 460–82; J. C. Davis, 'Political Thought during the English Revolution', in B. Coward (ed.), *A Companion to Stuart Britain* (Oxford: Oxford University Press, 2003), pp. 374–96; and Antony Black, 'Christianity and Republicanism: from St Cyprian to Rousseau', *American Political Science Review* 9 (1997), pp. 647–56.

[10] Worden, 'Factory of the Revolution', pp. 13–15; compare Skinner, *Liberty Before Liberalism*, p. 118 to Michael P. Zuckert, 'Appropriation and Understanding in the History of Political Philosophy: on Quentin Skinner's Method', *Interpretation* 13 (1985), pp. 403–24 on the Cambridge school's insistence on severing the history of political thought from one's own political life or action.

[11] For a brief preview of that history, see Quentin Skinner, 'States and the Freedom of Citizens', in Quentin Skinner and Bo Stråth (eds.) *States and Citizens* (Cambridge: Cambridge University Press, 2003), pp. 11–27.

[12] Skinner, *Liberty before Liberalism*, p. 112f. for the metaphor of archaeology; Peter Kjellstrom, 'The Narrator and the Archaeologist: Modes of Meaning and Discourse in Quentin Skinner and Michel Foucault', *Statsventenskaplig Tidskrift* 98 (1995), pp. 21–41.

own reading of *Utopia*, and of other related and contemporaneous humanist writings, as they bear on Skinner's archaeology. In my discussion, I will critically examine the explanatory power of 'neo-Romanism' as applied to More.

I

Most schematically described, the neo-Roman tradition is said by Skinner to have emerged from a synthesis of Roman law concepts glossed by Azo and his pupils in the thirteenth century and the classical writings of Cicero (in particular), Sallust, Livy and Tacitus; this underpinned the civic ideology, the ideal of republicanism, developed in the Italian city-states, especially Florence and Venice. Machiavelli makes the fullest and most influential, if unorthodox, statement and reappraisal of the neo-Roman theory in the *Discorsi* on Livy's *History of Rome*. Some of the elements of Italian republicanism – which remained in contestation with the theory of princely government – were imported into northern Europe in the first years of the sixteenth century, and found a particularly receptive audience in early-modern (and monarchical) England.[13] In the *Visions*, Skinner moves directly from considerations of the writings of the 'neo-Roman' Machiavelli on liberty and *virtù* to Thomas More's contemporaneous *Utopia* of 1516, which he there describes as the 'one of the earliest and most original attempts to introduce a classical (particularly Roman) understanding of civic virtue and self-government into English political thought'.[14] Skinner never explicitly labels More a neo-Roman theorist, or even a republican theorist; however, from 1998 More is implicitly assimilated into the 'neo-Roman' narrative. The More essay is a lightly revised version of 'Sir Thomas More's *Utopia* and the Language of Renaissance Humanism' of 1988, now entitled 'Thomas More's

---

[13] Recent research on the transmission of Italian humanism into early Tudor England lays emphasis on the education and/or diplomatic service in Italy of humanists such as Linacre, Tunstall, Pace, Starkey, Pole and Lupset. See J. Woolfson, *Padua and the Tudors: English Students in Italy, 1485–1603* (Cambridge: James Clarke and Co., 1998); C. Curtis, 'Richard Pace on Pedagogy, Counsel and Satire' (Cambridge: unpublished PhD thesis, 1996); J. Woolfson (ed.), *Reassessing Tudor Humanism* (Basingstoke: Palgrave Macmillan, 2002).

[14] Skinner's essays on More are 'More's *Utopia*', *Past and Present* 38 (1967), pp. 153–68; *Foundations*, I, ch. 9; the discussion at the end of 'Political Philosophy' in *Cambridge History of Renaissance Philosophy*, pp. 389–452; 'Sir Thomas More's *Utopia* and the Language of Renaissance Humanism', in A. Pagden (ed.), *The Languages of Political Theory in Early-Modern Europe* (Cambridge: Cambridge University Press, 1987), pp. 123–57; and the recent revision of the last-mentioned in *Visions*, II, as 'Thomas More's *Utopia* and the Virtue of True Nobility', pp. 213–44. See George Logan, 'Interpreting *Utopia*', *Moreana* 31 (1994), pp. 203–58 for a discussion of Skinner's treatment of *Utopia*. Skinner has incorporated some of Logan's criticisms about, for example, his blurring of the distinction between More as author and character and his equation of Utopia with the best state of the commonwealth, into the revised *Visions* essay. I cite the revised essay in order to avoid confusion, while acknowledging that it represents a more recent and altered reading, especially in its placement immediately following the essays: Skinner, 'Machiavelli on Virtù and the Maintenance of Liberty', *Visions*, II; and Skinner, 'The Idea of Negative Liberty: Machiavelli and Modern Perspectives', *Visions*, II.

Utopia and the Virtue of True Nobility' so as to refer more specifically, it seems, to the larger concern with the Renaissance virtues and neo-Roman liberty.

In *Liberty before Liberalism* More appears as an early advocate of self-government, in terms of individual citizens exercising a right of participation in the making of laws – *Utopia* suggests the ideal of the free city as realised in a federated republic. There is then a large gap in the explication of reception of neo-Roman liberty, or at least some of its constituent elements, in England, beyond the comment that it had 'already struck some deep and ramifying roots'.[15] The research of Patrick Collinson is cited as showing how 'quasi-republican modes of political reflection and action' were present in later Elizabethan society, and that of Markku Peltonen on the reception of Machiavellian ideas by humanists from the 1570s.[16] It is unclear to me whether it is implied that the elements of neo-Roman theory which Skinner identifies in the text of *Utopia* disappear from the horizon between More and the later Elizabethans; or whether, as is more likely, the ideal of the mixed constitution as developed by later Tudor humanists, such as Thomas Starkey (*Dialogue c.*1535), John Ponet (*Shorte Treatise of Politike Power* 1556) and Sir Thomas Smith (*De republica Anglorum* 1583) represents some sort of continuity.[17] More supporting scholarship is yet to be done by Tudor intellectual historians. Jonathan Woolfson's recent essay on the use made of Aristotle's *Politics* and the contemporary Venetian model by Tudor writers is an important contribution in this direction; Mark Goldie's study of office holding in early-modern England is another.[18] The *Visions* similarly

---

[15] Skinner, *Liberty before Liberalism*, p. 11.

[16] Patrick Collinson, *De Republica Anglorum Or, History with the Politics Put Back: Inaugural Lecture delivered 9 November 1989* (Cambridge: Cambridge University Press, 1990); 'The Monarchical Republic of Queen Elizabeth I', in J. Guy (ed.), *The Tudor Monarchy* (London: St Martin's Press, 1997), pp. 110–34; David Norbrook, 'Lucan, Thomas May, and the Creation of a Republican Literary Culture', in Kevin Sharpe and Peter Lake (eds.), *Culture and Politics in Early Stuart England* (Stanford: Stanford University Press 1993), pp. 45–66. Other relevant discussions include B. Worden, 'English Republicanism', in J. H. Burns (ed.), *The Cambridge History of Political Thought*, with the assistance of Mark Goldie (Cambridge: Cambridge University Press, 1991), pp. 443–75; M. Todd, *Christian Humanism and the Puritan Social Order* (Cambridge: Cambridge University Press, 1987); D. Norbrook, *Poetry and Politics in the English Renaissance* (London: Routledge, 1984); Richard Tuck, *Philosophy and Government, 1572–1651* (Cambridge: Cambridge University Press, 1993); Blair Worden, 'Republicanism, Regicide and Republic: the English Experience', in Martin van Gelderen and Quentin Skinner (eds.), *Republicanism: a Shared European Heritage*, 2 vols. (Cambridge: Cambridge University Press, 2002), I, pp. 307–27.

[17] Skinner, 'Political Philosophy', pp. 445–7; J. Woolfson, 'Between Bruni and Hobbes: Aristotle's Politics in Tudor Intellectual Culture', in his *Reassessing Tudor Humanism*, pp. 197–222.

[18] Mark Goldie, 'The Unacknowledged Republic: Officeholding in Early Modern England', in Tim Harris (ed.), *The Politics of the Excluded, c.1500–1850* (New York: Palgrave, 2001), pp. 153–94. Worden sounds a cautionary note, warning historians not to confuse participatory features in pre-Civil War English public and communal life, which are being increasingly recovered, with constitutional republicanism: Worden, 'Republicanism, Regicide and Republic', p. 313. My thanks to Conal Condren for allowing me to read the manuscript of his book, *Argument and Authority in Early Modern England: The Presupposition of Oaths and Offices*, which further develops this line of stimulating research and questions whether negative concepts of liberty have any place at all in this period.

moves from More directly to the British civil wars. In any case, a native version of fully fledged neo-Roman theory is said to appear in the seventeenth century, with Machiavelli's *Discourses* serving as an obvious source of inspiration and culminating in James Harrington's *Oceana* of 1656 (Harrington was, it should be said, an admirer of More, and *Utopia* informs the *Oceana*).[19] The 'rise and temporary triumph' of neo-Roman theory is traced into the early decades of the eighteenth century in the *Visions*; it helped to destabilise the Stuart monarchy and aided the legitimation of the short-lived 'free state' established after the regicide in 1649.

And what are the most distinctive characteristics of neo-Roman theory as Skinner reconstructs it from classical and humanist sources? Drawing explanatory power from the metaphor of the body politic, neo-Roman thought had as its fundamental premise the idea that sovereignty in a free state must remain in the possession of the citizen-body as a whole.[20] It is the will of its citizens that is recognised as the basis of law and government. The standing of the *civis* or citizen is in contrast to that of the *subditus* or subject; and *libertas*, the freedom of individual citizens as well as of communities, is defined in terms of the absence of arbitrary domination, or even the potential for arbitrary domination, by others and in contrast with the condition of slavery. The nurturing of a virtuous and educated citizenry is necessary to guarantee and maintain the liberty of states and individuals alike. The humanist contention that *virtus vera nobilitas est* is identified as an important element of neo-Roman theory: virtue alone, rather than hereditary wealth and lineage, enables us to play our part as citizens of true nobility and worth. Citizenship is also linked with the value of the life of *negotium*, of active political service, in preference to that of *otium*, contemplative withdrawal in pursuit of religious or philosophical truth. Tyranny, on the other hand, renders the body politic unfree 'if it is forcibly or coercively deprived of its ability to act at will in the pursuit of its chosen ends'.[21]

This constitutes Skinner's third concept of liberty, the fruit of his continuing engagement with theorists of liberty, especially Isaiah Berlin, Phillip Pettit and Gerald MacCallum, and his reading of authors such as Henry Parker, Francis Osborne, Henry Neville, Edward Littleton, Marchamont Nedham, Henry Vane and John Milton in the seventeenth century.[22] In addition to Berlin's two

---

[19] M. Peltonen, *Classical Humanism and Republicanism in English Political Thought, 1570–1640* (Cambridge: Cambridge University Press, 1995); B. Worden, 'English Republicanism'.

[20] Skinner, *Visions*, II, p. 9; Alison Brown's 'De-masking Renaissance republicanism', in Hankins's *Renaissance Civic Humanism*, pp. 179–99 is excellent on the rhetoric of liberty and the increasing scepticism about the republican ideal in the late fifteenth and early sixteenth century.

[21] Skinner, *Liberty before Liberalism*, p. 47; Skinner, 'Classical Liberty and the Coming of the English Civil War', in van Gelderen and Skinner, *Republicanism*, II, pp. 9–28.

[22] Quentin Skinner, 'A Third Concept of Liberty', *Proceedings of the British Academy* 117 (2002), pp. 237–68.

concepts of liberty, positive and negative in the sense of freedom from constraint, Skinner sets forth an alternative theory of liberty – negative liberty in the sense of freedom from the potential for the exercise of discretionary powers held by those on whom those who are ruled depend. In the context of the clash between crown and Parliament in the seventeenth century, Skinner argues that the critics of the royal prerogative (particularly with respect to extra-parliamentary taxation and the negative voice or power of veto) develop arguments that insist that if a king retains any discretionary powers whatsoever the realm cannot be a free state, but rather a state of dependent servitude. If many of Skinner's seventeenth-century 'neo-Romans' allow for the possibility for a monarch to be a ruler of a free state, safeguards must be imposed to ensure that the body of the commonwealth can never be reduced to a condition of dependence on his/her personal will or on the prerogative powers of the crown.[23] Some, like Francis Osborne, deny that any community living under a monarch can be considered a free state – any king inclines to the arbitrary exercise of power. In the English context, Skinner concedes that the 'immediate inspiration for this way of thinking appears to have come from a number of medieval common-law texts', such as those of Henry de Bracton and Sir Thomas Littleton.[24] But Skinner continues on to argue that the definitions found in these authorities derive from the *Digest*, and so from Roman law.

The fiction of *Utopia*, as is well recognised, bears the mark of More's close reading of Greek philosophy as much as Roman. More was a translator of Lucian and, along with Richard Pace, supported the causes of Erasmus's Greek New Testament and education in the Greek language as the basis for study in the liberal sciences.[25] Skinner's previously mentioned essay (revised for *Visions*), 'Thomas More's *Utopia* and the Virtue of True Nobility', does not concern itself with the details of the structure of the mixed constitution of the newly discovered island of Nowhere, formed with reference to Sparta, Greece, Rome and the primitive Christian church, as internal evidence and the parerga of the text suggest.[26] Nor does it consider *Utopia* from a rhetorical or literary perspective, or in detailed historical context. Skinner chooses instead to concentrate on two idioms or contested vocabularies in the so-called dialogue of counsel in book I

---

[23] Skinner, *Liberty before Liberalism*, pp. 53–5.

[24] Skinner, 'States and the Freedom of Citizens', pp. 12–13.

[25] C. Curtis, 'Richard Pace's *De fructu* and Early Tudor Pedagogy', in *Reassessing Tudor Humanism*, pp. 43–77; Eric Nelson, 'Greek Nonsense in More's *Utopia*', *The Historical Journal* 44 (2001), pp. 889–917.

[26] For example the prefatory letter of Jerome Busleyden to More, and Beatus Rhenanus to Wilibald Pirckheimer. Thomas More, *The Yale Edition of the Complete Works of St Thomas More*, ed. Edward Surtz and J. H. Hexter (New Haven: Yale University Press 1965), IV, *Utopia*, p. 317; R. J. Schoek, 'More, Plutarch and King Agis', *Philological Quarterly* 35 (1956), pp. 366–75; M. N. Raitere, 'More's *Utopia* and *The City of God*', *Studies in the Renaissance* 20 (1973), pp. 144–68; Dominic Baker-Smith, *More's Utopia* (New York: HarperCollins, 1991); George Logan, *The Meaning of More's Utopia* (Princeton: Princeton University Press, 1983).

of *Utopia* which are familiar from neo-Roman theory: of *otium* versus *negotium*, and *vera nobilitas*, and to show how these relate directly to the issue of what constitutes the *optimus status reipublicae*, the best state of the commonwealth.

While acknowledging the insights of recent scholarship which stresses the equivocations and ambiguities of the text of *Utopia*, Skinner rejects the 'new orthodoxy' which he characterises as over-emphasising these, and argues that More's principal aim 'was to challenge his readers at least to consider seriously whether Utopia may not represent the best state of the commonwealth'.[27] Classical, humanist and scholastic debates over these issues contextualise Skinner's discussion of 'what orthodoxy More is questioning, what response he is offering, what exact position he is occupying on the spectrum of political debate'.[28]

There are several related conclusions, and these are important to Skinner's typology of early-modern English political thought; they underlie the ideal of the *vir civilis* which Skinner brilliantly discusses in *Reason and Rhetoric in the Philosophy of Hobbes* and inform the influential characterisation of English civic humanism which Peltonen presents from the mid-sixteenth century onwards.[29] The authorial More in book I sets 'civic' or Ciceronian humanism, as articulated by the figure of More, against a Platonic notion of contemplative withdrawal, argued by Hythloday. The figure of More is said to be restating the case for the 'ideal of civic self-government, based on an active and politically educated citizenship' to which the courts of northern Europe were becoming increasingly inhospitable. Skinner implies that this is closest to the understanding of the historical More, poised to enter the service of Henry VIII, of the proper relationship between philosophy and life.[30] And against the Aristotelian and scholastic view that distinguished birth and inherited wealth – and their attendant ethic of display, splendour and magnificence – are the foundations of nobility, and therefore necessary qualifications for public office, Hythloday counters with, in Skinner's words, 'a claim that soon became almost a slogan of humanist political thought: the claim that *virtus vera nobilitas est*, that the possession of virtue constitutes the only possible grounds for regarding someone as a person of true nobility'.[31] And this in turn relates to the question of what qualities in a citizen best serve the commonwealth: 'The Utopians believe that what is alone noble and deserving of honour is a willingness to labour for the common good. The qualities they think of as truly noble are accordingly the qualities of virtue that are indispensable for performing such civic tasks.'[32] Consequently, the laws and customs of Utopia prohibit *otium* and require *negotium* from all citizens. Civic virtue in

---

[27] Skinner, *Visions*, II, p. 214.   [28] Ibid., p. 220.
[29] Also see Guy, 'Tudor Monarchy and its Critiques', in Guy, *Tudor Monarchy*, pp. 78–109.
[30] Skinner, *Visions*, II, p. 224.   [31] Ibid., p. 223.   [32] Ibid., p. 231.

all its manifestations is encouraged. 'The Utopians, we learn, are all trained in virtue.'[33]

The true radicalism of the text, however, lies in the conclusion of Hythloday and the Utopians that the only means of achieving this is through the abolition of private property and money, so that all pride and inequity are pulled out by the roots. The figure of More reflects on Hythloday's description of Utopia in one of the concluding passages of book II that such a system 'utterly overthrows all the nobility, magnificence, splendour and majesty which are, in the estimation of the common people, the true glories and ornaments of the commonwealth'.[34]

Skinner considers that the authorial More is raising a doubt about the coherence of humanist political thought. If inherited wealth is prevented from being treated as criterion of true nobility, can humanists continue 'to insist on the indispensability of private property, of hereditability and in general of "degree, priority and place" as preconditions of any well-ordered society'?[35] Is it then enough to educate the nobility in virtue, or must a more radical restructuring of political life be effected? Here then is a point of conceptual change for Skinner, where More's 'humanist critique of humanism' has sought to alter the view of his countrymen about how political and ethical life may be reappraised by challenging and inverting inherited normative vocabularies.[36]

In the final essay in *Visions of Politics*, 'The State of Princes to the Person of the State', Skinner links *Utopia* with the series of linguistic moves that give rise to the modern understanding of the state. The Erasmian humanists transmitted the vocabulary and values of the *quattrocento* 'vision' of the *optimus status reipublicae* into northern Europe. Erasmus, Starkey and More are concerned with the *status* that allows the happiest and most justly ordered political life.[37] And furthermore, in its depiction of the arrival of the Anemolian ambassadors on the island, *Utopia* contains an 'early and devastating portrayal of public magnificence as nothing more than a form of infantile vanity'.[38] If Machiavelli still assumed that a ruler's capacity to maintain his state was connected with 'his condition of stateliness', More is said to begin the process by which that connection is severed. This is held to be part of the growing perception in the course of the sixteenth and seventeenth centuries that heads of state are simply holders of office, and the ascription of majesty to them as such was inappropriate.[39]

---

[33] Ibid. Nelson has recently argued that *Utopia* dramatises a 'confrontation between the values of the Roman republican tradition, as understood in More's time, and those of a rival commonwealth theory based on Greek ethics'. *Contra* Skinner, the ideology standing behind *virtus vera nobilitas*, Nelson argues, is essentially Platonic and Aristotelian, rather than Roman in the first place: 'Greek Nonsense in More's *Utopia*', pp. 889, 914–15.

[34] More, *Utopia*, pp. 224–5.   [35] Skinner, *Visions*, II, p. 242.

[36] Skinner, *Visions*, I, p. 178.   [37] Skinner, *Visions*, II, p. 373.

[38] Ibid., p. 412.   [39] Ibid., p. 412.

As mentioned previously, More is brought into the neo-Roman perspective in *Liberty before Liberalism*. *Utopia* is said to have put forward a possible solution to the problem of individual citizen participation in the framing of laws which was seized upon by John Milton. At 'a time when the ideal of the *civitas libera* was first being seriously canvassed in England', More suggested that a genuine *res publica* should be a federated republic, as in Utopia, with its self-governing cities managed through the agency of annually elected magistrates chosen from among themselves.[40] Additionally, More argues through the mouth of Hythloday that the virtuous citizen who would freely counsel his ruler is prevented from exercising his duty because of the corrupt conditions of European courtly life – little separates service to kings and servitude.[41] As Speaker of the House of Commons, the historical More upheld the exercise of the freedom of speech according to the dictates of conscience in the cause of the common good.[42]

II

It is worthwhile to 'excavate' more from *Utopia* and other Morean and humanist writings in the first decades of the sixteenth century with respect to the vocabularies and themes which relate to Skinner's representation of neo-Roman theory for two reasons. First, I wish to extend Skinner's study of early-modern English liberty and slavery. Second, I wish to challenge Skinner's adoption of More as a 'neo-Roman'. I leave the question of the value of 'neo-Romanism' as an explanatory category more generally in the period open at this time, although my discussion does suggest potential difficulties.

In October 1516 More wrote to Erasmus that he should like to win approval for *Utopia* from gifted humanists who held high office in their own countries and so were particularly suitable critics, as well as beneficiaries, of the wisdom of his fiction. They should favour such an invented polity with men like themselves in positions of leadership and influence; in their own countries, however, they must suffer inferior men as their equals, if not superiors. More is confident that men of their kind are not motivated by the desire to have 'many people under them, many subjects, as kings now call their peoples (something, that is, worse than slaves); for it is so much more honourable to bear rule among free men'.[43]

This subject/slave antithesis appears in one of fifteen Latin epigrams which are composed on the *topos* of responsible versus tyrannical rule, and clearly articulates More's preference for consultative government – this is important, for the reader of the ironic, undogmatic and contradictory *Utopia* is often denied

[40] Skinner, *Liberty before Liberalism*, p. 10.   [41] More, *Utopia*, p. 54.
[42] Skinner, *Liberty before Liberalism*, pp. 87–9.
[43] Erasmus, *The Complete Works of Erasmus* (Toronto: University of Toronto Press, 1974), IV, Ep. 481, p. 116.

clear access to authorial intention. These highly political epigrams were composed around the same time as *Utopia*, and Erasmus had hoped to publish an enormous volume containing *Utopia*, his own *Querela Pacis* and the Lucianic translations and Latin poems of both writers. In the end, More's Latin poems were printed with the third edition of the *Utopia*. More contrasts the tyrant and the king as follows, punning on the meaning of *liberi* as either freemen or children: 'A King who respects the law differs from cruel tyrants thus: a tyrant rules his subjects as slaves; a king thinks of his as his own children.'[44] This patriarchal understanding of government, and indeed the pun, is repeated in another epigram: 'A devoted king will never lack children; he is father to the whole kingdom. And so it is that a true king is abundantly blessed in having as many children as he has subjects.'[45] More appears to invite the translation of *civis* as citizen as much as subject.

The force of the other epigrams on good and bad rulers is similar, drawing on centuries-old discursive traditions of the *corpus reipublicae mysticum* and the king's two bodies based on Christological imagery and the Aristotelian ideal of kingship as paternal government.[46] They also cast the duties of ruler and subject in terms of office, as the Yale editors suggest. A good king acts as a shepherd or watchdog, protecting the interests of his subjects and so ensuring his own survival and peace of mind. In a well-governed kingdom there is a relationship of mutual protection, affection and obligation, in which the people risk their lives to save the king, and they each individually consider him as the head of their own body. It is not only a question of what is best for the subjects, but also what renders the ruler less vulnerable to either foreign attack or internal rebellion. Rulers should not feel free to abuse their position merely because they are surrounded with the trappings of majesty; in sleep they are no more elevated than beggars, and unless guarded by either virtue or force, their life may be disposed of by any man. On the other hand, tyrants who treat subjects as slaves have no right to hold authority and should retain command only as long as the *populus* allows, judging that there is no other who can promote its interests better.[47]

More's highly ambivalent encomiastic coronation odes for the young Henry VIII – who has just taken his oath – set out criteria against which his discharge

[44] Thomas More, Epigram 109, in Clarence Miller et al. (eds.), *The Latin Poems*, in *The Complete Works of St. Thomas More*, vol. III, part II (New Haven: Yale University Press, 1984), pp. 163, 164. *Quid inter Tyrannum et Principem*: 'Legitimus immanissimis/ Rex hoc tyrannis interest./ Seruos tyrannus quos regit,/Rex liberos putat suos'.

[45] More, Epigram 111, *Yale Complete Works*, III, part II, pp. 163, 164: *Bonum principem esse patrem non dominum*: 'Princeps pius nunquam carebit liberis./ Totius est regni pater./ Princeps abundat ergo felicissimus,/ Tot liberis, quot ciuibus.'

[46] Ernst Kantorowicz, *The King's Two Bodies: a Study in Medieval Political Theology* (Princeton: Princeton University Press, 1966) pp. 207–32. More, *Yale Complete Works*, III, part II, pp. 364–5; *Yale Complete Works*, IV, p. 367. Cf. John 10:12; Aristotle, *Eudemian Ethics* 2.1.15 (1219b).

[47] More, Epigrams 112, 114, 115, 120, 121, 201, in *Yale Complete Works*, III, part II.

of office might later be judged, and articulate his reservations concerning hereditary rule. One of the five odes is particularly pertinent given More's outspoken opposition in Parliament to Henry VII in 1504.

> This day is the limit of our slavery, the beginning of our freedom, the end of sadness, the source of joy, for this day consecrates a young man who is the everlasting glory of our time and makes him your king – a king who is worthy not merely to govern a single people but singly to rule the whole world – such a king as will wipe the tears from every eye and put joy in the place of our long distress . . .[48]

It appears here at least that More believes that it is possible to live in freedom under monarchical rule. But it is also clear that More looked to Henry VIII to undo the damage his father had inflicted upon the commonwealth through his abuse of royal prerogative and exploitation of attainder, as well as bonds and recognisances, in order to cow the nobility. He extols the son to restore the ancient laws and ranks of the realm, award honours and public offices appropriately rather than sell them to the undeserving, and even rescind the unjust laws enacted in the previous reign.[49] Henry VIII is warned that it is vital to attract the affection of his people by ensuring that they do not fear that their property is not secure from the royal prerogative. The anger of the people brings tumults.

How much faith More placed in the reforming power of the panegyric is unclear. More worked on the English and Latin versions of *The History of Richard III* between 1513 and 1518. Indebted to Sallust, Tacitus and Suetonius, it was another scarcely veiled exhortation to virtuous rule for Henry VIII, and certainly reveals More's pessimism about the likelihood of monarchical rule degenerating into arbitrariness. In the hypothetical council scene of book I of *Utopia*, Hythloday argues in terms very close to those of More's Latin poems and through him the authorial More alludes to specific sharp fiscal practices in

---

[48] More, Epigram 19, in *Yale Complete Works*, III, part II, 100–10, 101–10. 'Meta haec seruitij est, haec libertatis origo,/ Tristitiae finis, laetitiaeque caput./ Nam iuuenem secli decus O memorabile nostri/ Ungit, et in regem praeficit ista tuum./ Regem qui populi non unius usque, sed orbis/ Imperio dignus totius unus erat./ Regem qui cunctis lachrymas detergat ocellis,/ Gaudia pro longo substituat gemitu'. As described by Nicholas Harpsfield, More, using 'the ancient liberty of the Parliament House for freely speaking touching the public affairs', persuaded the Lower House to resist the king's request, based on custom, for moneys to provide for the marriage of Princess Margaret to James IV of Scotland. E. V. Hitchcock (ed.), *The Life and Death of Sir Thomas More* (London: Early English Text Society, 1932), pp. 60–1. More returned to the theme of tyranny in his translation of Lucian's exercise in forensic rhetoric, *Tyrannicide*. A man who has killed the son of a tyrant and so prompted the father's suicide claims that he is entitled to receive the reward due for freeing the state of its oppressor. More, *Translations of Lucian*, ed. C. R. Thompson, in *The Complete Works of St. Thomas More*, vol. III, part I (New Haven: Yale University Press, 1974).

[49] The Yale editors note that Henry VII exploited a thirteenth-century declaration of common law, the *Statuta de praerogativa regis*, in order to increase royal revenues. An obsolete text, it was revived and glossed to cover economic possibilities not previously envisioned. More, *Yale Complete Works*, III, part II, p. 328. Henry VIII did, in fact, cancel many bonds and recognisances in the early years of his reign.

the reigns of Edward IV, Henry VII and Henry VIII.[50] Again we find excoriating criticism of kings who regard their subjects' lives and properties as their own, of dishonourable counsellors who claim that poverty and lack of liberty blunts the spirit and grinds out of the oppressed the lofty spirit of rebellion,[51] and of judges who massage the law so that decisions are always made in favour of the king's treasury. Hythloday argues that a ruler can always fall back on the royal prerogative if other means of satisfying his will fail. But such a ruler is a jailer rather than a keeper of his kingdom. A ruler who does not know how to reform the lives of his citizens, except by depriving them of all of life's rewards, should admit that he is not competent to rule free men and abdicate. Hythloday cites the case of the Macarians, the 'happy people', who have had a succession of excellent rulers who take an oath on assuming office to have no more in the treasury than an amount of £1000, sufficient to safeguard the realm.

I want to underline a crucial element that arises from my discussion thus far, which is at variance with Skinner's account of neo-Roman theory. Where Skinner's neo-Romans decry the dependence of subjects on any monarch who wields discretionary power, More emphasises a mutual, and potentially beneficial, relationship between ruler and subject. Even a self-interested ruler might theoretically be made to see that a willing and loving people best advances the ruler's desire for internal and external security and prosperity. And More deploys an eclectic range of sources – Greek, Roman, Christian and scholastic – to persuade us of this.

How likely is it that a people may live in freedom under a ruler or monarch (precisely the question which Skinner argues was considered in the next century by his 'neo-Romans')? Another epigram echoes the title of *Utopia*, 'What is the Best State of the Commonwealth' (*Quis optimus reipublicae status*):

You ask which governs better, a king or a Senate. Neither, if (as is frequently the case) both are bad. But if both are good, then I think that the Senate, because of its numbers, is the better and that the greater good lies in numerous good men. Perhaps it is difficult to find a group of good men; even more frequently it is easy for a monarch to be bad. A senate would occupy a position between good and bad; but hardly ever will you have a king who is not either good or bad. An evil senator is influenced from better men than he; but a king is himself the ruler of his advisers. A senator is elected by the people to rule; a king attains this end by being born. In the one case blind chance is supreme; in the other, a reasonable agreement. The one feels that he was made a senator by the people; the other feels that the people were created for him so that, of course, he may have subjects to rule. A king in his first year is always very mild indeed, and so every year the consul will be like a new king. Over a long period a greedy king will gnaw away at his people. If a consul is evil, there is hope of improvement. But, you say, a serious

---

[50] *Utopia*, 92f. J. H. Lupton's commentary to his edition of *The Utopia of Sir Thomas More* (Oxford: Clarendon Press, 1895) supplies the details. See Baker-Smith, *More's Utopia*, pp. 121–3.

[51] *Utopia*, p. 94.

disagreement impedes a senate's decisions, while no one disagrees with a king. But that is the worse evil of the two, for when there is a difference of opinion about important matters – but say, what started you on the inquiry anyway? Is there anywhere a people upon whom you yourself, by your own decision, can impose either a king or a senate? If this does lie in your power, you are a king. Stop considering to whom you may give power. The more basic question is whether it would do any good if you could.[52]

Did the English republican or so-called neo-Roman theorists of the seventeenth century read this epigram along with their *Utopia* in the third edition? *Utopia* did endow More with the power of imposing his preferred constitution, with his humanist friends as senators. In a letter to Erasmus in 1516, More describes his vision of being crowned by the Utopians with the distinguished diadem of corn-ears, a splendid sight in his Franciscan robe and bearing the venerable sceptre of a sheaf of corn – but the dream ends. His consolation is that earthly kingdoms do not last much longer.[53]

So does More, like Francis Osborne, believe that the only form of constitution under which freedom is guaranteed a self-governing republic? In his second letter to Peter Giles, appended only to the third edition of *Utopia*, More acknowledges that, like other philosophers, he has included some absurdities in *Utopia*. The Utopian constitution is not a blueprint for reform, but rather encourages fresh insights in political thought which subsequent writers could appropriate, imitate or reject as a mere *jeu d'esprit*. That said, some aspects invite examination. The island's government is constructed around an elaborate system of institutional constraints and is conciliar – this may have extended to More's preference for the ordering of the church. It is a syncretic architecture, blending features of democracy, an elected aristocracy of the learned, and elective monarchy.[54]

Such a constitution, founded by the conquering first law-giver and absolute ruler Utopus, is based on the rule of law applied to all equally (although few

---

[52] More, Epigram 198, *Yale Complete Works*, III, part II, pp. 228–31. I depart from the Yale translation of the title.

[53] *Complete Works of Erasmus*, IV, Ep. 499, pp. 163–4.

[54] Baker-Smith, *More's Utopia*, has a good discussion of the Utopian constitution, pp. 151–200. There is a general council of the whole island, with an assembly of syphogrants and a senate of tranibors (one-tenth the size of the assembly). The syphogrants or phylarchs, who represent thirty households each, elect the chief magistrate or prince by secret ballot from among four men nominated by the people of the four sections of the city, and he holds the office for life. The tranibors are re-elected annually, and at each meeting of the senate, two syphogrants as well as the governor attend to guard against conspiracy and factionalism. No matter of public interest may be settled by the senate unless it has been aired at a previous meeting. The discussion of public matters outside the senate or assembly is a capital offence. There is, however, scope for wide public discussion within the institutional framework – the *comitia publica* in all likelihood refers to the forum of each syphogrant together with the thirty families he represents in the senate. It would appear, then, that every member of every family (the basic unit of the commonwealth) participates in decision-making regarding the administration of their city. These checks on the power of the prince and senate thus, says Hythloday, prevent the enslavement of the people.

laws are needed) and the practice of virtue. Utopus is the extraordinary and exceptional ruler in the line of Lycurgus, who is able to reconstitute a state fallen into corruption because of internal religious conflict and then deprives his office of the discretionary power of coercion.[55] The office of ruler is replaced by a system of multiple princes or governors, one for each city, who can be deposed for tyranny. The Utopians are the happiest of people, we are told, subject to no anxieties since they cannot be arbitrarily dispossessed of their property or deprived of their liberty or lives; the governors, one feels, sleep easily in their beds, while everyone values virtue as its own reward. If Plato's *Laws* and the Spartan constitution suggest features of the Utopian constitution, there would appear to be a parallel with the Venetian constitution with its doge, senate and grand council. One neglected parallel, I believe, is with the constitution of the church; the silver age of conciliarism is flourishing in precisely those years in which Hythloday lived in Utopia, 1510 to 1515.[56]

If More had no direct experience of the Venetian constitutional arrangement or of the debates surrounding the Pisan–Milan schism and the Fifth Lateran Council, his close friend, the diplomat and cleric Richard Pace, did. Pace's writings offer a fruitful context to those of More on conciliar and republican themes. Part of the Erasmus circle and patron to Starkey, Lupset and Pole in the Veneto, Pace considered that if he were not Venetian by birth, he was by inclination; the Venetians for their part claimed him as one of their own.[57] Unlike More, he was educated in the Italian universities. He studied at Padua, Bologna and Ferrara under the supervision of famous humanist scholars and translators in the areas of Latin, Greek, rhetoric, Roman law, and Platonic and Aristotelian philosophy. One of them was Niccolò Leonico Tomeo, a Paduan scholar and republican with links to Donato Giannotti, and by the 1520s at least Pace was well acquainted with Gasparo Contarini, as well as many other leading Italian humanists.[58] Pace entered the service of Christopher Bainbridge in Rome in 1509 as his Latin and Italian secretary. Bainbridge was made a cardinal in 1511, and Pace attended the conclave which elected Leo X in 1513 and sessions of the Fifth Lateran Council. He became First Secretary to

---

[55] Walker argues *contra* Skinner that there are two circumstances in which Livy and Machiavelli allow the rule of a single person – in the foundation of a commonwealth or in the reform of a corrupt one. '*Paradise Lost*', pp. 271–82.

[56] Black has argued in opposition to Skinner and Pocock that 'republican ideas could, like monarchical ones, be put about in a variety of languages, in terms of corporation theory and neo-Christian ecclesiology as well as neo-Roman or Machiavellian terms'. With Black I must agree that Skinner has implied that Christian thought has little to do with republicanism, neglecting the shared themes of public welfare and corporate decision-making: Black, 'Christianity and Republicanism', p. 654.

[57] Cathy Curtis, *Dictionary of National Biography*, 2004.

[58] T. Mayer, *Thomas Starkey and the Commonwealth* (Cambridge: Cambridge University Press, 1989); M. L. King, *Venetian Humanism in an Age of Patrician Dominance* (Princeton: Princeton University Press, 1986); Curtis, 'Richard Pace', ch. 1, esp. pp. 24–6.

Henry VIII in 1516, and had much experience of the princely courts of the empire and the operation of imperial legal codes.

Pace's *De fructu* of 1518, published by John Froben and sharing the same editors as *Utopia*, advances conciliarist theory and a plea for a counsellor's exercise of freedom of speech against the background of European war and peace, and the failures of the Pisa–Milan and the Fifth Lateran Councils to effect reform in the years 1511–17.[59] Like More, Pace connects *vera nobilitas* with civic virtue, and exhorts others to the life of *negotium*. With a note of extreme weariness, however, he makes the paradoxical complaint that if he is free by nature, he is not by choice, having bound himself to the service of Henry VIII as the servant of Wolsey. And to serve one's country exceeds all liberty.[60]

But Pace is not easily classified as a neo-Roman, despite his seal being the head of Cicero. Like his younger contemporary and friend Starkey, he was as deeply immersed in Aristotelian political thought as Roman and, like More, tended to a synthesis of these with an Erasmian Christian civic humanism. In *De fructu* Cicero is said to have been created by Demosthenes and Isocrates in oratory, and by Plato and Aristotle in philosophy. The satire itself is Menippean and encyclopaedic, a praise of classical and Renaissance learning in all its spheres. The conciliarism it obliquely expresses favours a strong oligarchical and mixed church structure, perhaps the analogue of his preference for oligarchic Venetian republicanism. Pace argues for wide participation by learned and lay members of the church, and the adherence by popes and cardinals to the rule of canon and civil law. The acts of previous popes cannot be rescinded at will in order to exact taxation which is justified as being necessary to defend ecclesiastical liberty. In *De fructu*, Pace contrasts Giles of Viterbo's Lateran address calling for reform of the church at the highest level with the debased classicising Ciceronian oratory of the papal court which asserted the church's ancient *libertas* in terms of a triumphant Roman *imperium*. Pace shared Erasmus's extreme distaste for appeals made by self-serving papal orators, such as Thomas Inghirami, to *necessitas* and *utilitas publica* to justify Julius II's prosecution of war on the papacy's Christian subjects. The classical Roman language of liberty and slavery could be put to specious uses by skilled and corrupt rhetoricians.[61]

Whether or not one of the most widely read and frequently published and translated satires of the sixteenth century – the *Julius exclusus* (composed and revised 1513–17, first edition 1518) – should be attributed to Pace rather than Erasmus, as I have argued, it should hold an important place in English political

---

[59] Richard Pace, *De fructu qui ex doctrina percipitur*, ed. and trans. F. Manley and R. S. Sylvester (New York: The Renaissance Society of America, 1967).
[60] Pace, *De fructu*, pp. 12–13.   [61] Curtis, 'Pace', pp. 150–63.

thought by virtue of its unambiguous theory of conciliarism, constitutionalism and resistance and its timely English editions and translations – *c*.1533 and 1535; and 1669, 1673 and 1680.[62] It is a companion text to *Utopia* and *De fructu*, probably never intended for publication by the author but pirated by German humanist Protestant reformers.

One of the major publishing successes of the sixteenth century, this pasquinade in dialogue form was well known to the Erasmian circle, and hence members of Henry VIII's court, from its circulation in manuscript at least from 1517.[63] The satire has two structuring devices, both of which have been entirely unrecognised in the large scholarship surrounding it. Inghirami's funeral oration for Julius II becomes the subject of parody, providing the form and content for Julius's ironic self-encomium. The debate between St Peter and Julius at the gates of heaven draws on the scholastic exchange between the papal apologist Tommaso de Vio (Cardinal Cajetan), and the Gallican conciliarist Jacques Almain, regarding the relationship of pope, general council and the universal church.[64] Voicing Almain's analogy between secular and ecclesiastical authority, the character of St Peter in the *Julius* argues against the protestations of the corrupt, law-breaking Pope Julius II that in cases of tyranny which threaten the survival of the community, a prince or pope may be deposed, or even put to death.[65] The authority to do so remains latent in the whole community. Like

---

[62] Ibid., pp. 255–6.

[63] The *Julius* went through twelve editions from 1518 to 1521 and was rendered into vernaculars rapidly.

[64] For translations of Almain's *Libellus de auctoritate ecclesiae* (Paris, 1512), Cajetan's *Auctoritas papae et concilii sive ecclesiae comparata* (Rome, 1511) and *Apologia de comparata auctoritate papae et concilii* (Venice, 1514) see J. H. Burns and Thomas M. Izbicki (eds.), *Conciliarism and Papalism* (Cambridge: Cambridge University Press, 1997). H. Jedin, *A History of the Council of Trent*, trans. Ernest Graf, 2 vols. (London, 1957–61), I, ch. 2; Olivier de la Brosse, *Le Pape et Le Concile. La comparaison de leurs pouvoirs à la veille de la Réforme* (Paris, 1965), ch. 10. Francis Oakley, 'Almain and Major: Conciliar Theory on the Eve of the Reformation', *American Historical Review* 70 (1965), pp. 673–90; 'Conciliarism in the Sixteenth Century: Jacques Almain again', *Archiv für Reformationsgeschichte* 68 (1977), pp. 111–32; and 'Conciliarism at the Fifth Lateran Council?', *Church History* 41 (1972), pp. 452–63; Brian Tierney, *Foundations of the Conciliar Theory: the Contribution of the Medieval Canonists from Gratian to the Great Schism* (Cambridge: Cambridge University Press 1955); Augustin Renaudet, *Préréforme et Humanisme à Paris pendant les premières guerres d'Italie. 1496–1517* ([1916]; Paris 1953). Skinner, *Foundations*, II, pp. 113ff. and 'Political Philosophy', pp. 389–452. J. H. Burns, 'Scholasticism: Survival and Revival', in *The Cambridge History of Political Thought: 1450–1700*, pp. 135–58; J. H. Burns, 'Conciliarism, Papalism and Power, 1511–1518', in D. Wood (ed.), *The Church and Sovereignty c.590–1918: Essays in Honour of Michael Wilks*, Studies in Church History, Subsidia 9 (Oxford: Oxford University Press 1991), pp. 409–28. Most recently, see Francis Oakley, 'Anxieties of Influence: Skinner, Figgis, Conciliarism and Early Modern Constitutionalism', in *Past and Present* 151 (1996), pp. 60–110 and Annabel Brett, *Liberty, Right and Nature: Individual Rights in Later Scholastic Thought* (Cambridge: Cambridge University Press, 1997).

[65] Erasmus, *Complete Works*, XXVII, pp. 179–81, at 193. *Erasmi Opuscula: A Supplement to the Opera omnia*, ed. W. K. Ferguson (The Hague: M. Nijhoff, 1933), p. 92, ll.460–70; p. 94, ll.517–37.

More, St Peter insists on the exercise of freedom of speech by learned and virtuous men in frequently convened public assemblies, be they church councils or senates, as an antidote to tyranny. Julius is censured for breaking his election capitulation to hold a general council within two years of his election. He is also taken to task for endangering the *respublica Christiana* through his policy of territorial expansion funded through illegal and punitive taxation and the sale of offices and indulgences, and by encouraging faction and dissent between European princes. Pope Julius, incredulous at his exclusion from heaven and threatening St Peter with excommunication, insists on those concepts in Roman law, carried into canon law and articulated by Cardinal Cajetan, which support absolutist rule of government: *quod principi placvit*, what pleases the prince has force of law, and *legibus solutus*, the ruler is the source of all law. According to the character Julius, a pope cannot be censured, even by a general council, or deposed even if publicly convicted of heresy, since he has the power to abrogate, limit, interpret and stretch the law itself if he should find it unsatisfactory. In any case who would dare challenge the pope, who is so well armed and protected? St Peter counters that it is Christ who is the true head and law-giver of the church; the welfare of the Christian commonwealth is more important than the *maiestas* of any individual pope.

It is well to recall here that More argued that tyrants who treat subjects as slaves have no right to hold authority and should not retain power if the people judge that there is another who can better promote their interests – abdication is one solution. More warns that a tyrant – a ruler who does not put the welfare of the commonwealth before his personal will – may meet death at the hand of an assassin. In the 1530s More would make the analogy between ecclesiastical and secular government – 'counsayles do represent the whole chyrch . . . as a parliament representeth ye hole realm'.[66] More wrote to Cromwell that he never thought the pope above the general council, or greatly advanced the pope's authority in any of his writings.

III

I wish to conclude with some further observations on *Utopia*, its interpretation and Skinner's methodological approach. I have argued that More and his best state of the commonwealth do not rest easily under the term 'neo-Roman', or republican, although More is clearly preoccupied with issues of freedom and servitude, tyranny and representative government, civic participation and true nobility. That More was deeply pessimistic about the corruptibility of early-modern European rulers is undeniable. Hythloday's discussion of the dangers

---

[66] More, *The Confutation of Tyndale's Answer*, in *Yale Complete Works*, VIII, part I, eds. L. A. Schuster, R. C. Marius and J. P. Lusardi (New Haven: Yale University Press, 1973), p. 146; E. Rogers, *The Correspondence of Thomas More* (Princeton: Princeton University Press, 1947), p. 499, ll.252–64.

inherent in discretionary rule in the hypothetical council allude to historical cases of abuse by past and present English kings, and *The History of Richard III* is a sombre study in kingship and hereditary rule.

But while the epigram on the best state of the commonwealth expresses a strong preference for senatorial rule and consultation, the author strategically interrupts his meditation and stops short of endorsing it in all cases. Hythloday's Macarian rulers and Utopus offer the prospect of freedom under a monarch, and a number of More's Latin poems may be read similarly. The notion of mutual dependency between ruler and ruled also fails to align with Skinner's account of neo-Romanism. And More was a common lawyer, and is introduced as such in *Utopia*. He could reach as easily for his Bracton or Littleton as for the *Digest* of Roman law for inspiration about these themes.

Furthermore, the generic and ironic literary forms which More employs are directed to a multi-layered audience, and although he assumes the mantle of the satirist he writes under the constraints of what can safely be said while serving as counsellor to a monarch who shows his father's tendencies to overbearing rule. If More was as intimately acquainted as any Renaissance humanist with the classical sources Skinner associates with neo-Roman theory, he also drew as much intellectual sustenance from Greek, scholastic and Christian thought. As a Democritus/Demonax reborn, Pace and Erasmus praised More for his philosophical eclecticism, moderation and prudence in adapting to circumstances.[67] Like Lucian, whom he so admired, More appropriated, fused and transformed earlier traditions so as to comment on the utility of those traditions in contemporary society and to generate debate and new insight. Such immensely complex writings often refuse to yield clean lines of argument, or if they appear to do so, only from within a particular context or in opposition with one another so as to prompt the rethinking of categories. More can appear as an Augustinian, neo-Platonist, Ciceronian, Lucianic satirist or indeed a monarchist. The Renaissance commonplace method, one organisational structure of *Utopia*, itself encourages the development of discrete themes; but this is undercut by More's ambiguous vocabulary, syntax and dialogic presentation. When More's writings are placed in the context of related humanist texts – such as Pace's conciliarist *De fructu* and the *Julius* – another category is suggested, that of the closet conciliarist who could well apply corporation theory to both church and secular authority.

Another difficulty concerns the transmission of More's *Utopia* into the seventeenth century. It is frequently cited and imitated in some of its generic aspects and institutional features, yet few authors and theorists discuss their interpretation explicitly or systematically.[68] I have yet to find a seventeenth-century

---

[67] Curtis, 'Pace', pp. 120–2.

[68] *Sir Thomas More in the English Renaissance: an Annotated Catalogue*, introduction by Anne Lake Prescott, *Medieval and Renaissance Texts and Studies* 83 (Tempe: Arizona University Press, 1994).

author making a direct comparison between Charles I and ship money and the questionable Tudor taxations alluded to in *Utopia*, despite the striking similarities in theme. It is only Harrington who gives as much constitutional specificity to his *Oceana* as More does in *Utopia*. In the case of Harrington and Robert Burton in his *Anatomy of Melancholy*, interpretation of *Utopia* is in turn embedded in their utopias which continue the transformational process. This is further compounded by More's ambivalent reputation acquired in the sixteenth century as both a witty corrector of folly and a deceitful mocker who prostituted his learning to the Catholic cause. The Utopians are allowed religious toleration, but not English Protestants. Protestant writers did not necessarily wish to claim this ancestry.

The final issue raised in my opening remarks concerns Worden's apprehensions about Skinner's historical-mindedness and present-mindedness in his writings on freedom and citizenship. Skinner has returned to this in a recent interview, reiterating his view that intellectual history, especially in the study of discontinuities, opens our eyes to the richness of our intellectual inheritance and our relationship to it. It does not contain lessons for the present. But again the passion of Skinner's language argues not only for his claim that the bringing to the surface of the neo-Roman vision helps give a new perspective on the hegemonic rival classical liberal view of politics, of the relations between 'freedom of citizens and the powers of the state', but that he in some way endorses a contemporary society which reconceptualises itself in the light of a neo-Roman theory of liberty.[69] He writes for an audience 'obsessed with notions of rights and interests' so that they can be awakened to the knowledge that there exists 'a completely different model, in which duty was prioritised and citizens were not encouraged to see themselves simply as consumers of government'.[70] It is difficult to draw the line in the sand.

[69] Maria Lucia Pallares-Burke, 'Quentin Skinner' in *The New History: Confessions and Conversations* (Cambridge: Polity Press, 2002), pp. 212–40. cf. Skinner's peroration, 'States and the Freedom of Citizens', pp. 24–5.
[70] Pallares-Burke, 'Quentin Skinner', p. 229.

H. M. Höpfl

Quentin Skinner blends scholarship with lightness of touch, and to do him justice one would have to be able to match both. The mildly revisionist comments on his account of scholasticism that I make in what follows in no way deny the debts that scholarship owes to him. He singles out three contributions which scholasticism made to the 'foundations': to the ideology of the republic against the *signori*, to the theory of popular sovereignty and to constitutionalism, especially its most radical version, and thus indirectly to the identification of the modern state.[1] This was in many respects a dramatic reinterpretation of the character and substance of early-modern political thought. As he has rightly pointed out, the fashionable historiography of Puritanism and constitutionalism at the time he was writing ignored this dimension altogether. And if Skinner's thought has been recruited for various contemporary ideological projects, notably the attempt to find some half-way intellectually respectable pedigree for participative politics, well, he can hardly be blamed for that. In any event, there are many worse things that could be drawn on than *Foundations*.

All the same, many of the organising ideas employed in *Foundations* are not problem free, as Skinner readily admits. Leaving aside period pieces like 'radical' and 'genuinely political', many of the terms he used to designate themes, doctrines, traditions, schools, authorities and 'ideologies' are proleptic. Republicanism, constitutionalism, humanism, absolutism are all coinages from the early nineteenth century or thereabouts, like so many other -isms. Of these, 'constitutionalism', for example, cannot (it seems to me) be paraphrased so as to bear a historically straightforward referent, and Skinner himself has never since *Foundations* been happy with 'republicanism'.[2] 'Scholasticism', too, is problematic. This -ism is no older than the later eighteenth century, and even the term 'scholastic' was not used either as a self- or a hostile identification much

---

[1] Quentin Skinner, *The Foundations of Modern Political thought*, 2 vols. (Cambridge: Cambridge University Press, 1978), I, pp. 22ff., 65ff., II, esp. pp. 323ff.
[2] In Quentin Skinner, *Liberty before Liberalism* (Cambridge: Cambridge University Press, 1998) he has suggested 'the neo-Roman concept of liberty'.

before the sixteenth century.[3] At the time when he wrote *Foundations* Skinner was sometimes curiously insouciant about the vocabulary that people actually used and their self-identifications. What he calls 'scholastics' and 'scholasticism' was identified in two ways before the sixteenth century. One was by neutral designations of institutions (the 'schools') and their custom and practice, faculties (e.g. 'the theologians'), and adherents of some doctrine, teacher or method (*methodus*, *mos*). The other was by means of terms of abuse. But even in the sixteenth century, the normal designation was *doctores*, *magistri*, *theologi*, *dialectici*, which could be used either neutrally or sarcastically. Luther, for example, seems always to have used expressions like *die Doctores in den hohen Schulen*,[4] *die Juristen*, etc., never 'scholastics'. *Foundations* examines how 'renaissance', and cognate ideas like 'middle' and/or 'dark' ages, spreading light, *humaniores litterae* or *studia humanitatis* and so forth[5] identified scholasticism by opposition and denigration, as it were. But this terminology is transparently self-glorificatory and implies an absurdly schematic periodisation. The only thing we can learn from it is that there was an established and powerful academic enterprise which, according to its opponents, fostered ignorance, arrogance and incomprehension of the classics (apparently the one thing necessary for the cultivated mind), and which was devoted to impractical, useless, frivolous, obscure, disputatious, point-scoring questions and topics, 'quillets and quiddities', *argutiae*, etc. All in a barbarous, dreadful kitchen-Latin which used words not to be found in Cicero, or even Augustine, such as *circumstantiae* and *entitas* and so forth.[6] No historical interpretation of scholasticism could treat such a caricature as more than symptomatic, and of course Skinner's bears no resemblance to it.

It seems most prudent, therefore, to begin with an identification of scholasticism which is impossibly restrictive, but historically unproblematic at least. It

---

[3] I owe this and other corrections to Annabel Brett. The *Constitutiones* of the Society of Jesus, adopted in 1558, but written by Ignatius himself and finished in 1551, pt 4, ch. 5, s. 1, and ch. 6, s. 4, have *theologia scholastica*, without explanation, whereas the first text qualifies '[theologia] positiva, ut dicant', presumably recognised as a neologism. The English term for 'scholasticism' was 'the schools', and 'school' philosophy, logic, divinity, etc. See for example Robert Persons SJ, *A Treatise tending to Mitigation towardes Catholicke Subjectes in England* (London, 1607), especially ch. 9: 'Schoole-Devines, Doctors and Lawyers', for an astonishingly well-informed account of the history of the schools.

[4] E.g. *Vermahnung an die geistlichen, versammlet auff dem Reichstag zu Augsburg, Anno 1530*, in Martin Luther, *Martin Luther's sämmtliche Werke*, ed. E. L. Enders, XXIV (Frankfurt: Evangelischer Verein, 1883), p. 375.

[5] Skinner, *Foundations*, I, pp. 105–12.

[6] For the entire vocabulary of abuse, self-praise and mutual recrimination from the fourteenth century onward see Erika Rummel, *The Humanist-Scholastic Debate in the Renaissance and Reformation* (Cambridge, Mass.: Harvard University Press, 1995). Regrettably she rarely cites the original terminology; I have been unable to check her sources for her citations in translation of 'scholastic' and in once place 'scholasticism' (p. 85), translating the Dominican theologian Melchior Cano, who by then (1563) may well have used the former term, but certainly not the latter.

is usually what Skinner himself had in mind. This identity of 'scholasticism' is gestured at by the term itself – from *scholasticus*, an instructor, a learned man, a master of 'scholars' (students) subject to his 'discipline'; hence the common schools term of approval *scholastice* (in a scholarly manner).[7] 'Scholasticism' in this sense is a shorthand for the teaching of the 'schools' or 'universities' of medieval Europe. It denotes an academic paradigm which specified both what was to be taught, an academic substance, and how it was to be taught, a method. The emphasis was on teaching, *doctrina* (from *docere*, to teach). The paradigm distributed this academic substance between faculties; the method was much the same, irrespective of faculty or discipline. It also ranked faculties in a hierarchy of honour. The three highest faculties, theology, law (civil and canon) and for some reason medicine, were in part valued for the vulgarly commercial reason that they produced the best job qualifications. But this cannot have been the only reason, because rhetoric, which was one of the lower faculties, had long since vindicated its utility as a marketable skill, whereas a theology degree, especially a doctorate, was rarely aimed at, and was by no means a precondition for a glittering career, unlike a law degree.[8] The lower disciplines, the 'liberal arts' and natural philosophy, were, however, just as much part of the scholastic curriculum as the highest faculties. In this sense, *humaniores litterae* or *studia humanitatis* were themselves scholastic disciplines, and the controversy between 'humanists' (sometimes called *auctoristas* in Spain) and 'scholastics' was a faculty turf-war about status and control of academic territory. Skinner rightly stresses that there were academies from the fourteenth century onwards where nothing but humanities was taught, especially in Italy, and 'humanists' who were not 'university'[9] academics. But all their work either was or could be reintegrated into that of the schools.

The ranking of faculties was always a matter of dispute. And what principles of inclusion and exclusion governed the curriculum seems not to have been clear even to scholastics themselves. But only *scientia* could be admitted, in other words, things about which certitude was in principle possible and which could be demonstrated and taught (which is Aquinas's definition of science and was still Hobbes's).[10] The criterion of demonstrability was the scholastic

---

[7] I am unsure of the force of the term *scholastica* in the standard biblical history textbook of the schools, the *Historia scholastica* of Petrus Comestor, mid-twelfth century.

[8] See A. Kenny and J. Pinborg, 'Medieval philosophical literature', in N. Kretzmann, A. Kenny and J. Pinborg (eds.), *Cambridge History of Later Medieval Philosophy* (Cambridge: Cambridge University Press, 1982), pp. 11–42, at pp. 14–17.

[9] Skinner, *Foundations*, I, pp. 197ff. *Universitas* was merely one of several medieval words for a corporation; the lower faculties of what we call medieval universities taught what would subsequently be taught in grammar schools plus logic to boys of (say) fifteen, and many 'universities' did not have some or all of the higher faculties; only *universitates studii generalis* taught everything, if they had the staff. Some of the convents of the religious orders had their own teaching even at theology level.

[10] Hobbes, *Leviathan*, ed. Michael Oakeshott (Oxford: Basil Blackwell, 1946), ch. 5, p. 30: 'the signs of Science are some certain and infallible; some uncertain. Certain, when he that pretendeth

method, and it is therefore impossible to identify anything as a 'scholastic' doctrine except by reference to both method and substance. *Sententiae, quaestiones, disputationes, divisio*, arguments *pro et contra, resolutiones, responsiones, conclusiones*, authorities, definitions, distinctions, syllogisms, demonstrations and all the other components of the method of the school had a rationale which linked method to substance. Both presupposed an inheritance of texts which were all authoritative but were discordant and sometimes contradictory. The 'method' was the set of instruments that promised to harmonise these authorities. The authorities, however, were not a permanently fixed corpus or canon. Aristotle and his Arab commentators in Latin translation became authorities of the first rank in the twelfth century, although they never superseded the authority of Augustine or Peter Lombard. Again: masters of the method themselves became authorities; some of them came to be of comparable authority to the authorities they themselves used: Lombard, Aquinas or Scotus in theology, or commentators such as the authors of the *Glossa* on the Bible, Bartolus on Roman law or Hostiensis on canon law. Even some who wrote commentaries on these commentators became authorities. Equally, the humanities for all their inferior status were quite capable of extending or diminishing the range of *auctores*, e.g. by making available previously unknown works by already known authors, or impugning the authenticity, status or worth of existing authorities (e.g. the Donations of Constantine, Pseudo-Dionysus, the Apostolic Canons, the pseudo-Aristotelean *Secretum Secretorum* and *Yconomica*), or revising translations or interpretations of texts, or providing and editing texts in the original languages, for example those of Aristotle, the Roman law or the Vulgate Bible and so forth. Thus sixteenth-century scholastics had available to them the Complutensian Polyglot Bible in Hebrew, Latin, Greek and Aramaic, published in 1520 by the university of Alcalá, home for a time of the scholastic luminary Domingo de Soto.[11] The scholastic corpus of authorities thus expanded, but on occasion also contracted; with the invention of printing, there was an exponential increase in the range of authorities directly available to any scholar.

In terms of this very narrow understanding, one can readily identify a continuous, uninterrupted though obviously anything but changeless or monolithic tradition of 'scholasticism', that is to say university teaching, stretching into the seventeenth century. So long, that is, as what Skinner slightly equivocally

the Science of any thing, can teach the same; that is to say, demonstrate the truth thereof perspicuously to another'; Aquinas, *Sententia libri Metaphysicae*, ed. E. Alarcón, bk I, lectio 1, no. 29 (81595): 'Signum scientiae est posse docere . . . Artifices autem docere possint, quia causas cognoscant, ex eis possunt demonstrare: demonstratio autem est syllogismus faciens scire'. All references to Aquinas's works are to the astonishing *Corpus Thomisticum* website edited by Enrique Alarcón.

[11] A *bon mot* of the time was 'Qui scit Sotum, scit totum', the person who knows Soto knows what there is to know.

termed 'the *revival* of Thomism' means only that Thomism attained a new vital-
ity and prestige under particularly able exponents like Mair, Almain, Vitoria and
their Dominican and Jesuit successors in Spain and elsewhere. But there is also
a different understanding of 'revival' in his account. The Thomists, he argued,
reconfigured their authorities and doctrine in such a way as to direct them
single-mindedly to the refutation and exclusion of the 'heretics of our age'.[12]
But what is arguably striking is just how little these preoccupations intruded on
the Second Scholastic: Suárez's *De legibus* and his *Opus sex dierum*, for example, hardly mention anything specifically related to the Reformation. Treatises
On justice and law, such as those of Soto, Molina, Lessius and Valentia, confined their comments about the heretics to add-ons, and even then tried as much
as possible to assimilate contemporary heresy to its ancient and medieval predecessors already dealt with *in extenso* in the schools, and thus requiring no
conceptual re-tooling.

This deliberately narrow understanding of scholasticism highlights the fact
that until the fifteenth century virtually all the scholastic 'contributions' to what
is now and was never then called 'political theory' were in fact extracurricular
productions, or polemical writings, *Publizistik*. But then the same could be said
of almost the entire 'canon' of political theory subsequent to the Greeks. And
it would be mere pedantry to deny the title 'scholastic' to writings by authors
whose day-job was as academics, whose every paragraph paraded its scholastic
provenance, and whose authority as polemicists was predicated on their academic status but almost never vice versa. The most striking exception here is
Marsiglio of Padua, who had no independent academic standing but could trade
quotations with the best of them. As I have said, the curriculum was not forever
fixed, and the content of polemical treatises could subsequently be interpolated
into the curriculum, partly by the later practice of *relectiones*, and before that
by the *quaestiones quodlibeticae* and *quaestiones disputatae*, which were part
of the ordinary conduct of academic business.[13] In sixteenth-century scholasticism the traditional limits of the curriculum were in any case being comprehen-
sively eroded, not least by the introduction of *Controversies*-theology towards
the end of the century. Its first and most conspicuous exponents were the Jesuits
Gregorio de Valentia at Ingolstadt and Robert Bellarmine at the Roman College,
subsequently the Gregorian University of Rome; the formal curricular incorpo-
ration of ecclesiology and casuistry had taken place much earlier.

But although this more relaxed identification of scholasticism to include
extracurricular as well as curricular activities is eminently reasonable, there

---

[12] Skinner, *Foundations*, II, ch. 5.
[13] M. Kempshall, *The Common Good in Late Medieval Political Thought* (Oxford: Clarendon Press,
1999), pp. 8–9, describes these as 'the two forms of academic disputation which provide perhaps
the most revealing index of issues of contemporary concern, but also the most "authoritative"
reflections of the personal opinions of individual masters.'

is a price to be paid for it. Stripped of any strictly academic location and of the methodological dimension, scholasticism rapidly loses its identity as a distinctive discursive genre in terms of tenets, authorities, vocabulary or anything else. It would be extravagant to say, as I formerly did, that there are no propositions, beliefs, attitudes or doctrines peculiar to 'scholasticism': some utterances are indelibly stamped with the mark of the schools. All the same, virtually all the authorities acknowledged by humanists were also authorities for scholastics, though obviously not vice versa. Scholastics believed just as emphatically as humanists did that the classics, pagan as well as patristic, were a treasury of wisdom and virtue. What is more, the premium that scholasticism placed on authorities and hence on short quotes summarising them, as well as on principles, axioms, maxims, free-standing and snappy one-line propositions of every sort demanded by the syllogistic and dialectical method, meant that a fund of such memorable one-liners was available for general public consumption, transportable from location to location, including from scholastic to humanist or polemical or even vernacular locations. 'Man is born free' (or as the case may be, equal), 'man is a political [or social] animal', 'peoples were not created for kings, but kings for peoples', 'it is permissible to repel force with force', 'what concerns all should be approved by all', 'no one may be a judge in his own cause', 'no one can give what they do not have': who held the copyright on such *dicta*? Their original source was often impeccably classical in any case. And humanists, Protestants, *politiques*, etc. could appropriate a 'scholastic' authority by the still familiar rhetorical ploy: 'even our enemies admit that', etc. The less ignorant or dogmatic among them had never denied the intelligence of at least some scholastics; misapplied intelligence no doubt, but intelligence for all that.

Consider an illustration: the two vernacular pieces of English political writing in the 1590s that created the greatest stir were Persons's *Conference concerning the Next Succession* (1594/5) and Hooker's *Laws of Ecclesiastical Polity* (preface and books I–IV, 1593, book V, 1597). The Anglican cleric Richard Hooker cited the 'Schoole-Divines' at every turn, writing, however, in mellifluous English (so there were no identifying stylistic barbarisms), and without the *quaestio* format. The Jesuit Robert Persons, the 'diabolical Machiavellian' hate-figure of English Protestants, wrote his scathing *Conference* in vigorous polemical English. As to its theoretical part it was very similar to Hooker's. But he did not cite a single scholastic authority, or indeed anything whatever that was not equally authoritative for a predominantly Protestant English lay public, or for humanists; he even adopted the latter's favourite dialogue form for his book. But then, as has already been said, grammar, rhetoric, philology, patristics and *humaniores litterae* were part of the scholastic curriculum and in 1599 they were methodically integrated into a systematic course of studies in the exemplary curriculum of the Jesuits, the *Ratio studiorum*. Hooker's and Persons's contemporary, the Jesuit Juan de Mariana, wrote much the same as they did in his notorious mirror for princes *De rege et regis institutione* (1599), which was in best humanist (indeed Tacitean) Latin, mentioned no scholastics, and incorporated a good deal of reason of state, as Persons had done. Are we to say that Mariana's and Persons's works were scholasticism in drag, so to speak? Surely a more sensible verdict would be that we are here witnessing the evaporation of anything specifically scholastic into the mainstream of European political thinking.

I alluded earlier to the opacity of the reasons why the scholastic curriculum in- or excluded substances of various kinds. The extracurricular character of scholastic writings on politics, however, is certainly not due to scholastics regarding politics as a dirty business which an academic ought not to allow to soil his hands, or because they considered it to be one of the 'practical arts', for so was medicine, which was one of the higher faculties. And scholastics, like academics throughout the ages, were not in the habit of underselling themselves or their products in point of usefulness. Nor was it because of any personal or professional dangers incident to political utterances. Scholasticism covers hundreds of years, and what was outright heresy or treason in one time or place was often precisely what secular and/or ecclesiastical authorities wanted to hear in another time or place. The reason for the disjuncture between academy and politics is rather that politics was the kind of discourse for which it was difficult to find a place in the academic curriculum, and for which there was no corps of academic experts. Who is authoritative (*peritus, expertus, sollers*) in respect of what matter was and remained a persistent preoccupation of scholasticism. As the maxim had it, *cuilibet experto in sua scientia credendum est*. It was clear enough who had authority to pronounce on canon or civil law, doctrine or morality or cases of conscience, or health, geometry or sound argument, or for that matter on plumbing. But who had any particular authority or *locus standi* in respect of politics? Ockham at one point seemed to be saying there were no such experts for politics at all: 'It is not necessary to believe everyone who is thought an expert [*peritus in scientia sua*], because in many arts and science no one can be perfect, but everyone can err.' But on closer inspection this turns out to be merely a highly polemical claim aimed at those who in Ockham's view simply had long memories but no speculative aptitude. Another similar remark about *periti* was equally polemical, being directed at those theologians who were in his view giving the wrong advice about the authority of the papacy.[14] Elsewhere his views on the authority of *theologi aut canonistae aut in legibus imperialibus eruditi* were assertive enough.[15]

---

[14] J. Miethke, 'Die mittelalterlichen Universitäten und das geschriebene Wort', *Historische Zeitschrift* 231 (1990), pp. 1–44, at p. 33 n. 80, p. 39.

[15] William of Ockham, *Ockham: Opera Politica*, IV, ed. H. S. Offler (Oxford: Oxford University Press, 1997), e.g. *Breviloquium de Principatu Tyrannico*, pp. 100, 103–5, 161: 'Non est expertis incognitum . . .'

Here are some generalisations, perilous as all such things are, but someone has to put their head above the parapet occasionally. In the first place, there was not only no academic discipline or faculty, but not even an identifiable academic field constituted by the term 'politics', or any of the variant grammatical forms derived from *polis*. I am happy to follow Maurizio Viroli's account of the use of the language of politics to distinguish a republican regime and the *civile vivere* from the *stato* of princes in *quattrocento* Italy.[16] But in Northern Europe *politica*, *politici*, *politique*, politicks, policy (distinguished only in English from 'politics' by a separate word, and then only uncertainly until the seventeenth century),[17] polity, *politisch* became a fashionable and vernacular vocabulary only in the course of the sixteenth century: one can positively see people rolling such words around on their tongues.[18] Even then the Latin substantive *politica* was still so unfamiliar that there was no agreement on whether it was a feminine singular (which it remains in the Romance languages and German) or a neuter plural (which it sometimes is in English). The same was true in the middle ages. Aquinas for example refers to the title of Aristotle's *Politics* in the plural,[19] as was usual, since this was how the Moerbeke translation rendered it. But he normally used the term in the singular, either as a short form for *scientia politica* (presumably after the precedent of *ethica*, also a singular except in the translation of the *Ethics*), or to designate the activity of ruling. On occasion, but very rarely, he and others used *politicus* as a substantive to mean a statesman or ruler.[20]

The whole family of words normally did no conceptual work at all that I can see. It was of course familiar from the Latin translations of Aristotle, and also from Cicero who had used *politia* for the title of Plato's *Republic*. But whether a writer used any term from this family seems to have depended largely on how closely he was tracking Aristotle's *Politics* or his *Ethics*. Aquinas used the adjective *politicus* freely in his commentary on Aristotle's *Politics*, but hardly at all in the *Summa theologiae*. But even in his commentary on the *Ethics*, he often preferred the adjective *civilis*, referring for example to *civilis scientia* or *civilis multitudo*.[21] He rendered Aristotle's description of man as *zoon politikon* as either *animal politicum*, or *sociale*, or both, indifferently. Again, Marsiglio and Ockham rarely used the adjective, let alone *politica* as a substantive, even though both referred regularly to *politia* (or *policia*, a spelling

---

[16] M. Viroli, *From Politics to Reason of State* (Cambridge: Cambridge University Press, 1992).

[17] Thomas Fitzherbert's two-part *Treatise concerning Policy and Religion* (London, 1606, 1610) used 'policy' indifferently to mean both politics and policy.

[18] For some supporting evidence, see my 'Orthodoxy and Reason of State', *History of Political Thought* 23 (2002), pp. 211–37, at pp. 215–18.

[19] Aquinas, *Sententia libri Metaphysicae*, proem, para. 81566: 'Sicut docet philosophus in politicis suis'.

[20] Aquinas, *Sententia libri Ethicorum*, bk I, lectio 2, no. 5 (para. 72731).

[21] Ibid, e.g. bk I, lectio 2, no. 7 (72729), and lectio 3, no. 1 (72736); bk I, lectio 1, no. 5 (para. 72709). See also the quotation from Aegidius Romanus, cited in n. 29 below.

which presumably explains the German word *Polizeyen*, sometimes used for 'polities', for which German had no current word, and for 'state', for which it had no word at all until the end of the sixteenth century). That term too, however, seems to have had no settled meaning, and was used equally for regime, form of government or as a variant for *civitas*. In the scholastic curriculum, Aristotle's *Ethics*, his *Metaphysics* and his writings on natural philosophy, even minor and falsely ascribed works, were vastly more significant than the *Politics*. Cicero's *De officiis* was a much more widely known text in any event, not least because it also figured in the arts curriculum. Even when the adjective 'political' was used (and Gerson, for one, writing three-quarters of a century later than Ockham, used it quite freely and also the peculiar *politizans*: reflecting about the polity), it was normally accompanied by an explanatory term: e.g. *politica vel civilis* (or *saecularis*), qualifying law, government, authority, *societas* or *dominium*. *Civilis* or *saecularis* were far more usual terms. The only author who made *politicus* do any conceptual work that I can find is Ptolemy of Lucca. In his mirror of princes *De regimine principum* he distinguished after a fashion between *political* and *despotic* rule, seemingly on the basis of Aristotle's mixed form. Aristotle had confusingly categorised the latter as the *politeia*, a term he otherwise used generically for the institutional order of any *polis*. If they knew of Ptolemy's work, neither Marsiglio, Ockham nor Gerson followed his usage, even though all of them were as deeply concerned with distinguishing tyrannical from legitimate rule, and were as respectful of Aristotle as he was.[22]

In short, *politica* did not demarcate a substance, such as (according to the opinion of the time) was presupposed by any science, art or discipline. And there was no other equivalent term either. So far as the topics dealt with in *Foundations* were given any general label before the sixteenth century, it was as matters concerned with *regimen, gubernatio, imperium, potestas*, the *civitas, respublica*, the *societas perfecta* and even less promisingly and more personalising, *dominium* or *principatus* or most commonly *regnum* or *imperium*. Knowledge of such matters was referred to by Aquinas in his unfinished[23] commentary on Aristotle's *Politics* and his commentary on the *Ethics* as *politica scientia* or *doctrina politica, id est civilis*. In deference to Aristotle's authority, he even

---

[22] Ockham in one place (*De Principatu Tyrannico* in *Ockham: Opera Politica*, IV, p. 184), referring to Aristotle's *Politics*, does however say: 'vir principatur uxori politice, et pater principatur liberis regaliter'. Similarly Aquinas, *Sententia libri Politicorum*, bk I, lectio 3.9 (para. 79129), distinguishes despotic *principatus* over *servi* from 'politicum [principatum] quo rector civitatis principatur liberis', but then explained his meaning as 'principatu politico *et regali* qui est ad liberos' (my italics). Compare however ibid., bk. 1, lectio 10.3 (para. 79218), where following Aristotle he distinguishes *principatus politici* from the regal in virtue of the fact that subjects and princes change positions from one year to the next.

[23] It was finished by Peter of Auvergne. Aquinas found time to complete commentaries on the *Ethics*, the *Metaphysics*, the *Posterior Analytics*, the *De Anima*, but did not write a commentary on Aristotle's other most eminently 'political' work, the *Rhetoric*, either.

described this *scientia* as the noblest and most architectonic of sciences in virtue of the eximious dignity of its subject matter, namely the common good.[24] But although the purpose of scholastic commentaries was expository and explanatory, Aquinas was extremely careful to limit the importance and also the scope of this *scientia*. In his commentary on Aristotle's *Metaphysics*, which began by citing 'the Philosopher in his *Politics*', he made it clear that metaphysics was the highest of the sciences, as being *maxime intellectualis*, and dealing with those things that are *maxime intelligibilia*, namely first causes. It is its (and not political science's) place to regulate and order (*regulatrix, ordinare*) all the other sciences. He explained that metaphysics, unlike politics, deals with the highest things under three titles, according to the subject matter: *scientia divina* (or theology), metaphysics and *prima philosophia*.[25] And in his *Ethics* commentary he made the point even more explicitly, attributing it to Aristotle: 'He does not say that *politica* (sing.) is the foremost science unconditionally (*simpliciter*), but foremost among the sciences dealing with action (*scientiarum activarum*)', for 'the foremost science with regard to all sciences is divine science'. Then, shifting from *scientia* to mean a discipline, to *scientia* meaning any body of knowledge, he explained that its ordering capacity extended only to the *scientiae* concerned with ends subordinate to the highest end of the polity, the common good, namely rhetoric, the military and 'operative *artes*', or *practicae scientiae*, dictating to them not only whether they shall or shall not be employed, but also what they shall be employed in doing. With respect to the higher-ranking speculative (i.e. theoretical)[26] sciences, *politica* (here meaning government and the kind of practical and ethical *scientia* it involves) determines only whether they shall be taught and which shall be taught (for example that geometry will be taught), but does not tell the practitioners of these sciences what they are to think (e.g. about the properties of triangles). He then repeated Aristotle's contention that the wise man demands no more certitude than the subject matter allows, and that in political and moral matters there was inevitably more uncertainty than in the speculative sciences. All of which amounted to saying that theology, not politics, was queen of the sciences, and that *scientia politica* was

---

[24] *Sententia libri Ethicorum*, bk 1, lectio 2, nos.7–8 (paras. 72729–30): 'Optimus finis pertinet ad principalissimam scientiam, et maximam architectonicam . . . Sed civilis scientia videtur esse talis . . . Duo autem pertinent ad scientiam architectonicam, quorum unum est, quod ipsa praecipit scientiae vel arti quae est sub ipsa quid debeat operari . . . Aliud autem est, quod utitur ea ad suum finem. Primum autem horum convenit politicae, vel civili, tam respectu speculativarum scientiarum, quam respectu practicarum'.

[25] Proemium (para. 81566).

[26] I do not know whether *theoria* or its adjective were ever used in medieval Latin; *theoria* was very rare in classical Latin and does not appear in its English form until the later sixteenth century. 'Speculative' and 'theoretical' have the same metaphor as their root: a spectacle, something to be contemplated. They certainly had no role in any curricular sphere, and 'political speculation' would hardly have the same meaning as 'political theory' or 'political science'.

essentially a practical art conversant with things about which certain knowledge (and knowledge and certitude are the same thing) was hard to come by, and therefore it could not pretend to any academic status, for all its salience and nobility among the practical arts. He then went on to endorse Aristotle's verdict that since it presupposed so much experience, it was not a *scientia* for which young persons (i.e. students) were suitable auditors.

But just because this was the verdict of Aquinas, it does not follow that it was therefore the verdict of scholastics as a body. But it was. Political science could pass the first hurdle for inclusion in the scholastic curriculum, because from 1265 there was a relevant text (in translation), Aristotle's *Politics*, and also his *Ethics*. Apart from Albert the Great's and Aquinas's commentaries, there is also evidence of commentaries produced by various arts faculties, but they are uncommon and not nearly as numerous as commentaries on Aristotle's other works, and attendance at lectures on the *Politica* was not compulsory for matriculation.[27] In any event commentaries were extremely sparing of discussions: they were intended to explain the 'mind' of the author, which given the character of Moerbeke's translation was labour enough. What is altogether missing is any paradigm in the *quaestio/responsio* format, until we get the *relectiones* (a way of pulling together topics that previously had only been dealt with separately and in a diffuse manner) of the sixteenth century, in particular those of Francisco de Vitoria. Even then, it is notable that there is not a single attempt to produce a coherent and sustained discussion of the foremost political concept of scholasticism, namely the common good.[28] In so far as *politica* had any academic *locus standi* at all, it was as a sub-branch of *scientia moralis* or ethics, where certain knowledge of at any rate moral principles was possible. And this explains an attractive but misleading comment of the extreme hierocrat Aegidius Romanus (Giles of Rome), which is in my view misinterpreted by Flüeler. In an occasional piece *De differentia rhetoricae, politicae et ethicae* of the late thirteenth century, Aegidius put the lawyers in their place, and Flüeler interprets this as an instance of political science having to defend its autonomy not only against theology but also against jurisprudence (p. 7):

27 C. Flüeler, *Rezeption und Interpretation der Aristotelischen Politica im späten Mittelalter*, 2 vols. (Amsterdam: B. Grüner, 1992), I, esp. pp. 33–44.
28 I am aware of only one treatise on the subject, the Dominican Remigio de' Girolami's *De bono communi* of *c*.1300. Aside from being more of a *florilegium*, a thesaurus of quotable quotes on the topic, than a treatise in due form, it was (for all the attention devoted to it by modern scholars) so obscure that it never achieved an *editio princeps* until the twentieth century, despite the enormous number of publication of scholastic works of all kinds immediately subsequent to the invention of printing, including encyclopaedic collections like Melchior Goldast's *Monarchia* of 1611. The common good was of course a frequently and intensively discussed topic in various contexts, which, however, were and remained separate; see Kempshall, *The Common Good*, cited above, *passim*.

Politica is divided into two parts: setting down laws and upholding laws (*legum conservativam*); deliberating about laws therefore concerns those whom we call *legistas* and also to [political science], but not in the same way. For *politica* delivers laws in the manner of an art [i.e. a science!]; but the *legistae* deliver laws without art. For they do not consider them in a scientific manner, but merely report (*per modum narrativum*). So *legistae* have the same relation to *politici* as the vulgar and lay-persons to dialectics . . . *Legistae* are political rustics (*ydiote politici*), because they use politics without art.[29]

But the art or science he is talking about is politics considered as a branch of ethics,[30] as Flüeler himself makes clear.

Moreover, in so far as anyone could be said to have any academic expertise in such matters, there was not even a conventional term for such persons, to correspond to *iurisperitus, canonista, theologus, magister, artista, expertus in logicalibus, medicus, auctorista*. Scholastics occasionally, but very rarely, used the word *politicus* where the meaning might be a person specialising in *doctrina politica*.[31] But then occasional references are to be found to *oeconomicus* as well, although no one pretends that household management was an academic subject in the middle ages. There were no professorships in politics, the infallible mark of academic status, until the late sixteenth century.[32] Cicero himself had twice, once in *De officiis*, referred to *philosophi politici*. But the very fact that the term floated in that eminently familiar text without ever being fished out and put to use by anyone as a job-specification – the term would not have been hard to invent in any case, given the facility for terminological innovation displayed by scholastics – demonstrates all too clearly that there was no place for anything of the sort in the mentality or (if you like) horizon of the time. But then 'philosophy' was not the name of a scholastic faculty or discipline either, except for the lower discipline of 'natural philosophy', but was a synonym for *scientia*, as in 'moral philosophy'. Presumably it was precisely because it had no curricular connotation that 'philosophy' was available to humanists as

---

[29] Aegidius Romanus, *De Differentia Rhetorica, Politicae et Ethicae*, as cited in Flüeler, *Rezeption und Interpretation* I, p. 7, my translation.

[30] Ibid. A very similar comment is attributed to Ockham; it is cited in G. de Lagarde, *La naissance de l'esprit laïque au déclin du moyen âge*, III, p. 207 and n. 207, where lay jurists are compared to 'vils mechaniques'; and Ockham, *Dialogus*, bk I, ch. 9.

[31] Aquinas, *Sententia libri Politicorum*, bk II, lectio.8.1 (para. 79319), used the cumbersome expression 'ordinationes quaedam . . . sunt adinventae a philosophis et a quibusdam hominibus, qui fuerunt prudentes et experti in civili conversatione'. For his normal usage of the substantive *politicus*, see ibid., bk II, lectio 3.6 (para. 79435) 'politicus, id est rector politiae'. There is an unexplained reference by Gerson in one place, and not I think anywhere else in his writings to 'sicut a *politicis* dicentibus, bonam fidem esse ubi non simulatur unum et alium agitur' (my italics); Jean Gerson, *Œuvres Complètes*, Mgr. Glorieux (ed.), (Tournai: Desclée, 1965), VI, p. 230.

[32] The first such professorship was, I think, founded in the Protestant University of Leyden, but I have been unable to trace the reference.

a label for their ostentatiously (and ostensibly) non-curricular conception of good letters.

The absence of politics or *principatus* and therefore of any corresponding experts from the curricular topography of scholasticism was neither casual nor devoid of substantive consequences. Much of the subject matter of what Skinner considers under the heading of 'political thought' was what scholastics regarded as matters on which there might be pragmatic knowledge, prudence (indeed *prudentia politica* was one of the three species of the genus prudence)[33] and wisdom, but no demonstrative knowledge, *scientia*. Prudence is a much neglected topic in *Foundations*: indeed it has no entry in the index. The scholastic curriculum certainly provided for the epistemological investigation of prudence, conventionally the chief of the cardinal virtues, along with justice, fortitude and temperance. Scholastic theologians discussed the prerequisites and nature of prudence, and what they termed its 'work' or 'operations'. But the exercise of prudence in regard to *regimen* by princes and their advisers, as well as judges and magistrates, and the entire business of the best order and working of a *respublica*, *civitas*, or more likely *regnum*, *regimen* or *principatus*, was not a *scientia* to be learnt in a university, and demonstrated and taught to students. Not that scholastics had any concept like the 'functioning' or 'working' of institutions in any event; in fact they had no word for 'institutions'. There were indeed academic repositories of political prudence in works handled by the lower faculties of grammar and rhetoric, which covered among other things the poets, orators and historians of Antiquity; history (or experience) being the mother of prudence, as the cliché had it. But primarily prudence was something to be learnt on location by prudent persons from other prudent persons, from experience, and from whatever sources of edifying knowledge were at hand, notably specifically *not* academic productions such as mirrors of princes and discourses and dialogues of various kinds. And mirrors of princes were notoriously not 'how to' books, but were concerned with improving princes' morals and conduct by instruction in virtue.

This is not to say that the higher faculties did not provide any professional knowledge for political consultancy work, so to speak. Indeed universities (especially law and theology faculties) were frequently consulted by spiritual and temporal authorities for their professional verdict on contentious political issues which had a strong theological, moral or religious dimension and thus fell within the professional sphere of some faculty. In the theology faculties, some matters of *regimen* were dealt with under the headings of *On Justice and Right* and *On Laws*, as well as incidentally on other subjects for commentary, as when Aquinas reflected on the ethical issue of tyrannicide in the context of a commentary on

---

[33] This was another Aristotelian cliché, piously reported by scholastics, but without any curricular valence or substantive exploration.

Lombard's *Sententiae*. All the same, it was one thing to consider, say, the principles of just taxation, and quite another to decide on the appropriate method and requisite level of taxation to meet some particular contigency. But for the most part the universities did not explore political concepts or issues in the way that issues in metaphysics, logic or theology were explored, unless some *topos* was already clearly established. I think I can confidently say, for example, that when contracts were discussed in the law faculties, this was never treated as an invitation to consider the possibility of any *contractus, foedus, conventio, pactio* or *pactum* between a ruler and the people or the commonwealth, or any other topic of that sort. For the most part lawyers confined themselves narrowly to the minutiae of their trade. But higher-level commentary on Roman and canon law as well as theology did allow all manner of speculative excursions: both had in particular to deal at some point with the authority of emperors and popes respectively, and by extension with the authority of all those who had some claim to exercise a legislative or coercive power. The topic here was normally *imperium*, and by extension *regnum* (*rex est imperator in regno suo*), or generically *principatus* or *dominium*. But it also on occasion included free cities, which could be elided with *respublicae* because the ambiguous term *civitas* was both a general term for the polity but also meant a city; there was not before the sixteenth century a going rate, or upper and lower threshold about size of territory, for what could count as a *regnum* or *principatus*. However, absolutely no curricular or other significance seems to have attached to the public law/private law distinction, which in Roman law at most vaguely approximated to modern distinctions between constitutional law and other forms of law. In any event, there was not, I think, any area marked out in any faculty as 'public law', which might give us an analogue for a constitution, and hence for constitutionalism by implication. In passing, I have not found any evidence that what Skinner terms the 'private law' argument for political resistance was designated or thought of in that way, and there is no reason to expect to find any evidence: in principle, any argument about individual rights or powers, such as the 'right of self-defence', could equally well attach to 'mystical bodies', that is to say bodies corporate of any kind, including the body politic.

One significant implication of this approach to discussions of *principatus* and *potestas* is that it brought into operation with a vengeance what C. S. Lewis somewhere describes as the 'insulating power of context'. The fact that some issue or some concept featured in one standard *quaestio* in one part of the curriculum of one faculty did not in the least imply that it would be treated in the same way even in another *quaestio* in the same faculty, let alone in other faculties or in connection with related matters in other faculties. The analytical and topic-based approach characteristic of the scholastic method did not encourage synoptic overviews of anything as a whole. Instead, in the best tradition of universities through the ages, subject matters were defined by the set of *quaestiones* of some master, and usually by his answers as well. The more routinised topics became, the less likely it was that their insulation would be broken through. So it was for example perfectly possible, and indeed usual, to assert the principle that 'man is naturally free (and/or equal)' in the context of discussions of whether slavery was legitimate or not, or whether a human being might be subject to *dominium proprietatis*, or might licitly sell him- or herself into slavery, or whether a free man might marry a *servus* or vice versa. The principle might however be ignored altogether in the context of the *potestas coactiva* of princes or commonwealths, where the justification was in terms of the naturalness and necessity of relationships of super- and subordination, of bodies needing heads, of the common good needing to be the special business of someone, lest it be attended to by no one. Again, the 'natural liberty' of individuals was not brought together with the idea of a pre-civil, and pre-political 'natural state', or 'state of nature', despite the fact that the legitimation of authority was standardly by reference to what Locke was still calling the 'original' of civil government, or the 'end' of civil government. These two were as often as not the same thing, namely some permanent requirement of human beings, considered as the origin if they did not as yet have it, or the end which it ought to continue to aim at, once it was established. Skinner is quite right to say that the terms and concepts of a *status purae naturae*, or *status naturalis*, or man *in puris naturalibus* were or became part of the standard repertory of Thomist concepts. But what they were used to address was the question of the operations and effect of grace and of divinely vouchsafed knowledge and laws: the 'natural condition' was a conjecture about what man would be like, were he not provided with saving grace and saving knowledge vouchsafed by revelation. So the 'natural condition', the condition when man knew only the natural law, was for example contrasted with the *status* of man under Mosaic law, and subsequently man's condition under the law of Christ. The insulating power of context ensured that there was absolutely no compulsion to bring this concept together either with any account of the origin or end of civil authority and the *respublica perfecta*, or with the concept of 'natural liberty' or 'natural right', which involved a different sense of the concept of 'nature'. In the same way, the context sometimes dictated that ownership of something in virtue of having worked for it, and thus merited it, counted as being by natural right. But in other contexts scholastics maintained with equal confidence and lack of qualification that only common property was by natural right and that all regimes of particular or private property and possession were creatures of the positive law or some regime of property created by rulers.

Skinner is therefore not in my view right to say, as he does, that according to Thomists, man's natural condition was pre-civil but not pre-social: until Suárez such an idea never entered their heads. Moreover the fact that one standard argument for the necessity of civil authority was in terms of what things would be like in the absence of civil authority does not entail that with or without the word, scholastics had the concept of the state of nature. You might as well say that Luther and Calvin had the concept of the state of nature, because they too both said that unless civil authority were there to restrain them, men (or at least the wicked) would tear each other apart. It was the genius of Hobbes, and to some extent of Suárez, that they invented the concept of a condition of nature as a methodical way of considering the bases and necessity of authority. Obviously they did not invent it out of nothing. They may even have got it from scholastic writings on grace and re-tooled it, seeing that grace was one of the most contested issues in Western Christendom both as between reformers and Catholics and within each denomination from the 1520s onwards. But that in no way detracts from it being an invention, and theirs.

Was there then no politically relevant substance at all which was peculiar to scholasticism? There was, at an extremely abstract level. Scholasticism offered the only methodical way of asking and answering the most abstract questions. Indeed it lends itself to misinterpretation precisely because it alone achieved that level of abstraction. Thus it is sometimes asked, for example, whether or to what extent Aquinas or Ockham advanced a positivistic theory of law and/or a subjective theory of rights, or whether the ethic of scholasticism was 'individualistic' or 'collectivistic'. Such questions are anachronistic, but the point is that the work of scholastics was abstract enough to tolerate them. For a methodical and theoretical account of concepts like law, or justice, or right, or contract, or for a general theory of political authority or the *respublica*, or the church, or order, or the relationship between the law-giver and the law, or law and command, or reason and law, or law and morality, or the commonwealth and the ruler, the only place to go was to go to the schools. Just as you had to go to the schools for anything resembling a discussion of epistemological questions. People, including scholastics, increasingly went to humanists for instruction in philology, for classical and patristic erudition, for *historiae*, for elegance of expression and copiousness of language, for practical political prudence, or moral edification, the *philosophia Christi* or *humanitas*. But for *scientia* it was the scholastics that provided both the materials and the method, even for vituperative critics like Hobbes.

The scholastics' way of dealing with such matters was in many respects far from ideal, given their passion for syllogisms, for knock-down arguments and for one-liners. It is also beyond contention that some of the topics on which scholastics thought certitude and demonstrative argument was possible seem to us the purest cases of metaphysical speculation, or 'dominant ideology', if that sort of language is preferred. Although it was questioned by some, for example inconclusively and on pragmatic grounds by Marsiglio of Padua, in an ambivalent way (with the arguments *pro et contra* being stated without resolution) by William of Ockham, and in a deeply confused way by Ptolemy of Lucca, it was almost universally regarded as a certain inference from first principles that monarchy was the best form of government in that it corresponds most closely to the first principles of order. It is also striking just how much did *not* figure among the standard *quaestiones* of the schools. A remarkable example is that everyone agreed that rulers, especially those in positions of highest authority, were in some sense 'absolute', *legibus soluti*, and in other respects not. But we have to wait until the later sixteenth century for attempts to distinguish the laws that bound them as 'fundamental laws', and until the seventeenth century for the idea that what binds them is an order of laws and institutions which are themselves changeable and human artefacts, and which together compose a 'constitution', a word which like 'institution' was in scholastic terminology merely one of the many variants for a law. Again, the whole topic of ecclesiology (until the fifteenth century), specifically the rights of the papacy with respect to secular rulers, and much of the discussion of the authority of the emperor versus that of the papacy, and then the authority of kings with respect to the emperor, and even more opaquely that of 'free cities' with regard to the emperor or the pope, was conducted in polemical treatises and not inside the academies. The position of Aquinas, who confined himself strictly to academic writing and teaching, in many of these questions remains almost indecipherable.

What would complete *Foundations*, then, would be an investigation of how scholasticism came to be assimilated and attenuated into the formats and approaches to methodical study (with method itself a philosophical or dog-matic issue of acute significance) which came to be common to the universities and academies of all Europe. And while the same account might be given of theology and philosophy, and (for all I know) of law, the particular focus of our story would be the absorption of scholasticism into a common manner of treating *methodice* what was increasingly clearly identified as the special academic field of *doctrina civilis* (or *politica*), or 'civil philosophy'. That in turn was distin-guished in curricular terms from the more clearly humanist and rhetoric-derived but equally academic areas of *prudentia civilis* and 'reason of state', which in turn furnished the resources for the discussion of 'institutional architecture' (Rahe), on which (*pace* Skinner) I think scholastics had virtually nothing to say, and for which they had virtually no vocabulary. And it is perhaps in these terms that we might for instance be able to explain why the echo of the schools is clearly audible in a thinker like Hobbes, for all his jibes at the schoolmen. It is hardly surprising that a philosopher should resemble schoolmen rather than rhetoricians.

8   Scholastic political thought and the modern concept of the state

Annabel Brett

Quentin Skinner accorded scholastic authors a prominent role in putting in place 'the foundations of modern political thought'. This much is plain if we consider the four essential preconditions for 'the acquisition of the modern concept of the State' that he listed in his conclusion.[1] Skinner postulated, first, that 'the sphere of politics should be envisaged as a distinct branch of moral philosophy, a branch concerned with the art of government'; secondly, that 'the independence of each *regnum* or *civitas* from any external and superior power should be vindicated and assured'; that 'the supreme authority within each independent *regnum* should be recognised as having no rivals within its own territories as a law-making power and an object of allegiance'; and finally that 'political society is held to exist solely for political purposes'. According to the narrative offered over the course of the two volumes of *Foundations*, thirteenth-century scholastic doctors at the university of Paris, together with those members of religious orders and others who developed their work in the context of the northern Italian city-states, were critical in establishing the first precondition, by vindicating Aristotle's vision of politics against conservative forces within the church. While Skinner tended to view the second precondition as owing more, at least initially, to the activity of Roman lawyers rather than scholastics (although he saw a close connection between medieval scholasticism and Roman law, both in content and in method), the work of scholastic theorists was crucial to the third: from Marsilius of Padua through the conciliarist theory of the church to the Counter-Reformation scholastics, whom Skinner saw as the forerunners of a natural-law theory of the state eventually developed by Grotius, Hobbes and Pufendorf.[2] Finally, Skinner

I would like to thank Harro Höpfl, Magnus Ryan and Jim Tully for exchanges, comments and conversations from which I have benefited immeasurably in what has proved to be a process of rethinking the foundations of my own work. My debt to Quentin Skinner goes beyond any words of acknowledgement, for teaching me with such grace how to think about these questions in the first place.

[1] Quentin Skinner, *The Foundations of Modern Political Thought*, 2 vols. (Cambridge: Cambridge University Press, 1978), II, pp. 349–52. The relationship between 'the foundations of modern political thought' and the 'acquisition of the modern concept of the State' (see also the preface, *Foundations*, I, p. ix) is never spelled out in the course of the two volumes, and leaves open a number of questions. I return to these at the end of the second section below.
[2] Skinner, *Foundations*, II, p. 184.

argued that the 'second-hand scholastic philosophy'[3] of the revolutionaries at the end of the sixteenth century developed, with Buchanan and Mariana, into a 'purely secular' theory of popular sovereignty which would culminate eventually in John Locke's *Two Treatises of Government*.[4] They thereby 'laid the foundations for the later challenge to the two main traditions of absolutist political theory' (patriarchalism and the natural-law theory of Grotius, Hobbes and Pufendorf), and hence played a significant role in the establishment of the 'modern "liberal" theory of constitutionalism' as well.[5]

In identifying 'the contribution of scholasticism'[6] in this way, Skinner perhaps laid himself open to the charge of working with an uncritical acceptance of the category 'scholasticism', as opposed principally to 'humanism'; and equally with the other contrasts that structure the work, for example between 'Renaissance' and 'Reformation' (which divides the volumes) or between 'constitutionalism' and 'absolutism' (which provides the central narrative of the second volume). And yet the ambition adverted to above, to understand the period as a whole as one *from which* the modern concept of the state resulted, transcended the habitual deployment of these contrasts. The same is true of his parallel ambition to understand the history of political thought not as a history of ideas but of texts, and of texts in context: interventions within shifting and overlapping normative vocabularies in different relationships with social and political realities.[7] Together these perspectives led Skinner to challenge and to revise, sometimes dramatically, the ways in which these inherited categories had previously been understood. So, for example, instead of a simple dichotomy between humanism and scholasticism, Skinner consistently insisted on a triad of scholasticism, humanism and the heritage of Roman law in the developments he was interested in. Again, he did not associate Renaissance political thought exclusively with humanist political thought, and he stretched both back to the thirteenth century, well beyond previously defined and celebrated contours.

---

[3] The phrase is David Wootton's in his essay on the Levellers in J. H. Burns (ed.), *The Cambridge History of Political Thought 1450–1700* (Cambridge: Cambridge University Press, 1991), p. 442; but true to Skinner's intentions, I think.

[4] Skinner, *Foundations*, II, pp. 347–8.

[5] Ibid., p. 347. Their works clearly constitute, therefore, part of the 'foundations of modern political thought'. But their relevance to the 'acquisition of the modern concept of the State' is unclear. Summing up on the subject of the state in the conclusion, Skinner does not mention these authors again: it is rather Bodin and the *politiques* who are said to be the key players in the establishment of the fourth precondition (that 'political society is held to exist solely for political purposes'). Skinner tackled this issue directly in his later article, 'The state', in T. Ball, J. Farr and R. L. Hanson (eds.), *Political Innovation and Conceptual Change* (Cambridge: Cambridge University Press, 1989), pp. 90–131, at 114–15: in the monarchomachs and their successors, principally Locke, 'no effective contrast is drawn between the power of the people and the powers of the state', and hence they cannot be seen as direct sources for the modern concept of the state.

[6] The phrase occurs for example in I, p. 144, discussing the role of scholastic thinking in *quattrocento* republicanism.

[7] See the preface in Skinner, *Foundations*, I, pp. x–xi.

The Reformation remained the Reformation, but had its roots in fourteenth- and fifteenth-century critiques of the papacy. In the case of constitutionalism, Skinner relocated the origin of the most popular forms of constitutionalism in Catholic rather than Calvinist circles.

In some sense, then, Skinner's allegiance to the traditional nomenclature of the history of ideas was actually part of his attempt decisively to shift the relations between the players. What strikes one forcibly in retrospect is the dialectical character of the book, as it moves forward in a series of steps and counter-steps in relation to existing paradigms within the history of ideas. But it also depicts the same kind of progression among the normative vocabularies that Skinner takes as the proper subject of that history. The result is a kind of split-level intellectual waltz concealed by its elegant narrative prose and indeed by its own success in making its dialectical moves part of the common currency of the history of political thought. Although my focus here is on 'scholasticism', therefore, it will be clear from what I have said that this thread cannot be isolated from the others without losing the sense of the book.

Scholasticism and liberty

Scholasticism[8] plays only a small part in the drama of liberty and virtue that occupies the first volume of *Foundations*, providing an alternative defence of liberty in the first half of the fourteenth century and later (in the figures of Savonarola and Salamonio) contributing to the survival of republican values in an age of princes.[9] Skinner began his chapter on 'Scholasticism and Liberty' with the recovery of Aristotelian moral and political thought at the university of Paris in the second half of the thirteenth century. As he argued, this made available to the Latin West a vision of politics based on the rational potentials of human nature in contrast to the prevalent Augustinian picture of the earthly city as a consequence of the corruption of human nature. The 'greatest exponent' of the new Aristotelianism was Thomas Aquinas – although Skinner said almost nothing about the way in which he integrated Aristotle into his theology or even his unfinished treatise on government, the *De regno* or *De regimine principum*, except to record the northern European, monar- chical cast of his political thought.[10] Skinner's emphasis was rather on the

---

[8] I have suggested in my introduction part of the motivation for the use of the term 'scholasticism' in Skinner's account. As a general point, I agree with Harro Höpfl (above, p. 113) that it can represent an artificial and anachronistic reification. But I do not think that the term 'scholasticism' is necessarily vicious as such, provided we understand it not as an 'ism' but as referring to the dynamic intellectual practice of the medieval universities or schools. An alternative is to follow continental usage and refer instead to 'the scholastic'. See the remarks in G. Wieland, *Ethica – scientia practica. Die Anfänge der philosophischen Ethik im 13. Jahrhundert* (Münster: Aschendorff, 1981), pp. 13–16 ('Bemerkungen zur Scholastik').
[9] Skinner, *Foundations*, I, ch. 2 *passim*; pp. 144–52.   [10] Ibid., I, p. 51.

translation of this Aristotelian political idiom to the communes of northern Italy in defence of republican liberty and the autonomy of the city-states *vis-à-vis* the empire and the church. The means of transmission were both Aquinas's Italian fellow-Dominicans, Remigio de' Girolami and Ptolemy of Lucca, and the Roman lawyers at Bologna, who 'began to incorporate the concepts and methods of Aristotelian political theory into their glosses and commentaries'.[11] In their hands, the Aristotelian emphasis on the rational potentials of human nature became a means of vindicating the claims of the people to self-government. The scholastic master of arts Marsilius of Padua and the Roman lawyer Bartolus of Sassoferrato used this republican Aristotelianism to find a new and radical solution to the problems of maintaining the liberty of the communes.[12]

I want to focus to begin with on the question of medieval scholastic political theory in general rather than the specific story about scholasticism and liberty. Skinner's account identified two key features: its Aristotelian cast and its close relations with legal discourse. To take the question of Aristotelianism first, the starting point of Skinner's analysis – the conflict between Aristotelianism and Augustinianism at the university of Paris and the role of Aquinas in the vindication of the former – was (curiously enough, perhaps) indebted to a neo-Thomist philosophical and theological perspective that makes Aquinas the central figure in Western theology for achieving a synthesis of Latin Christianity and Greek philosophy.[13] Recent work tends both to deconstruct the neo-Thomist paradigm[14] and to focus more on the institutional conditions for the reception of Aristotle (especially at the university of Paris)[15] – seeing those conditions as critical to understanding the philosophy and theology that resulted. The principal context for this reception was the expanding and developing curriculum of the faculty of arts at Oxford and Paris in the first half of the thirteenth century. But we can see this process as part of a broader 'turn to theory' in all the branches of medieval learning, including medicine, theology and law: a move away from a practice-based approach to one that can be studied and, equally importantly, taught in the increasingly formalised institutional context of the medieval university.[16] As the example of the revived study of the Roman law shows, a theoretical approach needed theoretical foundations, authoritative books (in this case the *Corpus iuris civilis*) on which to base itself. For the

---

[11] Ibid.   [12] Ibid., p. 61.

[13] The debt to Etienne Gilson is clear in the references at pp. 50–1.

[14] See the remarks – with especial reference to the work of Alain de Libera – in P. W. Rosemann, *Understanding Scholastic Thought with Foucault* (New York: St Martin's Press, 1999), pp. 2–9.

[15] See in particular O. M. Weijers, *Le maniement du savoir. Pratiques intellectuelles à l'époque des premières universités* (Turnhout: Brepols, 1996) and O. Weijers and L. Holtz (eds.), *L'enseignement des disciplines à la Faculté des arts (Paris et Oxford, XIII–XV siècles)* (Turnhout: Brepols, 1997).

[16] I borrow this analysis from Wieland, *Ethica – scientia practica*, pp. 15–18.

masters of arts, the newly translated texts of the Aristotelian corpus fulfilled this function.

As Harro Höpfl argues in his chapter in this book, the key issue *vis-à-vis* politics was the scholastic understanding of the Aristotelian corpus as *scientia* or 'science'. Here the influence of the Arab commentators on Aristotle was critical. It was the twelfth-century philosopher Ibn Rushd (Averroes) in particular who had stressed the scientific character of Aristotle's works: '[t]he Philosopher's conclusions are true and certain because they are the result of syllogistic demonstration based on causes'.[17] However, again under Arab influence, the texts that were translated in the first wave of the Aristotelian reception were, apart from the first four books of the *Nicomachean Ethics*, exclusively works of physics and metaphysics: that is, they were works of 'speculative' rather than 'practical' science. Medieval scholastics had inherited this Aristotelian distinction prior to the reception of the Aristotelian texts themselves, and had confidently put down ethics, economics and politics under the heading of practical science. But when the full texts of the *Nicomachean Ethics*, the (ps.-Aristotelian) *Economics* and the *Politics* came to be available in the second half of the thirteenth century, their interpreters had to face the problematic question of how a discipline could be both practical, concerned with the contingent particulars of action, and scientific, which to them meant conclusions demonstrated from universal principles and causes. In his commentary on *Ethics* book I, Albert the Great (Aquinas's teacher) solved the problem with a division of ethics into 'teaching' (*doctrina*, 'doctrine') and 'use'. Ethics as 'use' is the same as virtue, but 'with regard to the doctrine that considers virtue, it is a science of [virtue] and it is knowable [*scibilis*]'.[18] Aquinas in his commentary on *Ethics* book VI also argued that political science is not identical with the virtue of prudence:

> prudence does not exist purely in reason, but has something of itself in the appetite; all the things mentioned here are species of prudence insofar as they do not consist solely in reason, but have something of themselves in the appetite; for insofar as they exist purely in reason, they are called practical sciences, i.e. ethics, economics and politics.[19]

These defences of the scientific character of practical science come from commentary on the *Ethics*, a text that was officially part of the arts curriculum

---

[17] C. Lohr, 'The New Aristotle and "Science" in the Paris Arts Faculty (1255)', in Weijers and Holtz, *L'enseignement des disciplines*, 251–70, at 260–1; cf. pp. 262–3 for the Latin reception of the Averroist model.

[18] Albertus Magnus, *Ethicorum libri X*, in *Opera omnia* (Lyons, 1651), t. IV, tract. I, ch. 2 ('Can there be a science of virtue?'). Cf. the discussion in Wieland, *Ethica*, pp. 116–17.

[19] Thomas Aquinas *Sententia libri ethicorum*, in *Opera omnia iussu Leonis XIII P.M. edita*, t. 47.2 (Rome, 1969), p. 357. Aquinas had earlier (p. 347) specified that prudence is a virtue of the 'opinionative' faculty, since both opinion and prudence concern 'things that can be otherwise', i.e. non-universals. Thus, although prudence is an intellectual virtue, it does not exist purely as a matter of reason, like an art or a science, but requires in addition 'rectitude of the appetite'.

at Paris. Aristotle's *Politics* never achieved this status. None the less it was intensively studied and commented on there, as recent work has shown.[20] In a move that would be crucial for the future course of scholastic political thought, Aquinas incorporated extensive material from both the *Ethics* and the *Politics* into the second part of his *Summa theologiae*, which considers human action. For Aquinas, as for most of his thirteenth-century contemporaries, theology was a science: in so far as it concerns God, a speculative science; in so far as it considers human actions, a practical science.[21] Aristotle's work on politics, then, gave Aquinas the possibility of a scientific understanding of human communities and human law deriving from the nature of their constituent human beings. In his political treatise the *De regno*, this enabled him to develop a rationally demonstrable, causal analysis of the power of the prince and the nature of his government, in place of the reflective and moral practice-orientated 'mirror for princes' that had hitherto been the norm.[22] In the *Summa* it profoundly shaped his understanding of natural law and its relationship to human law and the virtues of justice and political prudence. The legacy of this for sixteenth-century scholastics was to allow them to raise explicitly political questions within the theology curriculum as part of the study of theology, the master-science of human actions.

The second key aspect of scholastic political thought identified by Skinner was its close relationship with the discipline of law, both in method and in content. Like the masters of arts, Roman lawyers (or at least some of them) used the model of science as a knowledge based on causes, understood law as a practical science, and incorporated some of the substantive principles of Aristotelian politics, for example that man is by nature a political animal, into their work.[23] We should not think of this as a one-way process, however: scholastic philosophers and theologians were heavily influenced in their turn by the concepts and vocabulary of legal discourse. In the Italian context, Skinner's focus was on Roman law; but there was also considerable exchange between scholastic theologians and canon lawyers, particularly as they wrestled with questions of the nature of the church and its government. It was principally from canon law, for example, that scholastic theologians gained the idea of the *universitas* or corporate body, which crucially extended the range of legal and political agents beyond the natural individuals of Aristotelian political science to include the

---

[20] The key work is Christoph Flüeler, *Rezeption und Interpretation der Aristotelischen Politica im späten Mittelalter*, 2 vols. (Amsterdam-Philadelphia: B. R. Grüner, 1992).

[21] Thomas Aquinas, *Summa theologiae*, in *Opera omnia iussu Leonis XIII P. M. edita*, t. 4 (Rome, 1888), pars prima, q. 1, a. 2 and a. 4.

[22] J. Miethke, *De potestate papae. Die päpstliche Amstcompetenz im Widerstreit der politischen Theorie von Thomas von Aquin bis Wilhelm von Ockham* (Tübingen: Mohr Siebeck, 2000), pp. 31–45.

[23] A good discussion can be found in J. Canning, *The Political Thought of Baldus de Ubaldis* (Cambridge: Cambridge University Press, 1987), pp. 159–84.

church and the political community.[24] One vitally important dimension of this legal or juridical cast was, however, entirely left aside in *Foundations*, although it was at the centre of the life both of the university of Paris and of the northern Italian cities in the period in question. This was the impact upon the scholastic vocabulary of politics of the so-called 'poverty controversy', the extended and destructive wrangle over the possibility – both legal and moral – of living the life of supreme poverty, which the Franciscans claimed to do in imitation of Christ. Thus, simultaneously with the reception of the Aristotelian understanding of human nature and its relation to political structures came the question of the relation of Christ and his life to the legal structures of the Roman empire: property and jurisdiction. The debate was, at one level, intricately legalistic in its exhaustive analysis of the different legal relations that human beings can be in with regard to other human beings and to goods. But it was forced to transcend the lawyers' perspective in so far as what was being argued over was the possibility of living *outside* such legal relations. The end result was, again, a recourse to human nature and its natural potentials, but this time cast in the juridical terms of *dominium* and rights – '*licit* powers', *potestates licitae*, as William of Ockham famously described them.[25] This dual heritage would be critical to the political thought of the second scholastic that Skinner discussed in volume II of *Foundations*.

Returning now to the question of scholasticism and liberty, Skinner's more recent lines of inquiry into republican liberty have bypassed the medieval scholastics almost entirely. He has seen the Aristotelian tradition as a tradition of positive liberty, stemming from one of its key premises ('taken up in particular by scholastic political philosophy', with the example of Aquinas), that 'the human animal is *naturale sociale et politicum*'.[26] Instead Skinner has stressed the Roman inheritance of republican thought: Cicero, Sallust and classical Roman law. But the sharp distinction this suggests between Roman law and scholasticism has left him open to the charge of ignoring the influence of legal thought on scholastic political Aristotelianism, which is not always or necessarily so 'eudaimonistic' as his brief characterisation suggests – even in Aquinas (not to mention Marsilius).[27] While Skinner has examined in detail

---

[24] The canon-law understanding and application of corporation theory to the church is classically discussed in Brian Tierney, *Foundations of the Conciliar Theory* (Cambridge: Cambridge University Press, 1955).

[25] See *The work of ninety days*, ch. 2, tr. in A. S. McGrade and J. Kilcullen (eds.), *William of Ockham: A letter to the Friars Minor and Other Writings* (Cambridge: Cambridge University Press, 1995), p. 24.

[26] Quentin Skinner, 'The Republican Ideal of Political Liberty', in G. Bock, Quentin Skinner and M. Viroli (eds.), *Machiavelli and Republicanism* (Cambridge: Cambridge University Press, 1990), pp. 293–309, at 296.

[27] See K. Übl, *Engelbert von Admont. Ein Gelehrter im Spannungsfeld zwischen Aristotelismus und christliche Überlieferung* (Vienna: Oldenbourg, 2000), pp. 119–21. However, the question of what constitutes 'political Aristotelianism', at least for the medieval period, is heavily debated. The account offered by Cary Nederman, 'The meaning of "Aristotelianism" in medieval moral

the classical texts of Roman law on liberty and servitude, he has not returned to any extensive consideration of how medieval and Renaissance Roman lawyers may themselves have understood and used those texts, nor to the medieval scholastics. To that extent the possibilities offered by the second chapter of *Foundations* for a rapprochement between republicanism and Aristotelianism remain open.[28]

Constitutionalism and the Counter-Reformation

The central story of the second volume of *Foundations* is clear and powerful. Luther's attack on the papacy fundamentally redrew the boundaries between spiritual and temporal. The resultant understanding of the temporal sphere as the kingdom of law, coupled with a particular interpretation of Romans 13.1 ('the powers that be are ordained of God'), introduced a new element of divine-right absolutism into European political thought. Against this the political theorists of the Counter-Reformation – principally the scholastics of the Iberian univer- sities and the Jesuit colleges – pitted the Catholic emphasis on human nature and its possibilities independently of grace, characteristically expressed by the scholastics in their revived and rearticulated Thomist language of natural law. This heritage enabled Catholic political theorists to build up the political com- munity from nature and to derive the ruler's power from the human community rather than immediately from God, and therefore to put a natural limit on legis- lation and the power of the prince. Hence Skinner's title for the central section of the second volume: 'Constitutionalism and the Counter-reformation'. As a natural-law theory of the state, this form of argument was taken up and devel- oped by the great seventeenth-century theorists of state sovereignty, Grotius, Hobbes and Pufendorf. But as a theory of popular sovereignty it was appropri- ated and radicalised in the context of the wars of religion that beset Europe from the mid-sixteenth to the mid-seventeenth century. Detached from its scholastic origins it was available to and employed by Catholic and Calvinist revolution- aries alike, and ultimately by the last of their line, John Locke. Paradoxically,

---

and political thought' (*Journal of the History of Ideas* 57 (1996), pp. 563–85), that 'Aristotelian- ism' necessarily entails a deep connection between the human good and the political order, fits well with Skinner's more recent approach. But then Nederman's position has the acknowledged, but still odd consequence that Marsilius of Padua, whose text is saturated with Aristotle citations, is not really an Aristotelian at all: ibid., pp. 583–4.

[28] The chapter entitled 'The Rediscovery of Republican Values', in Quentin Skinner, *Visions of Pol- itics*, 3 vols. (Cambridge: Cambridge University Press, 2002), II: *Renaissance Virtues*, pp. 10–38, contains a revised account of Aquinas's and other medieval scholastics' political thought which strongly stresses the elements of 'mixed constitution', election, and the goals of unity, justice and peace to provide a 'framework of security' for the pursuit of the good life (ibid., pp. 31–7), as well as their appreciation of the force of republican arguments. However, the following chap- ter, 'Lorenzetti and the Portrayal of Virtuous Government', maintains a clear contrast between early republicanism and Thomist Aristotelianism. Skinner says very little in either chapter about the good life and the human good itself, so it is not clear how 'eudaimonism' fits into these arguments.

then, the giants of seventeenth-century Protestant political theory rest on the shoulders of firm defenders of the papacy.

In a move typical of the way in which the overall narrative of *Foundations* progresses, Skinner started this story by going backwards. In the first chapter of the section, 'The background of constitutionalism', Skinner located the seeds of constitutionalism in the conciliar proposals of the later middle ages: the theory – if we want to reify it as such[29] – that power in the church is located ultimately in the body of the church, represented by a general council, rather than it its head, the pope, and that *in extremis* the council has the power to depose a theologically deviant, dangerous or simply 'useless' pope. In approaching the political thought of the sixteenth century from this direction, and in so far as his conclusion to the third section of the volume took the story into the seventeenth century by stressing Locke's intellectual debts to these figures, Skinner was (and acknowledged that he was)[30] to some extent retreading the 'road from Constance to 1688': the thesis that the constitutional settlement of the Glorious Revolution had its roots in a constitutional analysis of the church propounded in the late middle ages. Originating with the work of John Neville Figgis and developed by his pupil Harold Laski (to whom we owe the tag), this line of argument had more recently been articulated by James Burns and Francis Oakley. Indeed Oakley has quite lately referred to Skinner in *Foundations* as 'mainstreaming' his own theory.[31]

This 'continuity thesis' has latterly been dubbed the 'neo-Figgisite orthodoxy'[32] and attacked by Cary Nederman from the point of view of a historian of medieval political thought, provoking a debate with Oakley in the pages of the journal *History of Political Thought*. According to Nederman, the 'constitutionalism' of the conciliarists is something essentially 'medieval', organic in its understanding of the relationship between the different elements of a community, and as such something fundamentally different from the 'constitutionalism' of, for example, Locke, which is 'modern' in the sense of being based on individual rights and statutory limitations of different powers.[33] There is no direct road, that is, from Constance to 1688. Whatever we make of this argument,

---

[29] Cf. Constantin Fasolt, *Council and Hierarchy: the Political Thought of William Durant the Younger* (Cambridge: Cambridge University Press, 1991), p. 318: 'no such thing as the conciliar theory was ever a historical reality'.

[30] Skinner, *Foundations*, II, p. 123; Skinner insisted, however, on the Roman law element as well as the conciliarist.

[31] F. Oakley, 'Nederman, Gerson, Conciliar Theory and Constitutionalism: *Sed contra*', *History of Political Thought* 16 (1995), pp. 1–19, at 3; F. Oakley, '"Anxieties of Influence": Skinner, Figgis, Conciliarism and Early Modern Constitutionalism', *Past and Present* 151 (1996), pp. 60–110, at 77.

[32] Questionably so: see below, p. 147.

[33] C. Nederman, 'Conciliarism and Constitutionalism: Jean Gerson and Medieval Political Thought', *History of European Ideas* 12 (1990), pp. 189–209, at 193, gives a list of requirements for 'modern' constitutionalism; C. Nederman, 'Constitutionalism – Medieval and Modern:

it undoubtedly calls into question any uncritical usage of the term 'constitutionalism' *vis-à-vis* these authors. Oakley suggests that we can take it broadly as any political arrangement involving the governed as well as the governors, while Nederman draws to his side Constantin Fasolt's conclusions concerning the fourteenth-century (and so 'medieval') conciliarist William Durant the Younger: the so-called 'conciliarist' and 'papalist' position are not two opposed theories of the church, but two parts of an understanding of the community which both involves and transcends the two aspects, council and hierarchy.[34] Fasolt's historically engaged and subtle analysis offers, however, another perspective: that for all the scholastic writers with whom we are concerned, we might do better to abandon these dualisms altogether. In the authors we are considering, the dynamics of legitimate *potestas* run both up and down, from the individual and/or the community to the head and back again, in different contexts and depending on what needs to be done or what aspect is in question. It is a distinctive way of thinking about the interlocking and conflicting powers and agency of the different bodies and individuals that make up human life in common, be this the life of the political community or the life of the church.

Returning to the sixteenth- and early seventeenth-century scholastics who are the subject of Skinner's analysis (and whose position between 'medieval' and 'modern' is an issue to which I shall return in conclusion), I suggest that their political theory both resists and is obscured by the antithesis between 'constitutionalism' and 'absolutism' – which moreover renders the debate interminable. Take, for example, the treatment of Suárez in *The Cambridge History of Political Thought 1450–1700*: was he ultimately an absolutist, even if he 'accommodated significant aspects of the constitutionalist tradition' (Howell Lloyd), or did he on the contrary tend to endorse 'contractarian doctrines of resistance' (John Salmon)?[35] The answer is, both; or, better, neither. Most of the Spanish scholastics have a strong conception both of the extent of royal power and of the rights of individuals and communities: they are two sides of the same coin. And in fact Skinner himself was quite well aware that scholastic political thought strains at his categories of analysis. His final chapter in the central section is called 'The limits of constitutionalism', and shows how their thinking contains elements of both 'radicalism' (especially in the concept of individual rights) and 'absolutism'; its heirs are both Mariana and Buchanan (the radical side) and 'the modern natural-law theory of the state' in Grotius, Hobbes and Pufendorf (which tends to absolutism). The chapter might perhaps

against Neo-Figgisite Orthodoxy', *History of Political Thought* 17 (1996), pp. 179–94, develops these themes.
[34] See Fasolt, *Council and Hierarchy*, introduction (pp. 1–25); cited by Nederman, 'Constitutionalism – Medieval and Modern', pp. 185–6.
[35] H. A. Lloyd, 'Constitutionalism', and J. H. M. Salmon, 'Catholic Resistance Theory', both in Burns, *Cambridge History*, pp. 254–97, at 296–7; and pp. 219–53, at 238–9.

better have been called 'The limits of "constitutionalism"' – at least in this context.

Laying aside these questions for the present, however, Skinner's rich and multifaceted analysis is in many ways acute and convincing, and powerfully captures and motivates some of the most prominent motifs in their thinking.[36] There is no doubt that the question of what political positions were entailed by Catholic religious allegiances was of central concern to these scholastic theologians, who were many of them not simply academics but employed by princes and other nobility in positions as confessors and political advisers. It is true that the arguments are not always so clear cut as Skinner suggests. In the case of Francisco de Vitoria, for example, Skinner acknowledges that his views on the origins of royal power are 'curiously similar' to those of the Lutherans, but he does not make it sufficiently clear that this is because it is not the divine-right implications of the apostates that disturb Vitoria, but the anarchic implications of 'evangelical liberty'.[37] Moreover one should always remember that the main lines of sixteenth-century scholastic political thought predate the Reformation, being set by the Italian Dominican Tommaso de Vio, Cardinal Cajetan, in his exchange with the Sorbonne theologian Jacques Almain over the question of power within the church.[38] It is church reform, not counter-reform, which was the original context for the defining motifs of this way of thinking: the argument for the natural and human origins of political communities and power within them is not in order to combat a rival understanding of political power, but the understanding of the church as a political community and of power within it as stemming from the community rather than from God. It is this that prompted Cajetan to agree with Almain in positing no difference in the source of power, whatever the superficial constitution of a political community – even a divinely instituted monarchy – and it is this that is the underlying target of Vitoria's attack.[39] Nevertheless, it is still open to Skinner to argue – and quite correctly in my view – that these same lines of thinking could be, and were, effectively redeployed against the heretics.

One of the effects, however, of this Counter-Reformation perspective on the second scholastic is that Skinner tends to treat the school as homogeneous.[40]

---

[36] For a recent restatement of Skinner's case, see M. Walther, 'Potestas multitudinis bei Suárez und potentia multitudinis bei Spinoza', in F. Grünert and K. Seelmann (eds.), *Die Ordnung der Praxis. Neue Studien zur spanische Spätscholastik* (Tübingen: Niemeyer, 2001), pp. 281–97, at 281–2.

[37] Skinner, *Foundations*, II, p. 140; Francisco de Vitoria, *On Civil Power*, transl. in *Vitoria: Political Writings*, ed. A. Pagden and J. Lawrance (Cambridge: Cambridge University Press, 1991), p. 16.

[38] This exchange has now been translated into English in J. Burns and T. M. Izbicki (eds.), *Conciliarism and Papalism* (Cambridge: Cambridge University Press, 1997).

[39] As is apparent from Vitoria's commentary on the *Summa theologiae*, 1a2ae q. 90 a. 3, in *Francisco de Vitoria. Comentario al tratado de la ley*, ed. V. Beltrán de Heredia (Madrid: CSIC, 1952).

[40] Skinner, *Foundations*, II, p. 138: 'remarkably homogeneous outlook'.

Here again he is clearly aware of the strain that this imposes in some respects, but he none the less he sees the members of the school as broadly putting forward the same pattern of political argument. This is certainly justified up to a point. Skinner called his book *The Foundations of Modern Political Thought*: his enterprise was not to give an exhaustive account of the second scholastic, but to identify its predominant features, the unarguably characteristic linguistic formulations, motifs and argumentative strategies that it bequeathed to the seventeenth century and beyond. Compare the summary of scholastic political thought given by Filmer in his *Patriarcha*, and we see that contemporaries too felt that they could identify with confidence the broad outlines of the scholastic 'tenet'.[41] Furthermore, Skinner's approach has the merit of taking seriously the entirety of the second scholastic from Vitoria to Suárez and integrating it fully within a Europe-wide history of political thought, contrary to the tendency within Anglo-American historiography to discuss only those aspects and figures (principally the later Jesuits, and especially Suárez because of his role in the controversy with James VI and I) that impinge upon a basically northern European and indeed Atlantic perspective on the political thought of the early-modern period. The *Cambridge History* mentioned above aptly demonstrates the impoverishment of thinking on the second scholastic within anglophone circles in the years following *Foundations*: the Iberian peninsula receives hardly any attention at all, as Burns acknowledges in his introduction with little apparent regret.[42]

None the less, this unification of the school in terms of its fundamental political motifs and their motivation has its drawbacks. There are major differences between the authors and in particular between the Dominican and the Jesuit members of the school: the context (both political and institutional), the aims and the theology had important differences. As I have indicated, Skinner does take some account of this. But those distinctions that he draws do not affect the substance of his discussion. Specifically – and this will be the focus of the rest of this paper – to take Suárez as in some sense a spokesperson[43] elides what I am tempted, in view of this volume, to call 'the Dominican moment', roughly coinciding with the reign of Charles V: the period in which principally Dominican theologians engaged simultaneously with questions of church reform and counter-reform, extra-European and intra-European empire. Their

---

[41] 'Mankind is naturally endowed with and born with freedom from all subjection, and at liberty to choose what form of government it please, and that the power which any one man hath over others was at the first by human right bestowed according to the discretion of the multitude': Sir Robert Filmer, *Patriarcha and other writings*, ed. Johann P. Sommerville (Cambridge: Cambridge University Press, 1991), p. 2.

[42] Burns, *Cambridge History*, p. 5. It is a merit of his introduction, however, that he squarely and honestly confronts the issue of anglocentrism.

[43] Skinner, *Foundations*, II, p. 138.

understanding of the political commonwealth was forged with all these different dimensions in view, not simply the necessity of combating an heretical understanding of political power or of the church. Precisely by – quite rightly – giving the second scholastic such a central place in European political thought, and precisely by insisting that we include Vitoria and Soto in this perspective as well as the Jesuits Molina and Suárez, Skinner sidelined the extra-European dimension of their thought and did not directly address the question of empire at all. Equally, by subordinating or even reducing the issue of the church to a question of constitutionalism versus absolutism in church government[44] (parallel with the question over secular government), he gave little consideration to the supranational dimension of this element of their thinking as well.

Globally speaking, then, Skinner's approach has the effect of marginalising the universalist elements of second scholastic political thought, by which I mean precisely those aspects that surpass the limits of the modern state, which is – according to the second and third criteria mentioned at the outset of this paper – by definition particularist and territorial. This is not to say that he ignores them completely. His scrupulous discussion covers both their attitude towards the American Indians and their understanding of the *ius gentium* ('international law'). But Vitoria's discussion of the American Indians is seen only as a part of the more general Counter-Reformation inflection of his theology and its rebuttal of the heretical thesis of *dominium* founded upon grace. Equally, the *ius gentium* is introduced in the course of discussing the revival of Thomist natural law theory, not overseas expansion, and while Skinner recognises that Vitoria held a less positivist view of international law than the later Jesuits, he does not examine its context or implications, concentrating instead on the development towards Suárez and the modern theory of international law as a positive law between sovereign states. The universalist elements, then, are there as addenda, a function of a Counter-Reformation constitutionalism that is essentially a theory of government within a single commonwealth, rather than partly constitutive of that theory.

Now one could argue that here again the governing metaphor of 'foundations' allowed Skinner to follow just this procedure. Under its protection, he was free to pick and choose which bits of what authors or movements constitute 'foundations' of modern political thought, seen as the theory of the modern state, and leave behind those bits that do not seem to go in that direction or just mention them as additional aspects. But what I am concerned to argue here is that this misrepresents the thought of the second scholastic. It was born out of a period in which the boundaries of the modern state were not yet fixed. The Habsburg empire was being fought over both inside and outside Europe. The relationship

---

[44] For example, Skinner's discussion of Ockham's analysis of the papacy is cast throughout in terms of a 'constitutional' as opposed to an 'absolute' monarchy, rather than addressing the different *kind* of community that Ockham thought the church to be: Skinner, *Foundations*, II, p. 38.

between national monarchies and church was in question. The rights of individuals within and outside these communities were in question too. The important thing about the theorists of the second scholastic, especially its Dominican members, is that they did not think about these questions independently of each other.

Let me fill that out. One of the surprising things about the handling of scholastics in volume II as opposed to volume I is that whereas in the latter the local Italian identity and political allegiances of the authors in question are central to the story, in the former Skinner gives very little attention to the peculiarly Spanish circumstances surrounding and involving the first members of the school of Salamanca. He highlights, rightly, the Parisian training of both Vitoria and Soto and the extent to which they took the lessons of Almain back to Spain with them. And yet Vitoria returned to Spain in 1524 and spent two years at the Dominican convent in Valladolid, one of the towns at the centre of the revolt of the *comuneros* against the new government of Charles V, a revolt generated partly by concerns over Spain's place within the new dimensions of the Habsburg empire and the refusal to be governed by foreigners.[45] Empire within Europe was therefore a central issue from the start, especially given the emphasis within Spanish humanist circles around Charles V on celebrating an idea of renewed world empire, a new Rome.[46] In respect of empire outside Europe, the Dominicans Vitoria, Soto, Melchor Cano, Bartolomé Carranza and others inherited the critique of Spanish conquistador activity begun by the Dominican missionary Antonio de Montesinos in Hispaniola in 1512 and continued – though without explicit reference to the Indies – by Cardinal Cajetan in his commentary on question 66 of the *Secunda secundae*, a key text for the Spanish school.[47] On the question of relations between empire and church, Vitoria had hardly taken up his chair at the University of Salamanca when Charles V's troops sacked Rome in 1527; and it was Charles again who was the prime mover in calling for a general council to address the problems of the Reformation.[48]

---

[45] The context of the *comuneros* revolt is brought out by J. A. Fernández-Santamaría, *The State, War and Peace: Spanish Political Thought in the Renaissance, 1516–1559* (Cambridge: Cambridge University Press, 1977), in his discussion of Vitoria at pp. 54–87. It is this – the fear of popular uprising – that offers at least part of the explanation for Vitoria's more divine-right monarchism in the lecture *On Civil Power*. However, Fernández-Santamaría's book came too late for Skinner fully to make use of it, which he regrets: Skinner, *Foundations*, II, p. 138n.

[46] See A. R. D. Pagden, *Lords of all the World: Ideologies of Empire in Spain, Britain and France c.1500–c.1800* (New Haven: Yale University Press, 1995), pp. 40–3.

[47] Las Casas reported that Cajetan's commentary on this locus, with its famous insistence that taking the possessions of infidels who had never been subject to Christian rule was nothing more that *magna latrocinia* ('great robberies', from Augustine) and liable to restitution, was written as a direct response to news of the Indies: see J. Höffner, *Kolonialismus und Evangelium. Spanische Kolonialethik im goldenen Zeitalter* (Trier: Paulinus Verlag, 1969), p. 251.

[48] Skinner acknowledges the more conciliarist dimensions of Vitoria's thought (as opposed to the Jesuits'), though he does not set this in the Spanish context: Skinner, *Foundations*, II, p. 145.

Spanish scholastics addressed these interlocking problems both in their occasional *relectiones* and in systematic discussions embedded throughout their voluminous commentaries on Aquinas's questions on the laws and on justice and right. From Aquinas they inherited the idea of natural law as a way to gain a critical understanding of contemporary political reality through being able causally to account for the legitimacy of human political arrangements. Key to their enterprise, however, was the idea not merely of natural law but of natural subjective rights – an element outside the resources of strictly Thomist discourse, but one which they made distinctively their own: partly through their exposure to the language of Almain at Paris, partly by appropriating the *via moderna* discussion of *dominium* from its home in commentary on the *Sentences* book IV, distinction 15, to Aquinas's question 62 of the *Secunda secundae*. Skinner did not see rights as central to the political thought of the scholastic: he put them down as part of its 'radical' edge, and did not really allow that the Dominicans made use of the concept at all.[49] But a renewed examination of the texts reveals that this is not the case. For Vitoria and Soto just as for Suárez and indeed for Ockham – whatever their differences – natural rights are the juridical expression and claim of the natural potentialities of human beings under natural law, and they allow human beings to be juridically creative in their own right: to create new structures not immediately given in natural law. To understand rights is to understand what structures they can have created and how to recognise them. They do not necessarily either limit rulers' powers (thus making them by definition part of the 'radical' side of scholastic thinking) or support them (feeding into its 'absolutist' strand): they can go both ways. In this way they function more as a kind of political hermeneutic than as a specific political doctrine. A classic case is Vitoria's handling of the question of the American Indians: they are humans, therefore they have *dominium*, therefore their jurisdictions and properties are legitimate jurisdiction and property.[50] Again, from Soto: all individuals have the natural right to physical and moral well-being. It is in order to exercise it that they form a political community; that community then necessarily transfers this right or 'faculty' to a ruler, who will exercise the entire power of the community for the common good.[51] But a political community beyond a certain size can neither convene to transfer its power, nor can its ruler carry out the function for which it was created.[52] The implication is that an empire can only be a conglomeration of separately formed, territorially limited commonwealths: there is no political unit called 'empire' that can be a legitimate holder of political power.

[49] Skinner, *Foundations*, II, p. 176.
[50] Vitoria, *On the American Indians* 1.4–6, in *Vitoria*, ed. Pagden and Lawrance, pp. 247–51.
[51] Domingo de Soto, *De justitia et jure. De la justicia y del derecho* (bilingual Latin-Spanish edition, Madrid: Instituto de Estudios Políticos, 1967), book IV, q. 4, a. 1, p. 302, col. 1.
[52] Soto, *De justitia et jure*, book IV, q. 4, a. 2, p. 304, cols. 1–2.

These conclusions, which contain the essence of Soto's theory of the genesis of the commonwealth and the origin of political power, are formulated in two questions entitled 'Is any man lord of all the world?' and 'Is the emperor lord of the world?' That is, what we might call Soto's 'political theory' is formed not just as a deduction from Thomist natural law principles, or in response to an heretical understanding of government – though it certainly involves that – but as part of a meditation on structures and activities that transcend the boundaries of the individual commonwealth. And this brings me on to the second major strategy of Dominican political reflection, intimately connected with the first: the Dominican habit of 'cross-referencing' the phenomena with which they were presented, understanding the juridical status of one with reference to that of another, and so involving all the dimensions of their political meditation in a kind of mutual implication. A critical grasp of extra-European juridical structures and the relations between them involves a similarly critical grasp of their European counterparts. So, to continue with Vitoria's lecture on the American Indians: having established on natural-law principles that they are human, he then faces the classic objection that they do not look very human to us. His reply is to insist that this is an accident of upbringing, not an essential difference, and to confirm this he refers to his own Spain: 'Even among us we see many peasants who are little different from brute animals.'[53] He also concludes that the Europeans have no just cause to invade American commonwealths purely on the grounds that they are offending against natural law: for otherwise 'the king of France has a perfect right to conquer Italy'.[54] On the issue of relations between temporal commonwealths and the church, Vitoria argues for the difference between them on grounds taken from Aristotle and Aquinas, but supplements his explanation with the remark that therefore 'it is not correct to think of civil and spiritual powers as two disparate and distinct commonwealths, like England and France'.[55]

One of the most telling examples of this practice of cross-reference was the controversy generated within the school by Vitoria's invocation of the *ius communicandi* or 'right of communication' in support of European travel to and through the New World. As we have seen, he formally recognises American Indian political structures as equivalent in nature and juridical status to those of Europe. But he uses the *ius communicandi* to argue that these structures cannot exclude travellers from other countries, who must (if they come in peace) be allowed passage and also given the right of citizenship if they decide

---

[53] Vitoria, *On the American Indians*, 1.5, in *Vitoria*, ed. Pagden and Lawrance, p. 250.

[54] Vitoria, *On Dietary Laws, or Self-Restraint*, 1.5, in *Vitoria*, ed. Pagden and Lawrance, p. 225. As the note there explains, this involves a joke in questionable taste about the sexual predilections of the Italians and an indirect reference to the Sack of Rome.

[55] Vitoria, *Relection I On the Power of the Church*, 5.6, in *Vitoria*, ed. Pagden and Lawrance, p. 90.

to stay.[56] Vitoria's pupil Melchor Cano made a classic Vitorian move in relating Vitoria's argument to the European context: the Spanish come to the Indies not as travellers but as invaders, 'and the Spanish would not tolerate this at the hands of the French'.[57] But Vitoria's closest associate Soto turned the argument back in a different way. In his *Deliberation in the cause of the poor*, Soto's principal thesis concerned internal migration and the right of cities within Spain to exclude travelling mendicants. His first argument against this right was the natural right of travel: 'by natural law and the law of nations highways and cities lie open to all indifferently'.[58] His third was that the kingdom constitutes one body, in which there are wealthier and poorer regions, and that (as members of the same body) the wealthier cannot bar the poor from elsewhere.[59] But he developed this point about the unity of the body of the realm to argue not just for the unity of all Christians in one body – a conclusion from St Paul, and therefore of divine law – but ('if we refer the matter higher, to natural law') for the conjunction of all humanity in the same nature: 'so that, unless they were our enemies, or we feared some detriment to our faith from them, it would not be rightful [*fas*] to eject even infidel mendicants from our commonwealth'.[60]

As we have seen, Vitoria's (and, to some extent, Soto's) position was challenged even within their own Dominican circle. Beyond it, the Jesuit Luis de Molina definitively rejected the position that a breach of the *ius communicandi* constitutes grounds for a just war: any commonwealth may licitly forbid access, commerce and the use of its assets (e.g. harbours, rivers, mines) to strangers – all the more so if these strangers appear to be more powerful than it is and might be a threat in future (although this is not a necessary condition).[61] But it would be wrong to see the later generations of the school of Salamanca in terms of a generalised shift in their theory towards positivism in the field of the *ius gentium* and (in parallel) towards legal voluntarism and absolutism within political commonwealths. Although some of these traits are present in Suárez – and not unambiguously, as I have hinted – the position of his *De legibus*

---

[56] Vitoria, *On the American Indians*, 3.1, in Pagden and Lawrance, *Vitoria*, pp. 278–84.

[57] Melchor Cano, *De dominio indorum*: Apéndice II in L. Pereña et al. (eds.), *Juan de la Peña. De bello contra insulanos* (Madrid: CSIC, 1982), p. 579; discussed in comparison with Vitoria by M. Delgado, 'Die Zustimmung des Volkes in der politischen Theorie von Francisco de Vitoria, Bartolomé de las Casas und Francisco Suárez', in Grünert and Seelmann, *Die Ordnung der Praxis*, pp. 157–81, at 175.

[58] Domingo de Soto, *In causa pauperum deliberatio* (ed. together with his *Relectio de ratione tegendi et detegendi secretum* (Salamanca, 1566)), fo. 102.

[59] Ibid., fo. 103.

[60] Ibid. Interestingly, this precise point does not appear in Soto's vernacular version of this treatise, perhaps indicating its controversial nature: see his *Deliberación en la causa de los pobres*, ed. Felix Santolaria Sierra, *El gran debate sobre los pobres en el siglo XVI. Domingo de Soto y Juan de Robles 1545* (Barcelona: Ariel, 2003), p. 65.

[61] Luis De Molina, *De iustitia et iure*, q. 40 'De bello' (bilingual Latin-Spanish edn. in M. Fraga Iribarne, *Luis de Molina y el derecho de la guerra* (Madrid: CSIC, 1947), Apéndice I), disp. 105, pp. 335–9. See the discussion in D. Janssen, 'Die Theorie des gerechten Krieges im Denken des Francisco de Vitoria' in Grünert and Seelmann, *Die Ordnung der Praxis*, pp. 205–43, at 231.

as some kind of 'culmination' of the political meditation of the school should not lead us to ignore alternative (and still under-explored) avenues offered by later Jesuit writers.[62] Nevertheless, the purpose of this discussion has been to highlight the distinctive theoretical achievements of the first generation of the school, which, precisely in developing an understanding of the territoriality of political power, developed at the same time and as part of it the understanding that political commonwealths are not entirely separate, juridically 'sealed' entities, exclusive and exhaustive of human community.

This extensive understanding of the natural communication of humanity and the resulting 'porosity' of commonwealths does not fit happily into Skinner's story of 'the acquisition of the modern concept of the State'. Nor does it fit happily into the development of the 'modern "liberal" theory of constitutionalism' that he attributes to the scholastics' radical heirs, which – in the hands of its more recent proponents – is essentially a theory of the internal arrangements of a sovereign state. The 'neo-Figgisite orthodoxy' is a more parochial and thinned-down version of Figgis's own thesis, in which the Jesuit insistence upon the external and supranational communities of the Catholic church and of universal human society was a key part of the internal constitutionalist story.[63] But if it does not belong to either of these modes of political modernity, what place does it have in the foundations of modern political thought? Two possible answers suggest themselves. The first is that this distinctive form of political meditation belongs to an 'interim period' between medieval and modern, after the demise of medieval universalism but before the enshrinement of the modern system of nation states, symbolised by the treaty of Westphalia of 1648. It is thus not part of the foundations of modern political thought, but is instead a resource for postmodern political and international thought, seeking to overcome the limitations and excesses of the nation-state system and the impermeable theoretical boundary between 'inside' and 'outside' that it carries with it.[64] But a second answer is to suggest that the symbolic force of the treaty of Westphalia is itself

---

[62] J.-F. Courtine, *Nature et empire de la loi. Études suaréziennes* (Paris: Vrin, 1999), esp. ch. 2, offers an analysis of Suárez's political thought in terms of the Jesuit shift away from the authentically Thomist anthropology of Vitoria and Soto, underpinning a more voluntarist and positivist understanding of law. Similar lines of thought, developing the Augustinian theme, can be found in D. Ferraro, *Itinerari del volontarismo. Teologia e politica al tempo di Luis de León* (Milan: FrancoAngeli, 1995). For a detailed new study with a completely different approach, see H. Höpfl, *Jesuit Political Thought: the Society of Jesus and the State, c. 1540–1630* (Cambridge: Cambridge University Press, 2004).

[63] See J. N. Figgis, *Studies of Political Thought from Gerson to Grotius, 1414–1625*, 2nd edn. (Cambridge: Cambridge University Press, 1923), lecture VI ('The Jesuits') *passim* and lecture VII ('The Netherlands revolt'), esp. p. 186 (Grotius and the Jesuits against, in the first place, 'the radical separateness of states'). See also his lecture 'On some political theories of the early Jesuits', in *Transactions of the Royal Historical Society* NS 11 (1897), pp. 89–112.

[64] See for example R. B. J. Walker, *Inside/Outside: International Relations as Political Theory* (Cambridge: Cambridge University Press, 1993); cf. the thoughtful discussion in R. Specht, 'Spanisches Naturrecht: Klassik und Gegenwart', *Zeitschrift für philosophische Forschung* 41 (1987), pp. 169–82.

part of a process of enshrinement of the nation-state system which is actually quite recent, and which serves to mask the presence of more pluralistic and open systems of government operating in large parts of the world throughout the early-modern and modern periods.[65] In this perspective, the political meditation of the second scholastic is as much a part of the foundations of modern political thought as the acquisition of the concept of the state or of liberal constitutionalism. Either way the conclusion seems clear: we do ourselves a grave disservice if we write these authors out of our histories of political thought. I have argued for a shift in the balance of Skinner's interpretation, but the fact remains that, in a book called *The Foundations of Modern Political Thought*, they are richly and centrally there.

---

[65] See James Tully, *Strange Multiplicity: Constitutionalism in an Age of Diversity* (Cambridge: Cambridge University Press, 1999) and *Understanding Imperialism Today* (Cambridge: Cambridge University Press forthcoming), esp. section 4.

'So meerly humane': theories of resistance in early-modern Europe

Martin van Gelderen

> It is time, my lords, to conclude, for I have talked for much longer than I believed I would. And now you clearly see, that the Sovereign Magistrate, whichever title he has been given, has not been sent from Heaven, but is established by the common consent of the Citizens; that, if he wants to act in a way that is worthy of a Prince or Magistrate, he should recognise himself to stand under all Laws; that he cannot wield his Power at will, but as required by the Public Good; and that if he does otherwise, he does not act as a Prince or Magistrate, but as a Tyrant; and that he then may be bridled by his Subjects, in virtue of all Divine and Human Law.[1]

With this powerful summary Gerard Noodt concluded his farewell lecture as Rector of the University of Leiden. It was February 1699 and Noodt had chosen 'The Power of Sovereigns' as the title of a lecture that was a synthesis of seventeenth-century debates on natural liberty, the formation of the commonwealth, the nature of sovereignty and the legitimacy of resistance against tyranny. Noodt presented his conclusions as mere common sense, underpinned by references to the leading authorities on the subject, to George Buchanan, the *Vindiciae contra Tyrannos*, Hugo Grotius and Samuel Pufendorf.

One of the most important legacies of Quentin Skinner's *Foundations* is its systematic study of theories of resistance in early-modern Europe – from Luther to Locke. It is a journey that takes the reader right across Europe, from the Lutheran heart of Saxony to the centres of constitutionalist thought in Paris, moving on to the revival of Thomism in Salamanca and to Calvin's rise in Geneva, ending with the elaboration of full-fledged theories of resistance by Calvinists in France, Scotland and England – the authors and works Gerard Noodt knew so well. Along thematic lines it is a journey from Luther's initial insistence on obedience to the theory of revolution of Calvinists such as François Hotman, Theodore Beza, Hubert Languet, Philippe du Plessis Mornay, Christopher Goodman and George Buchanan, whose theories culminate in 'the

---

[1] Gerard Noodt, *Du pouvoir des souverains et de la liberté de conscience*, ed. Jean Barbeyrac (Amsterdam, 1714), p. 302.

classic text of radical Calvinist politics',[2] Locke's *Two Treatises of Government*. This journey not only offers a comprehensive overview of the development of early-modern theories of resistance, which in many ways surpasses previous pathbreaking twentieth-century studies of the subject, most notably those of Allen and Mesnard.[3] The aim of the itinerary is also to offer a sustained critique of Michael Walzer's thesis about the origins of radical politics. In *The Revolution of the Saints* Walzer argued that 'it was due to their Calvinist allegiances that writers like Buchanan felt moved to adopt their radical stance'.[4] While granting that 'the *writers* who mounted and theorised about the revolutions of sixteenth-century Europe were in general self-proclaimed Calvinists', the vital question for the second volume of *Foundations* is whether it 'was also the case that the *arguments*' these writers 'invoked were specifically Calvinist in provenance and character'.[5]

One of the crucial arguments in *Foundations* is that Lutherans, not Calvinists, set the tone for the development of Protestant political thought. Faced with the possibility that the emperor, Charles V, might take up arms against them, Lutheran leaders set up the Torgau disputation in October 1530. Admitting that as theologians they had so far 'taught not to resist secular authority', Luther now recognised the argument of a number of leading jurists that the laws of the Empire allowed defence against unwanted violence. Culminating in the famous Magdeburg Confession of April 1550 Lutherans developed a constitutionalist interpretation that endowed inferior magistrates with the duty to resist the higher magistrate when the latter, to quote the Confession, 'wants to force the people to renounce God's Word and the true religion and to take on idolatry'.[6] The Confession also refers to the justification of resistance that Lutherans developed on the basis of the Roman law maxim *vim vi repellere licet*, which holds that it is lawful to repel unjust force with force. The Magdeburg Confession argues that when the secular magistrate 'prosecutes the true Religion and honesty', he steps outside his 'honour and office' and falls back into the status of a private person, whose private use of force should, as Roman law teaches, be resisted.

One of the main chapters of *Foundations* elucidates how in the 1550s Calvinists 'took over and reiterated the arguments in favour of forcible resistance which

---

[2] Quentin Skinner, *The Foundations of Modern Political Thought*, 2 vols. (Cambridge: Cambridge University Press, 1978), II, p. 239.

[3] See J. W. Allen, *A History of Political Thought in the Sixteenth Century*, rev. edn (London: Methuen, 1957) and Pierre Mesnard, *L'essor de la Philosophie Politique au XVIe siècle*, 3rd edn (Paris: Editions Vrin, 1969).

[4] Quentin Skinner, 'Humanism, Scholasticism and Popular Sovereignty', in Quentin Skinner, *Visions of Politics*, 3 vols. (Cambridge: Cambridge University Press, 2002), II: *Renaissance Virtues*, pp. 249–50. The reference is to Michael Walzer, *The Revolution of the Saints* (London: Weidenfeld and Nicolson, 1966).

[5] Ibid., pp. 249–50.

[6] *Bekentnis Unterricht und vermanung, der Pfarrhern und Prediger, der Christlichen Kirchen zu Magdeburg* (Magdeburg, 1550) fol. Hiij (v).

the Lutherans had already developed'.[7] English Calvinists such as Ponet and Goodman endorsed the private law justification of armed resistance. In Geneva and France Calvinists elaborated the constitutionalist defence of the duty of inferior magistrates to resist a godless higher magistrate. Calvin and his followers presented these inferior magistrates as 'ephoral' authorities. The reference to the Ephors of Sparta emphasised that these magistrates were elected; they were popular magistrates. Calvinists embedded their reflections on the authority and duty of inferior and popular magistrates in a contractual theory, where princes, faithful subjects and God were bound together by covenant.

The idea of the covenant was central to the political thought of the French Huguenots, culminating in the contractual analysis of the *Vindiciae contra Tyrannos*, published in 1579 and now available in English in George Garnett's fine edition.[8] The argument of the *Vindiciae* is centred around two covenants. The first is a contract between God, king and inferior magistrates. On the basis of this covenant the *Vindiciae* argues that as both king and inferior magistrates are 'ordained by God to govern justly and rule on his behalf', inferior magistrates have the religious duty to resist a king 'who overturns the law and Church of God'.

The second covenant is only between king and people. The *Vindiciae* argues that, in a position of natural liberty, the people had decided to create a king, to pursue their welfare and to uphold their rights. Kings should always remember, the *Vindiciae* writes, 'that it is from God, but by the people and for the people's sake that they do reign'. Since it was impossible for all inhabitants to get together and conclude a contract with the king, the people had, the *Vindiciae* asserts, vested its authority in a body of inferior magistrates. If the king 'fails in his promise' to uphold the covenant, 'the people are exempt from obedience, the contract is made void' and on behalf of the people the inferior magistrates are entitled and obliged to resist the tyrant. In the words of the *Vindiciae*, 'every magistrate is bound to relieve, and as much as it in him lies, to redress the miseries of the commonwealth'.

The *Vindiciae*'s emphasis on the contract between king and people exemplifies what in *Foundations* is called 'the epoch-making move' the Huguenot monarchomachs make

from a purely religious theory of resistance, depending on the idea of a covenant to uphold the laws of God, to a genuinely political theory of revolution, based on the idea of a contract which gives rise to a moral right (and not merely a religious duty) to resist any ruler who fails in his corresponding obligation to pursue the welfare of the people in all his public acts.[9]

---

[7] Skinner, *Foundations*, II, p. 207.
[8] Stephanus Junius Brutus, *Vindiciae contra Tyrannos*, ed. and trans. George Garnett (Cambridge: Cambridge University Press, 1994).
[9] Skinner, *Foundations*, II, p. 335.

The most radical affirmation of such a political right of resistance was articulated by George Buchanan in his dialogues on *The Right of the Kingdom in Scotland,* published, like the *Vindiciae,* in 1579.[10]

Both Calvin and Buchanan had been pupils of John Mair. In one of its most innovative moments *Foundations* argues that Lutheran and Calvinist theories of resistance are deeply indebted to the late medieval discussions of commentators and conciliarists. The legacy of conciliarism and Roman law was brought to the Calvinists by their own teachers, and *Foundations* highlights the importance of Mair and Almain, who revived the conciliarist tradition at the Sorbonne, and of jurists such as Mario Salomonio, whose *De Principatu* argues that the prince was not *legibus solutus,* but a 'minister of the commonwealth' bound by contract to the people, who, to quote Salomonio, 'as the creator of the prince must be greater than the prince whom they create'.[11]

The conclusion, stated at the end of *Foundations,* is that, to quote,

as will by now be clear, the concepts in terms of which Locke and his successors developed their views on popular sovereignty and the right of revolution had already been largely articulated and refined over a century earlier in legal writings of such radical jurists as Salomonio, in the theological treatises of such Ockhamists as Almain and Mair, as well as in the more famous but derivative writings of the Calvinist revolutionaries.[12]

The main theorists of resistance may have been self-proclaimed Calvinists, but their theories were legal and political, rooted in the legacy of late medieval conciliarism and constitutionalism. Moreover, the shift to radical politics was never the preserve of Calvinists alone. Buchanan's move to what is called 'a highly individualist and even anarchic view of the right of political resistance'[13] is paralleled by the account of popular sovereignty given by the Spanish Jesuit Juan de Mariana in the first book of *De Rege et Regis Institutione,* published in Toledo in 1599.[14]

Lutheranism

While the arguments in *Foundations* are mainly directed against Michael Walzer's work, they entail the fundamental rejection of a long historiographic tradition, going back to the work of Max Weber and Ernst Troeltsch, that presented Calvinists as studious contributors to the rise of capitalism and democracy, the hallmarks of modernity, while poor Lutherans remained stuck in their unqualified reverence for absolutist princes.[15] In the past decades German historians have contributed strongly to the revision of the theories of Weber

[10] George Buchanan, *De Iure Regni apud Scotos, Dialogus* (Edinburgh, 1579).
[11] Mario Salomonio, *De Principatu* (Rome, 1544), fol. 12, also 17 and 21.
[12] Skinner, *Foundations,* II, pp. 347–8.   [13] Ibid., p. 343.
[14] Juan de Mariana, *De Rege et Regis Institutione* (Toledo, 1599).
[15] Key works include Max Weber, *The Protestant Ethic and the 'Spirit' of Capitalism and Other Writings* (New York: Penguin Books, 2002) and, perhaps even more importantly, Ernst Troeltsch,

and Troeltsch, which form such an important part of their intellectual heritage. Research on Lutheran theories of authority, obedience and resistance has played an important role in this revision.

Scholars such as Diethelm Böttcher, Gabriele Haug-Moritz and Robert von Friedeburg have delved deeper into the connections between Lutheran political thought and late medieval legal traditions.[16] Their research shows how the jurists and princes who sympathised with Luther almost self-evidently appealed to Roman law commentators such as Bartolus and Baldus and to the long-standing constitutional practices of the Empire, including the 1519 *Wahlkapitulation* of the emperor Charles V. To their notable astonishment Luther refused to accept their refined interpretations of imperial and Roman law, superseding them – and this was the real novelty of the debate – with a much more straightforward hierarchical and centralistic image of the political order as a divine ordination with the emperor as its sole apex and all others, including proud princes and imperial cities, reduced to the status of subjects whose duty was to obey. Luther's verdict in 1529 was simple: 'a Christian should bear violence and injustice, especially from his own secular authority'.[17] Grudgingly, as only Luther could grudge, the Wittenberg theologians recognised the legal – but not the theological – validity of the arguments of the jurists in October 1530.

John, elector of Saxony, and Philip, landgrave of Hessen, did not see themselves as subjects of the emperor. They recognised Charles V as their overlord, to whom they owed dutiful obedience. But they also insisted on the highness and authority of their own office, as set out by divine and natural law, by the rules of Roman and canon law and by the charters of the Empire. Legal and classical conceptions of office smoothly merged with the feudal concepts of tutelage, of lord and vassal, who were tied to each other in a pact of mutual rights and obligations, not in the one-way street of king and subject. Admittedly, as *Obrigkeit* the position of the elector of Saxony and the landgrave of Hessen within the constitutional patchwork of the empire was inferior in status to that of the emperor, but if Charles V, the higher magistrate, stepped outside the bounden duty of his office, then it was the *officium* of the princes of Hessen and Saxony to defend themselves and those under their authority and protection against the deliberate use of unjust force.

The Social Teaching of the Christian Churches (London: Macmillan, 1931). For recent assessments see Hartmut Lehmann and Günther Roth (eds.), *Weber's 'Protestant Ethic': Origins, Evidence, Contexts* (Cambridge: Cambridge University Press, 1993).

[16] See Diethelm Böttcher, *Ungehorsam oder Widerstand? Zum Fortleben des mittelalterlichen Widerstandsrechtes in der Reformationszeit (1529–1530)* (Berlin: Duncker & Humblot, 1991); Robert von Friedeburg, *Self-defence and Religious Strife in Early Modern Europe: England and Germany, 1530–1680* (London: Ashgate, 2002) and Gabriele Haug-Moritz, 'Widerstand als "Gegenwehr". Die schmalkaldische Konzeption der "Gegenwehr" und der "gegenwehrliche Krieg" des Jahres 1542', in Robert von Friedeburg (ed.), *Widerstandsrecht in der frühen Neuzeit. Erträge und Perspektiven der Forschung im deutsch-britischen Vergleich* (Berlin: Duncker & Humblot, 2001), pp. 141–61.

[17] Luther, WA Briefwechsel 5, 258.

In discussing the natural and legal entitlement to defence against unjust violence Lutheran jurists were keen to use the concepts of *Gegenwehr* and *Notwehr*. The Magdeburg Confession is built on the principle 'that an inferior magistrate may use self-defence against a higher one, if the latter wants to root out the Christian religion with force'.[18] As the equivalents of the Latin concept of *defensio*, *Notwehr* and *Gegenwehr* refer to the immediate and proportional defensive response to the use of unjust force. The element of proportionality is vital. Matthias Flacius, the leader of defiant Magdeburg, declares emphatically in 1551 that it is as plain 'as clear, lightning sunshine, that this war and this persecution are there because of the Gospel of Jesus Christ and that we have not overreacted in our self-defence'.[19]

To appreciate this particular emphasis on self-defence it is vital to recognise, as Luise Schorn-Schütte has highlighted in a number of studies, that Lutheran reflections on issues of obedience and resistance are embedded in a more comprehensive theory of the social order. By divine ordination society is composed of three orders. As Luther puts it in 1528: 'These are the three holy orders and right establishments [*stiffte*], ordained by God: the office of the minister, the state of marriage, the secular authority'.[20] From the distinction between *status ecclesiasticus*, *status politicus* and *status oeconomicus* Lutherans started to derive more specific conceptions of the three offices. As the Magdeburg Confession explains, God 'has separated the three regiments in such a way, that he has given each his specific office and duty and his own specific way of punishment'. But the three orders are also interdependent and, to quote the Confession, as God wants it, 'each of them should serve the other'.[21]

[18] *Bekentnis Unterricht und vermanung, der Pfarrhern und Prediger, der Christlichen Kirchen zu Magdeburg*, fol. H4 (r).

[19] Matthias Flacius Illyricus, *Ein Geistlicher Trost dieser betrübten Magdeburgischen Kirchen Christi: daß sie die Verfolgung umb Gottes Worts, und keinen andern Ursachen halben, leidet*, in Friedrich Hortleder, *Der Römischen Keyser und königlichen Maiestete, auch des heiligen Rö(mischen) Reichs, geistlicher und weltlicher Stände . . . Handlungen und Ausschreiben . . . Von Rechtmässigkeit, Anfang, Fort- und endlichen Außgang deß Teutschen Kriegs, Keijser Carls deß Fünfften, wider die Schmalkaldischen Bundsoberste, Chur und Fürsten, Sachsen und Hessen . . . Vom Jahr 1546 bis auff das Jahr 1558*, 2nd edn (Gota, 1645), IV:13, s. 1152. For Flacius see Oliver K. Olsen, *Matthias Flacius and the survival of Luther's reform*, Wolfenbütteler Abhandlungen zur Renaissanceforschung (Wiesbaden: Harrassowitz, 2002).

[20] Luise Schorn-Schütte, 'Die Drei-Stände-Lehre im reformatorischen Umbruch', in Bernd Moeller, *Die frühe Reformation in Deutschland als Umbruch* (Gütersloh: Gütersloher Verlagshaus, 1998), p. 439. See also Luise Schorn-Schütte, *Evangelische Geistlichkeit in der Frühneuzeit. Deren Anteil an der Entfaltung frühmoderner Staatlichkeit und Gesellschaft* (Gütersloh: Gütersloher Verlagshaus, 1996), pp. 390–452 and Luise Schorn-Schütte, 'Obrigkeitskritik und Widerstandsrecht. Die *politica christiana* als Legitimitätsgrundlage', in Luise Schorn-Schütte (ed.), *Aspekte der politischen Kommunikation im Europa des 16. und 17. Jahrhunderts*, Historische Zeitschrift, Beiheft 39 (Munich: R. Oldenbourg Verlag, 2004), pp. 195–232.

[21] *Bekentnis Unterricht und vermanung, der Pfarrhern und Prediger, der Christlichen Kirchen zu Magdeburg*, fol. Giij.

As this Lutheran conception elevates the father of the household to a distinct office, he also obtains the duty of self-defence, especially, as Luther writes in 1539, when attacked by a 'bearwolf', an animal 'that may look like a wolf, but that is possessed by the devil and destroys and tears apart everything'.[22] Needless to say, the pope and his *Schuß-Herrn*, his toy dogs, were the bear-wolves Luther had in mind. In addition, the Lutheran theory of the social order urges office-holders to assist and admonish each other, especially when the 'true knowledge and honour of God' are at stake. Interlocking the three offices empowers ministers to take a critical stance towards secular authorities, when-ever their office requires them to do so. Instead of being slavish followers of their princes, Lutheran ministers can, at times, become staunch critics of princely politics. Censuring princes becomes an important part of the office of Lutheran ministers, especially of those who sympathise with the Magdeburg Confession.[23] In his *Regentenspiegel* from 1605 Polycarp Leyser, the Saxon court chaplain, repudiates the slander that ministers are wont 'to have one foot on the pulpit and another one in the town hall'. But, he immediately adds,

as God's Word deals with everything that is of this world, it truly happens often that a minister, especially when the text and word of God require so, must punish the sin and slander that occur in the secular and domestic regiment, in Chancelleries, in town halls and in other halls.

As Leyser insists, in doing so, the Lutheran minister 'is neither intruding into another office, nor is he falling into worldliness'. On the contrary 'it is appropriate to his office . . . to warn his beloved ruler [*Oberkeit*] and his beloved neighbour'.[24]

Thanks to the research of the past twenty-five years a more nuanced picture of Lutheran political thought starts to emerge. Firmly rooted in late medieval legal and feudal traditions, Lutherans – and Lutheran jurists in particular – give particular twists to such crucial concepts as *defensio*, *officium* and to the theory of estates. Within the Lutheran conception of society as a divine ordination

---

[22] *Etliche Schluß-Reden D. Martini Lutheri in offentlicher Disputation verthädigt Anno 1539*, in Hortleder, *Der Römischen Keyser*, book II, cap. 18, p. 97.

[23] See Schorn-Schütte, *Evangelische Geistlichkeit in der Frühneuzeit*; Luise Schorn-Schütte, 'Obrigkeitskritik im Luthertum? Anlässe und Rechtfertigungsmuster im ausgehenden 16. und 17. Jahrhundert', in Michael Erbe et al. (eds.), *Querdenken. Dissens und Toleranz in Wandel der Geschichte* (Mannheim: Palatium Verlag im J & J, 1995), pp. 253–70; Wolfgang Sommer, *Gottesfurcht und Fürstenherrschaft* (Göttingen: Vandenhoeck & Ruprecht, 1988) and Wolfgang Sommer, 'Obrigkeitskritik und die politische Funktion der Frömmigkeit im deutschen Luthertum des konfessionellen Zeitalters', in Von Friedeburg, *Widerstandsrecht in der frühen Neuzeit*, pp. 245–63.

[24] Polycarp Leyser, *Regenten Spiegel, Gepredigt aus dem C i. Psalm, des königlichen Propheten Davids, auff gehaltenem Landtage zu Torgau dieses 1605. Jahres im Iunio* (Leipzig, 1605), pp. 76–7. I owe this reference to Matthias Weiss, whose forthcoming doctoral thesis offers a seminal reinterpretation of *politica christiana* in general and Lutheran mirrors of magistrates and princes in particular. See Matthias Weiss, *Die Politica Christiana. Grundzüge einer christlichen Staatslehre im Alten Reich* (Frankfurt, 2005).

consisting of three interdependent offices, minister, *paterfamilias* and magistrate, it is appropriate to react defensively against a breach of office of higher magistrates that involves the application of unjust force.

Lutherans and Calvinists

The idea of the entitlement to *Notwehr*, to *defensio*, is picked up by almost all Calvinist brands in Europe.[25] It would, however, be wrong to suggest a smooth and easy blend of Lutheran and Calvinist ideas on obedience and resistance. Most notably, in 1566 Lutheran ministers such as Matthias Flacius, who had led the resistance at Magdeburg and now served the Lutheran community of Antwerp, clashed fiercely with the Calvinist leaders of the uprising and iconoclastic fury that marked the beginning of the revolt in the Low Countries against the government of their overlord, Philip II. The Confession of the Antwerp Lutheran ministers, written by Flacius, follows German traditions and distinguishes between 'different offices', presenting the secular authorities as 'an estate . . . ordained by God, to whom has been given the sword and who have been ordered to command'.[26]

The actions of Dutch Calvinists were, in Flacius's view, not in accordance with Lutheran teaching. In October 1566 Flacius expressed his great fear 'that there will be troubles here similar to those in France, because the Calvinists are infected with the spirit of rebellion'. As Flacius saw it, the Calvinists of the Low Countries were not committed to defensive and proportional self-defence but to rebellion: 'This is not written in the scriptures: when you are persecuted by the secular authorities, take up your sword and chase them away.'[27] The break between Lutherans and Calvinists became irreparable in December 1566 when the Calvinist synod discussed the question 'whether in the Low Countries a number of the vassals and a number of subjects may resist their magistrates with force, when he does not uphold the privileges, but violates them'. Dryly, almost wryly, the Calvinist synod concluded that this is indeed 'permitted, when one can find the right instruments to do so; one should have one or more leaders, money and people'.[28] Two years later, one of the intellectual leaders of the Dutch

---

[25] For attempts to find traces of Lutheran theories in English and Scottish political thought see Von Friedeburg, *Self-defence and Religious Strife in Early Modern Europe.*

[26] *Bekendtnus derer Kirchen binnen Antorff, so der waren Augspurgischen Confession zugethan* (Schmalkalden, 1567), fol. O8 (r).

[27] Wilhelm Preger, *Matthias Flacius Illyricus und seine Zeit*, II (Erlangen: T. Bläsing, 1859–61), pp. 288–9.

[28] See L. A. van Langeraad, *Guido de Bray, zijn leven en werken* (Zierikzee: S. Ochtman 1884), p. lxviii and R. van Roosbroeck, 'Wunderjahr oder Hungerjahr? Antwerpen 1566', in Franz Petri (ed.), *Kirche und gesellschaftlicher Wandel in Deutschen und Niederländischen Städten der werdenden Neuzeit* (Cologne/Vienna: Böhlau, 1980), pp. 187ff. For what follows see Martin van Gelderen, *The Political Thought of the Dutch Revolt 1555–1590* (Cambridge: Cambridge University Press, 1992), ch. 3 and 4.

Revolt, Marnix van St Aldegonde, decisively rejected the proposal to limit the entitlement to resistance to the 'high magistrate and the States of the country' with the exclusion of 'the lowest magistrates and private persons'. Marnix's reply that the legitimacy of resistance depends in particular on whether civil government has been established 'with certain contracts and mutual obligations' indicates the move away from the Lutheran emphasis on self-defence.

In legitimating their resistance against the government of Philip II Dutch authors represent the charters in terms of contracts as essential parts of the 'ancient constitution' which has been created by wise ancestors to safeguard Dutch liberty. Within the 'ancient constitution' the charters function as constitutional guarantees of liberty. They are the fundamental laws of the country, which no prince is allowed to violate or change; they are the bridles of the prince and they contain the conditions on which the prince has been accepted by the States on behalf of the people. While the charters are the constitutional and legal guarantees of liberty, the parliamentary assemblies and the citizens of the Netherlands are presented as its virtuous guardians. In the course of the 1570s the Dutch rebels develop an interpretation of the Dutch political order as based on liberty, constitutional charters, representative assemblies and civic virtue. In 1581 the Frisian humanist Aggaeus van Albada is the first Dutch author to give a full account of popular sovereignty as the foundation of the constitution. Being educated in Paris, Orléans, Bourges and Italy[29] he underpins his arguments with references to Plato, Aristotle and Cicero, to Bartolus and Baldus, to Salomonio and the *Vindiciae contra Tyrannos* and, perhaps most surprisingly and cleverly, to the work of Domingo de Soto and Fernando Vázquez de Menchaca, counsellors to Charles V and Philip II, whose vital contributions to early modern theories of civil power and resistance are highlighted in Annabel Brett's study *Liberty, Right and Nature*.[30]

Vázquez develops his radical theory of civil power in his main work, the *Controversies*, published in 1564 and dedicated to Philip II. The foundation of Vázquez's account of civil power is the presumption that before the establishment of the first acts of human law all *res* are in a state of natural liberty. In the case of some *res*, most famously the sea, this natural liberty can never be relinquished. In the case of human beings 'the natural appetite for society, the *naturalis appetitus socialis,* and the necessity of human beings to protect themselves against wrongdoers leads to the formation of society and civil power.[31]

---

[29] For Albada see Wiebe Bergsma, *Aggaeus van Albada (c. 1525–1587), schwenckfeldiaan, staatsman en strijder voor verdraagzaamheid* (Groningen: Meppel, 1985).

[30] Annabel S. Brett, *Liberty, Right and Nature: Individual Rights in Later Scholastic Thought* (Cambridge: Cambridge University Press, 1997) especially ch. 5, pp. 165–204.

[31] Fernando Vázquez de Menchaca, *Controversiarum Illustrium aliarumque usu frequentium libri tres* (Venice, 1564), preface, nos. 121–2. I have used the edition of Fidel Rodriguez Alcalde, which also has a Spanish translation (Valverde: Valladolid, 1931).

In strong contrast with Soto, Vázquez draws a sharp line between the natural movement to society and the artificial establishment of civil power.[32] Natural sociability leads to the congregation of free citizens in society. But men do not naturally live at peace with each other, and so society will suffer from discord and dissent. For their own protection free citizens will then decide to establish civil power. As Vázquez puts it, all kings 'are understood as created, elected or given not for their own sake or that of their own utility, but for the sake of the citizens and the utility of the citizens'.[33] In Vázquez's theory *civilis potestas* is power conceded by free citizens to the king, who should govern them to their own good.

Vázquez's theory raises the question of the legitimacy of resistance in situations where the king abuses his *imperium et potestas* and turns into a tyrant. In the case of Vázquez the radical answer is that if the jurisdiction of the king is based on the consent of the citizens, 'then that consent is of its nature revocable, since they are seen to have subjected themselves for their own utility, not that of their prince'.[34]

Albada refers to Vázquez at almost all stages of his legitimation of the Dutch revolt and of the civil power of the Dutch parliamentary assemblies, the provincial States and the States General. The basic premise of Albada's argument, 'that all forms of government, kingdoms, empires and legitimate authorities are founded for the common utility of the citizens, and not of the rulers' is directly taken from the *Controversies*;[35] it is followed by a long reflection on Salomonio's *De Principatu* which leads to Albada's endorsement of popular sovereignty. The argument that all princes are bound by the laws and that Philip II in particular is tied to the charters of the Low Countries is supported with references to both Soto and Vázquez.[36] The defence of the active policy of intervention by the States is based on Vázquez's theory of jurisdiction and 'natural protection'. The legitimacy of Dutch resistance against Philip II is supported with the argument 'that if a community is oppressed by its Prince or Stadholder, it shall take recourse to its overlord; but if there is no overlord, the community is entitled to take up arms'. According to Albada this argument was first formulated by Soto and then endorsed by Vázquez.[37]

The Dutch reception of Vázquez's theory of the origins of civil power finds its climax in the work of Hugo Grotius.[38] The turn to Vázquez, 'the pride of

---

[32] See for this point in particular Brett, *Liberty, Right and Nature*, p. 173.

[33] Vázquez, *Controversiarum*, preface, no. 119.   [34] Ibid., book II, ch. lxxxii, no. 6.

[35] Aggaeus van Albada, *Acten*, 166 referring to Vázquez, *Controversiarum,* book I, ch. 1, no. 40.

[36] Albada, *Acten*, 16, 106 and 121.

[37] Ibid., 122 referring to Soto, *De justitia et iure*, book V, question 1, art. 3 and Vázquez, *Controversiarum*, book I, ch. 8, no. 33.

[38] Hugo Grotius, *De Iure Praedae Commentarius*, ed. H. G. Hamaker (The Hague, 1868). References are also to the English translation: Hugo Grotius, *De Iure Praedae Commentarius: Commentary on the Law of Prize and Booty*, vol. I, ed. Gwladys L. Williams and Walther H. Zeydel (Oxford: Clarendon Press, 1950).

Spain',[39] begins in *De Iure Praedae*, Grotius's first main attempt to formulate a comprehensive legal and political theory. Having argued that self-preservation, *sui-amor* and friendship, *amicitia*, are the main characteristics of individuals in the state of natural liberty, where each is 'free and *sui iuris*', Grotius follows Vázquez to elucidate the move from natural liberty to human society and the establishment of civil power. For reasons of demographic growth, better protection and greater economic convenience individuals decide to create smaller societies, which are 'formed by general consent for the sake of the common good'.[40] Explicitly Grotius endorses Vázquez's view that while 'human society does indeed have its origin in nature, civil society as such is based on deliberate institution'.[41] Grotius uses the concept of *respublica* to refer to a multitude of private persons who have come together to increase their protection through mutual aid and to assist each other in acquiring the necessities of life. Referring again to Vázquez, Grotius emphasises the 'will of individuals' (*singulorum voluntas*) as the constitutive force for their union by way of civil contract – Grotius uses the term *foedus* – in a 'unified and permanent body' with its own set of laws. From *singuli* the individuals taking this seminal decision turn themselves into *cives*, citizens.

The laws of the commonwealth emanate from its will as a unified body based on consent. With references to Vázquez, Vitoria and Covarruvias Grotius argues that 'civil power, manifesting itself in laws and judgements, resides primarily and essentially in the bosom of the commonwealth itself'.[42] Of course not everybody has the time to devote himself to the administration of civil affairs. The exercise of lawful power is therefore entrusted to a number of magistrates, who act for the common good. By mandate the magistrates have the authority to make laws for the *respublica*, which bind all citizens.

Grotius uses the concept of *magistratus* to emphasise that those who exercise civil power, be they king, princes, counts, state assemblies or town councils, are administrators. Arguing that 'just as every right of the magistrate comes from the commonwealth, so every right of the commonwealth comes from private persons', Grotius reaffirms in *De Iure Praedae* that 'public power is constituted by collective consent'.[43] Civil power is neither absolute nor eternal. Grotius endorses the position of Vázquez that 'the power of the commonwealth remains intact even after the establishment of the principate'. Going back to Vitoria, Grotius accepts the argument of 'the Spanish theologian . . . that the commonwealth may change one prince for another or transfer the principate from one dynasty to another'.[44]

[39] Grotius, *De Iure Praedae,* p. 236; *Commentary*, pp. 249–50.
[40] Grotius, *De Iure Praedae,* pp. 19–20; *Commentary*, p. 20.
[41] Grotius, *De Iure Praedae,* p. 92; *Commentary*, p. 92.
[42] Grotius, *De Iure Praedae,* p. 25; *Commentary*, p. 25.
[43] Grotius, *De Iure Praedae,* p. 91; *Commentary*, p. 92.
[44] Grotius, *De Iure Praedae,* p. 269; *Commentary*, p. 284.

This argument lies at the heart of Grotius's justification of the Dutch revolt. First, in line with the revolt's traditions, Grotius defends the authority of the parliamentary assemblies with reference to the old charters. He characterises the assembly of the States as the 'supreme magistrate which maintains the law of the commonwealth and the citizenry'. Faced with the 'foreign arms' of the Spaniards it was their duty to uphold 'the pacts which had been sanctified by the oath of the prince, and which gave continuity to the form of government' (*forma imperii*); it was their duty to 'liberate the commonwealth and the individual citizens from exactions, which directly contravened not only the law but also the common liberty of mankind because, as the Spanish Doctor argues, these exactions lead to immediate pillage and to future servitude'.[45]

When Grotius moves on to justify the abjuration of Philip II, he appeals to Vázquez not only as the 'Spanish Doctor' but also as one of Philip's own 'senators'. Grotius endorses Vázquez's view that when 'superiors' such as Philip 'refuse justice to the subjects, they are not only deprived *ipso jure* of supreme jurisdiction, but also become forever incapacitated from recovering that jurisdiction'.[46] Grotius places full weight on the basic principles that the commonwealth is the source of civil power and that government is based on contractual consent. He upholds the 'doctrine which has maximum support among the Spaniards themselves that the power which has been given to the prince can be revoked, particularly when the prince exceeds his bounds, because then *ipso facto* he ceases to be regarded as a prince'. With a final blow Grotius reiterates – with a further reference to Vázquez – that 'he who abuses supreme power renders himself unworthy of it, and ceases to be a prince in consequence of what he does to make himself a tyrant'.[47]

Like Salomonio and Albada, Grotius and Vázquez are key figures in an intellectual tradition of humanists who blend the languages of jurisprudence and neo-scholasticism, of Roman law and the school of Salamanca, with the Renaissance vocabulary of civic humanism and republicanism to discuss the issues of civil power and resistance. The contrasts with the Lutheran theory of self-defence are striking. In terms of vocabulary there is an important shift from the language of divine ordination, of divine orders, of defence and self-defence by inferior magistrates to the language of popular sovereignty, civil power, civic rights and, especially in Grotius's Dutch writings, active citizenship. The political order is not the outcome of divine ordination but of civic creation; social order is not a divinely ordained hierarchy but a civil society of citizens whose position, at least in the face of the law, is characterised by the principles of civil liberty and equality. Resistance is not the ultimate resort of inferior magistrates

---

[45] Grotius, *De Iure Praedae,* p. 271; *Commentary,* p. 286.
[46] Grotius, *De Iure Praedae,* p. 272; *Commentary,* p. 286.
[47] Grotius, *De Iure Praedae,* p. 274; *Commentary,* p. 289.

acting in self-defence but the active right of the sovereign people and their representatives, who have been given this right by the collective consent of the citizens.

Like Grotius, some of the monarchomachs, most notably, as John Salmon has highlighted, Buchanan and Rossaeus, had grounded their radical theories of resistance on the 'acceptance of a presocial state of nature' and 'the belief that the people really did exercise authority'.[48] As in Grotius's case, these reflections on the origins of civil society were deeply informed by Cicero's analysis in *De inventione* and *De officiis*. Unlike Grotius, Buchanan and Rossaeus are less willing to see civil society purely as the artificial outcome of private calculations on the basis of self-preservation and utility; Buchanan still sees 'a certain force of nature' and 'a light divinely shed upon our souls' moving men to the formation of society.[49]

English receptions: Filmer, Parker and Milton

A number of studies, including those of Hugh Trevor-Roper, Richard Tuck and Jonathan Scott, have confirmed and refined John Salmon's thesis that Grotius was one of the key figures in the intellectual exchange between English and continental political thought.[50] As a result of the recent focus on whether we should read Hobbes with or without Grotius,[51] the wider reception of Grotius's works has been neglected. Grotius's theological works, especially *De Veritate Religionis Christianae* and the *Annotations to the New Testament,* were essential reading in England. Readings varied, indeed clashed. Grotius became the main intellectual inspiration of the Great Tew circle. One of its leading members, the eminent Anglican theologian Henry Hammond, published a whole series of

---

[48] J. H. M. Salmon, 'An Alternative Theory of Popular Resistance: Buchanan, Rossaeus, and Locke', in J. H. M. Salmon, *Renaissance and Revolt: Essays in the Intellectual and Social History of Early Modern France* (Cambridge: Cambridge University Press, 1987), p. 138. For Buchanan see also J. H. Burns, 'George Buchanan and the Anti-monarchomachs', in Nicholas Phillipson and Quentin Skinner (eds.), *Political Discourse in Early Modern Britain* (Cambridge: Cambridge University Press, 1993), pp. 3–22; J. H. Burns, *The True Law of Kingship: Concepts of Monarchy in Early Modern Scotland* (Oxford: Oxford University Press, 1996), pp. 191–209 and Roger Mason, 'People Power? George Buchanan on Resistance and the Common Man', in Von Friedeburg, *Widerstandsrecht in der frühen Neuzeit*, pp. 163–81.

[49] Buchanan, *De Iure Regni apud Scotos, Dialogus* pp. 10–11. The point is highlighted by Salmon, 'An Alternative Theory of Popular Resistance', especially p. 152.

[50] J. H. M. Salmon, *'The French Religious Wars in English Political Thought* (Oxford: Oxford University Press, 1959). See Hugh Trevor-Roper, 'The Great Tew Circle', in Hugh Trevor-Roper (ed.), *Catholics, Anglicans and Puritans: Seventeenth Century Essays* (London: Fontana, 1989), pp. 166–230; Richard Tuck, *Philosophy and Government, 1572–1651* (Cambridge: Cambridge University Press, 1993); Jonathan Scott, *England's Troubles: Seventeenth-Century English Political Instability in European Context* (Cambridge: Cambridge University Press, 2000).

[51] See Perez Zagorin, 'Hobbes without Grotius', *History of Political Thought* 21 (2000), pp. 16–40.

works to defend Grotius against the attacks of the puritan John Bidle.[52] Another Puritan, Richard Baxter, borrowed – as William Lamont has pointed out – 'the bits of Grotius he liked – particularly, the recognition of self-preservation as the ultimate criterion – and turned them against the bits of Grotius he didn't like', most notably Grotius's irenicism, which Baxter interpreted as a disastrous programme for the reunion of the churches.[53] Meanwhile during the 1660s John Locke, whose inclinations were rather different from Baxter's, started to recommend the irenicist works of Grotius – in particular *De Veritate Religionis Christianae* – to his students at Christ Church in Oxford, while taking notes himself from Henry Hammond's *Pacifick Discourse of God's Grace and Decrees*.[54]

Grotius's theory of resistance became, as Jonathan Scott has pointed out, 'one of the most quoted political sources in England'.[55] For most, if not all English readers, the principal source of Grotius's theory was not *De Iure Praedae*, but Grotius's much more cautious account of civil power and resistance in the fourth chapter of the first book of *De iure belli ac pacis*. Making a remarkable move Grotius now explicitly rejected the opinion of those 'who will have the Supreme Power to be always, and without exception, in the people'.[56] The key argument against the absolute primacy of popular sovereignty is the absolute liberty of the people. Grotius argues that people are perfectly free to transfer their natural right of self-government to one – or more – persons, relinquishing it, if they want to, forever. Just as it is 'lawful for any man to engage himself as a slave to whom he pleases', so it is 'lawful for a people that are at their own disposal, to deliver up themselves to any or more persons, and transfer the right of governing them upon him or them, without reserving any share of that right to themselves'. Just as individual persons are entitled to choose their own 'way of living', so the people 'may choose what form of government they please'. Being on the 'Brink of Ruin' or 'in great Want', the people may well 'find no other Means to save themselves' but to 'yield all Sovereignty to another'.[57]

---

[52] See Henry Hammond, *A Second Defence of the Learned Hugo Grotius* (London, 1655); *A Continuation of the Defence of Hugo Grotius in an Answer to the Review of his Annotations* (London, 1657). For Hammond see John W. Packer, *The Transformation of Anglicanism, 1643–1660, with Special Reference to Henry Hammond* (Manchester: Manchester University Press 1969); Trevor-Roper, 'The Great Tew Circle', pp. 215–27 and Neil Lettinga, 'Covenant Theology turned upside down: Henry Hammond and Caroline Anglican Moralism, 1643–1660', *Sixteenth Century Journal* 24 (1993), pp. 653–69.

[53] William Lamont, 'Arminianism: the Controversy that Never Was', in Phillipson and Skinner, *Political Discourse in Early Modern Britain*, pp. 45–66, at p. 59.

[54] See John Marshall, *John Locke: Resistance, Religion and Responsibility* (Cambridge: Cambridge University Press, 1994), pp. 25–6.

[55] Jonathan Scott, *England's Troubles*, p. 149.

[56] Hugo Grotius, *De iure belli ac pacis*, book I, ch. IV, para. VIII. The translation is based on Hugo Grotius, *The Rights of War and Peace*, ed. and trans. Jean Barbeyrac (London, 1738).

[57] Ibid.

In the judgement of Grotius's strongest English critic, Sir Robert Filmer, this is still dangerous radicalism. Filmer recognises the doctrines 'that civil power depends on the will of the people' and 'that private men or petty multitudes may take up arms against their princes'.[58] As Filmer sees it, these doctrines are 'the desperate inconveniences which attend upon the doctrine of the natural freedom and community of all things'.[59] From Filmer's perspective Grotius is affiliated with a group of 'Jesuits and some over zealous favourers of the Geneva discipline'– for an Anglican such as Filmer an unholy alliance if ever there was one. Membership of the unholy alliance included Cardinal Bellarmine, Francisco Suárez and Buchanan.

To begin with, Filmer abhorred Grotius's argument that the political order is not the outcome of divine ordination but of civic creation; that social order is not a divinely ordained hierarchy but a civil society of citizens whose position, at least in the face of the law, was characterised by the principles of, as Filmer writes with great disdain, 'the Natural Liberty and Equality of Mankind'. Grotius 'teacheth', Filmer writes with strong disapproval, 'that the people may choose what form of government they please, and their will is the rule of right'.[60] And as Filmer notes, even when the people choose monarchy as their form of government, 'lawful kings have no property in their kingdoms, but a usufructuary right only as if the people were the lords and the kings but their tenants'. Worse is to follow. The theory of resistance that Grotius goes on to derive in *De iure belli ac pacis* alarms Filmer even more. While Grotius underpins his theory of resistance with frequent references to the work of William Barclay, the arch anti-monarchomach, Filmer argues that the great peril of Grotius's theory of resistance is that, given the foundational principles of Grotian political thought, on the issue of whether a king has become a tyrant, an 'enemy of the whole people', as Grotius now puts it,[61] 'every private man may be judge'.[62]

For Henry Parker, 'the most aggressive, thoughtful, and provocative parliamentarian writer in the early years of the Long parliament and civil war era',[63] whose own writings were also heavily attacked by Filmer, Grotius did not go far enough. As Michael Mendle has shown, Parker's staunch defence of parliamentary sovereignty was grounded on the assumption that all power, as

---

[58] Sir Robert Filmer, *Observations Concerning the Originall of Government upon Mr Hobs* Leviathan, *Mr Milton against* Salmasius, *H. Grotius* De Jure Belli (1652) in Sir Robert Filmer, *Patriarcha and Other Writings*, ed. Johann P. Sommerville (Cambridge: Cambridge University Press, 1991), p. 222.

[59] Ibid., p. 225.   [60] Ibid., p. 221.

[61] Grotius, *The Rights of War and Peace*, book I, ch. IV, para. XI.

[62] Filmer, *The Originall of Government*, p. 220.

[63] Michael Mendle, *Henry Parker and the English Civil War: the Political Thought of the Public's 'privado'* (Cambridge: Cambridge University Press, 1995), p. xi; for a similar judgement see Quentin Skinner, 'John Milton and the politics of slavery', in Skinner, *Visions,* II, pp. 286–307, at p. 293.

Parker put it in the pamphlet from 1642 that gave him the name and fame of the *Observator*, 'is originally inherent in the people, and is nothing else but that might and vigour which such or such a societie of men containes in itselfe'.[64] Parker insisted on the identity of people and Parliament; popular sovereignty implied parliamentary sovereignty. Parliament, wrote the *Observator*, was 'the State it self'.[65]

Like Grotius Parker saw government as a civic creation. In *Jus Populi,* Parker's most systematic and 'frontal assault upon the organic and patriarchal assumptions about the naturalness of government',[66] the *Observator* explicitly praised Grotius's 'qualification of political rule, that he accounts *so meerly humane*', and fully endorsed Grotius's argument, 'that if the King seek to alter it, he may be . . . *opposed by the people*'.[67] But Parker strongly rejected Grotius's new permissiveness towards absolute monarchy. The key issue was whether the people can, as Grotius argued, choose to relinquish their natural liberty and put themselves under the subjection of a monarch. While accepting the legitimacy of absolute monarchy, Grotius had later on in *De iure belli ac pacis* drawn parallels between slavery and monarchy, asserting that 'as then personal liberty excludes the Dominion of a Master, so does civil Liberty exclude royalty, and all manner of Sovereignty properly so called'.[68] Right at this point Grotius quotes Livy, who, in Grotius's poignant summary of the crux of the republican argument, 'oppose those Peoples that were free, to them that lived under Kings'. Livy is joined by Cicero and of course Tacitus. To top it all, Grotius reminds his readers that 'even the Stoicks acknowledge there is a kind of servitude in subjection and in the Holy Scriptures the Subjects of Kings are called their servants'.[69] Parker drew the conclusion. 'By favour of Grotius' Parker argued 'there is stronger reason, that no Nation yet ever did voluntarily or compulsorily embrace servitude, or intend submission to it'.[70] With this conclusion Parker made Filmer's nightmare come true. While Grotius had, as Filmer saw it, 'in words' acknowledged the legitimacy of monarchy, his 'circular suppositions' were brought to their radical conclusion by Parker. True lovers of liberty, cherished deeply by both Parker and Grotius, would never opt for monarchy.

Along these lines the abolition of monarchy should be seen as an act of self-liberation by the free and sovereign people. As Martin Dzelzainis and Skinner have argued, this argument lay at the heart of John Milton's defence of the

---

[64] Henry Parker, *Observations upon Some of His Majesties Late Answers and Expresses* (London, 1642), p. 1.

[65] Parker, *Observations*, p. 34.   [66] Mendle, *Henry Parker and the English Civil War*, p. 127.

[67] Henry Parker, *Jus Populi. Or, a Discourse wherein Clear Satisfaction is given, as well Concerning the Right of Subiects, as the Right of Princes* (London, 1644), p. 7; see Mendle, *Henry Parker and the English Civil War*, pp. xiv, 131–2.

[68] Grotius, *The Rights of War and Peace*, book I, ch. III, para. XII.

[69] Ibid.   [70] Parker, *Jus Populi*, p. 66.

1649 regicide.[71] Milton asserted that no man 'can be so stupid to deny that all men naturally were borne free . . . born to command and not to obey'. After the Fall men had formed 'Citties, Towns and Common-wealths'. They had done so 'by common league to bind each other from mutual injury, and joyntly to defend themselves against any that gave disturbance or opposition to such agreement'. For reasons of 'ease' and 'order, and least each man should be his own partial Judge', men had 'communicated' their natural 'authoritie and power of self-defence and preservation' to those called kings and magistrates, 'not to be thir lords and Maisters', Milton insisted, but to be their 'Deputies and Commissioners', their trustees.[72] The 'power of kings and magistrates' is 'only derivative', 'committed to them in trust from the People to the Common good of them all'.[73] 'Kingdom and magistracy' are, as Milton puts it with reference to the first letter of the apostle Peter, 'a human ordinance'.[74] 'Fundamentally', Milton argued, the power of self-government remained with the people; to take it away from them was 'a violation of thir natural birthright'.[75] In defending the regicide, Milton combined the 'classical – and more specifically a Roman law – conception of freedom and slavery' with elaborate appeals to the arguments of the monarchomachs, referring at length to Buchanan, Goodman, and to Luther and Calvin themselves.[76] But given the endurance and inalienability of popular sovereignty the language of resistance was no longer needed to justify the people intervening with the 'tenure of kings and magistrates'. 'As oft as they shall judge it for the best', the people may either 'choose' or 'reject' a ruling king or magistrate, 'retaine him or depose him, though no tyrant, merely by the liberty and right of free born Men to be govern'd as seems to them best'.[77] From this perspective the regicide, seen as 'justice don upon a Tyrant' was, Milton writes, 'no more but the necessary self-defence of a whole Common-wealth'.[78]

There was no doubt in the minds of England's revolutionaries that Charles I was a tyrant; indeed for many he was directly associated with popery and the Antichrist. As Volker Leppin has shown, Luther had turned the Antichrist into a central concept of Reformation theology, identifying not just individual popes, but the institution of the papacy itself as the Antichrist, the figure who, as announced in II Thes. 2:4, puts himself above everything, including, most

---

[71] See Martin Dzelzainis, Introduction in John Milton, *Political Writings*, ed. Martin Dzelzainis (Cambridge: Cambridge University Press, 1991), pp. ix–xxv; Martin Dzelzainis, 'Milton's politics' in Dennis Danielson (ed.), *The Cambridge Companion to Milton*, 2nd edn. (Cambridge: Cambridge University Press, 1999), pp. 70–83 and Skinner, 'John Milton and the politics of slavery'.

[72] John Milton, *The Tenure of Kings and Magistrates*, in Milton, *Political Writings*, pp. 8–9.

[73] Ibid., p. 10.   [74] Ibid., p. 15. The reference is to 1 Pet. 2.13.   [75] Ibid., p. 10.

[76] Skinner, 'John Milton and the Politics of Slavery', p. 302 and Dzelzainis, *Milton's Politics*.

[77] Milton, *The Tenure of Kings and Magistrates*, p. 33.   [78] Ibid., p. 45.

importantly from Luther's perspective, the Word of God.[79] Moreover, as Luther saw it, the Antichrist did not only work in the church, the Temple of God, but also in the world, where the papacy subjected the social order as ordained by God to its wilful authority. At this point the Antichrist incorporated the tyrant. From this distinctly Protestant perspective Charles V was *miles papae*, soldier of the Antichrist, which was bad enough, but presumably not quite as bad as being the Antichrist himself. Dutch pamphleteers had argued at length that Philip II's attempt to 'rule over the soul' was a main element of his tyranny, but in elucidating the king of Spain's tyranny treatises such as *Political Education*, the main defence of the abjuration in 1581, explicitly adopted the classical definition of Bartolus. In the following decades the concept of tyranny changed; in some cases the distinction between the classical tyrant and the Antichrist broke down almost completely.[80] In a sermon at Knole, which was, as its title put it, *An alarme beat up in Sion, to war against Babylon*, Joseph Boden went as far as to raise the almost diabolical question whether 'our King should be one of those tenne, of whom we read, Revel. 17.13, that have one mind, and shall give their power and strength unto the beast?'[81] Other Protestants were less millennarian in delineating the relationships between 'popery' and tyranny. Milton, as David Norbrook has pointed out, greatly feared the dangers of 'the interdependency of religious and civil corruptions', declaring that tyranny is 'an ambiguous monster, and to be slaine in two shapes'.[82] Protestants like Milton saw 'popery' as a threat to liberty and civil society, embodied by tyrants seeking to rule over the liberty of conscience, over man's soul. Others defined popery as the very embodiment of the Antichrist. There was a wide spectrum of opinions here, but the definition of tyranny in terms of 'popery' was the one moment where Protestant and Catholic theories of resistance stood distinctly apart.

The diabolic tyrant now also appeared on the popular stage. Ben Jonson's *Sejanus, his Fall* presented the classical tyrant, as did – in stark republican poetics – Joost van den Vondel's *Batavian Brothers*; Shakespeare's *Richard III* gave depth to the English tyrant. The tyrant was presented as a complex figure, driven by his passions, deeply wily and untrustworthy, spreading shrewd webs of lies. The tyrant was a deformed, almost diabolic monster, recognisable to all.

---

[79] See Volker Leppin, *Antichrist und Jüngster Tag. Das Profil apokalyptischer Flugschriftenpublizistik im deutschen Luthertum 1548–1618* (Gütersloh: Gütersloher Verlagshaus, 1999), especially ch. 7, pp. 207–43.

[80] Robert Zaller, 'The Figure of the Tyrant in English Revolutionary Thought', *Journal of the History of Ideas* 54 (1993), p. 594.

[81] Joseph Boden, *An alarme beat up in Sion, to vvar against Babylon. Or: The summe of a sermon upon Revelation 18. and the 6. Preached at Knowle, before the Honourable the Committee of the county of Kent, on the 13. of Iune, anno 1644. and by the said Honourable Committee required to be published* (London, 1644), p. 29. See Zaller, 'The Figure of the Tyrant in English Revolutionary Thought', p. 596.

[82] David Norbrook, *Writing the English Republic: Poetry, Rhetoric and Politics, 1627–1660* (Cambridge: Cambridge University Press, 1999), p. 114.

In one of his boldest moves, when asking 'what the people may lawfully doe' against tyranny, 'a common pest, and destroyer of mankinde', Milton declared that 'no man of cleare judgement need goe further to be guided then by the very principles of nature in him'.[83] Milton, to be sure, was one of Filmer's other nightmares.

The Glorious Revolution

That '*every Man* is *Judge* for himself' is the answer John Locke gave famously to the question '*Who shall be Judge* whether the Prince or Legislative act contrary to their Trust?'[84] How Locke moved from the legacy of Buchanan, Grotius and the *Vindiciae* to the theory of revolution that awards individuals the right of resistance has been elucidated in numerous studies, including, most notably, those of Richard Ashcraft, James Tully, Jonathan Scott and John Marshall.[85] Locke had read Grotius's works in the early 1660s and he recommended *De iure belli ac pacis*, in addition to Samuel Pufendorf's *De iure naturae et gentium*, to those who wished to be instructed 'in the natural rights of Men, and the Original and Foundations of Society, and the Duties resulting from thence'. *The Two Treatises* are not only indebted to Grotius because, like Algernon Sidney's *Discourses on Government* they are a direct rebuttal of Filmer, but also because key moments of Grotius's civil philosophy – the natural liberty of the private person in the state of nature, the formation of civil society as an act of civic creation, the nature of consent as the basis of government and the law of war – are central to Locke's reflections on civil power and resistance.[86]

Given that men are, as Locke puts it, 'born . . . with a Title to perfect Freedom, and an uncontrouled enjoyment of all the Rights and Privilidges of the Law of Nature', each human being 'hath by Nature a Power, not only to preserve his Property, that is, his Life, Liberty and Estate, against the Injuries and Attempts of other Men; but to judge of and punish the breaches of that Law in others'.[87] As Locke emphasises, 'the only way whereby one devests himself of his Natural Liberty, and *puts on the bonds of Civil Society* is by agreeing with other Men to joyn and unite into a Community'.[88] With government based on consent and trust, Locke's reflections on resistance focus on the situations in which

[83] Ibid., p. 17.

[84] John Locke, *Two Treatises of Government*, ed. Peter Laslett (Cambridge: Cambridge University Press, 1988), II. 240 (pp. 426–7).

[85] Richard Ashcraft, *Revolutionary Politics and Locke's Two Treatises of Government* (Princeton: Princeton University Press, 1986); James Tully, *An Approach to Political Philosophy: Locke in Contexts* (Cambridge: Cambridge University Press, 1993); Jonathan Scott, 'The Law of War: Grotius, Sidney, Locke and the Political Theory of Rebellion', *History of Political Thought* 13 (1992), pp. 565–85; John Marshall, *John Locke: Resistance, Religion and Responsibility* (Cambridge: Cambridge University Press, 1994).

[86] As emphasised in Scott, 'The Law of War'.   [87] Locke, *Two Treatises*, II. 87 (p. 323).

[88] Ibid., II. 95 (p. 331).

government dissolves the legitimating bond of trust between itself and the incorporated people by, as John Marshall puts it, 'acting beyond its trust or unjustly – that is, by arbitrarily taking property, or by removing or corrupting the legal processes by which such arbitrary action could be prevented and thus directly threatening the people'.[89] If government goes as far as actually declaring and perpetrating war on the people, it dissolves civil society itself, bringing back a state of nature. In breaching the trust of the people and governing arbitrarily, a king steps out of the bounds of his authority and, as Locke argues in a dramatic passage, declares war against the people, for whom it is perfectly legitimate to repel unjust force with force: 'When a King has Dethron'd himself, and put himself in a state of War with his People, what shall hinder them from prosecuting him who is no King, as they would any other Man, who has put himself into a state of War with them'.[90] As Jonathan Scott has highlighted, in his defence of rebellion Algernon Sidney makes a very similar move.[91] Sidney argues that it is perfectly legitimate to act

against a legal magistrate, who takes upon him (tho within the time prescribed by the law) to exercise a power which the law does not give; for in that respect he is a private man, *Quia*, as Grotius says, *eatenus non habet imperium*; and may be restrain'd as well as any other, because he is not set up to do what he lists, but what the law appoints for the good of the people.[92]

As on other occasions, Sidney takes recourse here to *De iure belli ac pacis*, which he identified in 1677 'as the most important influence' upon his own political thought.[93]

Many other pamphlets and treatises justifying the Glorious Revolution invoked Grotius. The most explicit, though perhaps not the most illuminating, example was *The Proceedings of the Present Parliament Justified by the Opinion of the most Judicious and Learned Hugo Grotius*, a pamphlet that tried to convince

some of the *Reverend Clergy* who yet seem to labour under some Scruples concerning the *Original Right of Kings,* their *Abdication of Empire*, and the Peoples inseparable Right of *Resistance, Deposing*, and of *Disposing and Settling of the Succession to the Crown*.[94]

---

[89] Marshall, *John Locke*, p. 270.   [90] Locke, *Two Treatises*, II. 239 (pp. 424–5).

[91] For Sidney's political thought see Jonathan Scott, *Algernon Sidney and the Restoration Crisis, 1677–1683* (Cambridge: Cambridge University Press, 2002); Blair Worden, 'The Commonwealth Kidney of Algernon Sidney', *The Journal of British Studies* 24 (1985), pp. 1–40; Alan Craig Houston, *Algernon Sidney and the Republican Heritage in England and America* (Princeton: Princeton University Press, 1991) and Blair Worden, 'Republicanism and the Restoration, 1660–1683', in David Wootton (ed.), *Republicanism, Liberty, and Commercial Society, 1649–1776* (Stanford: Stanford University Press, 1994), pp. 139–93, esp. 153–74.

[92] Sidney, *Discourses concerning Government*, ch. II, section 24, para. 3, p. 222.

[93] See Scott, 'The Law of War', p. 569.

[94] Anon, *The Proceedings of the Present Parliament Justified by the Opinion of the most Judicious and Learned Hugo Grotius* (London, 1689), title page.

The presence of Grotius in the debates of 1689 and in the work of authors such as Locke and Sidney indicates the common ground but also the variety of the political ideas employed to defend the turnover of the English monarchy, the abdication of James II, the invasion of William III and the establishment of William and Mary as king and queen. Grotius, Locke and Sidney share some of the crucial arguments that are at the heart of the debate; they advocate natural liberty, see political society and government as the outcomes of civic creation, and justify resistance against kings who have fallen into tyranny and make war on the people. These were the foundational elements of Gerard Noodt's synthesis from 1699, which underlined that all of this was, in Parker's words, 'so meerly humane'. As Noodt put it, 'it is certain that the names of *Sovereign* and of *Subject*, of *Master* and of *Slave* are unknown to Nature: they were simply given to us by men'.[95]

There are, of course, also substantial differences between Grotius, Locke and Sidney. Much more than Locke, both Grotius and Sidney indulge in historical argumentation, buttressing their arguments with lengthy studies of past and present societies and governments, of Rome, Israel, Sparta, Venice, Aragon, France, England.[96] Locke and Grotius try to be as precise as possible in identifying and limiting the cases when rebellion is justified. Sidney, however, learning from Machiavelli and Tacitus, starts to recognise the positive value of 'civil wars and tumults', arguing that while

it is ill, that men should kill one another in seditions, tumults and wars . . . it is worse, to bring nations to such misery, weakness and baseness, as to have neither strength nor courage to contend for anything; to have nothing left worth defending, and to give the name of peace to desolation.[97]

This appreciation of civil discord is an important part of Sidney's republican dwellings, entailing many points of difference with Locke. While Locke – in the words of John Marshall[98] – 'made no declaration of rights of political agency within political society', Sidney celebrated the free republics, glorified Rome and venerated Israel in a language of passionate love of liberty, 'that is half-English, half-Roman; half-Christian, half-classical'.[99]

The debates of the Glorious Revolution have been studied extensively – at least on the English side. What is missing is a genuine comparative, 'transnational' dimension, a defect that still characterises so much of early-modern intellectual history. Recent research in political history – most notably the work of Jonathan Israel – has highlighted that while the events of 1688–9 may have been a Glorious Revolution from the English perspective, from the Dutch viewpoint they were a Glorious Invasion, a daring and controversial intervention

[95] Noodt, *Du pouvoir des souverains et de la liberté de conscience*, pp. 219–20.
[96] See Worden, *Republicanism and the Restoration*, p. 159.
[97] Sidney, *Discourses*, ch. 2, section 26, p. 259.   [98] Marshall, *John Locke*, p. 264.
[99] Worden, *Republicanism and the Restoration*, p. 174.

in a foreign country.[100] In his *Declaration*, printed and distributed in massive numbers, William of Orange defends his personal involvement with the argument that 'our Dearest and most Entirely Beloved Consort, the Princesse, and likewise Wee our selves, have so great an Interest in this Matter, and such a Right, as all the world knows, to the Succession to the Crown'.[101] This line of argument can of course not be adopted by the other leaders of the Dutch Republic. The Amsterdam town council, the States of Holland and all others who decided to support William's invasion, justified the move to intervene in England, to upset James II and to establish the new regime of William and Mary along different lines. The Dutch States General declared 'that the welfare of the State' was at stake. The public resolution of the States General, published in several languages, points to the 'close and particular alliance' between the indomitable tyrants James II and Louis XIV. If James were 'able to achieve his aim and to obtain absolute power over his people, the two kings would try, out of Interest of State, and out of hate and envy towards the Protestant Religion, to bring this State [the Dutch Republic] into confusion and, if possible, to destroy it'.[102] The invasion of England is publicly defended as a pre-emptive strike against threatening tyrants. Once again Europeans turned for guidance to Grotius, who in ch. 25 of the second book of *De iure belli ac pacis* had analysed the legitimation of foreign intervention in highly cautious terms. Grotius wavered between a general principle of non-intervention, cautioning against 'provoking wars by usurping the care for things under the control of others', and the principle that, in cases of manifest oppression, when the people themselves cannot rise against tyranny, it is legitimate for others 'to take up arms' on their behalf.[103] The conflict between the two principles has continued to trouble Europeans, not only in 1689 but also after 1789, when, for example, Edmund Burke sought to justify British intervention in the French Revolution.[104] In 2006 it still troubles us.

---

[100] See Jonathan Israel, 'The Dutch Role in the Glorious Revolution', in Jonathan Israel (ed.), *The Anglo-Dutch Moment: Essays on the Glorious Revolution and its World Impact* (Cambridge: Cambridge University Press, 1991) and Jonathan Israel, *The Dutch Republic: its Rise, Greatness, and Fall 1477–1806* (Oxford: Oxford University Press, 1995).

[101] *The Declaration of His Highness, William Henry, By the Grace of God, Prince of Orange, &c. Of the Reasons inducing him to appear in Armes in the Kindome of England, for Preserving of the Protestant Religion, and for Restoring the Lawes and Liberties of ENGLAND, SCOTLAND and IRELAND* (The Hague, 1688) p. 7.

[102] *Resolutie, Inhoudende de redenen, die haer Hoogh Mogende Hebben bewogen, om Syne Hoogheydt, in Persoon naer Engelandt overgaende, met Schepen ende Militie te assisteren* (The Hague, 1688), p. 5.

[103] Grotius, *The Rights of War and Peace*, book II, ch. XXV, par. VIII, especially 1 and 3.

[104] See Iain Hampsher-Monk, 'Edmund Burke's Changing Justification for Intervention', *Historical Journal* 48 (2005), pp. 65–100.

10 Hobbes and democracy

Richard Tuck

I think that what Quentin Skinner's pupils learned first from him, before they absorbed any particular ideas, and even before they understood his methodological advice, was how to live an intellectually adventurous and courageous life. I remember as an undergraduate the excitement of his lectures in 1967 and 1968, which were the basis (as it later emerged) for *The Foundations of Modern Political Thought*; we watched in awe as this rather slight figure on the podium showed that one need be beholden to no one in developing one's own ideas, and that what mattered was how elegantly and powerfully one could defend them. Almost forty years of thinking about this same material has not dimmed my admiration for the lectures, for the subsequent book and for its author; everything I have thought has begun (and sometimes – surprisingly often, actually – ended) with his ideas. This paper is an example of the process.

What I want to raise in it is a question which has increasingly seemed to me to be worth putting directly to the account of modern politics implicit in the book, and in much of Skinner's subsequent work. It is about the role in this account not of republicanism but of democracy. As we all know, many of the republican theorists whom he has studied, and from whom he increasingly wants to bring lessons home to modern politics, were not democrats in anything like our sense of the word; most of them were principally (in so far as they had clear constitutional ideas) supporters of a kind of mixed government. On the other hand, if we want to find a sophisticated and deep theorist of democracy, as it has been understood since the French Revolution, then the most plausible candidate I believe is the writer whom Skinner has always posed as the great opponent of this politics, Thomas Hobbes. This may seem an extraordinary claim, such is the strength and pervasiveness of the conventional view that Hobbes was a theorist of 'despotism' or (in Skinner's own words) 'counter-revolution'. But this view, as I hope to show, rests on a mistaken history of the idea of democracy; read against a different history, Hobbes's contribution to democratic theory becomes clear, and perhaps one of his most important legacies. I should say to start with that there are two aspects to this claim. The first is that Hobbes had a specific and interesting theory of democracy, even though it may (to some extent) have been a by-product of his desire to defend an idealised monarchy; the second is that his political theory in general was more influenced by his reflections on the character of democratic government than we often realise. Though he was indeed a theorist of despotism, it was the despotic democracy which was the clearest example of what he had in mind, and he was well aware of that fact.

In this paper I shall be concentrating on Hobbes's earlier works, and not on *Leviathan*. There are two reasons for this. The first and most important is that if one is interested in Hobbes's influence on eighteenth- and even nineteenth-century European ideas of democracy, then *De Cive* is by far the most significant work. It was frequently reprinted by major publishers in its original Latin, and copies seem to have been readily available of the authorised translation into French by Hobbes's friend Samuel Sorbière,[1] whereas the Latin *Leviathan* was not reprinted after 1678, and was essentially available only as part of the 1668 *Opera Omnia*; *Leviathan* was, extraordinarily, not fully translated into French until 1971! Rousseau, for example, who was a most attentive reader of Hobbes, was primarily interested in *De Cive*. The second reason is that Hobbes presented his political theory in somewhat different terms in *Leviathan* from those which he had used in the early works; in particular, he allowed the notion of representation to do much of the expository work. This may have made a difference in the underlying theory, and a full discussion of that difficult question would require a separate paper; though I myself think that in the end the new terminology did not fundamentally alter his ideas – after all, he reprinted *De Cive* in his *Opera Omnia* alongside the Latin translation of *Leviathan*, and so presumably believed at that point that they were broadly compatible. At all events, what I present here is an account of Hobbes as he would have been understood if he had died (as he nearly did) in 1647. If it is a plausible account, then the question of what happened in *Leviathan* has to be answered in the light of it.

By the end of October 1641 Hobbes had put together a distinctive and (he claimed) original theory of political association, embedded in three connected works – a sketch (at the very least) of the second section of his great and ongoing project, the *Elementa Philosophiae*; a full version of the third section; and an English summary of both sections, in the form of a treatise on law. At the heart of this theory was a distinction between what he called in English 'concord' and 'union' (in Latin *consensio* or *concordia*[2] and *unio*). He proclaimed the novelty of this theory in ch. 8 of part II of *The Elements of Law*, in which he was dealing with those opinions which 'are maintained in the books of the dogmatics, and divers of them taught in public chairs, and nevertheless are most

---

[1] Latin texts: Paris 1642, Amsterdam 1647 (bis), Amsterdam 1657, Amsterdam 1668 (part of the *Opera Omnia*), Amsterdam 1669 (bis), Amsterdam 1696, Halle 1704, Amsterdam 1742, Lausanne 1760. The Sorbière translation was published in 1649.

[2] Rather oddly, the term *consensio* is used in the body of *De Cive*'s text, and *concordia* in the marginal notes and chapter summaries.

incompatible with peace and government, and contradictory to the necessary and demonstrable rules of the same'.[3] The third of these opinions is 'that the sovereign power may be divided':

> If there were a commonwealth, wherein the rights of sovereignty were divided, we must confess with Bodin, Lib. II. chap.I. *De Republica*, that they are not rightly to be called commonwealths, but the corruption of commonwealths. For if one part should have power to make the laws for all, they would by their laws, at their pleasure, forbid others to make peace or war, to levy taxes, or to yield fealty and homage without their leave; and they that had the right to make peace and war, and command the militia, would forbid the making of other laws, than what themselves liked . . . The error concerning mixed government hath proceeded from want of understanding of what is meant by this word *body politic*, and how it signifieth not the concord, but the union of many men. And though in the charters of subordinate corporations, a corporation be declared to be one person in law, yet the same hath not been taken notice of in the body of a commonwealth or city, nor have any of those innumerable writers of politics observed any such union.[4]

This is the plainest declaration of where his own originality lay that is to be found in either *The Elements of Law* or *De Cive*, and it shows that this distinction was seen by Hobbes as central to his whole political enterprise. The distinction seems to have been worked out most exactly in a passage of the draft *De Homine*[5] which, like much of the projected work, is presumably translated or summarised in part I of *The Elements*:

> when the wills of many concur to some one and the same action, or effect, this concourse of their wills is called CONSENT; by which we must not understand one will of many men, for every man hath his several will; but many wills to the producing of one effect . . . When many wills are involved or included in the will of one or more consenting, (which how it may be, shall be hereafter declared) then is that involving of many wills in one or more called UNION.[6]

But the fullest discussion was in ch. 5 of *De Cive*:

> However many come together in a coalition for defence, nothing will be gained if they fail to agree on the best way of doing so, and each one uses his resources in his own fashion. The reason is that, having conflicting ideas, they will obstruct each other, or if in the expectation of victory or booty or revenge, they do achieve sufficient agreement for an action, they will still be so divided afterwards by differences of purpose and policy or by envy and rivalry (natural causes of conflict) that they will not be willing to help each other or to keep peace among themselves, unless compelled to do so by a common fear. It follows from this that an *accord* [*consensio*] between several parties, i.e. an association

---

[3] Thomas Hobbes, *The Elements of Law Natural and Politic,* ed. Ferdinand Tönnies, 2nd edn (London: Frank Cass, 1969), II 8.5.

[4] Ibid., II.8.7.

[5] See the passage from *De Cive*, V.4 quoted below – 'the last section' refers (as *sectio* always did in Hobbes's Latin works) to a *sectio* of the *Elementa Philosophiae*. For additional references to the other sections, see *De Cive*, preface 18 and ch. IX.8.

[6] Hobbes, *The Elements*, I.12.7,8.

[*societas*] formed only for mutual aid, does not afford to the parties to the accord or association the security which we are looking for, to practise, in their relations with each other, the *laws of nature* given above. (An *accord* of several persons, as defined in the last section, consists only in their all directing their actions to the same end and to a *common good*.). But something more needs to be done, so that an accord on peace and mutual assistance for a *common good* may be prevented by fear from collapsing in discord when a *private good* subsequently comes into conflict with the *common good*.[7]

This 'something more' was that, because 'a *combination* of several wills in the same end is not adequate to the preservation of peace and stable defence',

it is required that there be a *single will* [*una voluntas*] among all of them in matters essential to peace and defence. This can only happen if each man subjects his *will* to the *will* of a *single* other, to the *will*, that is, of one *Man* or of one *Assembly*, in such a way that whatever that one *wills* on matters essential to the common peace may be taken as the *will* of all and each [*omnes et singuli*].[8]

General submission or subjection 'is called UNION', and

A Union so made is called a *commonwealth* [*civitas*] or *civil society* [*societas civilis*] and also a *civil person* [*persona civilis*]; for since there is *one will* of all of them, it is to be taken as *one person*; and is to be distinguished and differentiated by *a unique* name from all particular men, having its own rights and its own property [*res sibi proprias*]. Consequently, no single citizen nor all together (except him whose will stands for the will of all) are to be *regarded as the commonwealth*. A COMMONWEALTH, then, (to define it) is *one person*, whose *will*, by the agreement of several men, is to be taken as the *will* of them all; so that he may make use of their strength and resources for the common peace and defence.[9]

Everyone 'directing their actions to the same end and to *a common good*' sounds on the face of it like a desirable state of affairs, but Hobbes's central idea was that it is not *politics* – as he said in *De Cive* V.5, social animals such as bees or ants 'should not be called *political*; for their government is only an accord, or many wills with one object, not (as a commonwealth needs) one will'. Politics requires precisely the renunciation of one's own desires and projects in the interests of a united course of action, and this should not be seen (Hobbes always argued) merely as the alignment of the citizens' wills towards a generally defined end such as (say) a well-ordered common life.[10] The union of the citizens was total, in the sense that they did not preserve (even internally, I would argue) a separateness of purpose: each citizen genuinely took the will of the person or group of people who were the *civitas* to be his will, and this public

---

[7] Thomas Hobbes, *De Cive*, V.4. I have slightly altered the translation of this sentence from that found in the Cambridge edition. The original reads '*sed oportere amplius quiddam fieri, ut qui semel ad pacem, & mutuum auxilium, causa communis boni consenserint, ne postea, cum bonum suum aliquod privatum a communi discrepaverit, iterum dissentiant, metu prohibeantur*'.

[8] Ibid., V.7 (slightly corrected from Cambridge translation).   [9] Ibid., 5.9.

[10] Contrast Grotius's remarks in the Prolegomena to *De iure belli ac pacis, libri tres* §6.

will became in the process his own conscience – 'the conscience being nothing else but a man's settled judgment and opinion, when he hath once transferred his right of judging to another, that which shall be commanded, is no less his judgment, than the judgment of that other; so that in obedience to laws, a man doth still according to his conscience'.[11] This was indeed a startling idea, and it remains so; but the puzzle Hobbes wished to solve was the pre-eminent modern puzzle. Given the absence of any agreement among the citizens about matters of substance (either because as a matter of fact such agreement is not to be extracted from a culturally disparate population, or because, as Hobbes himself believed, there can be no reasonable consensus about anything), how can there be politics? His answer (as I have argued in a number of places) was that, at least for political purposes, citizens have to be ready to accept the irrelevancy of their own views, and genuinely transfer their own judgements about all contentious issues to a single agent who will make a conclusive judgement on their behalf.[12]

As I have said, total union of this kind sounds extraordinary, and there were no contemporary European states which claimed to be examples of such a thing. Indeed, Hobbes himself may have supposed that there never had been such a state – see his distinctly utopian remarks in the Epistle Dedicatory to *De Cive*, and the rather similar remarks in part IV of *Leviathan*.[13] The governing ideology of most states, whether monarchies or republics, was that they were mixed constitutions of some sort, and of course the essence of a mixed constitution

---

[11] Hobbes, *The Elements*, II.6.12. Some people are misled by the fact that this passage continues, 'but not his private conscience' into supposing that Hobbes imagined that one could have a 'public' and a 'private' conscience with respect to the same thing. But it is clear from what comes later in paragraph 12 that he meant that one would have a 'private' conscience only if the issue with which the conscience was concerned had not yet come under the consideration of the sovereign. Obeying law is as much a matter of internal assent as is acting on one's own judgement.

[12] The one exception to this – and it is a subtle and complex issue – is that citizens of a special kingdom of God are exempt in religious matters from this requirement internally to assent to the judgements of the (pagan) sovereign, though not necessarily from externally assenting. Fully to discuss this question would require again another paper.

[13] If the patterns of human action were known with the same certainty as the relations of magnitude in figures, ambition and greed, whose power rests on the false opinions of the common people about right and wrong, would be disarmed, and the human race would enjoy such secure peace that (apart from conflicts over space as the population grew) it seems unlikely that it would ever have to fight again. But as things are, the war of the sword and the war of the pens is perpetual (*De Cive*). 'Whence comes it, that in Christendome there has been, almost from the time of the Apostles, such justling of one another out of their places, both by forraign, and Civill war? such stumbling at every little asperity of their own fortune, and every little eminence of that of other men? and such diversity of ways of running to the same mark, *Felicity*, if it be not Night amongst us, or at least a Mist? [W]ee are therefore yet in the Dark' (*Leviathan*, ch. 44, p. 334 of the original). For Hobbes's utopianism, see now Richard Tuck, 'The Utopianism of Leviathan', in Tom Sorell and Luc Foisneau (eds.), *Leviathan after 350 Years* (Oxford: Oxford University Press, 2004) pp. 125–38.

was that the different elements were (to use Hobbes's terminology) in accord rather than united.

Even if the parts of the state were not articulated in the classic mixed fashion, into a single person, an aristocratic or oligarchic council, and a more democratic assembly, the conventional idea of the 'body politic' (as Hobbes spotted) still rested on the notion of accord between the individual citizens, as in the story in Livy from which the imagery was so often drawn (that is, the speech of Menenius Agrippa at the Secession of the Plebs, II.32).

But this traditional view had itself come into being in opposition to a vision of politics much closer to that which Hobbes wanted to introduce (or re-introduce) into the modern world, and the striking thing about this alternative vision was that it was explicitly and systematically a theory of democracy. The story begins, as one might have supposed, with Aristotle, and in particular with the distinction in the *Politics* between two kinds of democracy, which were (on the Aristotelian account) fundamentally at odds with one another. The discussion which was to be most relevant to Hobbes's theory came in book IV, in the section of the *Politics* which is probably a separate and free-standing work on constitutional forms from Aristotle's later years, and which is almost certainly closely related to the *Constitution of Athens*. In this book, Aristotle, after distinguishing between four types of democracy according to their differing levels of citizen participation, turned to a more fundamental distinction. In all the four types which he had so far dealt with, 'the law [νομοι, *nomoi*] is supreme'. But there is a fifth,

in which not the law, but the multitude, have the supreme power, and supersede the law by their decrees [ψηφισματα, *psephismata* or plebiscites]. This is a state of affairs brought about by the demagogues. For in democracies which are subject to the law the best citizens hold the first place, and there are no demagogues; but where the laws are not supreme, there demagogues spring up. For the people becomes a monarch, and is many in one; and the many have the power in their hand, not as individuals, but collectively . . . This sort of democracy, which is now a monarchy, and no longer under the control of law, seeks to exercise monarchical sway, and grows into a despot; the flatterer is held in honour; this sort of democracy is to other democracies what tyranny is to other forms of monarchy . . . (1292a5–20)

Elsewhere, Aristotle terms this kind of regime 'extreme democracy' (δημος ἐσχατος, *dēmos eschatos*) (1296a1).

Modern scholars have become clearer about what Aristotle had in mind in this passage, after the discovery in 1890 of a nearly complete text of Aristotle's *Constitution of Athens*. By a 'democracy subject to the law' he had in mind the restored constitution of Athens after 403, in which a body of νομοθεται (*nomothetai*) elected from the roll of jurors decided on any amendments to existing legislation, following a quasi-judicial proceeding in which witnesses for and against a proposal were heard. The democratic Assembly's ψηφισματα (*psēphismata*) were no longer allowed (as they had been under the Periclean democracy) to decide legislative issues on the basis of general discussion and majority vote. Hansen has observed, intriguingly, that the very word δημος (*dēmos*), while it is often used as a synonym for the Assembly, is never used as a synonym for the jury.[14] The Athens of Aristotle's time, in other words, had tried to erect a system of constitutional law which was to a degree immune to ordinary democratic activity, and which called for judicial reflection rather than political discussion, in a very modern way; Aristotle like many of his contemporaries appears to have thought that this was a restoration of the original Solonic democracy, which had gradually been corrupted from the time of Aristides onwards, and which was turned into an extreme democracy by Cleon. Medieval readers lacked this precise knowledge, but they were aware of the general point of Aristotle's remarks, and usually associated them (reasonably enough) with the defence in the *Politics* of the πολιτεια (*politeia*) or 'mixed democracy', in which a variety of institutions reined in the power of the δημος (*dēmos*), and in which the balance of the institutions was preserved by a relatively inviolable underlying structure of law.

Extreme democracy, according to Aristotle, was thus a constitution which had too high a degree of unity among its citizens. In book I he had attacked the Socrates of the *Republic* for arguing that the city should be united, arguing instead that 'freemen and equals . . . cannot all rule together' and that rotation of magistracies among them preserved equality without sacrificing diversity (1261a30); in book II he repeated that 'there is a point at which a state may attain such a degree of unity as to be no longer a state, or at which, without actually ceasing to exist, it will become an inferior state . . . The state is a plurality [πληθος, *plēthos*], which should be united and made into a community by education' (1263b30–40). It is clear throughout Aristotle's discussion of constitutions that he envisaged a well-founded democracy to be a mode of government in which there was a certain amount of agreement on common ends among the citizens, but not total agreement, and in which there was no one sovereign source of authority over their lives. And through the rediscovered *Politics* this system of distributed powers became the standard constitutional model for medieval Europe, and beyond.

A similar system had already come to be regarded as the model for Rome, though with some straining of the facts. On the face of it, the Roman Republic from the third century BCE onwards was a clear example of an Aristotelian extreme democracy. There was no distinction between νομοι (*nomoi*) and

---

14 Mogens Herman Hansen, 'The Sovereignty of the People's Court in Athens in the Fourth Century BC and the Public Action Against Unconstitutional Proposals', in *Odense University Classical Studies* 4 (Odense: Odense University Press, 1974), pp. 19–21. Hansen argues persuasively that Aristotle did not count Athens as a 'radical democracy' (p. 14), but as a 'mixed democracy' (p. 60).

ψηφισματα (*psēphismata*) at Rome; every piece of legislation, even the ancient Twelve Tables themselves, could be changed by a *plebiscitum* passed by a simple majority vote in the *concilium plebis* presided over by the tribunes.[15] Moreover, the Republic was not a deliberative democracy: the various assemblies were the means by which a mass voting population (910,000 registered citizens in the census of 70/69, compared with a good estimate of 30,000 in fourth-century Athens) could express their wishes, while discussion and deliberation were expressly confined to the Senate, which consisted (in the classical period of the Republic) of magistrates and ex-magistrates who had previously been elected to their offices in the assemblies. One might say that the classical Roman republican constitution was the reverse of the post-403 Athenian constitution: at Athens, policy matters were discussed in the democratic assembly, but important legislation took place in an elected body, while at Rome the Senate discussed policy, and the assemblies voted on the plebiscites.

The fact that Rome was an extreme or tyrannical democracy according to the Aristotelian classification was obscured by a division among the Romans themselves over how to characterise their republic. The most influential tradition for later readers stemmed from the circle of Scipio Africanus the Younger, who befriended Polybius and appears as an interlocutor in Cicero's *De republica*; the view of this tradition, expressed by both Polybius and Cicero, was that Rome was a mixed constitution and was therefore close in form to a *politeia*. Cicero in particular insisted repeatedly that pure democracy was dangerous – 'the principle which ought always to be adhered to in the commonwealth [is] that the greatest number should not have the greatest power'[16] – and that democratic equality (*aequabilitas*) was undesirable.[17] Clearly, this was partly an attempt to rescue Rome from the opprobrium of democratic tyranny with which it might be invested in the Greek world; indeed, many Greeks did see Rome in this light, as is shown by the accounts of its constitution in Dionysius of Halicarnassus, and in the constitutional theory put by Cassius Dio into the mouth of Agrippa in the fascinating debate at the court of Augustus about whether truly to restore the republic.[18] But it was also presumably an attempt to force the constitution into

---

[15] See the excellent discussion in Andrew Lintott, *The Constitution of the Roman Republic* (Oxford: Oxford University Press 1999), e.g. p. 63. Other popular assemblies could also change any existing legislation by majority vote – the differing methods for legislating under the Republic are notoriously complicated.

[16] Cicero, *De Republica*, II.39.

[17] See in particular *De Republica*, I.43 and I.53, in which *aequabilitas* is contrasted unfavourably with *aequitas*, the recognition of merited distinction. Lactantius (*Divine Institutes*, V.14) powerfully denounced these passages of Cicero, concluding that 'neither the Romans nor the Greeks could hold justice, because they had men distinguished by many grades, from the poor to the rich, from the lowly to the powerful, from private citizens even to the most sublime heights of kings'. The contrast of *aequabilitas* with *aequitas* was preserved for medieval and Renaissance writers in this section of Lactantius, as the relevant parts of the *De Republica* were not known until 1820.

[18] Cicero, *De Republica*, LII.9.

a form which was congenial to the *optimates* towards the end of the Republic. More radical and *popularis* Latin writers such as Sallust seem to have thought of Rome straightforwardly as an unmixed democracy, though the passage in which Sallust says this most clearly is a fragment from a lost work.[19] In the absence of the Greek texts, this view was more or less unknown in the middle ages, and even when they came to be known, their discovery was balanced by the discovery of Polybius which (then as now) was the most systematic and authoritative statement of the 'mixed' interpretation.

A plural state of the Aristotelian or Polybian kind is of course in some sense a single agent. At the beginning of the *Politics*, Aristotle uses the comparison between a state and a body: 'the state is by nature clearly prior to the family and to the individual, since the whole is of necessity prior to the part; for example, if the whole body be destroyed, there will be no foot or hand, except homonymously, as we might speak of a stone hand' (1253a20). This image became extremely popular among Roman writers; thus Cicero talked of the *corpus reipublicae*,[20] and I have already mentioned Livy's famous use of the image. The lawyers used the term (Digest 41.3.30, 6.1.23.5), and Seneca expounded it approximately in terms of Stoic philosophy:

there are certain continuous bodies, such as a man; there are certain composite bodies, – as ships, houses, and everything which is the result of joining separate parts into one sum total: there are certain others made up of things that are distinct, each member remaining separate – like an army, a populace [*populus*], or a senate. For the persons who go to make up such bodies are united by virtue of law or function [*iure aut officio*]; but by their nature they are distinct and individual.[21]

As Seneca's remarks illustrate, the notion of the *corpus rei publicae* did not in any way preclude the kind of plurality which both Aristotle and Cicero advocated. The different parts of the body politic remained distinct but collaborating, as in the fable told by Menenius Agrippa, and the unity of the whole was given by this agreement – it was a prime example of the kind of *consensus* and *concordia* which Cicero extolled.

The language of the *corpus rei publicae* or (in less good Latin) the *corpus politicum* persisted all through the middle ages and the Renaissance. At some point it came to be joined by the language of the *persona publica*; although Gierke declared that the notion of the 'person' was not applied to the state (as distinct from the private corporation) by medieval writers,[22] subsequent scholarship has uncovered many such instances, notably in the writings of the

[19] The speech of Macer the tribune (from the lost *Historiae*) 15–17, 24.

[20] See *De Officiis*, I.85; *In Pisonem*, 25; *Pro Murena*, 51.

[21] Seneca, *Epistulae Morales*, trans. Richard Gummere, Loeb Classical Library LXXVII (Cambridge, Mass: Harvard University Press), pp. 170–1.

[22] Otto von Gierke was already arguing this in his 1880 essay on Althusius: Otto von Gierke, *The Development of Political Theory*, trans. Bernard Freyd (New York: H. Fertig, 1939) – see e.g. p. 150.

fifteenth-century conciliarist John of Segovia, which Antony Black drew to our attention thirty years ago. What Segovia called the *presidens*, that is, the ruler,

> ceases to be a private and is made a public person; he loses in a sense his isolated unity, and puts on the united people [*perdit quodammodo solitariam unitatem, et induit unitam multitudinem*], so that he may be said to bear the person not of one but of many.[23]

Superficially, this sounds strikingly like Hobbes, but the key difference is that Segovia presumed that the *multitudo* had a separate collective existence from the *presidens*, and that it could exercise authority over itself whenever it gathered itself in one place,

> since truth itself is preferred to fiction. For the truth is that this people is many persons; while the fiction is that the president himself, who in truth is a single person, is said to be many by representation. But, when someone is said to have authority simply on the ground that he represents one or many others, by the very fact that those represented are present, their authority, and not his, is heeded . . .[24]

In other words, the *presidens* represented the unity of the *corpus politicum*, but the *corpus* continued to be seen as a unity composed of disparate elements, whose capacity to act as a single entity came from the natural (the 'truthful') alignment of their wills – still concord of the Aristotelian or the Ciceronian type.

The first, slight, indications of an interest in the possibilities of 'extreme' democracy came in the translations of and commentaries on book IV of the *Politics*. William of Moerbeke's translation, the standard translation until the fifteenth century, had described extreme democracy as being when the *dominus* is the *multitudo* and not the *lex*, and when the people rule through their *sententiae*, encouraged by *demagogi*. Then *monarchus enim fit populus compositus unus ex multis*.[25] The Thomist commentary on this (now known to be by Pierre d'Auvergne) explained it by saying that these *sententiae* were concerned with particulars, not generalities, and that this was what made the democracy tyrannical.[26] But Renaissance writers began to see a different possibility. Bruni's new translation of Aristotle described the acts of the radical democracy with the neutral Latin term *decreta*, but commenting on his translation the mid-fifteenth-century Florentine humanist Donato Acciaiuoli pointed out that what

---

[23] Antony Black, *Monarchy and Community: Political Ideas in the Later Conciliar Controversy 1430–1450* (Cambridge, Cambridge University Press, 1970), pp. 25, 143.

[24] Ibid., pp. 27, 143.

[25] See the text in Aquinas, *Octo Libros Politicorum Aristotelis Expositio*, ed. Raymund M. Spiazzi (Turin: Marietti, 1966), p. 201 (liber IV, lectio iv).

[26] Ibid., p. 203. The text is corrupt, among other things reading *decreta* for *sententiae*. This was the result of the Renaissance reworking of the Thomist texts to bring them in line with Bruni's translation of Aristotle: see Aquinas, *Sententia libri Politicorum*, in *Opera Omnia iussu Leonis XIII P. M. edita*, t. 48 (Rome, 1971), A17–18. There is no accurate edition of books IV–VIII of this commentary, unlike I–III, which are by Aquinas.

Bruni had called the *ductores populi* who led the radical democracy were people like the tribunes at Rome.[27] This hint was picked up in the mid-sixteenth century, largely by French Aristotelians, who began to translate ψηφισματα (*psephismata*) as *plebiscita*,[28] thereby firmly associating Aristotle's tyrannical democracy with Rome. The most widely read new translation of the *Politics*, by the Italian Pietro Vettori, used the term, and also included a commentary on the phrase 'the people becomes a monarch' which must have been a source of Hobbes's thinking on the subject:

Princeps enim populus fit, iunctus unus e multis. The passage shows the difference between this, and a monarch properly so called. For a monarch is a mortal being who does everything in his own right; this kind of democracy is made up of many beings, even though they are all mortal, out of whom a people [*populus*] is formed by all coming together and making one man [*unus homo*] . . .[29]

This passage is worth some reflection. Though it is always risky to claim that there are no earlier instances of a particular turn of phrase (Gierke himself, as we have seen, was caught out by this), I can say at least that I have not come across the plain statement that a people is 'one man' before Vettori. The *corpus politicum*, as the passage from Seneca which I quoted earlier illustrates, was not the same as a man, precisely because it consisted of disaggregated parts which were only combined together through some kind of *consensus*; to picture the actual human body as functioning through agreement of the members was to talk the language of fable and not of anatomy. Writers in the Aristotelian or Ciceronian tradition (and one or other of those descriptions encompasses almost everyone for a thousand years) were thus rather wary of describing the *res publica* as 'one man', precisely because it emphasised the undesirable unity of the state.

What was to prove the decisive move in the assimilation of Rome to the category of extreme democracy was made by another French humanist of the midcentury, Nicholas Grouchy, in the first comprehensive and historically accurate analysis of the voting assemblies at Rome. Grouchy explained his interest in the *comitia* in the preface, in the following words:

As long as the Roman Republic was free, it was formed from the three kinds of republic (as Polybius shows), βασιλεια, αριστοκρατια, δημοκρατια: but it seems to me that δημοκρατια [democracy] had much the greatest role. While a kind of royal power can be seen in the consulate, and aristocratic power in the Senate, the people had such

---

[27] Donato Acciaiuoli, *In Aristotelis Libros Octo Politicorum Commentarii* (Venice, 1566), p. 131.

[28] See Joachim Périon (trans.), *De Republica, qui Politicorum dicitur, libri VIII* (Basle, 1549), p. 128.

[29] Pietro Vettori, *Politicorum libri octo ex Dion. Lambini & P. Victorii interpretationibus* (Basle, 1582), pp. 352–3, 357. (Vettori's translation is the left column, Lambin's right – see p. 2. Lambin was more circumspect – in place of *plebiscita* he said *decreta, quae psephismata Graeci dicunt*).

authority over all the magistrates, and the Senate, that it is not unjustified to say that all the sovereignty of the Republic [*omne imperium, omnem maiestatem illius Reip.*] was with the people . . . Passing laws, making peace and war, contracting or dissolving associations with others, and making treaties, were all in the power of the people. So great was the reward of virtue in the Republic, that no one could seek the offices and honours which everyone wanted except *via* the people . . .[30]

Grouchy's new interpretation was immediately attacked, notably by the Italian Carlo Sigonio and (despite his practice in translating) Joachim Périon, but it was also quickly endorsed by other scholars, such as the influential Onofrio Panvinio.[31] The quarrel about how to construe the Republic continued into the next century, with opinion evenly divided;[32] it continues, indeed, down to our own time. But Grouchy had for the very first time since Antiquity given political theorists a well-documented example of a functioning radical democracy, complete with full details of its complex voting systems and an analysis of how they worked to solve various problems inherent in electoral politics.[33] The theorists responded quickly, though not necessarily in the way Grouchy might have welcomed. Jean Bodin in his *Methodus* of 1566 picked up Grouchy's interpretation of the Republic; but he made clear that he did not share Grouchy's esteem for the Republic itself.[34] Whereas Grouchy had seen the Republic as a model political system, Bodin both in the *Methodus* and in the later *Six Books of the Republic* was intensely critical of democratic politics as represented by Rome, and used the new understanding of the Republic as a democracy principally as a means of attacking it. For Bodin, as is well known, political authority was the same kind of thing as paternal authority: his political ideas were driven by a profound anti-Aristotelianism, in which both the distinction which Aristotle had made between the city and the family, and the concept of a mixed constitution, were to be swept away. As a consequence, democracy on Bodin's account became clearly a debased form of government, in which

[30] Nicholas Grouchy, *De Comitiis Romanorum Libri Tres* (Paris, 1555), p. 3r.

[31] For Sigonio see William McCuaig, *Carlo Sigonio: the Changing World of the Late Renaissance* (Princeton: Princeton University Press, 1989); for Périon, see his *De Romanorum et Graecorum Magistratibus Libri Tres* (Paris 1559, 2nd edn Strasbourg 1607), p. 294; for Panvinio see *Reipublicae Romanae Commentariorum libri III* (Venice, 1558), p. 302.

[32] Paulus Merula thought that the republic was clearly democratic – see his *De Legibus Romanorum*, II.12, posthumously published in his *Opera Posthuma* (Leiden 1684) p. 51, but Zamoscus in his *De Senatu Romano* (Strasbourg 1607) said that it was *temperatio civitatis* (pp. 171ff).

[33] Notably the rule which prevented Condorcet or Arrow effects in majority voting between three or more candidates (cyclic majorities). This was always a risk in the annual election of the ten tribunes, who were selected by the assembly on the basis of a preference ordering among the candidates. The rule was that the tribes (the voting units) voted in a random sequence, with a candidate being declared elected once he had secured the votes of more than half the tribes, and the tribes who had not yet voted then choosing among the candidates who remained.

[34] Though it should be said that Grouchy did praise Bodin in his *Refutatio*, p. 5v.

the merits of paternal authority were obscured. Although Bodin's attack on the mixed constitution was followed by a number of early seventeenth-century writers, notably Grotius, they also tended not to construe the Republic as a model democracy – for Grotius it was a model, but its constitution was aristocratic, not democratic.[35]

So the idea that Rome had been an admirable radical democracy (as distinct, of course, from an admirable mixed constitution – a sentiment widely shared) remained the preserve of those historians who agreed with Grouchy, and did not form the basis of a more general political theory, until – it can be claimed – the work of Hobbes. Particularly in *De Cive*, Hobbes granted democracy a very special status, in a way which was quite unprecedented. It is true that he was (from the point of view of his liberal readers) an advocate of despotism or tyranny, but the clearest example of tyranny, as far as he was concerned, was the tyrannical democracy which Aristotle had attacked in book IV, and his whole theory of the body politic was designed to show how the union which Aristotle had criticised in that passage was in fact the only legitimate form of political association. The Aristotelians were therefore wrong in supposing that it was possible to think of a political association in which the different elements worked together but kept their individuality. As he had spotted, the traditional idea of the 'body politic' presupposed that the ruler was separate from the ruled, and that it was the agreement between ruler and ruled which kept the body functioning. In place of this, he insisted that the commonwealth was genuinely (as Vettori had said) *unus homo*, which was itself the 'monarch' or 'prince'. Hobbes clearly referred to Aristotle's observation that (in Vettori's translation) the tyrannical democracy was where the *princeps populus fit*, when he said in *De Cive* that

men do not make a clear enough distinction between a *people* and a *crowd*. A *people* is a *single* entity, with *a single will*; you can attribute *an act* to it. None of this can be said of a crowd. In every commonwealth the *People* reigns; for even in *Monarchies* the *People* exercises power [*imperat*]; for the *people* wills through the will of *one man*. But the citizens, i.e. the subjects, are a *crowd*. In a *Democracy* and in an *Aristocracy* the citizens are a *crowd*, but the *council* is the *people*; in a *Monarchy* the subjects are the *crowd*, and (paradoxically) the *King* is the *people*.[36]

---

[35] By the time of *De iure belli ac pacis* in 1625, Bodin was saying things which to some extent anticipate Hobbes – see his remarks at I.3.19 about Polybius: 'At the Time in which he wrote, the Government [of Rome] was merely popular, if we consider the Right and not the Manner of acting; since not only the Authority of the Senate, which he refers to Aristocracy, but also that of the Consuls, which he compares to Monarchy, were both dependent on the People. What I have said of Polybius, I say likewise of other Authors, who, in writing on Politicks, may think it more agreeable to their Purpose, to regard the external Form of Government, and the Manner in which Affairs are commonly administered, than the Nature itself of Sovereignty.'

[36] Hobbes, *De Cive*, XII.8.

If the people can be thought of as a king (according to Aristotle), then by the same token, Hobbes thought, a king can be thought of as the people.

But Hobbes's sense that tyrannical democracy was in some way the paradigm for his well-founded commonwealth goes further than this. Particularly in *De Cive*, he made clear that democracy was foundational and special:

Let us now see what the founders do in the formation of each kind of commonwealth. When men have met to erect a commonwealth, they are, almost by the very fact that they have met, a *Democracy*. From the fact that they have gathered voluntarily, they are understood to be bound by the decisions made by agreement of the majority. And that is a *Democracy*, as long as the convention lasts, or is set to reconvene at certain times and places. For a convention whose will is the will of all the citizens has *sovereign power*. And because it is assumed that each man in this convention has the right to vote, it follows that it is a *Democracy*, by the definition given in the first article of this chapter [i.e. a democracy is 'where *sovereign power* lies with an *Assembly* in which any citizen has the right to vote'].[37]

Majority voting, he made clear, was critical: 'Two things . . . constitute a *Democracy*, of which one (an uninterrupted schedule of meetings) constitutes a δημος [*dēmos*], and the other (which is majority voting) constitutes το κράτος or authority [*potestas*]'.[38] And it was this fact, that an extreme democracy is the paradigm commonwealth, which enabled Hobbes to argue forcefully for one of his key political ideas, which differentiated him from virtually all theorists before Rousseau, that the state was constituted by merely one contract.

It is usually thought, and not unreasonably, that the primary point of this idea was (as Pufendorf was to put it later) 'to oppose those seditious and turbulent Spirits, who, in his Time, laboured to bring down the regal Power to their own Model . . . [and] to cut off from these Men their ordinary Plea for Rebellion, which was, that there is a reciprocal Faith between the Prince and the People'.[39] But the most powerful argument which Hobbes had at his disposal to make this point was that it was ridiculous to conceive of a radical democracy in this light: as he remarked in a note added to *De Cive* VI.13 in 1647,

A popular state obviously requires absolute power, and the citizens do not object. For even the politically unaware see the face of the commonwealth in the popular assembly and recognise that affairs are being managed by its counsel.[40] A Monarchy is no less a commonwealth than a Democracy, and absolute Kings have their Counsellors, by whom they wish to be advised and to have their commands in all important matters reviewed, though not revoked. But to most people it is less obvious that the commonwealth is contained in the person of the King.[41]

---

[37] Ibid., VII.5.   [38] Ibid.

[39] Samuel Pufendorf, *Of the Law of Nature and of Nations*, trans. Basil Kennett (Oxford, 1703), VII.2.9.

[40] The Cambridge translation has 'deliberations' instead of 'counsel'; the original is *consilio*, and in this context 'deliberations' may confusingly suggest a deliberative assembly.

[41] Hobbes, *De Cive*, VI.13n.

Or, as he said at VII.7, 'after a commonwealth has been formed, any agreement by a citizen with the *People* is without effect, because the *People* absorbs into its own will the will of the citizen . . . [*populus voluntate sua voluntatem civis . . . complectitur*]'.[42] Pufendorf himself recognised the force of this when he conceded that his own account of the two contracts might not convince his reader in the case of a democracy, 'yet he cannot fairly take Occasion thence to exclude it from other Forms, where those who command, and those who obey, are really and naturally different Persons'.[43] In a sense, one could say that whereas earlier writers (including Aristotle himself) had taken something like a mixed state to be paradigmatic, and had interpreted democracy as ideally a kind of mixed government, Hobbes took democracy to be paradigmatic, and ruthlessly interpreted all other forms (even monarchy) as like democracy.

It goes without saying, and it is on the face of it the great difference between him and later democratic theorists such as Rousseau, that Hobbes supposed that implicit in the power of an actual democracy was the power to dissolve itself and transfer its sovereignty to a single person; this is, after all, why he has normally been seen as an apologist for monarchy and as profoundly unrepublican. But two things should be said about this. The first and most important is that there are many ways of being dominated by other men, and socially approved arguments can oppress us as surely as laws. The power of Hobbes's extreme democracy was total precisely because (on his general account of politics) no room should be left for any contentious principles to govern and restrain the people's actions. The logic of this, or so he not implausibly believed, was that the democracy had *inter alia* the right to decide that another agent could exercise its power, since otherwise a constitutional principle would be constraining the popular will; and if that principle, why not others? This is potentially a bleak view of democratic politics, and it is possible that Rousseau thought of a way out of it, but it is a real dilemma for anyone as bitterly opposed as Hobbes to the informal structures of coercion which proliferate in modern liberal democratic societies.

The second thing to say is that the outlook might not have been as bleak as it appears at first glance. There were actually two separate concerns in the parts of *De Cive* devoted to constitutional matters (and, though to a lesser extent, in the equivalent parts of *The Elements of Law*). One, with which we are very familiar, was a desire to show that the king of England was an absolute monarch in the sense that he did not owe his authority to Parliament;[44] but the other and much

---

[42] Intriguingly, one of the meanings of *complector* is 'represent' – this may count as the first use of the notion of 'representation' in this context in Hobbes, and illustrates how the elaborate discussion of the concept in *Leviathan* may simply spell out in detail an idea which was already effectively present in the earlier work.

[43] Pufendorf, *Of the Law of Nature and Nations*, VII.2.12.

[44] The specifics of the English constitution are not dealt with explicitly in *De Cive*, but the anti-Parliamentary thrust of the argument is abundantly clear.

more surprising desire was to establish that democratic sovereignty could in principle be both legitimate and practically effective. Hobbes indeed signalled this latter desire with a remark in the preface to the 1647 edition that it had been among his aims

> not to give the impression that citizens owe less obedience to an Aristocratic commonwealth or a Democratic commonwealth than they owe to a Monarchical commonwealth. For though I have deployed some arguments in the tenth chapter to press the point that Monarchy has more advantages than other forms of commonwealth (the only thing in this book which I admit is not demonstrated but put with probability), I say everywhere explicitly that every commonwealth must be allowed supreme and equal power (para. 22).

He made good on this commitment by paying more than lip service to the principle of equality between the constitutional forms, and by documenting in some detail the way in which democracies might be as effective and admirable as monarchies.

The discussion of the issue in chs. VII, X and XII, which are the chapters in which practical political issues are primarily discussed, turns on an important but often neglected distinction in Hobbes between 'government' (*imperium*) and 'administration of government' (*administratio gubernandi*):

> For government is a *capacity*, administration of government is an *act*. *Power* is equal in every kind of commonwealth; what differs are the acts, i.e. the *motions* and *actions* of the commonwealth, depending on whether they originate from the deliberations of many or of a few, of the competent or the incompetent. This implies that the advantages and disadvantages of a regime do not depend upon him in whom the authority of the commonwealth resides, but upon the ministers of government. Hence it is no obstacle to the good government of a commonwealth if the *Monarch* is a woman, boy, or infant, provided that the holders of the ministries and public offices are competent to handle the business . . .[45]

In a related passage in ch. XIII, he drew a striking analogy:

> We must distinguish between the *right* [*ius*] and the *exercise* [*exercitium*] of sovereign power [*summum imperium*]; for they can be separated; for instance, he who has the right may be unwilling or unable to play a personal role in conducting trials or deliberating issues . . . When *right* and *exercise* are separated, the government of the commonwealth is like the ordinary government of the world, in which God the first mover of all things, produces natural effects through the order of secondary causes. But when he who has the right to reign wishes to participate himself in all judgements, consultations, and public actions, it is a way of running things comparable to God's attending directly to every thing himself, contrary to the order of nature.[46]

So Hobbes supposed that under normal circumstances government and its administration would be separated, and that this was the most 'natural' state

---

[45] Hobbes, *De Cive*, X.16.   [46] Ibid., XIII.1.

of affairs. The superiority of one type of sovereign constitutional order over its rivals then rested purely on the kind of administration to which it was likely to give rise, and it was quite possible to have a democratic sovereign whose administration met Hobbes's standards of effectiveness. Such an administration could not be a deliberative assembly: he made abundantly clear in all his discussions of commonwealths that such assemblies are the antithesis of a well-founded democracy. In popular states, for example, he remarked, 'there may be as many *Neros* as there are *Orators* who fawn on the *people*'.[47] And in a most powerful passage from the same chapter, a passage which in many ways lies at the emotional heart of Hobbes's whole enterprise, he mocked those who defended democracy as a forum for deliberation:

Perhaps someone will say that the *popular state* is immensely preferable to *Monarchy*, because in that state, in which of course everyone manages public business, everyone has been given leave to publicly display his prudence knowledge and eloquence in deliberations about matters of the greatest difficulty and importance; and because the love of praise is innate in human nature, this is the most attractive of all things to all those who surpass others in such talents or seem to themselves to do so; but in *Monarchy* that road to winning praise and rank is blocked for most of the citizens. What is a disadvantage, if this is not? I will tell you. To see the proposal of a man whom we despise preferred to our own; to see our wisdom ignored before our eyes; to incur certain enmity in an uncertain struggle for empty glory (for this cannot be avoided, whether we win or lose); to hate and be hated because of differences of opinion; to reveal our plans and wishes when there is no need to and to get nothing by it; to neglect our private affairs. These, I say, are disadvantages. But to lose the opportunity to pit your wits against another man, however enjoyable such contests may be to clever debaters, is not such a disadvantage for them, unless we shall say that it is a disadvantage for brave men to be forbidden to fight, for the simple reason that they enjoy it.[48]

And it was of course true for Hobbes that democratic sovereignty might readily imply deliberative government, and that the great merit of monarchical sovereignty was that it was less likely to (though the – from his perspective – depressing history of English Parliaments showed that this was far from being necessarily true). But a democracy without a deliberative assembly was not at all inferior to a monarchy:

These disadvantages found in the deliberations of large assemblies prove that *Monarchy* is better than *Democracy* insofar as in *Democracy* questions of great importance are more often passed to such assemblies for discussion than in a *Monarchy*; it cannot easily be otherwise. There is no reason why anyone would not prefer to spend his time on his *private business* rather than on *public affairs*, except that he sees scope for his eloquence, to acquire a reputation for intelligence and good sense, and to return home and enjoy his triumph with his friends, parents and family for his great achievements. The whole pleasure which *Marcus Coriolanus* drew from his deeds in war was seeing

---

[47] Ibid., X.7.   [48] Ibid., X.9.

that the praises of him pleased his mother. But if in a *Democracy* the *people* chose to concentrate deliberations about war and peace and legislation in the hands of just one man or a very small number of men, content themselves with the appointment of magistrates and public ministers, content, that is, to have authority without executive function, then it must be admitted that *Democracy* and *Monarchy* would be equal in this matter.[49]

This is of course effectively a description of the Roman Republic, in which deliberation was restricted to the Senate, and the *comitia* simply voted on the laws presented to it and on the election of magistrates. In *The Elements* he provided a second example:

But though the sovereignty be not mixed, but be always either simple democracy, or simple aristocracy, or pure monarchy; nevertheless in the administration thereof, all those sorts of government may have place subordinate. For suppose the sovereign power be democracy, as it was sometimes in Rome, yet at the same time they may have a council aristocratical, such as was the senate; and at the same time they may have a subordinate monarch, such as was their dictator, who had for a time the exercise of the whole sovereignty, and such as are all generals in war. So also in a monarchy there may be a council aristocratical of men chosen by the monarch; or democratical of men chosen by the consent (the monarch permitting) of all the particular men of the commonwealth. And this mixture is it that imposeth; as if it were the mixture of sovereignty. As if a man should think, because the great council of Venice doth nothing ordinarily but choose magistrates, ministers of state, captains, and governors of towns, ambassadors, counsellors, and the like; that therefore their part of the sovereignty is only choosing of magistrates; and that the making of war, and peace, and laws, were not theirs, but the part of such councillors as they appointed thereto; whereas it is the part of these to do it but subordinately, the supreme authority thereof being in the great council that choose them.[50]

As the analogy with the God who is First Mover illustrates, Hobbes was also quite prepared to envisage a situation where the democratic sovereign (unlike at Rome or Venice) had virtually no power to intervene in the daily running of the state. Sovereignty anyway, he argued, was general in scope – 'the sovereign as such provides for the citizens' safety only by means of laws, which are universal'[51] – and there would normally be no occasion for genuinely arbitrary

---

[49] Ibid., X.15.   [50] Ibid., II.1.17.

[51] Ibid., XIII.3. This rather surprising claim was not a temporary aberration, but was repeated by Hobbes very plainly as late as *Behemoth*. In this dialogue on the Civil War in England, the interlocutor (B) asks the sage (A), 'Must tyrants . . . be obeyed in everything actively? Or is there nothing wherein a lawful King's command may be disobeyed? What if he should command me with my own hands to execute my father, in case he should be condemned to die by the law?' A answers, 'This is a case that need not be put. We never have read nor heard of any King or tyrant so inhuman as to command it. If any did, we are to consider whether that command were one of his laws. For by disobeying Kings, we mean the disobeying of his laws, those his laws that were made before they were applied to any particular person; for the King, though as a father of children, and a master of domestic servants[,] command many things which bind those

acts of sovereignty by a monarch or a democracy. The only condition which had to be met in order for a constitution to be democratic was that all the citizens could meet or otherwise declare their will on at least one occasion without being summoned by a monarch or aristocratic council. *De Cive* explained this by an extended comparison between a democracy and a sleeping monarch:

The intervals between meetings of the citizens may be compared to the times when a *Monarch* is asleep; for the power is retained though there are no acts of commanding[;] . . . the dissolution of a meeting on the terms that it may not reconvene is the death of a *people*, just as so to sleep that one can never wake is the death of a man. If a King without an heir is about to go to sleep and not wake up again, (i.e., is about to die) and hands sovereign power to someone to exercise until he awakes, he is handing him also the succession; likewise if a *people*[52] in choosing a temporary Monarch, at the same time abolishes its own power of reconvening, it is passing dominion over the commonwealth to him. Further, a king who is going to sleep for a while gives sovereign power to someone else to exercise, and takes it back when he wakes up; just so *a people, on the election of a temporary Monarch*, retains the right of meeting again at a certain time and place, and on that day resumes its power. A king who has given his power to someone else to exercise, while he himself stays awake, can resume it again when he wishes; just so a *people* which duly meets throughout the term set for a *time-limited Monarch* can strip him of power if it so wishes. Finally a king who gives the exercise of his power to another person while he sleeps, and can wake up again only with the consent of that person, has lost his life and his power together; just so a *people* which has committed power to a *time-limited Monarch* on the terms that it cannot meet again without his command, is radically dissolved, and its power rests with the person it has elected.[53]

This idea of a democracy as potentially a sleeping monarch, in which all administration might be conducted by a non-democratic institution, but which is characterisable as a democracy because the people possess some ultimate authority over what is done in their name, is of course a very powerful and flexible idea. Applied for example to the American Constitution, it would imply that America is a democracy in so far as the people can revise the Constitution, even though on a straightforward Hobbesian analysis of the USA it is an aristocracy ruled by the Supreme Court (who possess the power of interpreting law which is the principal mark of sovereignty). It is also substantially the idea which Siéyès had about the revolutionary French constitution, and which has in various ways become the standard view of democratic constitutions in the modern world. It is customary to say that this view is the result of trying to combine both democratic legitimacy and safeguards against the obvious practical hazards of democratic politics in a single constitution; but if this is correct, then it was

children and servants[,] yet he commands the people in general never but by a precedent law, and as a politic, not a natural person' (Thomas Hobbes, *Behemoth; or, the Long Parliament*, ed. Ferdinand Tönnies, intr. Stephen Holmes (Chicago: University of Chicago Press, 1990), p. 51).
[52] The Cambridge trans. simply has 'people', not 'a people'.   [53] Hobbes, *De Cive*, VII.16.

Hobbes who first posed this problem and provided the modern solution to it. His interest in this possibility, and in the general implications for democracies of his distinction between government and its administration, testifies to the fact that he did not think of his ideas as fundamentally anti-democratic, but rather as providing, alongside a new constitutional theory of monarchy, an equally plausible new theory of democracy.

Furthermore, we may have to face the fact that the modern image of the extreme democracy – the type of society in which for good or ill its citizens are arbiters of both law and morality, and in which the liberal constraints on political power are absent – is transmitted to us from republican Rome not so much by the 'republican' theorists of the seventeenth century but by their principal opponent. Even to put the thought in this way, however, though in some respects it poses a question to Skinner's interpretation of these matters, acknowledges a debt to him; the terms in which we might think of politics have been permanently changed by his work, and as we play with re-arranging the ideas, we should recognise that it was Skinner who handed us all the ideas in the first place – and that in the end he will probably have the last word.

11   A lion in the house: Hobbes and democracy

Kinch Hoekstra

In *Foundations*, Quentin Skinner presented a powerful interpretation of the origins of the modern Western understanding of popular sovereignty. With his customary clarity and erudition, Skinner began with the rise of government by the *popolo* in northern Italy early in the last millennium, and went on to show how the conception of popular sovereignty evolved via scores of thinkers: Bartolus, Marsilius and Gerson in the fourteenth and fifteenth centuries, for example; Goodman, Salamonius and Hotman in the sixteenth. Skinner's study of the development of the theory of popular sovereignty culminated with its articulation by Buchanan and Mariana in the later sixteenth century, which was 'available to be used by all parties in the coming constitutional struggles of the seventeenth century'.[1] In subsequent work, Skinner has shown in detail how elements of this theory of popular sovereignty were used in those struggles: not only by republicans, Levellers and moderate constitutionalists, but also by Thomas Hobbes, who opposed all of these groups.

Popular Hobbes

In contrasting Hobbes with some of his contemporaries, Skinner has made much of Hobbes's sardonic characterisation of them as 'democratical gentlemen'.[2] A number of scholars have none the less claimed that Hobbes's own writings form the foundation of the modern theory of political democracy.[3] The label

I would like to thank the editors for their helpful guidance.

[1] Quentin Skinner, *The Foundations of Modern Political Thought*, 2 vols. (Cambridge: Cambridge University Press, 1978), II, p. 347.

[2] Hobbes employs this apparent oxymoron in *Behemoth*, ed. Ferdinand Tönnies (Chicago: University of Chicago Press, 1990), pp. 26, 39; see Skinner, 'Classical Liberty and the Coming of the English Civil War,' in Martin van Gelderen and Quentin Skinner (eds.), *Republicanism: a Shared European Heritage*, 2 vols. (Cambridge: Cambridge University Press, 2002), II, pp. 9–28, esp. pp. 15–28.

[3] The wording of the claim is adapted from Gianfranco Borrelli, 'Hobbes e la teoria moderna della democrazia. Rappresentanza assoluta e scambio politico', *Trimestre* 24 (1991), pp. 243–63, at pp. 244 and 259; cf. e.g. Alexandre Matheron, 'The theoretical function of democracy in Spinoza and Hobbes', in Warren Montag and Ted Stolze (eds.), *The New Spinoza* (Minneapolis: University of Minnesota Press, 1998).

of 'democratical gentlemen' is deliberately paradoxical, suggesting the untenability of a position that can be summed up by a contradiction in terms. Such incompatibility also inheres, I shall argue, in the position of the democratical Hobbesians.

That position incorporates and extends two commonplace claims. The first of these is that Hobbes was, regardless of his aims, the founder of liberalism, or perhaps even of liberal democracy. According to this view, which has justly been described as canonical,[4] Hobbes's premises of the equal natural rights and liberties of all human beings, and of the need to establish government on the consent of the governed, set in motion the argument for modern liberalism or democracy, which overwhelmed whatever anti-liberal or anti-democratic conclusions Hobbes himself attempted to derive from those premises. The second widely accepted view is that Hobbes 'argued that democracy was the origination of all forms of government . . . because in the initial coming together of a group of people, their agreement to found a body politic was a democratic one'.[5] The democratical Hobbesians agree on the importance of the second claim, and typically espouse some version of the first. Some of Hobbes's contemporaries, including Robert Filmer and John Bramhall, seized on elements of his theory – such as the right of self-preservation, the requirement of the consent of the people, and the idea of original democracy – and charged Hobbes with handing the traditional authority of the monarch to the people. George Mace's declaration is typical of more recent commentators who interpret Hobbes in this vein: 'Although most commentators consider . . . Hobbes the foe of democracy, I believe the birthrights in our heritage are Hobbesian.'[6] Richard Tuck's characteristically learned and intrepid essay shows how a democratical Hobbesian may go further in arguing that Hobbes's theory was not just an accidental cornerstone of liberalism but was itself democratic by design.[7] He maintains that Aristotle's 'extreme democracy is the paradigm commonwealth' for Hobbes; that Hobbes construed the Roman republic as 'an admirable radical

---

[4] Roberto Farneti develops this thesis at length in *Il canone moderno. Filosofia politica e genealogia* (Turin: Bollati Boringhieri, 2002). A recent variant of the canonical view is in Vickie B. Sullivan, *Machiavelli, Hobbes, and the Formation of a Liberal Republicanism in England* (Cambridge: Cambridge University Press, 2004): see esp. pp. 83, 105, 110.

[5] Ingrid Creppell, 'The Democratic Element in Hobbes's *Behemoth*', *Filozofski vestnik* 24 (2003), pp. 7–35, at pp. 29–30n. citing works by Richard Tuck, Deborah Baumgold and Murray Forsyth.

[6] George Mace, *Locke, Hobbes, and the Federalist Papers: an Essay on the Genesis of the American Political Heritage* (Carbondale and Edwardsville: Southern Illinois University Press, 1979), p. x. Cf. Frank M. Coleman, *Hobbes and America: Exploring the Constitutional Foundations* (Toronto: University of Toronto Press, 1977), p. 3: 'Hobbes is the true ancestor of constitutional liberal democracy.'

[7] That Tuck believes the democratic freight of Hobbes's theory is intentional can be seen, for example, in his argument that 'he did not think of his ideas as fundamentally anti-democratic, but rather as providing . . . [a] plausible new theory of democracy' (Richard Tuck, 'Hobbes and democracy', p. 190; all subsequent references to this piece will be to 'Tuck').

democracy'; that he influenced the conception of democracy in subsequent centuries; and that he was the first to pose the problem of how to achieve democratic legitimacy while guarding against democratic dangers, and the first to provide 'the modern solution to it' by distinguishing between government and its administration.[8]

I will examine some of Hobbes's views on democracy or popular sovereignty, and will call into question claims made by the democratical Hobbesians. These include the following propositions: (1) that our conception of democracy, either representative or radical, derives from Hobbes; (2) that this conception is consistent with Hobbes's purposes; (3) that Hobbes relies on democratic sources that impart a democratic character to his theory; and (4) that Hobbes maintains that all commonwealths are originally democratic and derive their legitimacy from that original democracy. I think that each of these claims is, on balance, mistaken. A number of alternatives to the first view can be found in the two volumes of Skinner's *Foundations*; I will therefore focus more on the remaining three claims.[9] I argue not only that Hobbes's discussions of the relative merits of forms of government do not yield an endorsement of democracy, but also that the underlying structure of his theory is not democratic.[10]

How can Hobbes be democratic, given his vociferous criticisms of democracy? Most democratical Hobbesians answer that he is democratic despite himself, but Tuck offers an ingenious solution that would allow Hobbes to be deliberately democratic. He picks up Hobbes's distinction between sovereignty and the administration of government, and argues that Hobbes denounces democratic administration rather than democratic sovereignty.[11] If the people hold

---

[8] Tuck, pp. 184; 183; 171–2, 190; 189–90.

[9] The contention that it is from Hobbes that we have inherited our conception of radical democracy would require an account of how that inheritance was transmitted that is more plausible than accounts traced from other sources. Beyond those treated by Skinner in *Foundations*, such sources might include a gradual radicalisation of parliamentarian or republican ideas; a diffusion of ideas from figures in other civil war movements, such as the Levellers, the Independents, or the antinomians; or a transmission via other interpreters of Athens or Rome. An introduction to some alternative candidates for who conveyed a positive view of Rome is Fergus Millar's *The Roman Republic in Political Thought* (Hanover, NH: University Press of New England, 2002). Tuck argues that Hobbes's theory was democratic, but he provides neither a history of how that came to influence our conceptions of democracy, nor argument against the adequacy of rival accounts of this inheritance.

[10] I am not, therefore, primarily concerned to argue that Hobbes is a monarchist rather than a democrat. On a related issue, see my criticisms of the characterisation of Hobbes as a royalist in section I of Kinch Hoekstra, 'The *De Facto* Turn in Hobbes's Political Philosophy', in Tom Sorell and Luc Foisneau (eds.), *Leviathan After 350 Years* (Oxford: Oxford University Press, 2004), pp. 33–73, at pp. 35–48.

[11] I draw the distinction between sovereignty and administration (rather than, as Tuck does, between government and the administration of government), because Hobbes and his contemporaries sometimes use 'government' as a synonym for sovereignty, and sometimes as a synonym for administration.

ultimate sovereignty, but do not meet as a deliberative body, a democracy can be absolute and effective without the usual pitfalls of that form of government.[12]

Tuck argues that for Hobbes 'a democracy without a deliberative assembly was not at all inferior to a monarchy'.[13] Hobbes's claim, however, is more limited. He says that such a democracy – which he points out would not be easy to realise – would be equal to monarchy in the specific matter of not allowing assemblies to determine questions of great importance.[14] Hobbes is just saying that if a democracy does not discuss and decide in assembly, then it will not have the attendant defects of that procedure of deliberation. On the one hand, this is a minor point: in discussing the relative merits of forms of government, Hobbes says that democracies will not have a characteristic democratic weakness if they are uncharacteristic in this way. More significantly, note that Hobbes here allows that democracy can avoid some of its usual weaknesses if the people do not deliberate in assembly *and* they surrender executive power.[15] The people retain sovereignty as a potential or capacity but do not act upon it.[16] It is here that I think we can look to Aristotle for a paradigm that Hobbes may be inverting.

Toward the end of book V of the *Politics*, Aristotle systematically carries through his consideration of how each regime he has analysed may be best preserved, and considers how a vicious tyrant may prevent the collapse of his regime. He provides the answer that the best thing such a tyrant can do is to rule less viciously. The tyrant is immoderate and extreme; to stay in power he must become moderate. The tyrant is above all concerned with retaining power, but to retain power he should become less tyrannical and more king-like. The tyrant must above all aim to have the people consent to his rule if he wants his tyranny to be stable. Given that what distinguishes kingship from tyranny is the consent

---

[12] Tuck, pp. 186–9; this expands the suggestion in his introduction to Thomas Hobbes, *Leviathan*, ed. Richard Tuck (Cambridge: Cambridge University Press, 1996), esp. p. xxxvii.

[13] Tuck, p. 187.

[14] Thomas Hobbes, *On the Citizen*, ed. Richard Tuck and Michael Silverthorne (Cambridge: Cambridge University Press, 1998), 10.15: 'then it must be admitted that *Democracy* and *Monarchy* would be equal *in this matter*' (my concluding emphasis; references to *De Cive* will be to this edition). Specific disadvantages of deliberating in assemblies are laid out in sections 9–14 of *De Cive*, ch. 10. In section 6, arguing that the disadvantages of favourites are more serious in a democracy, Hobbes shows that his most frequent complaint about democracy, the effect of orators or demagogues, is not just a function of a democracy that deliberates, but of any democracy (for such demagogues will try to sway whatever decisions the people make, in whatever way they can). He would presumably find fault even with the proposed assembly in James Harrington's *Oceana*, in which all debate is banned and the people simply vote yes or no in silence. In ch. 19 of *Leviathan*, Hobbes makes clear that the drawbacks he discusses are of democracy *per se* rather than of deliberative democracy only, and points out the difficulties that attend any democratic assembly's attempts to procure counsel (including the influence of rhetoric, the tendency to division, and the impossibility of secrecy).

[15] I.e. 'if in a *Democracy* the *people* chose to concentrate deliberations about war and peace and legislation in the hands of just one man or a very small number, and content themselves . . . to have authority without executive function (Hobbes, *De Cive*, 10.15).

[16] Hobbes, *De Cive*, 10.16.

of the people, however, it seems that the tyrant has succeeded in preserving himself in power only by destroying his tyranny *per se*.[17] Similarly, Hobbes argues that a democracy will crumble unless the people forswear deliberation 'about war and peace and legislation' and hand over their executive power to one or a few. Democracy is self-defeating unless it is self-effacing – that is, unless it effectively becomes a monarchy or aristocracy.

The democracy without deliberation that Hobbes treats with such respect, Tuck maintains, is a close description of the Roman republic.[18] Two sections after the passage that Tuck offers as evidence, however, Hobbes makes his point about the Romans explicit:

> The most evident sign that the most absolute *Monarchy* is the best of all conditions for a commonwealth, is that not only kings but also commonwealths which are subject to the *people* and the *optimates* invariably confer full power to conduct a war on one man alone; and that power is the most absolute power possible . . . A *Monarchy* therefore is the best government of all in an army camp. And what else are countries but so many camps fortified against each other . . .?[19]

That is, Hobbes praises the Romans for abandoning such democracy as they had, and censures them for not realising that they should have abandoned it for good, rather than just in cases of emergency.[20] The idea that Rome was an admirable radical democracy because policy was not decided there in a deliberative assembly, far from forming the basis of Hobbes's political theory, is rejected by him.[21] In fact, in *The Elements of Law* Hobbes goes so far as to say that Rome was an aristocracy with a large deliberative assembly.[22]

---

[17] That said, it may be that Aristotle would keep these two distinct in principle, because the motivational state of the tyrant is different from that of the king: the tyrant mirrors the king, but has a different end for the same actions and thus is vicious.

[18] Tuck, pp. 187–8, on Hobbes, *De Cive*, 10.15.

[19] Hobbes, *De Cive*, 10.17. Hobbes here apparently draws on Jean Bodin, who builds his case primarily on Livy: see *The Six Bookes of a Common-weale*, trans. Richard Knolles (London, 1606), 6.4, pp. 715–17. Cf. Robert Filmer, *Patriarcha and Other Political Works of Sir Robert Filmer*, ed. Peter Laslett (Oxford: Basil Blackwell, 1949), ch. 16, pp. 86–7.

[20] Cf. William Petty, *The Petty Papers*, ed. Marquis of Lansdowne, II (London: Constable, 1927), p. 35. Hobbes also argues that although the Romans governed themselves by an assembly (each wanting 'to participate of government'), they implicitly admitted the superiority of monarchy by governing their provinces 'alwaies by Presidents, and Praetors' (*Leviathan*, 22.16 (p. 118); cf. 19.10 (p. 98), 19.13 (p. 99), and 23.3 (p. 124)).

[21] *Pace* Tuck, p. 183.

[22] Hobbes, *The Elements of Law*, 2.5.8, re. 'aristocracies . . . where the affairs of state are debated in great and numerous assemblies, as they were anciently in Athens, and in Rome'. In *Leviathan* he treats the Roman republic as riven by faction and sedition: cf. 22.32 (p. 122) and esp. 29.4 (p. 168). (Citations of *The Elements of Law* are to part, chapter and section number of the edition of Ferdinand Tönnies (London: Frank Cass, 1969); citations of *Leviathan* are to page number of the 'Head' edition of 1651, preceded by chapter and paragraph number.) In the Latin edition, he again brings in the possibility that the Roman Republic was an aristocracy: see how he alters 19.13 (p. 99) and 22.32 (p. 122). In *The Elements of Law*, 2.1.17, he says that Rome was 'sometimes' a democracy, but immediately makes clear that this democracy

In the next section we will see why Hobbes denied that Rome was a democracy (along with Athens, the usual early modern exemplar of an extreme democracy). Before doing so, it is worth making two preliminary points about the distinction between sovereignty and the administration of government (on which Hobbes's 'new theory of democracy' is purportedly based). First, the idea that Hobbes advocates such a division does not sit well with the idea that he reintroduces the Aristotelian conception of radical democracy into the modern world.[23] Tuck argues that for Hobbes the sovereign rules only by universal laws and 'there would normally be no occasion for genuinely arbitrary acts of sovereignty by a monarch or a democracy'.[24] This would mean, however, that a Hobbesian democracy would rule by established general *nomoi* rather than occurrent particular *psēphismata* – the opposite of Aristotle's primary constitutional claim about radical democracy.[25] Hobbes says that a democracy may

was not radical, for sovereignty could be exercised or administered by a dictator, by the generals, or by the senate. Nor is it clear that Hobbes would have accepted the assimilation of *plebiscita* with the *psēphismata* of radical democracy, for he identifies the demos not with the *plebs* but with the *populus* (cf. *De Cive*, 7.1, 7.5). Bodin excoriates Polybius *inter alia* for confusing *plebs* and *populus*, and thus for regarding *plebiscita* as the pronouncements of the people rather than of a faction (*Method for the Easy Comprehension of History*, trans. Beatrice Reynolds (New York: W. W. Norton, 1969), pp. 181–4, 236–8; cf. John Case, *Sphaera Civitatis* (Oxford, 1588), 4.4.8). Hobbes identifies the plebeians not with the people, but with an unlawful faction (*Leviathan*, 22.32, p. 122), so he seems to follow this line (which can be traced back to Sallust's lost *Histories* via the first decade of Livy and Augustine's *City of God*).

If Hobbes had a specific state in mind when he considered the possibility of a democracy in which 'the *people* should choose to concentrate deliberations about war and peace and legislation in the hands of just one man or of a very small number of men, and were happy to appoint magistrates and public ministers, i.e. to have authority without executive power' (*De Cive*, 10.15), it was probably not Rome but Venice. In *The Elements of Law*, Hobbes reduces all democracies to aristocracies, and so judges that Athens, Rome, and Venice are all aristocracies. But whereas the former, ancient regimes are condemned for debating affairs of state in large assemblies, and thus for their 'aptitude to dissolve into civil war', Hobbes is careful to explain that this aptitude is not to be found 'in such as do nothing else in great assemblies, but choose magistrates and counsellors, and commit the handling of state affairs to a few; such as is the aristocracy of Venice at this day' (*The Elements of Law*, 2.5.8). This may be Hobbes's way of squaring his theory with the myth of Venice', according to which that republic was a paragon of stability and longevity; if he also has it in mind in *De Cive*, he may classify it as a democracy because, as Contarini and others explained, all of the citizens participated in the sovereign assembly and authority resided in the *popolo* – though only aristocrats were citizens and only the citizen body constituted the *popolo*. (Cf. Harrington, *The Prerogative of Popular Government* (1658), p. 482 of *The Political Works of James Harrington*, ed. J. G. A. Pocock (Cambridge: Cambridge University Press, 1977); for a more complicated view, see James S. Grubb, 'Elite Citizens', in John Martin and Dennis Romano (eds.), *Venice Reconsidered* (Baltimore: Johns Hopkins University Press, 2000).)

[23] Tuck defends both ideas: see pp. 189–90 and 176.   [24] Tuck, pp. 188–9.

[25] See the passage Tuck treats as central, *Politics* 1292a5–37 (references to this work are to the edition of Franz Susemihl (Leipzig, 1872)). Even if we emphasise Tuck's qualification that rule in the Hobbesian commonwealth would 'normally' be by precedent law rather than arbitrary act, this marks a sharp difference from Aristotle's picture of radical democracy, in which the assembly of the citizens rules by arbitrary decrees rather than precedent universal law. Note too that Aristotle says that extreme democracy is undertaken for the interests of these rulers rather than for the common interest, whereas Hobbes rejects this distinction.

avoid some of the pitfalls of that form of government if it is administered by one or a few, and if the many do not themselves participate 'in all judgements, consultations, and public actions'.[26] This is the inverse of Aristotle's extreme democracy, however, in which magistrates have the least amount of independent power and the democratic assembly participates in the greatest range of deliberations and decisions. Aristotle characterises radical democracy as 'when all [citizens] convene to deliberate about everything, and the magistrates decide nothing'.[27] Moreover, Hobbes repudiates the idea of a 'democratic sovereign' with 'virtually no power to intervene in the daily running of the state'.[28] The sovereign has absolute authority, and may exercise it in accordance with precedent law or by immediate command: the choice is his.[29] So 'to take away a subject's property on the ground that *the Lord has need* is absolute Power.'[30] The sovereign may exercise such power in accordance with established laws, but in doing so his prevailing occurrent will is expressed rather than overridden.[31] Nor would it be coherent to restrict the sovereign to act only according to established and general laws, for when a question arises of how such a law bears on a particular case, it is up to the sovereign to interpret however he wishes. 'Legal action may sometimes be taken against the holder of *sovereign power*', but the question then is to identify his will rather than his right; 'hence he himself will be the judge.'[32] The sovereign can adhere to his own previous commands, but he cannot bind himself by them, and so any command he gives for a departure from them is itself the new law, superseding the old. 'When the sovereign commandeth anything to be done against his own former law, the command, as to that particular fact, is an abrogation of the law.'[33]

The second point concerns the claim that by proposing the idea of a democracy which is administered non-democratically Hobbes provides the first modern solution to the problem of how to have democratic legitimacy while avoiding its hazards.[34] I doubt that Hobbes thought that democracy either provided or required special legitimacy, but in any case we can be sure that Hobbes was not the first to put forward this idea. Aristotle himself draws a comparable distinction; and some of the figures mentioned in the opening paragraph did

[26] Tuck, pp. 186–9. The quotation, from *De Cive*, 13.1, is on p. 186.

[27] *Politics* 1298a29–30: 'to pantas peri pantōn bouleuesthai suniontas, tas d'archas peri mēdenos krinein', This characterisation of radical democracy changes little in the intervening centuries (a compact formulation is provided in 1596 by Pierre Grégoire, in *De republica*, 4.5.16 and 5.2.3). Writers sometimes reserve the name of 'ochlocracy' for this form of government.

[28] Tuck, p. XXX.

[29] I follow Hobbes in referring to the generic sovereign as 'him', but it should be understood that this stands for 'him, or her, or them'. In an aristocracy or democracy, the sovereign will is that of the assembly.

[30] Hobbes, *De Cive*, 11.6.

[31] See e.g. Hobbes, *De Cive*, 12.4 and the annotation to 6.15; Hobbes, *Leviathan*, 21.19, p. 113.

[32] Hobbes, *De Cive*, 6.15.   [33] Hobbes, *Leviathan*, 27.27, p. 157.   [34] Tuck, pp. 189–90.

so in order to maintain that the people retain authority and only ever delegate administration.[35] We can even be fairly confident about Hobbes's immediate modern source for the idea, for Hobbes first articulates the distinction between sovereignty and its administration in a stretch of argument that is heavily indebted to Jean Bodin.[36] The distinction between the state (or sovereignty) and government (or the administration of sovereignty) is common in Bodin, but the clearest cases, including instances where a democracy is administered non-democratically, come in book II, ch. 7. One salient case is that of Rome. Bodin judged that during most of the time of the republic, sovereignty in Rome was popular while its administration was not ('the gouernment was in the magistrats, the authoritie and councell in the Senate, but the soueraigne power and maiestie of the Commonweale was in the people').[37] From these cases, Bodin concludes: 'let vs firmely set downe and resolue that there are but three formes of Commonweales, and no more, and those simple also, and without any confused mixture one of them with an other; albeit that *the gouernment be sometimes contrarie to the state.*'[38]

Not really democracy

The story of Hobbes and democracy does not begin with Bodin, or with Aristotle, but with Thucydides. Hobbes not only made a careful study of Thucydides, he proudly claimed to be the first to translate him directly from Greek into a modern language, and went to great lengths to provide a reliable scholarly edition.[39] It was in Thucydides that Renaissance and early-modern readers

---

[35] Aristotle, *Politics* 1292b11–21; cf. Case, *Sphaera Civitatis*, 3.1.8. See also the distinction between two basic kinds of democracy in e.g. Besold's 1623 *Discursus Politici*, 3.2–3 (pp. 46–58 of the version printed in Christoph Besold, *Operis Politici Editio Nova* (Strasbourg, 1626)). By the time Grotius came to write *De iure belli ac pacis*, he was concerned to refute the opinion of those who had argued that everywhere and without exception the people retain sovereign power (1.3.8).

[36] See Hobbes, *The Elements of Law*, 2.1.15–17, and the reference to book II of Bodin's *De Republica* in 2.8.7, at which point Hobbes has just referred back to *The Elements of Law*, 2.1.16–17 (though the explicit citation is to 2.1.15).

[37] *Six Bookes*, 1.10, pp. 156–7; 2.1, pp. 185–90, 195–7 (where there are underlying differences between the French and Latin versions); 2.7, pp. 245–6; Bodin, *Method*, pp. 179–85. Quotation from *Six Bookes*, 2.1, p. 190.

[38] Bodin, *Six Bookes*, p. 250; my emphasis. Cf. Bodin, *Method*, p. 201: 'it is popular power, not royal, when the state is governed by the king according to the will of the people, since in this case the government depends upon the people'. The use in the *Six Bookes* of 'government' to signify the administration of sovereignty and not sovereignty itself serves as a reminder that some of the republicans that Skinner has studied, even if they advocate mixed government, should after all count as democratic in what Tuck takes to be Hobbes's sense. It was not an uncommon view that the people necessarily retain ultimate authority (seen especially in the right to resist at least some kind of tyrant), and yet that the government or administration was best when a mixture of the traditional three kinds.

[39] Thucydides, *Eight Bookes of the Peloponnesian Warre*, trans. Thomas Hobbes (London, 1629); hereafter 'Thucydides, Hobbes edn'. Tuck says that in 1555 Nicholas Grouchy 'had for the

found the greatest encomium of a direct democracy, in the funeral oration delivered by Pericles. It might be no great surprise, therefore, that we find Anthony Hammond writing that Hobbes 'translated this booke to teach Popular Oratory & in favour of a Democratical Governm[t]'.[40]

This view is surprising, however, because it is so wrong-headed. Writing a few years earlier, Pierre Bayle captures Hobbes's professed intention more accurately: 'to arouse in the English a disgust for the Republican spirit, he produced a translation of Thucydides'.[41] In his prefatory essay 'Of the Life and History of Thucydides', Hobbes commends Thucydides warmly, observing that 'it is manifest that he least of all liked the *Democracy*',[42] and providing a summary of what he takes to be Thucydides' indictment of it. At the other end of his literary career, Hobbes singles out Thucydides' work for praise in both his prose and verse autobiographies. In the former, he writes that he translated the history to reveal to his fellow citizens the folly of the Athenian democracy; in the latter, he says that Thucydides 'showed me how foolish Democracy is, and how much wiser one man is than an assembly'.[43] Hammond managed to get it completely backward.

very first time since antiquity given political theorists a well-documented example of a functioning radical democracy' (p. 182). If Tuck is right that Aristotle thought that Athens from the time of Cleon was an extreme or radical democracy (pp. 176–7), then they already had available to them a vivid account of radical democracy in the text of Thucydides, which was by then in Greek, Latin, French, German, Italian and English. And it would then be hard to avoid the conclusion that the model for Aristotle's view of radical democracy served Hobbes not as a pattern for his well-founded commonwealth, but as a paradigm of political disaster.

It is not clear, however, that Aristotle had Athens in mind when describing extreme democracy. Commentators disagree not only with one another on this issue, but even with themselves: compare W. L. Newman, *The Politics of Aristotle*, 4 vols. (Oxford: Clarendon Press, 1887–1902), 1:504 and n. 2 with 4:xli; and Peter L. Phillips Simpson, *A Philosophical Commentary on the Politics of Aristotle* (Chapel Hill, NC: University of North Carolina Press, 1998), 307 n. 39 with 381 n. 36. Robin Osborne points out that whereas it 'is generally accused of being Aristotle's model of the worst form of democracy', Athens had elements of his best democracy, especially in so far as it was agrarian and without frequent participation in assemblies (*Demos: the Discovery of Classical Attica* (Cambridge: Cambridge University Press, 1985), pp. 71–2). Bodin observes that Xenophon's characterisation of the Athenians as holding the will of the people to supplant the law fits Aristotle's characterisation of extreme democracy (*Method*, p. 241). Contrast Pericles (in Thucydides, 2.37.3, Hobbes edn, p. 102), who commends the Athenian people for obeying the magistrates and the laws. Also, note that Aristotle (e.g. at *Politics* 1298a31) repeatedly considers extreme democracy as it is 'now', whereas the Athenian democracy of Aristotle's day was not extreme (though cf. the Aristotelian *Constitution of Athens*, 41.2).

[40] Bodleian MS Rawl. D 174, fol. 8[r], dated 4 September 1699.

[41] Pierre Bayle, *Dictionaire Historique et Critique* (Rotterdam, 1697), vol. II, part 2, *sub* Pericles (p. 806 n. O): 'Thomas Hobbes voulant inspirer aux Anglois quelque degoût pour l'esprit Republicain, fit une version de Thucydide.'

[42] Thucydides, Hobbes edn, sig. a1[v].

[43] *Thomae Hobbes Malmesburiensis Opera Philosophica Quae Latine Scripsit Omnia*, ed. William Molesworth, vol. I (London, 1839), pp. xiv, lxxxviii ('Democratia ostendit mihi quam sit inepta, / Et quantum coetu plus sapit unus homo').

Hobbes is particularly struck by Thucydides' judgement of the government of Athens under Pericles, which he thinks serves to undercut Pericles' own panegyric of the democracy. In the words of Hobbes's translation, 'it was in name a State *Democraticall*, but in fact, *A gouernment of the principall Man*'.[44] This is a characteristic Thucydidean thought pattern: he explains how something is formally or nominally, and then reveals that it is something else effectively or in fact. Hobbes's translation is strewn with what the 'pretence' or 'pretext' is in cases where the underlying reality is often quite different.[45] Hobbes enthusiastically adopts this thought pattern, not only in the prefatory materials of his edition, but throughout his works.[46] He emphasises Thucydides' judgement of the so-called democracy under Pericles, observing that the historian reserves his greatest praise of the government of Athens for 'when in the beginning of this Warre, it was *Democraticall* in name, but in effect *Monarchicall* vnder *Pericles*'.[47] It might be thought that this fits with the idea that Hobbes supports democracy when it is administered by one person: the Athenian people 'committed the whole State to his administration', but they elected him and could in theory vote against his recommendations or oust him.[48] As far as Hobbes is concerned, however, it was none the less 'in effect' or 'in fact' not a democracy at all, but a monarchy; and he takes Thucydides' approval of this arrangement to be evidence not that he admired the democracy in this form, but that 'he best approued of the *Regall Gouernment*'.[49]

Hobbes universalises this reductive analysis in *The Elements of Law*. 'In *all* democracies, though the right of sovereignty be in the assembly, which is virtually the whole body; yet the use thereof is *always* in one, or a few particular men'.[50] This, Hobbes thinks, is because the arts of persuasion accompany all democracies, thus concentrating power in the hands of the most persuasive.

---

[44] Thucydides, Hobbes edn, p. 117 (2.65.9). Cf. Herodotus 3.82.4 (democracy idolises the champion of the people and becomes tyranny: cf. also Solon fr. 9); Plato, *Republic* 562a–569c, esp. 565d–566a (tyranny necessarily arises from democracy, via a leader of the people who gets a taste for blood and turns into a wolf against his fellow citizens); Plato, *Menexenus* 238cd (it is called democracy, but is in truth aristocracy with popular consent); Plutarch, *Moralia* 802c and *Pericles* 9, 11, 15, 16, and 39 (Pericles was thought to be monarchical and tyrannical, using rhetoric to control the people in a way incompatible with democracy).

[45] Thucydides deploys this distinction in various ways. For a subtle study, see Adam Milman Parry's 1959 dissertation, *Logos and Ergon in Thucydides* (New York: Arno Press, 1981).

[46] This is not to say that he necessarily adopted it from Thucydides, or from Thucydides alone; the thought pattern is also to be found in other traditions that influenced Hobbes, such as that of the Machiavellians. Hobbes may have been the author of the earlier 'Discourse upon the beginning of Tacitus', who writes about the popular forms Augustus was careful to retain in order to preempt republican demands: 'Few remained that had seene the ancient Republique. . . . whereas they might haue heard of the names of Consuls, Tribunes, Censors, and the like, the same they found also in the present State; though the authoritie of them all, remained onely in *Augustus*' (*Horae Subsecivae. Observations and Discovrses* (London, 1620), pp. 304–5).

[47] Thucydides, Hobbes edn, sig. a2ʳ.   [48] Ibid., p. 116 (2.65.4).   [49] Ibid., sig. a2ʳ.

[50] Hobbes, *Elements of Law*, 2.2.5, emphases added.

'One or few must of necessity sway the whole; insomuch, that a democracy, in effect, is no more than an aristocracy of orators, interrupted sometimes with the temporary monarchy of one orator.'[51] This judgement is not restricted to deliberative democracies. When he comes to compare the three forms of government in general, 'namely, democracy, aristocracy, and monarchy,' it turns out that 'the two former are in effect but one'. This is, again, because 'democracy is but the government of a few orators'.[52] Because all democracies end up effectively controlled by one or a few, there is in fact no such thing as a democracy.[53]

Others take up and displace the point that a sovereign who delegates administration may effectively shift sovereignty to that administrator. So Harrington argues that an aristocracy either rules via a king in order to protect its power from the people, or via the people in order to protect it from a king; and that all popular governments must rely on a senate or aristocratic element. 'Whence, though for discourse sake politicians speak of pure aristocracy and pure democracy, there is no such thing as either in nature, art or example.'[54] Hobbes cannot accept these mixed forms, so if he decides that something is not a pure or absolute democracy he must declare it another form of government or no form

---

[51] Ibid., 2.2.5.

[52] Ibid., 2.5.3; cf. Hobbes's note on Thucydides 8.48.5–6 (Hobbes edn, p. 497). Satan follows Hobbes (*Paradise Regained*, book IV, 267–70):

> Thence to the famous Orators repair,
> Those antient, whose resistless eloquence
> Wielded at will that fierce Democratie,
> Shook the Arsenal and fulmin'd over *Greece*.

In saying that the orators controlled the supposed democracy 'at will', Milton specifically refers to Pericles: the final line is from Aristophanes, *Acharnians*, 532 ('[Perikleēs houlumpios] ēstrapten, ebronta, sunekuka tēn Hellada'; reported in Diodorus Siculus, 12.40.6), which is quoted by Hobbes in his *De Cive*, 5.5. (It also makes its way into ch. 17 of the first translation of *Leviathan*, the 1667 Dutch edition (p. 173).)

[53] Cf. Filmer, writing shortly after the appearance of *Leviathan* about that work and *De Cive*: 'in conclusion the poore people are deprived of their government, if there can be no democracy by his principles' (preface to the *Observations* upon Hobbes, in *Patriarcha*, p. 239). A few months later, Filmer builds on this view in his *Observations upon Aristotles Politiques*. He says that 'those governments that seem to be popular are kinds of petty monarchies', and concludes that 'there is no form of government, but monarchy only', drawing the corollary that 'there is no such thing as an aristocracy or democracy' (Filmer, *Patriarcha*, pp. 227, 229). Filmer here draws on Bodin, *De Republica*, 6.4, where Bodin writes: 'And although we imagin a bodie of many lords, or of a whole people to hold the soueraigntie; yet hath it no true ground, nor support, if there bee not a head with absolute and soueraigne power, to vnite them together: the which a simple magistrat without soueraigne authoritie cannot do': thus, 'the chiefe point of a commonweale, which is the right of soueraigntie, cannot be, nor subsist (to speake properly) but in a Monarchie: for none can be soueraigne in a commonweale but one alone: if they be two, or three, or more, no one is soueraigne, for that no one of them can giue or take a law from his companion' (Bodin, *Six Bookes*, 6.4, p. 715).

[54] James Harrington, *The Art of Lawgiving* (London, 1659), p. 611 of *The Political Works*. Cf. Filmer, *Patriarcha*, pp. 226–7.

of government. Spinoza responds that democracy is the only form of absolute government,[55] and that there is in fact no such thing as a pure monarchy. 'Those who believe that one alone can hold the supreme Right of the Commonwealth err greatly . . . the government which is believed to be an absolute Monarchy is really an Aristocracy in practice', for the would-be monarch cannot run the government himself.[56]

Hobbes alleges that those who take up the cause of democracy do so to further their own power. The so-called 'democratical gentlemen' in fact 'desired the whole and absolute sovereignty, and to change the monarchical government into an oligarchy'.[57] They fulfilled this desire, but did not adequately understand that sovereignty shifts with effective power, so that one's servants can swiftly become one's masters. 'He that would set up democracy with an army', Hobbes observes, 'should have an army to maintain it.' Otherwise there will soon be a sovereign army, not a sovereign democracy. 'For they that keep an army, and cannot master it, must be subject to it as much as he that keeps a lion in his house.'[58] So, too, if the people forsake their deliberative and

---

[55] This point is touched upon by Bodin: cf. *Six Bookes*, 1.8, p. 99, which contains the gist of Hobbes's annotation of *De Cive*, 6.13, discussed by Tuck on pp. 184–5.

[56] Spinoza, *Tractatus Politicus*, 6.5: 'qui credunt posse fieri, ut unus solus summum Civitatis Jus obtineat, longè errant . . . imperium, quod absolutè Monarchicum esse creditur, sit reverâ in praxi Aristocraticum.' Hobbes does recognise the necessity of 'public ministers of sovereign power,' to use the title of ch. 23 of *Leviathan*, and would presumably argue that in those instances the ministers are doing the sovereign's bidding (whereas in the case of Pericles as understood by Thucydides and Hobbes, the people are doing the magistrate's bidding, and so sovereignty does not truly inhere in the people).

[57] Hobbes, *Behemoth*, p. 75. I do not have space here to explore the complexity of Hobbes's treatment of democracy in this and other works of the Restoration; for a stimulating analysis, see Tomaž Mastnak, '*Behemoth*: Democraticals and Religious Fanatics', *Filozofski vestnik* 24 (2003), pp. 139–68. James I anticipated many of the themes of *Behemoth*, pointing out in *Basilicon Doron* that Puritans appealed to Athens and Rome as models for how to gain power for themselves by trumpeting democracy. 'Some fierie spirited men in the ministerie, got such a guiding of the people at that time of confusion, as finding the gust of gouernment sweete, they begouth to fantasie to themselues a Democraticke forme of gouernment: and . . . settled themselues so fast vpon that imagined Democracie [margin: '*Such were the Demagogi at Athens*'], as they fed themselues with the hope to become *Tribuni plebes*: and so in a popular gouernment by leading the people by the nose, to beare the sway of all the rule . . . ' (James I, *Political Writings*, ed. Johann P. Sommerville (Cambridge: Cambridge University Press, 1994), p. 26).

[58] Hobbes, *Behemoth*, pp. 155, 193. Hobbes draws on the simile of the man who raised a lion in his house from Aeschylus, *Agamemnon*, 717–36. This was picked up by the character of Aeschylus in the *Frogs* of Aristophanes, in reply to the question of whether the people of Athens should recall Alcibiades in order to save the city. (Alcibiades was in exile in 405 BC, when this play was produced; a year later the Athenian democracy was defeated in the Peloponnesian war.) Aeschylus' judgement – 'It is best not to raise a lion in the city' (*Frogs*, 1431) – is in turn put to use by Plutarch, in his life of Alcibiades (16). The Thucydidean matrix for this passage is considered in Francis Macdonald Cornford, *Thucydides Mythistoricus* (London: Edward Arnold, 1907), chs. 11 and 12. Cf. also Herodotus, 5.92β.3 and 6.131.2; Aristophanes, *Knights*, 1037–40; Valerius Maximus, 7.2; and Erasmus, *Adagia*, 2.3.77, 2.1.86, and 1.1.2.

executive activities, they may find they have unwittingly enthroned their erstwhile administrators.[59]

Hobbes's Thucydidean penchant for the underlying fact of the matter brings him to insist upon effective rather than nominal sovereignty. This is in tension, however, with a more formal and juridical strand of his thought, in which he develops what he learned from Bodin, and reckons from the consequences of established names – so, for example, limiting the forms of sovereignty to three, with no mixture or limitation.[60] The former is the tradition of thought that has been neglected in this context, yet it may well be the dominant one. For Hobbes argues that *de jure* sovereignty follows from *de facto* sovereignty, and not the other way around.[61] None the less, he attempts to interweave these ways of thinking, simultaneously deploying prudence and reason and addressing both humanist and scientific concerns.[62]

By paying attention to the Thucydidean Hobbes, we can see a central problem with the suggestion that a democracy should delegate its deliberative and executive powers. For the question is not just a formal one of the ultimate source of sovereignty, but also a pragmatic one of who really holds the reins of power.[63] Delegation may shade over silently into abdication.

'You the people'

At the heart of the suggestion that Hobbes is the vital link in transmitting the idea of extreme democracy to us is the claim that Hobbes ultimately drew on

---

[59] In the annotation of *De Cive*, 6.13, Hobbes indicates why it may be prudent to forgo the exercise of some rights of sovereignty; in *De Cive*, 6.8, he argues that the executive power carries with it the sovereign right of judgement. Note that the democratic sovereign is required by the law of nature to preserve the absoluteness of sovereignty, and would be forbidden to delegate power or authority if that would compromise the safety of the people or the absoluteness of their sovereignty. There is a further potential problem with delegating the exercise of sovereignty, for it can happen 'that when the exercise of the Power layd by, is for the publique safety to be resumed, it hath the resemblance of an unjust act; which disposeth great numbers of men (when occasion is presented) to rebellion' (Hobbes, *Leviathan*, 29.3, p. 167).

[60] It should be noted, however, that both strands are already prominent in Bodin's own work.

[61] For defence of this point see Hoekstra, 'The *De Facto* Turn'.

[62] Quentin Skinner's *Reason and Rhetoric in the Philosophy of Hobbes* (Cambridge: Cambridge University Press, 1996) can be supplemented by further facets of both Hobbes's humanism (which draws on a tradition that is not just rhetorical, but also includes reason of state, political prudence, etc.) and his scientific procedure (which is modeled not just on Euclid, but on Bodin et al.); and it can be questioned in so far as it suggests that e.g. Hobbes's Thucydides is humanist but not scientific, whereas his *Elements of Law* is scientific but not humanist. See my review in *Filosofia Politica* 11 (1997), pp. 139–43.

[63] It may be that Hobbes employs both kinds of argument in the service of the aim of his philosophy. On the one hand, formal arguments that appeal to the absoluteness of sovereignty are designed to forestall dissension by those who would encroach with demands for limitation or mixture. On the other, arguments that appeal to effective power may promote peace, for example by allowing one's former obligation to lapse and a new one to arise when one falls under another's control. Peace and security may be best served by drawing on both formal and effective strategies, even if there are cases in which they could contradict one another.

Aristotle's characterisation of extreme democracy in formulating his theory that 'a *people* is a *single* entity, with *a single will*' and that 'the *King* is the *people*'.[64] Upon this claim Tuck constructs his alternative history of the idea of democracy, from which Hobbes emerges not as a theorist of 'counter-revolution' – a view which rests on 'a mistaken history' – but as 'a sophisticated and deep theorist of democracy':[65]

Hobbes clearly referred to Aristotle's observation that (in Vettori's translation) the tyrannical democracy was where the *princeps populus fit*, when he said in *De Cive* that '. . . In every commonwealth the *People* reigns; for even in *Monarchies* the *People* exercises power [*imperat*]; for the *people* wills through the will of *one man*. . . . in a *Monarchy* the subjects are the *crowd*, and (paradoxically) the *King* is the *people*.' If the people can be thought of as a king (according to Aristotle), then by the same token, Hobbes thought, a king can be thought of as the people.[66]

Tuck concludes from this that Aristotle's 'tyrannical democracy was in some way the paradigm for [Hobbes's] well-founded commonwealth'.[67]

On the one hand, it is not clear that the source for the idea that a people is one man, or that the king is the people, must be Aristotle's analysis of extreme democracy as a monarch or tyrant, transmitted to Hobbes by Vettori.[68] If a source is required, it could, for example, be from Aeschylus, transmitted (if an intermediary is needed) via Grotius: 'For in the Argive Tragedy of the Suppliants by Aeschylus, the people address the King thus: "You are the commonwealth, you the people; a ruler subject to no judge, you govern the altar of the country's hearth by your single vote, by your nod."'[69] In Aristophanes (one of the seven poets Hobbes specifies having read in his verse autobiography), Demos, or People, is represented as a tyrant surrounded by flatterers, and is elsewhere

---

[64] Tuck makes the suggestion on pp. 183–4, 190; the quotations from Hobbes, *De Cive*, 12.8 are in Tuck, p. 183.

[65] Tuck, pp. 171.

[66] Tuck, pp. 183–4, quoting Hobbes, *De Cive* 12.8 (translating *multitudo* as 'crowd').

[67] Tuck, p. 184.

[68] Tuck holds (p. 181) that Vettori's comment that a people is formed out of many by all coming together and making one man 'must have been a source of Hobbes's thinking on the subject'.

[69] Grotius, *De iure belli ac pacis libri tres* (Paris, 1625), 1.3.8, pp. 70–1 (quoting *Suppliants*, 370–3): 'nam in Argiua Tragoedia Supplicibus, sic populus Regem affatur apud Aeschylum:

> *Su toi polis, su de to dēmion,*
> *Prutanis akritos ōn,*
> *Kratuneis bōmon hestian chthonos,*
> *Monopsēphoisi neumasi[n] sethen.*'

It is striking that Grotius extracts this quotation, given that before and after it the king insists that he must consult the people to obtain their consent, and cannot act without persuading them: he acts only after the people have authorised him to do so by unanimous vote (see 942–3: 'mia psēphos', as one man – cf. line 373, above). On this Argive king as a constitutional monarch in a democracy, see A. F. Garvie, *Aeschylus' Supplices: Play and Trilogy* (Cambridge: Cambridge University Press, 1969), pp. 143–54.

compared to a monarch.[70] And in Hobbes's translation of Thucydides, Pericles addresses the assembled people of Athens and tells them that 'your gouernment is in the nature of a tyranny'.[71] These are all sources that antedate Aristotle.[72] We have no particular reason, however, to believe that Hobbes derived this idea from classical writers or their commentators. For example, it may well have been born from reflection on the civil law conception of a *persona* as a number of individuals brought together in a unity, or a radicalisation of a contemporary constitutional claim. So, around the time of *De Cive*, Dudley Digges writes that 'the King is the whole people, and what he doth is legally their Act': stripped of Digges's qualifications about the legitimate limits Parliament can impose on regal sovereignty, what remains is the Hobbesian claim.[73]

On the other hand, if Hobbes does employ the Aristotelian paradigm, he does so, to use his word, paradoxically: he does not follow it as an ideal, but inverts it. It is revealing that Hobbes does not use the equation of king and people in discussing a democracy, as Aristotle does: like Aeschylus as reported by Grotius, Hobbes employs it in relation to a monarchy. Far from the people being king, the king is instead the people.[74] The people rule in every

---

[70] *Knights*, 1087, 1111–14 and 1330–3.

[71] Thucydides, 2.63.2 (Hobbes edn, p. 115); cf. 1.122.3 (p. 64), 1.124.3 (p. 64), 3.37.2 (p. 163), 6.85.1 (p. 397). In 1.122.3 e.g. the Corinthian ambassadors identify the Athenian *polis* as a tyrant. Hornblower comments on this passage: 'As so often . . . Th. makes a speaker assimilate states and individuals, using about states the kind of moral language or metaphor appropriate to individuals: a tyrant is essentially an individual. The point is perhaps illustrated most clearly by the expression used by Euphemos at vi.85.1 . . . lit. "a tyrant man or *polis*"' (Simon Hornblower, *A Commentary on Thucydides*, vol. I (Oxford: Clarendon Press, 1991), pp. 200–1). Cf. the emphatic construction of *Knights*, 1114: Demos is a 'tyrant man' ('andra turannon'). On the idea of the 'polis turannos', see Cristopher Tuplin, 'Imperial Tyranny: some Reflections on a Classical Greek Political Metaphor', in P. A. Cartledge and F. D. Harvey (eds.), *Crux: Essays Presented to G. E. M. de Ste. Croix* (Exeter: Imprint Academic, 1985), pp. 348–75, and the essays referred to there (esp. those by Raaflaub and Connor).

[72] Cf. also Euripides, *Suppliants*, 352–3 (another *dēmos monarchos*); Isocrates, *Areopagiticus*, 7.26 and *On the Peace*, 8.115.

[73] [Dudley Digges], *The Vnlavvfulnesse of Subjects taking up Armes against their Soveraigne, in what case soever* ([Oxford], 1643), p. 151. Digges here adduces the same passage from Aeschylus that Grotius does, quoting and translating *Suppliants*, ll. 370–1 (cf. n. 69 above). Thomason had a copy of Digges's work by January 15, 1644; it is possible that Digges had seen one of the very few copies of the first edition of *De Cive*, which had been circulated to a handful of people in 1642.

The distinct idea of the people as king or prince crops up when democracy is explained within a monarchic political paradigm, and 'kingdom' or 'principate' is taken as tantamount to 'state' or 'commonwealth'. In the mid-sixteenth century, for example, Francesco Baldelli refers to democracy as the principate of the people (*democrazia, cioè principato popolare*).

[74] Cf. Giuseppe Sorgi, *Quale Hobbes? Dalla paura alla rappresentanza* (Milan: Franco Angeli, 1989), p. 105: 'It is not that sovereignty inheres in the people, but the people in sovereignty.' Tuck argues in his 1998 introduction to *De Cive* (p. xxxiii) that 'to say that the people of England was sovereign was on the face of it to make an anti-royalist claim, and the king's cause would not be helped much by the gloss that the "people" here meant the king!' There can be little confusion of Hobbes for an anti-royalist in the passage to which Tuck refers (12.8). Hobbes here clearly and repeatedly distinguishes 'people' from 'crowd' or 'multitude',

government, so it would be absurd to overthrow or alter the government in order to bring about the rule of the people. In all commonwealths, the demos rules: therefore, all states are democracies. This appears to be the opposite of the idea discussed in the last section, that no states are democracies. The intended effect, however, is the same: to disable the democratic activist. That all states are democracies and that no states are democracies are not contradictory positions, for they function on different levels, and so can be employed in tandem against the democratically inclined discontent.[75] To the complaint that popular representation or participation is inadequate, Hobbes can retort that the people are sovereign. To the reply that what is required is not just formal popular sovereignty but the actual control of the many, Hobbes has a practical and a formal rejoinder. The practical point is that one or a few always end up in control. The formal point is that the many cannot be in control and retain their independent many identities, for collective action requires unity. The people is not manifold, but one.

Rousseau argues that for a people to give itself to a king, it must first constitute itself as a people.[76] Aquinas and many others share this intuition. Hobbes diverts its force, arguing that for a people to be constituted as a people, it must give itself a sovereign representative. Further, the ruling people must, according to Hobbes, be constituted by a single will and a single voice; they are 'united as one person'.[77] There is thus a sense in which all commonwealths are monarchic.[78] We can see how stipulative is the notion that all sovereignty is of the people when we see that it requires this univocality, and that the people counts as such only in so far as it is unified in one sovereign person: the people does not exist without the sovereign, so the people cannot overthrow the sovereign without self-destruction. Like Spinoza, say, Hobbes insists that all sovereignty is irrevocably popular. In Hobbes's hands, however, the thesis of the inevitability of the sovereignty of the people serves to subvert the aim of the advocates of popular sovereignty.

---

arguing that in a monarchy the king is the people and the subjects a powerless and disunited multitude – and that to maintain that the multitude is the people (or, therefore, to maintain that the multitude is the king) is to be guilty of treason, as undermining the majesty of the king.

[75] For discussion of this point I am grateful to Victoria Kamsler.

[76] Rousseau, *Du Contrat social*, 1.5, in *Oeuvres complètes*, ed. Bernard Gagnebin and Marcel Raymond, vol. III (Paris: Gallimard, 1964), p. 359.

[77] Hobbes, *Elements of Law*, 1.19.8. Although the upshot of his argument is quite different, cf. Althusius: 'Monarchy is represented in Aristocracy and Democracy by the concord and consensus of the rulers, whose many voices are considered as one voice and will; without such a will Democracy and Aristocracy cannot endure, but perish immediately' (translated from *Politica methodice digesta*, ed. Carl Joachim Friedrich (Cambridge, Mass.: Harvard University Press, 1932 (3rd edn 1614)), p. 405 (39.14)). See also the distinction drawn by Francisco Suárez between an apolitical multitude and a political unity in which all are tied by consent to obey a common power, in *De legibus ac Deo legislatore* (Coimbra, 1612), 3.2.4.

[78] Cf. n. 53, above.

But is it original?

Democratical Hobbesians appeal, none the less, to the idea that each and every individual who submits to government must consent, and in so consenting they form an initial democracy. All political obligation in Hobbes thus derives from the consent of the governed, they argue, and from consensual alterations to the democratic foundations. In the chapter of *The Elements of Law* entitled 'Of the three sorts of commonwealth', Hobbes writes: 'The first in order of time of these three sorts is democracy.'[79] In *De Cive*, he says much the same thing, arguing that a democracy essentially exists when those who wish to form a government meet.[80] Harrington is just one contemporary who understandably thought the meaning of this was obvious: 'Mr Hobbes holdeth democracy to be of all governments the first in order of time.'[81] Later experts agree that Hobbes held that any kind of government begins by democratic election, and that democracy is the fundamental political order.[82] Tuck insists that 'democracy was foundational and special' for Hobbes, and that extreme democracy was 'the paradigm for his well-founded commonwealth'.[83] In *Philosophy and Government*, he made the same sort of case:

in the *Elements* [Hobbes] assumed that a sovereign must be elected by the people. In a democracy, acts of sovereignty were necessarily decided by votes; and democracy was prior both chronologically and logically to other forms of government . . . He clearly envisaged that civil society was formed by a general agreement to form a democratic republic, and that any other form of government must be voted in on a majoritarian basis – an even more explicitly republican idea than Selden's . . . or Grotius'.[84]

And Tuck says that Hobbes continued to emphasise the democratic nature of sovereignty in *De Cive* and *Leviathan*.[85]

Hobbes does say that democracy is 'first in order of time' of the sorts of commonwealth. This is not a claim of logical priority; but even the claim of temporal priority is puzzling. For Hobbes repeatedly asserts that *monarchy*

---

[79] Hobbes, *Elements of Law*, 2.2.1.   [80] Hobbes, *De Cive*, 7.5. Cf. n. 108, below.

[81] James Harrington, *Politicaster* (1659), p. 712 of *The Political Works*.

[82] Among the many who clearly subscribe to this position (sometimes restricting the claim to *Elements of Law* and *De Cive*) are George Croom Robertson, Ferdinand Tönnies, Leo Strauss, Manfred Riedel, Tito Magri, Glenn Burgess, Lucien Jaume and Karlfriedrich Herb.

[83] Tuck, p. 184.

[84] Richard Tuck, *Philosophy and Government, 1572–1651* (Cambridge: Cambridge University Press, 1993), pp. 310–11.

[85] See below, n. 99, and Tuck's introduction to his 1998 edition of *De Cive*, p. xxxii. Cf. also his introduction to his 1996 edition of *Leviathan*: 'in the *Elements of Law* and *De Cive*, Hobbes had gone to some lengths to depict the original sovereign created by the inhabitants of the state of nature as necessarily a democratic assembly, which could only transfer the rights of sovereignty to a single person or small group by a majority vote of its members. . . . [In *Leviathan*,] Hobbes still presupposed that something like a majority vote among the inhabitants of the state of nature would be necessary to create any sovereign other than a democratic assembly' (p. xxxv).

is chronologically prior (while sometimes suggesting that commonwealths of moment did not arise until petty monarchs banded together to form an aristocracy). In *The Elements of Law* Hobbes affirms

that the world, as it was created, so also it is governed by one God Almighty; and that all the ancients have preferred monarchy before other governments, both in opinion, because they feigned a monarchical government amongst their gods; and also by their custom, for that in the most ancient times all people were so governed; and that paternal government, which is monarchy, was instituted in the beginning from the creation; and that other governments have proceeded from the dissolution thereof, caused by the rebellious nature of mankind, and be but pieces of broken monarchies cemented by human wit.[86]

Hobbes treats it as obvious that 'there was paternal government in Adam', and holds that the initial form of government in Greece, Rome and Germany, 'as all other Countries, in their beginnings', was monarchic or aristocratic.[87] 'In Rome', for example, 'rebellion against Kings produced Democracy.'[88] More generally, the lords of families either grew into 'great Monarchies' or 'by a voluntary conjunction of many Lords of Families into one great Aristocracie'. It is only when rebellion against monarchy or aristocracy led to anarchy that democracy sometimes arose.[89] And Hobbes is quick to disclaim the view that all governments began with election by the people. He protests that although Bramhall 'hath said that I built upon a wrong foundation, namely, "that all magistrates were at first elective" . . . I never said nor thought it'.[90]

How, then, can Hobbes claim that democracy is 'first in order of time'? He can do so because he restricts this claim to polities that are set up by institution, that is, those that are established by the votes of all. 'Having spoken in general concerning *instituted* policy in the former chapter, I come in this to speak of the sorts thereof in special, how every one of them is *instituted*. The first in order of time of *these* three sorts is democracy.'[91] I suspect that scholars have been misled because this chapter is entitled 'Of the three sorts of commonwealth',

---

[86] Hobbes, *Elements of Law*, 2.5.3. Hobbes here says he will 'omit' these points in order to focus on others, but he is affirming them by paraleipsis. Cf. *De Cive*, 10.3–4 and the annotation to 10.3.

[87] Thomas Hobbes, *The Questions Concerning Liberty, Necessity, and Chance*, ed. William Molesworth, *The English Works of Thomas Hobbes*, vol. V (London, 1841), p. 184; Hobbes, *Leviathan*, 10.51 (pp. 45–6). Cf. *Leviathan* 12.12 (p. 54), 12.20 (p. 57), 30.25 (p. 184); Hobbes, *Behemoth*, pp. 76–8.

[88] In *Leviathan*, 12.20, p. 57, Hobbes makes clear that along with the other 'first Founders, and Legislators of Common-wealths' there mentioned, the original government of Rome was monarchic. This follows the traditional view that both Athens and Rome were born in violence and first found government under a warrior king (see e.g. Plutarch's parallel lives of Theseus and Romulus).

[89] Thomas Hobbes, *A Dialogue Between a Philosopher and a Student of the Common-Laws of England*, pp. 195–6; cf. pp. 198–9. I follow Joseph Cropsey's edition (Chicago: University of Chicago Press, 1971), citing the supplied page numbers of the edition of 1681.

[90] Hobbes, *Questions Concerning Liberty, Necessity, and Chance*, p. 181; cf. p. 158.

[91] Hobbes, *Elements of Law* 2.1.1, my emphases.

and in *Leviathan* a 'commonwealth' is simply any sovereign state.[92] But in *The Elements of Law*, the referent is more specific, as the last sentence of the previous part of the work indicates: 'I shall speak in the first place of commonwealths, and afterward of bodies politic, patrimonial and despotical.' In this work, a 'commonwealth' is a body politic which arises 'by mutual agreement amongst many'.[93] 'There be two ways of erecting a body politic; one by arbitrary institution of many men assembled together, which is like a creation out of nothing by human wit; the other by compulsion, which is as it were a generation thereof out of natural force.' The former is a commonwealth, which 'proceedeth from the assembly and consent of a multitude';[94] and it is unsurprising that this kind of civil society begins as a democracy.[95] What is remarkable, however, is that Hobbes compares the origin of this sort of body politic to creation *ex nihilo*, which he regarded as incomprehensible.[96] A body politic that arises from the consent of a democratic assembly is like a divine mystery that cannot properly be considered within philosophy.[97] Perhaps the focus of the civil philosophy, therefore, is really on the bodies politic that arise from compulsion, which Hobbes likens to the products of natural generation.[98]

A similar case can be made for *De Cive* and *Leviathan*.[99] Hobbes did not think that a body politic must begin as a democracy, for he was unambivalent about the centrality of commonwealths by acquisition, which arise instead

---

[92] In most of his works, Hobbes keeps to the usage found in *Leviathan*, which scholars have accordingly followed. In his earliest works, however, his meaning is different. Cf. Thucydides 4.78, and Hobbes's remarks thereon (Thucydides, Hobbes edn, p. 255).

[93] Hobbes, *Elements of Law*, 1.19.11.   [94] Ibid., 2.1.1.

[95] Deborah Baumgold notices that on the assumption that Hobbes endorses the democratic origin of all kinds of government in *Elements of Law* 2.2.1, his argument is 'anomalous', 'aberrant' and 'redundant' ('The Composition of Hobbes's *Elements of Law*', *History of Political Thought*, 25 (2004), pp. 16–43, at pp. 27–8). Rather than seeing this as reason to reject the assumption, she regards it as evidence that the argument was 'cobbled together to bring an ongoing project to a hasty conclusion' (p. 17; cf. pp. 29–30, 35).

[96] Cf. *Elementorum philosophiae sectio prima de corpore*, 2.8.20 (ed. William Molesworth, *Opera Philosophica*, I (London, 1839), p. 103).

[97] He does make an attempt to find instances of instituted bodies politic, but it may be worth noting that they are scriptural (see *De Cive*, 11.1).

[98] Contrast the usual view that 'civil philosophy is a study of the commonwealth by institution' (F. C. Hood, *The Divine Politics of Thomas Hobbes: an Interpretation of Leviathan* (Oxford: Clarendon Press, 1964), p. 127).

[99] Tuck argues that in *De Cive* 'Hobbes once again emphasised the elective, republican character of the sovereign' (*Philosophy and Government*, p. 316); but Hobbes makes clear that he is talking here only of instituted sovereigns (cf. *De Cive*, 7.1 and 8.1). Only the instituted sovereign can be said to be elective, and Hobbes goes on at the outset of ch. 8 to emphasise the unelected and monarchical origin of sovereignty in what he calls 'the *natural commonwealth*, which may also be called the commonwealth *by Acquisition* since it is acquired by natural power and strength'. Similarly, Tuck maintains (ibid., p. 328) that in *Leviathan* 'Hobbes retained some features of an elective sovereign; as he said at the beginning of Chapter 18: "A *Common-wealth* is said to be *Instituted*, when a *Multitude* of men do Agree, and *Covenant*, every one, with every one. . . ."' What should by now be clear is that this 'elective' sovereign is specifically a feature of (what in this work Hobbes calls) a commonwealth by institution, whereas 'A *Common-wealth by Acquisition*, is that, where the Sovereign Power is acquired by Force' (*Leviathan*, 20.1, p. 101).

from conquest or parental dominion.[100] Moreover, it would not suffice to make his theory democratic if he did. To insist on a radical democratic moment in the initial institution of government is not to make radical democracy the model of the well-founded commonwealth. According to this form of argument, Machiavelli in the *Discorsi* takes absolute princedom to be the model political order, given that he thinks such a prince is initially necessary to set up other orders, including republics. Again, Hobbes is more plausibly interpreted as undermining those who do take democracy to be paradigmatic: if, as they maintain, all power is originally in the people, and legitimacy is thus granted to the government they choose, it follows that the people have consensually ceded sovereignty to the monarch under whom they now live. Any democratic foundation there may be serves only to support the edifice of present power, however undemocratic.

To aver that the sovereign is authorised by the people is not yet to side with the democrats or the anti-democrats. For centuries before Hobbes, those who agreed on this premise then diverged sharply. According to the Roman *lex regia*, the people were the origin of the emperor's rule and power.[101] Glossators, canonists and philosophers distinguished between an *alienatio* and a *concessio*, and split into camps over the revocability of the transfer. Gierke sums up the situation:

One school explained this as a definitive and irrevocable alienation of power, the other as a mere concession of its use and exercise. The dispute was generalized and led to the most widely different theories of the relation between ruler and people. On the one hand from the people's abdication the most absolute sovereignty of the prince might be deduced. . . . On the other hand the assumption of a mere 'concessio imperii' led to the doctrine of popular sovereignty.[102]

However he may have distinguished himself in other ways, Hobbes is on this subject an enthusiastic pupil of the former school. This consideration sharply limits, if it does not eliminate, the democratic weight of Hobbes's theory of instituted commonwealths.

---

[100] The main discussions are chs. 2.3 and 2.4 of *Elements of Law*, chs. 8 and 9 of *De Cive*, and ch. 20 of *Leviathan*.

[101] *Institutes*, 1.2.6; cf. *Digest*, 1.4.1.

[102] Otto von Gierke, *The Development of Political Theory*, trans. Bernard Freyd (New York: W. W. Norton, 1939), pp. 93–4. Yves Simon is emphatic: 'Among the obnoxious simplifications which fill the treatises of political science, let us single out the proposition that the divine-right theory is theocratic and the sovereignty-of-the-people theory democratic. . . . Historians often described the views of Bellarmine and Suarez as expressions of the democratic theory of sovereignty; yet neither of these thinkers meant to recommend democracy. . . . This should be stressed: the transmission theory [i.e., that the people alienate sovereign right rather than revocably delegate it] is not understood by its proponents to be distinctly democratic.' (Yves Simon, *Philosophy of Democratic Government* (Chicago: University of Chicago Press, 1951), pp. 176–7.)

The democratical Hobbesians may here object to the restriction to commonwealths by institution, appealing to the idea that even commonwealths by acquisition are basically democratic because founded on the consent of the subjects. First, however, if Hobbes requires consent for there to be sovereignty, this does not by itself make his theory democratic.[103] Even according to Hobbes's theory, consent to slavery is not sufficient to render it something other than slavery.[104] Nor would a theory that legitimised the abolition of democracy on the basis of consent to that abolition necessarily count as a democratic theory. Second, it is not clear that Hobbes requires consent in a way that would render his theory democratic even in this very attenuated sense. Hobbes argues that consent to submission should be presumed or attributed whenever we are given a realistic option of stable protection (while sometimes excepting cases where we explicitly refuse). Although Hobbes stipulates that we must consent in order to be conquered, it is a sufficient sign of our consent (and therefore of our obligation) that we are in the power of another, alive and unchained.[105] This is hardly a model of democracy. Hobbes is above all concerned to legitimate present sovereign power, of whatever form; he emphasises that sovereign right does not derive from the legitimacy of the way in which the sovereign power originates or is exercised, but from the possession of that power; and he worries that if sovereignty is made to depend on the rightness of its origin, 'there would perhaps be no tie of the Subjects obedience to their Soveraign at this day in all the world'.[106] Third, the consent that is supposedly given to a sovereign by acquisition is not democratic, for it is not the consent of an assembled multitude. It is given *seriatim*: each individual who has his life spared is understood to have consented 'one by one' – normally without any undertaking to his fellows or assembly with them.[107]

---

[103] As the moderate royalist Clarendon observes, the indisputable dependence of government on the consent of the people is quite different from the doubtful idea that all government was originally democratically instituted. 'There is no doubt there are in all Governments many things don by, and with the consent of the People; nay all Government so much depends upon the consent of the People, that without their consent and submission it must be dissolved, since where no body will obey, there can be no command, nor can one man compel a million to do what they have no mind to do' (Edward Hyde, Earl of Clarendon, *A Brief View and Survey of the Dangerous and pernicious Errors to Church and State, in Mr. Hobbes's Book, Entitled Leviathan* (Oxford, 1676), p. 45). Cf. below, pp. 216–17.

[104] In *De Cive*, 8.2–9, for example, Hobbes argues that those who are kept in chains remain slaves rather than subjects: this presumably would hold even for slaves who are shackled but do not wish to be unshackled.

[105] Argument for this interpretation is in Hoekstra, 'The *De Facto* Turn'.

[106] *Leviathan*, 'A Review, and Conclusion', para. 8, p. 391.

[107] *Leviathan*, 26.8, p. 138: 'every subject in a Common-wealth, hath covenanted to obey the Civill Law, (either one with another, as when they assemble to make a common Representative, or with the Representative it selfe one by one, when subdued by the Sword they promise obedience, that they may receive life).' In *Leviathan*, 20.1, pp. 101–2, Hobbes does say that a commonwealth by acquisition may itself come about either way, i.e. 'when men singly, or many together by

Many scholars have discussed Hobbes's view of original democracy largely in order to offer explanations for why Hobbes drops the idea in *Leviathan*.[108] So Alexandre Matheron argues that Hobbes comes to reject it because 'it was paradoxical to derive the legitimacy of the best form of sovereignty from that of the worst form', and because it was added to the earlier works to guard against the 'catastrophic' effect on his theory of the admission that a sovereign can abandon rights and engage in contracts.[109] The paradox is just the sort that Hobbes relished, however; and he would have rejected Matheron's contention that a sovereign who violated a contract thus ruptured the fundamental covenant binding citizens to obey and returned them to the state of nature (as is indicated by the fact that he did not think that the 'supplement' of original democracy was needed to solve this problem in the case of sovereignty by acquisition). The puzzle of this theoretical shift has probably been blown out of proportion, for Hobbes continues to suggest that sovereignty by institution essentially begins as a democracy.[110] There may none the less be an explanation for why Hobbes does not repeat his forthright earlier statement to this effect. One reason may be that by 1651 the associations with the idea of original democracy were unwelcome ones, or that by then he had more than enough experience of its volatility. Another possibility is that he had considered the ramifications of his model of sovereignty by acquisition. At one point he suggests that sovereignty may be acquired when those who have fallen under the power of another submit either singly or by the majority of votes in an assembly. The underlying mechanism of authorisation works due to the consent of the individual, for which neither a popular assembly nor a democratic voting procedure is necessary. The general theory of authorisation that supports both the model of acquisition and that of

plurality of voyces . . . do authorise all the actions of that Man, or Assembly, that hath their lives and liberty in his Power'.

[108] Baumgold goes further: 'Hobbes, in fact . . . jettison[s] "democracy first" from the revised theory presented in *De Cive* and *Leviathan*, presumably due to the argument's unfortunate implication that England had once upon a time had a popular government' ('The Composition of Hobbes's *Elements of Law*', p. 17, citing A. P. Martinich). She says that in *De Cive* Hobbes inserts 'the crucial modifier . . ."almost"' (p. 27). Hobbes says: 'When men have met to erect a commonwealth, they are, almost by the very fact that they have met, a *Democracy*. From the fact that they have gathered voluntarily, they are understood to be bound by the decisions made by agreement of the majority. And that is a *Democracy* . . .' (*De Cive*, 7.5). That is, there is a kind of initial democracy in all commonwealths by institution. Those who assemble to institute a commonwealth *are* a democracy, almost by the act of assembly itself ('Qui coïerunt ad ciuitatem erigendam, pene eo ipso coïerunt, *Democratia* est'). 'Almost', because there is only necessary the understanding of what this voluntary meeting commits them to; but this is an understanding that is taken to follow from such voluntary assembly itself, so commonwealths by institution do begin as democracies. Elsewhere in *De Cive* (cf. 7.8 and 7.11), Hobbes makes clear that both monarchies and aristocracies by institution have their origin in the transfer of right from the precedent democracy.

[109] Alexandre Matheron, 'The theoretical function of democracy in Spinoza and Hobbes', pp. 210–12.

[110] See Hobbes, *Leviathan* 18.1, (p. 88) and 18.5 (p. 90); cf. nn. 99 and 108 above.

institution cannot itself depend on initial democracy, and in *Leviathan* Hobbes comes to focus on that underlying theory.

Such a theory does not require democratic foundations, and supports any regime regardless of its democratic credentials. In so far as Hobbes did argue for the original authority of the people (that is, particularly in the case of sovereignty by institution), he was hardly original. Such a position was common, but protean. As Filmer remarks in the opening section on Milton of *Observations Concerning the Originall of Government*: 'what the word people means is not agreed upon.' He later explains: 'If it be demanded what is meant by the word people? 1. Sometimes it is *populus universus*, and then every child must have his consent asked, which is impossible. 2. Sometimes it is *pars major*, and sometimes it is *pars potior et sanior*.'[111] Sometimes, too, it means all of the people in their right or natural place and order. The valence of popular sovereignty depends on what the *populus* is. Molina and Suárez and a number of other predecessors hold the view that authority is originally in the people.[112] The crucial question is what they meant by this. The answer in Hobbes's case is that his construal of 'the people' is not democratic. Without a sovereign, there is only an inchoate and impotent multitude in a state of nature, and the people does not exist; within a commonwealth, the authority of the people is always invested in the present sovereign, however he came to power and whatever he does to remain in power.

Putting democracy to sleep

Among other things, I have argued in the preceding sections that Hobbes insists on the possibility, and indeed the practical certainty, that legitimate commonwealths will have non-democratic origins; that he maintains that what are nominally democracies turn out in fact to be monarchies or aristocracies; and that he contends that the people rule in all commonwealths in order to grind down the point of the doctrine of popular sovereignty. These are issues not only of textual interpretation, but also of contemporary consequence. It is true that in passages of major works Hobbes claims that a democracy may help to ensure its stability if it delegates deliberative and executive powers. If it is not put forward to suggest that a democracy should effectively abolish itself, this recommendation is apparently in tension with Hobbes's more 'realistic' view that such an arrangement (at least in tendency) will not be a democracy.[113] Both

---

[111] In Filmer, *Patriarcha*, pp. 252, 255.

[112] For a catalogue, consult Gierke, *The Development of Political Theory*, esp. pp. 143–240.

[113] In *De Cive*, 13.1, Hobbes treats the delegation of power as a way for kings 'to exercise their power through' their magistrates. The parallel with God's operation via secondary causes suggests that to be sovereign one must still be the effective power, whose ministers act according to one's ongoing will. If to be sovereign it were sufficient to have been the initial source of

argumentative strategies can make sense, however, in light of his overall aim of security and peace. To pre-empt the frustration of that aim by an active and divisive democracy, Hobbes would have the democracy be like a sleeping monarch, delegating all administration to a non-democratic body. To lull the democracy to sleep is to tranquillise the threat – it does not matter so much whether the body politic still counts as a democracy when it is asleep. The important thing is that it is at peace, and asleep.

Hobbes does share some starting points with many democratic theories, including the emphasis on individual rights, the formal importance of the consent of the people, the denial of a privileged epistemological standpoint, and a doctrine of natural equality. Moreover, at a time when many who were branded as democrats in fact endorsed mixed sovereignty in order to check democracy, Hobbes's absolutism brings him to reject mixture and, strikingly, to accept the legitimacy of thoroughgoing democracy. These positions, however, are consistent with a broadly undemocratic argument. Hobbes's view that democracy must be as absolute and legitimate as any other form of government is not ultimately a call for or a defence of democracy in particular; rather, it is an argument for absolute government and the legitimacy of present power regardless of form.

If any democratic stirrings remain in Hobbes's thought, perhaps they are to be detected in three areas that have not been explored by the democratical Hobbesians. I will sketch these three very briefly and conclude that they are suggestive but do not suffice to give Hobbes a place in the democratic fold.

First, there are passages in *The Elements of Law* that appear democratic. The most striking is this:

> Now seeing freedom cannot stand together with subjection, liberty in a commonwealth is nothing but government and rule, which because it cannot be divided, men must expect in common; and that can be no where but in the popular state, or democracy. And Aristotle saith well (lib. 6, cap 2 of his *Politics*), *The ground or intention of a democracy, is liberty*; which he confirmeth in these words: *For men ordinarily say this: that no man can partake of liberty, but only in a popular commonwealth.* Whosoever therefore in a monarchical estate, where the sovereign power is absolutely in one man, claimeth liberty, claimeth (if the hardest construction should be made thereof) either to have the sovereignty in his turn, or to be colleague with him that hath it, or to have the monarchy changed into a democracy.

Moreover, Hobbes says, 'a few only' can receive honour from the sovereign, 'unless it be in a democracy; the rest therefore must be discontent. And so much

---

the acting governor's authority (cf. Tuck, p. 189 on 'the only condition'), then the body of the people could never transfer or surrender their sovereignty – a proposition that Hobbes vigorously denies.

of the first thing that disposeth to rebellion, namely, discontent, consisting in fear and ambition.'[114] Although this shares with Hobbes's later deflationary analyses the idea that the usual demands for liberty under a monarch are outrageous, this way of making the point suggests that there is greater liberty in a democracy than in a monarchy or aristocracy, and that there may be less discontent, and thus less rebellion, therein.

One reason this argument appears only in *The Elements of Law* may be that this work was written for an audience different from those for whom *De Cive* and *Leviathan* were intended. Hobbes circulated manuscript copies of *The Elements of Law* only within a restricted circle, and may have addressed this argument to those who would identify themselves as (or who would be concerned to persuade those who identified themselves as) members of an élite.[115] And there is special reason to think that this particular argument is geared to the élite. The argument quoted above does not appear in the general discussions of forms of government. Rather, it occurs in a chapter on 'the things that dispose to rebellion', of which 'the first is discontent'.[116] In one section, Hobbes considers the discontent of 'a great multitude, or heap of people', and of those who are in 'fear of want'.[117] In the next section, he analyses 'the other sort of discontent which troubleth the mind of them who otherwise live at ease, without fear of want'; and it is here that Hobbes puts forth his argument about democracy. This discontent arises because these gentlemen are not honoured as they think they should be, and are 'grieved with the state' that has not preferred them, thinking themselves 'regarded but as slaves'.[118] Hobbes then gives the above reply. In this context, we can see that the reply urges the ambitious gentlemen to be content with their lot.[119] The alternatives are either to claim rule instead of or along with the monarch, or to change the monarchy into democracy. The first is treason, the second rebellion. Attempting either will alienate the affection of the one from whom they seek preferment. And even if the latter succeeds, it is likely to leave the gentlemen with less than they had initially, for the honour and liberty will then be shared by all.[120] On this reading, the liberty promised by democracy is to be seen by the addressees of this argument, who think 'they excel in virtue

[114] Hobbes, *The Elements of Law*, 2.8.3.

[115] Together with an increasing awareness that the rebellious gentlemen furthered their ambitions with a democratic appeal, the difference in intended audience may explain why in *The Elements of Law*, 2.5 the advantages and disadvantages of forms of government are compared between monarchy and aristocracy, and in *De Cive*, 10 between monarchy and democracy.

[116] Hobbes, *The Elements of Law*, 2.8.1 and section heading thereof.   [117] Ibid., 2.8.2.

[118] Ibid., 2.8.3.

[119] Moreover, Hobbes insinuates that the rhetoric of liberty and anti-slavery is in the service of the wounded pride of the ambitious, thus encouraging suspicion of that rhetoric.

[120] And Hobbes makes clear that in a democracy 'the whole number . . . assembled together, are the sovereign, and every particular man a subject' (*The Elements of Law*, 2.1.3). Thus, even within a democracy, any individual's claim to general liberty is illegitimate and rebellious.

and ability to govern', as a likely diminution of their lot.[121] Hobbes is concerned here with those who chafe at their superiority not being recognised, and so strive for greater power or liberty. He aims to show them that such a state of liberty would either be a democracy or a state of nature.[122] Writing in monarchical England around 1639, Hobbes would have had reason to think that his select audience would find the former nearly as unacceptable as the latter.

Second, Hobbes's arguments for the superiority of monarchy and the inferiority of democracy must be understood in the context of his hope, as he puts it in addressing the readers of *De Cive*, 'that you will think it better to enjoy your present state (though it may not be the best) rather than go to war'.[123] Hobbes is largely anti-utopian:[124] the important thing is not that the government is of the best form, but that it is stable, which requires that it be obeyed. Hobbes writes this under the protection of a monarch, and is therefore required by the law of nature to support the monarchy and undermine democratic or aristocratic threats against it. Which form of government 'is the best, is not to be disputed, where any one of them is already established; but the present ought alwaies to be preferred, maintained, and accounted best'.[125] Hobbes singles out democracy for criticism, but his 'presentism' suggests the possibility that on this subject he may not think what he says or say what he thinks.

Third, it is worth noting that Hobbes sometimes refers to the greater power of the many, and thus to the effective sway of the mass of the people. Hobbes remains a student of Thucydides even when he insists on the actual power of the many over the formal power of one or a few – and despite the risk to the vital mechanism of authorisation, which is supposed to ensure that the multitude are comparatively weak because disunited. So he says in a different context that 'it is evident that the multitude's demand is much more powerful than an individual's'.[126] In the civil wars, it was 'the common people, whose hands were to decide the controversy'; the preponderant power is theirs:[127]

For the common people are the strongest element of the commonwealth. . . . If the great, because they are great, demand to be honored on account of their power, why are not the common people to be honored, because they are many and much more powerful. The sedition of those in Holland, called the Beggars, ought to serve as a warning how

---

[121] Hobbes, *The Elements of Law*, 2.8.3. Cf. the argument in 1.14.12 that 'he therefore that desireth to live in such an estate, as is the estate of liberty and right of all to all, contradicteth himself'.

[122] See Hobbes, *Elements of Law*, 2.5.2.

[123] Hobbes, *De Cive*, 'Preface to the readers', p. 14.

[124] Against this characterisation, see Richard Tuck, 'The Utopianism of *Leviathan*' in *Leviathan After 350 Years*; for it, see Hoekstra, 'The *De Facto* Turn'.

[125] Hobbes, *Leviathan*, 42.82, p. 301. Cf. Alcibiades in Thucydides, Hobbes edn, pp. 361–2 (6.18.7): 'they of all men are most surely planted, that with most vnity obserue the present Lawes and customes, though not alwaies of the best'.

[126] Hobbes, *De Homine*, 14.8: 'scilicet postulante multitudine singulis multò potentiore'.

[127] Hobbes, *Behemoth*, p. 115.

dangerous it is to the commonwealth to scorn citizens of modest means. . . . Kings, indeed, ought not to provoke the common people.[128]

This is not a constitutional view or a formal argument about government, but a more empirical consideration. Similarly, although the sovereign is not subject to artificial punishment, that is, he cannot justly be punished,[129] he is liable to natural punishments that will none the less come about as a matter of fact. Just as 'Intemperance, is naturally punished with Diseases', and 'Injustice, with the Violence of Enemies', so is 'Negligent government of Princes, with Rebellion'. These punishments for breaches of the laws of nature follow as 'their naturall, not arbitrary effects'.[130] Without the anthropological warning (in the relevant case the nature in question is human nature), the juridical deduction (that princes cannot be punished) would be dangerously misleading. Even the great artifice Leviathan must inhabit the natural world.

The first consideration turns out to present democracy as unattractive and untenable.[131] The second consideration is not evidence of Hobbes's predilection for democracy, or of the democratic character of his theory, but of the constraints we must observe in interpreting his criticisms of democracy. The third may suggest a kind of ultimate democracy akin to that limned by La Boétie or Spinoza; but this would be a power-based theory with consequences that most democrats are keen to denounce.[132] More decisively, such a suggestion is outweighed by Hobbes's arguments about the incapacity of the unrepresented multitude.[133] Not least, Hobbes's admission of the greater power of the masses is not necessarily democratic, given that he emphasises the ability of one or a few to control them by controlling their minds.

As Aristotle recognised, a radical democracy must be democratic both in sovereignty and in administration; thus, Hobbes does not provide a model of radical democracy. Any thoroughgoing democracy must be of, by, and for the people. With serious irony, Hobbes tries to undermine these requirements with

---

[128] This translation from ch. 30 of the Latin *Leviathan* is by Curley, who notes that Clarendon compared even the more subdued English version (*Leviathan*, 30.16, p. 180) to the outlook of the Levellers (Hobbes, *Leviathan*, ed. Edwin Curley (Indianapolis: Hackett, 1994), pp. 227–8n.).

[129] Hobbes, *Leviathan*, 18.7, p. 90.

[130] Ibid., 31.40, p. 193. Cf. Hobbes, *The Elements of Law*, 2.8.2.

[131] I have argued that in *The Elements of Law* Hobbes maintains that there is no greater liberty for subjects (considered as such) in a democracy; in his later works, Hobbes's repudiation of this democratic commonplace is unambiguous (cf. e.g. *De Cive*, 10.8).

[132] Also, as is made clear in Clarendon's case (n. 103 above), a view of the superior power of the multitude may provoke a demand for the management and restraint of that power rather than an endorsement of, or a belief in the ineluctability of, democracy.

[133] That is, Hobbes emphasises the latter arguments and puts them at the centre of his general theory. The clearest statement of the argument against the view that 'Soveraign Kings, though they be *singulis majores*, of greater Power than every one of their Subjects, yet they be *Universis minores*, of lesse power than them all together', is in *Leviathan*, 18.18, p. 93.

his claims to fulfil them. The government must be for the people, and Hobbes agrees that the proper end of government is *salus populi*. The government must be by the people, and he argues that in all commonwealths the people rule. And the government must be of the people, a condition Hobbes contends is met by the consent of the governed. Entrusting the sovereign with the *salus populi* does not make a democracy, however, and there is no democratic purchase in Hobbes's claims that the people always rule or that the people have consented to government, for they are made for all governments, however tyrannical and whatever their form. Sheep's clothing does not mean that the lion is one of the sheep after all, but that he plans to devour them.

12   Hobbes and the foundations of modern international thought

David Armitage

Profecto utrumque verè dictum est, *Homo homini Deus, & Homo homini Lupus.*
Illud si concives inter se; Hoc, si civitates comparemus.   (Hobbes, *De Cive*)[1]

Quentin Skinner concluded *The Foundations of Modern Political Thought*
(1978) with the claim that '[b]y the beginning of the seventeenth century, the
concept of the State – its nature, its powers, its right to command obedience –
had come to be regarded as the most important object of analysis in European
political thought'. For confirmation of this, he quoted Thomas Hobbes who,
in the preface to *De Cive* (1642), declared that 'the aim of "civil science" is
"to make a more curious search into the rights of states and duties of subjects"'.[2] *Foundations* was dedicated to the historical examination of just how
the state became the central analytical object of political thought and how the
groundwork for a recognisably modern concept of the state had been laid. Fundamental to this concept was the state's independence from 'any external or
superior power'.[3] Yet, save for a brief but suggestive account of neo-scholastic
conceptions of the law of nations, *Foundations* included no treatment of the
state in its nature, its powers or its rights as an international actor.[4] The concept
of the state traced by Skinner defined it almost entirely in terms of its internal,

I am especially grateful to Annabel Brett, Michael Doyle, Tim Hochstrasser, Quentin Skinner,
James Tully and Lars Vinx for their comments on earlier versions of this essay.

[1] Thomas Hobbes, *De Cive: the Latin Version*, ed. Howard Warrender (Oxford: Oxford University Press, 1983), p. 73; 'There are two maxims which are surely both true: Man is a God to
man, and Man is a wolf to Man. The former is true of the relations of citizens with each other,
the latter of relations between commonwealths': Thomas Hobbes, *On the Citizen*, ed. Richard
Tuck and Michael Silverthorne (Cambridge: Cambridge University Press, 1998), p. 3. (Subsequent references to these works will be to these editions, unless otherwise indicated.) On
this passage see François Tricaud, '"Homo homini Deus", "Homo homini Lupus": Recherche
des Sources des deux Formules de Hobbes', in Reinhart Koselleck and Roman Schnur (eds.),
Hobbes-Forschungen (Berlin: Duncker and Humblot, 1969), pp. 61–70.

[2] Quentin Skinner, *The Foundations of Modern Political Thought*, 2 vols. (Cambridge: Cambridge
University Press, 1978), II, 349; 'in jure civitatis, civiumque officiis investigandis opus est':
Hobbes, *De Cive*, p. 78. Compare Skinner, 'From the State of Princes to the Person of the State',
in Quentin Skinner, *Visions of Politics*, 3 vols. (Cambridge: Cambridge University Press, 2002),
II: *Renaissance Virtues*, pp. 368–413; Skinner, 'Hobbes and the Purely Artificial Person of the
State', in Skinner, *Visions*, III: *Hobbes and Civil Science*, pp. 177–208.

[3] Skinner, *Foundations*, II, p. 351.   [4] Ibid., pp. 151–4.

domestic or municipal capacities. The relations between states had apparently not yet become an important object of political or historical analysis.

The absence from *Foundations* of any extended treatment of what might be called the foundations of modern international thought was typical for the time at which the book appeared. In the same year that *Foundations* was published, W. B. Gallie, Skinner's predecessor in the Cambridge Chair of Political Science, commented that 'thoughts . . . about the roles and causes of war and the possibilities of peace between the peoples of the world' had formed 'an enterprise which the ablest minds of previous ages had, with very few exceptions, either ignored or by-passed.' Gallie argued that the foundations of modern international thought were laid much later, during the eighteenth century, 'in the writings of Montesquieu, Voltaire, Rousseau, and Vattel among others'.[5] Taken together, Skinner's and Gallie's accounts implied that the foundations of modern political thought were distinct from those of modern international thought and that each possessed a distinct chronology, genealogy and canon of fundamental thinkers.

For Skinner, as for most political theorists, Hobbes was the 'first . . . modern theorist of the sovereign state'.[6] This was the state as sovereign over its subjects rather than as a sovereign among sovereigns. The balance of Hobbes's own writings justified this focus on the internal dimension of the state. Hobbes had much less to say about the relations between states than many scholars – particularly theorists of international relations – would like him to have said. In comparison with his treatment of the domestic powers and rights of the sovereign, his reflections on the law of nations, on the rights of states as international actors and on the behaviour of states in relation to one another were scattered and terse. For this reason, students of Hobbes's political theory have generally seen his international theory as marginal to the central concerns of his civil science: 'The external relations of Leviathan are for them on the fringe of Hobbes' theory.'[7]

The relative silence of Hobbes and of his philosophical commentators on this matter contrasts starkly with his canonical position among the founding fathers of international thought: 'No student of international relations theory, it seems, can afford to disregard Hobbes's contribution to that field.'[8] Within

---

[5] W. B. Gallie, *Philosophers of Peace and War: Kant, Clausewitz, Marx, Engels and Tolstoy* (Cambridge: Cambridge University Press, 1978), p. 1; compare F. H. Hinsley, *Power and the Pursuit of Peace: Theory and Practice in the Relations between States* (Cambridge: Cambridge University Press, 1963).

[6] Skinner, 'From the State of Princes to the Person of the State', p. 413.

[7] Murray Forsyth, 'Thomas Hobbes and the External Relations of States', *British Journal of International Studies* 5 (1979), p. 196. For an early exception, see David Gauthier, *The Logic of Leviathan: the Moral and Political Theory of Thomas Hobbes* (Oxford: Clarendon Press, 1969), pp. 207–12.

[8] Noel Malcolm, 'Hobbes's Theory of International Relations', in Noel Malcolm, *Aspects of Hobbes* (Oxford: Oxford University Press, 2002), pp. 432–56, at p. 432.

the conventional typologies of international relations theory, Hobbes stands between Hugo Grotius and Immanuel Kant as the presiding genius of one of three major traditions of international theory: the Hobbesian 'realist' theory of international anarchy, the Grotian 'rationalist' theory of international solidarity, and the Kantian 'revolutionist' theory of international society.[9] There is clearly a problem here for historians, political theorists and international relations theorists alike. If Hobbes's contribution to international thought was so fundamental, how could it have been overlooked for so long? And how did he come to be accepted as a foundational figure in the history of international thought if his reflections on the subject were so meagre?

Amid the vast amount of commentary on Hobbes as an international theorist there is little that could be described as being of a genuinely historical character.[10] Accordingly, the first part of this essay will lay out Hobbes's conceptions of the relation between states across the course of his career.[11] As this survey will show, the full range of Hobbes's writings provides a more expansive and

---

[9] Martin Wight, 'An Anatomy of International Thought', *Review of International Studies* 13 (1987), pp. 221–7; Martin Wight, *International Theory: the Three Traditions*, eds. Gabriele Wight and Brian Porter (Leicester: Continuum 1991).

[10] As well as Forsyth, 'Thomas Hobbes and the External Relations of States', and Malcolm, 'Hobbes's Theory of International Relations', see especially Mark A. Heller, 'The Use and Abuse of Hobbes: the State of Nature in International Relations', *Polity* 13 (1980), pp. 21–32; Hedley Bull, 'Hobbes and the International Anarchy', *Social Research* 48 (1981), pp. 717–38; Cornelia Navari, 'Hobbes and the "Hobbesian Tradition" in International Thought', *Millennium: Journal of International Studies* 11 (1982), pp. 203–22; Donald W. Hanson, 'Thomas Hobbes's "Highway to Peace"', *International Organization* 38 (1984), pp. 329–54; Timo Airaksinen and Martin A. Bertman (eds.), *Hobbes: War Among Nations* (Aldershot: Avebury, 1989); Peter Caws (ed.), *The Causes of Quarrel: Essays on Peace, War, and Thomas Hobbes* (Boston: Beacon Press, 1989); Laurie M. Johnson, *Thucydides, Hobbes, and the Interpretation of Realism* (DeKalb: Northern Illinois University Press 1993); Raino Malnes, *The Hobbesian Theory of International Conflict* (Oslo: Scandinavian University Press, 1993); Michael W. Doyle, *Ways of War and Peace: Realism, Liberalism, and Socialism* (New York: Norton, 1997), pp. 111–36; David Boucher, *Political Theories of International Relations: from Thucydides to the Present* (Oxford: Oxford University Press, 1998), pp. 145–67; Dieter Hüning, '"Inter arma silent leges": Naturrecht, Staat und Völkerrecht bei Thomas Hobbes', in Rüdiger Voigt (ed.), *Der Leviathan* (Baden-Baden: Nomos, 2000), pp. 129–63; Richard Tuck, *The Rights of War and Peace: Political Thought and the International Order from Grotius to Kant* (Oxford: Oxford University Press 1999), pp. 126–39; Kinji Akashi, 'Hobbes's Relevance to the Modern Law of Nations', *Journal of the History of International Law* 2 (2000), pp. 199–216; Georg Cavallar, *The Rights of Strangers: Theories of International Hospitality, the Global Community, and Political Justice since Vitoria* (Aldershot: Ashgate, 2002), pp. 173–91; Peter Schröder, 'Natural Law, Sovereignty and International Law: a Comparative Perspective', in Ian Hunter and David Saunders (eds.), *Natural Law and Civil Sovereignty: Moral Right and State Authority in Early Modern Political Thought* (New York: Palgrave, 2002), pp. 204–18; Howard Williams, *Kant's Critique of Hobbes: Sovereignty and Cosmopolitanism* (Cardiff: University of Wales Press, 2003).

[11] This essay deals only with Hobbes's firsthand statements; any full survey of his knowledge of international relations would also have to include his translations of Fulgenzio Micanzio's letters to the second earl of Devonshire on foreign affairs (1615–26), Chatsworth, Hobbes MS 73.Aa, transcribed in British Library, Additional MS 11309, and of Thucydides, *Eight Bookes of the Peloponnesian Warre* (London, 1629).

nuanced set of reflections on the state in its international capacity than could be inferred from most treatments of the subject. No previous attempt has been made to trace the afterlife of Hobbes's reflections, in large part because there has been little study of the reception of his works more generally in the period since the mid-eighteenth century.[12] The second part of the essay will then survey the afterlife of Hobbes's international thought from the seventeenth century to the twentieth in order to show just how recent is the adoption of Hobbes as a – if not the – theorist of international anarchy.

The earliest statement on the subject of international relations attributable to Hobbes comes from the 'Discourse of Laws' contained in the *Horae Subsecivae* (1620), a volume of essays credited to Hobbes's pupil, William Cavendish, later the second earl of Devonshire. There the author (who, stylometric analysis has suggested, may have been Hobbes)[13] provided the following entirely conventional definition of the 'three branches that mens Lawes do spread themselves into, every one stricter then other':

> The Law of Nature, which we enjoy in common with al other living creatures. *The Law of Nations*, which is common to all men in generall: and the *Municipall Law* of every Nation, which is peculiar and proper to this or that Country, and ours to us as Englishmen.
> That of *Nature*, which is the ground or foundation of the rest, produceth such actions amongst us, as are common to every living creature, and not only incident to men: as for example, the commixture of severall sexes, which we call *Marriage*, generation, education, and the like; these actions belong to all living creatures as well as to us. The *Lawes of Nations* bee those rules which reason hath prescribed to all men in generall, and such as all Nations one with another doe allow and observe for just.[14]

This definition was conventional because drawn almost word for word from the opening pages of the *Digest* of Roman law, a text whose fundamental importance for early-modern political thought Skinner has repeatedly stressed.[15] The first paragraph of the *Digest* distinguished public law (which concerned religious affairs, the priesthood and offices of state) from private law. It then divided private law into three parts: the *ius naturale*, the *ius gentium* and the *ius civile* [*collectum etenim est ex naturalibus praeceptis aut gentium aut civilibus*]. In

---

[12] There is as yet no comprehensive survey of Hobbes's late eighteenth- and nineteenth-century reception comparable to Noel Malcolm, 'Hobbes and the European Republic of Letters', in Malcolm, *Aspects of Hobbes*, pp. 457–545, or Yves Glaziou, *Hobbes en France au XVIIIe siècle* (Paris: PUF, 1993), though see Richard Tuck, *Hobbes* (Oxford: Oxford University Press, 1989), pp. 96–8, and James E. Crimmins, 'Bentham and Hobbes: an Issue of Influence', *Journal of the History of Ideas* 63 (2002), pp. 677–96.

[13] Noel B. Reynolds and John L. Hilton, 'Thomas Hobbes and the Authorship of the *Horae Subsecivae*', *History of Political Thought* 14 (1994), pp. 361–80.

[14] [William Cavendish], *Horae Subsecivae, Observations and Discourses* (London, 1620), pp. 517–18 (contractions expanded).

[15] Quentin Skinner, *Liberty before Liberalism* (Cambridge: Cambridge University Press, 1998), pp. 39–41; Skinner, 'John Milton and the Politics of Slavery' and 'Liberty and the English Civil War', in Skinner, *Visions*, II, pp. 289–91, 313.

words that would be followed exactly by the author of the 'Discourse of Laws', it stated that the *ius naturale* is common to all animals and out of it comes marriage, procreation and child-rearing, while the *ius gentium* 'the law of nations, is that which all human peoples observe'. The source of the *ius naturale* was instinct; that of the *ius gentium*, human agreement. They therefore obliged human beings in different ways. It could thus be concluded of the *ius gentium*: 'That it is not co-extensive with natural law can be grasped easily, since this latter is common to all animals whereas *ius gentium* is common only to human beings among themselves.'[16] Though both could be distinguished from the *ius civile*, the internal law of particular communities, the *ius gentium* could not be assimilated to the *ius naturale*. The medieval and early-modern theory of natural law would thereafter rest on this trichotomy with its fundamental distinction between the law of nature and the law of nations.[17]

The definitions of the laws of nature and of nations in the *Horae Subsecivae* stand in marked contrast to what would become Hobbes's standard account in the successive versions of his civil science from the *Elements of Law* (1640) through *De Cive* (1642) to *Leviathan* (1651; 1668). If the passage from the 'Discourse of Laws' can be attributed to Hobbes, then his later treatments of the law of nature and of nations represented a clear break with that early triadic definition.[18] Hobbes's mature conception of the law of nations differed in three basic ways from the account offered in the 'Discourse of Laws': first, it derived the law of nature from reason alone; second, it distinguished firmly between the law of nature and the right of nature (a distinction that later writers, such as Samuel Pufendorf, would not observe as scrupulously as Hobbes); and, third, it collapsed the law of nations into the law of nature.

Hobbes's later statements were much closer to the jurist Gaius's definition, also found in the first chapter of the *Digest*, which distinguished the *ius civile* proper to each particular society from 'the law which natural reason has

---

[16] *The Digest of Justinian*, ed. Theodor Mommsen and Paul Krueger, trans. Alan Watson, 4 vols. (Philadelphia: University of Pennsylvania Press, 1985), I.1. pp. 1, 2–4: 'Ius gentium est quo, gentes humanae utuntur. quod a naturali recedere facile intellegere licet, quia illud omnibus animalibus, hoc solis hominibus inter se commune sit'; Max Kaser, *Ius gentium* (Cologne: Böhlau, 1993), pp. 64–70. This passage is usually attributed to Ulpian.

[17] Merio Scattola, 'Before and After Natural Law: Models of Natural Law in Ancient and Modern Times', in T. J. Hochstrasser and Peter Schröder (eds.), *Early Modern Natural Law Theories: Contexts and Strategies in the Early Enlightenment* (Dordrecht: Kluwer, 2003), pp. 10–11.

[18] The fact that the passage is such a literal paraphrase of the *Digest* makes it inapt for the kind of analysis applied in Reynolds and Hilton, 'Thomas Hobbes and the Authorship of the *Horae Subsecivae*'; likewise, *Thomas Hobbes, Three Discourses: a Critical Modern Edition of a Newly Identified Work of the Young Hobbes*, ed. Noel B. Reynolds and Arlene W. Saxonhouse (Chicago: University of Chicago Press, 1995), supplies little information on the sources of the discourses and, hence, no indication of whether other passages might also be paraphrases. For further evidence of such borrowing in the text see Andrew Huxley, 'The *Aphorismi* and *A Discourse of Laws*: Bacon, Cavendish, and Hobbes 1615–1620', *Historical Journal* 47 (2004), pp. 399–412.

established among all human beings . . . among all observed in equal measure . . . called *ius gentium*, as being the law which all nations observe'.[19] This produced a dichotomous taxonomy of law in which the law of nature applied both to individuals and to commonwealths and the civil law was distinguished from it as the positive commands of sovereigns. Hobbes's use of the distinction between the law of nations and the civil law would help to create two competing afterlives for him as a foundational figure both for the seventeenth- and eighteenth-century discipline of the law of nature and nations and for nineteenth-century legal positivism. His later reputation as a denier of international law and as a theorist of international anarchy would spring from these competing conceptions of him as at once a naturalist and a positivist, depending on whether he was considered as an international theorist or as a political theorist.

In his first mature account of the law of nations, Hobbes noted in the *Elements of Law* that previous writers on the law of nature could not agree whether it represents 'the consent of all nations, or the wisest and most civil nations' or 'the consent of all mankind' because 'it is not agreed upon, who shall judge which nations are the wisest'. He concluded instead that '[t]here can be . . . no other law of nature than reason, nor no other precepts of NATURAL LAW, than those which declare unto us the ways of peace'. Later in the work, he asserted that 'right [*ius*] is that liberty which law leaveth us; and laws [*leges*] those restraints by which we agree mutually to abridge one another's liberty' before applying that distinction to a tripartite division of law crucially different from that found in the *Digest* and in the *Horae Subsecivae*: 'whatsoever a man does that liveth in a commonwealth, *jure*, he doth it *jure civili*, *jure naturae*, and *jure divino*'. This division omitted the law of nations as strictly impertinent to the internal affairs of a commonwealth and irrelevant to its citizens as individuals and substituted instead the *ius divinum* as the third source of obligation in civil society. Individuals are not the subjects of the *ius gentium*; commonwealths in their capacity as artificial persons are. The *ius gentium* therefore only appeared as an afterthought in the very last sentence of the *Elements of Law*:

And thus much concerning the elements and general grounds of law natural and politic. As for the law of nations, it is the same with the law of nature. For that which is the law of nature between man and man, before the constitution of commonwealth, is the law of nations between sovereign and sovereign after.[20]

Hobbes elaborated this rather cursory statement in *De Cive*, a work whose central themes – 'men's duties, first as men, then as citizens and lastly as

---

[19] Gaius, *Institutiones*, I.3: 'quod vero naturalis ratio inter omnes homines constituit, id apud omnes populos peraeque custoditur vocaturque ius gentium, quasi quo iure omnes gentes utuntur' (also in *Digest*, I.1.9); Kaser, *Ius gentium*, pp. 20–2.

[20] Thomas Hobbes, *The Elements of Law, Natural and Politic*, ed. Ferdinand Tönnies, intr. M. M. Goldsmith, 2nd edn, (London: Macmillan, 1969), pp. 75, 186, 190.

Christians' – he defined as constituting 'the elements of the law of nature and of nations [*iuris naturalis gentiumque elementa*], the origin and force of justice, and the essence of the Christian Religion'.[21] After once more distinguishing law from right, Hobbes elaborated his definition of natural law in its application first to individuals and then to states:

Natural law can again be divided into the natural law of *men*, which alone has come to be called the *law of nature*, and the natural law of *commonwealths*, which may be spoken of as the *law of nations* [*lex Gentium*], but which is commonly called the *right of nations* [*ius Gentium*]. The precepts of both are the same: but because commonwealths once instituted take on the personal qualities of men, what we call a *natural law* in speaking of the duties of individual men is called the *right of Nations*, when applied to whole commonwealths, peoples or nations. And the Elements of *natural law* and *natural right* which we have been teaching may, when transferred to whole *commonwealths* and *nations*, be regarded as the Elements of the *laws* and of the *right of Nations* [*Et quae legis & iuris naturalis Elementa hactenus tradita sunt, translata ad civitates et gentes integras, pro legum et iuris Gentium Elementis sumi possunt*].[22]

This was the clearest statement Hobbes would ever give of his rationale for identifying the law of nations with the law of nature. In the *Leviathan*, he would say only, 'Concerning the Offices of one Sovereign to another, which are comprehended in that Law, which is commonly called the *Law of Nations*, I need not say any thing in this place; because the Law of Nations, and the Law of Nature, is the same thing' in so far as 'every Sovereign hath the same Right, in procuring the safety of his People, that any particular man can have, in procuring his own safety.'[23] This left implicit what Hobbes had made explicit in *De Cive*: that the commonwealth once constituted as an artificial person took on the characteristics and the capacities of the fearful, self-defensive individuals who fabricated it. However, he did not necessarily imply that individuals in the state of nature could be understood reciprocally as possessing 'the characteristics of sovereign states'.[24] The analogy between pre-civil individuals and commonwealths was imperfect and only made sense for Hobbes once states had been constituted as persons; to describe individuals as possessing the characteristics of states would beg the question of just what characteristics a state in fact possessed.

When Hobbes came to offer the final version of his account of the relation between the law of nature and the law of nations in the Latin *Leviathan* (1668), he repeated that they are the same [*idem sunt*] and expanded his definition in the English *Leviathan* by asserting that 'whatever a particular man could do before commonwealths were constituted, a commonwealth can do according to the *ius*

[21] Hobbes, *De Cive*, p. 77; Hobbes, *On the Citizen*, p. 7.
[22] Hobbes, *De Cive*, pp. 207–8 (*De Cive*, XIV.4); Hobbes, *On the Citizen*, p. 156.
[23] Thomas Hobbes, *Leviathan*, ed. Richard Tuck, rev. edn (Cambridge: Cambridge University Press, 1996), p. 244 (subsequent references will be to this edition).
[24] Tuck, *The Rights of War and Peace*, p. 129.

gentium'.[25] What exactly a commonwealth could do, he said, could be found in the list of the laws of nature earlier in his work. Hobbes left it to his readers to provide an account of the rights of commonwealths in the state of nature, though without any recognition that his account had changed over time. For example, in the *Elements of Law*, Hobbes had specified (as the twelfth law of nature), '*That men allow commerce and traffic indifferently to one another*' and illustrated the principle with the example (also used earlier by Grotius in the same connection) of the war between the Athenians and the Megareans.[26] Hobbes's subsequent enumerations of the laws of nature in *De Cive* and *Leviathan* omitted without explanation this stipulation that commerce must be unhindered. By contrast, the thirteenth law of nature, '*That all messengers of peace, and such as are employed to maintain amity between man and man, may safely come and go*', did recur in those later enumerations, even though in *De Cive* it was one of the very few laws of nature to have no equivalent in the divine law.[27] Hobbes may have come to think that the right of free trade needed no separate stipulation once the general law of treating everyone else equally had been stated, but he clearly came to believe that it was unenforceable in the state of nature, where there is 'no Culture of the Earth; no Navigation, nor use of the commodities that may be imported by Sea'.[28] He thereby accommodated his account of the law of nations to his account of the law of nature: what could not be rightfully (or practicably) claimed by individuals in the state of nature could hardly be claimed by commonwealths in their relations with one another.

It was on the basis of his assimilation of the law of nations to the law of nature that Hobbes identified the international arena as a still existing state of nature. Indeed, apart from 'the savage people in many places of *America*', commonwealths in their relations with one another provided his most striking and enduring evidence for the existence of that state of nature.[29] Hobbes seems to have made that discovery between writing the *Elements of Law* and *De Cive*. In the *Elements*, his account of the foundations of international relations was as cursory as his treatment of the *ius gentium*. Hobbes there took the *ius in bello* to be a specifically personal matter: '[t]here is . . . little to be said concerning the laws that men are to observe towards one another in time of war, wherein

---

[25] 'De officiis summorum imperantium versus se invicem nihil dicam, nisi quod contineatur in legibus supra commemoratis. Nam *jus gentium* et *jus naturae* idem sunt. Quod potuit fieri ante civitates constitutas a quolibet homine, idem fieri potest per jus gentium a qualibet civitate': Hobbes, *Leviathan* (1668), in *Thomae Hobbes Malmesburiensis Opera Philosophica Quae Latine Scripsit Omnia*, ed. Sir William Molesworth, 5 vols. (London, 1839–45), III, p. 253.

[26] Hobbes, *The Elements of Law*, ed. Tönnies, p. 87; [Hugo Grotius], *Mare Liberum* (Leiden, 1609), 3 (alluding to Diodorus Siculus, *Bibliotheca historica*, XII.39, and Plutarch, *Pericles*, XXIX).

[27] Hobbes, *De Cive*, p. 115 (*De Cive*, III.19, where diplomatic immunity becomes the fourteenth law of nature); Hobbes, *On the Citizen*, p. 51; Hobbes, *Leviathan*, p. 108 (where it is the fifteenth law of nature).

[28] Hobbes, *Leviathan*, p. 89.   [29] Ibid.

every man's being and well-being is the rule of his actions'. Beyond that, his treatment of commonwealths as international actors was descriptive rather than normative and concerned only 'the means of levying soldiers, and of having money, arms, ships, and fortified places in readiness for defence; and partly, in the avoiding of unnecessary wars'.[30]

In *De Cive*, Hobbes offered for the first time the full range of descriptive and normative characteristics of commonwealths as international actors that would also be found, with some modification and elaboration, in *Leviathan*. Answering the criticism that he had overestimated the primacy of fear as the fundamental motive for human action in the state of nature, Hobbes adduced the evidence of the relations between commonwealths, which 'guard their frontiers with fortresses, their cities with walls, through fear of neighbouring countries'; '[a]ll commonwealths and individuals behave in this way, and thus admit their fear and distrust of each other'. That fearful defensiveness defined the very nature of commonwealths when seen from the outside: 'And what else are countries but so many camps fortified against each other with garrisons and arms [*totidem castra praesidiis et armis contra se invicem munita*], and their state . . . is to be regarded as a natural state, i. e. a state of war?' Thus, Hobbes concluded,

hostility is adequately shown by distrust, and by the fact that the borders of their common-wealths, Kingdoms and empires, armed and garrisoned, with the posture and appearance of gladiators [*statu vultuque gladiatorio*], look across at each other like enemies, even when they are not striking each other.[31]

In the *Leviathan*, this image would become even more decisive evidence for the existence of the state of nature:

though there had never been any time, wherein particular men were in a condition of warre one against another; yet in all times, Kings, and Persons of Soveraigne authority, because of their Independency, are in continuall jealousies, and in the state and posture of Gladiators; having their weapons pointing, and their eyes fixed on one another; that is, their Forts, Garrisons, and Guns upon the Frontiers of their Kingdomes; and continuall Spyes upon their neighbours, which is a posture of War.[32]

On this basis, there could be no hope of peace among commonwealths: as the Lawyer explained in Hobbes's *Dialogue Between a Phylosopher and a Student, of the Common-Laws of England* (1666), 'You are not to expect such a Peace between two Nations, because there is no Common Power in this World to

---

[30] Hobbes, *The Elements of Law*, ed. Tönnies, pp. 101, 184.
[31] Hobbes, *De Cive*, pp. 93, 180, 277–78 (*De Cive*, I.2, X.17, XV.27); Hobbes, *On the Citizen*, pp. 25, 126, 231–2. The source of information on gladiators most readily accessible to Hobbes would have been Justus Lipsius, *Saturnalium Sermonum libri duo, Qui de Gladiatoribus* (Antwerp, 1585, and later editions).
[32] Hobbes, *Leviathan*, p. 90.

punish their Injustice: mutual fear may keep them quiet for a time, but upon every visible advantage they will invade one another.'[33] However, Hobbes did not infer from this posture of hostility that mutual fear would give rise to an international Leviathan, to liberate commonwealths from the dangers of the state of nature as the institution of the sovereign freed individuals from those perils. The two cases were incomparable 'because [sovereigns] uphold thereby, the Industry of their Subjects; there does not follow from it, that misery, which accompanies the Liberty of particular men'.[34] The international state of nature was not equivalent to the interpersonal state of nature and was therefore insusceptible to parallel remedies for its inconveniencies.[35]

Hobbes's scattered reflections on the law of nations, on the behaviour of states and on the relations between them, gave rise to two major but distinguishable conceptions with which his name would become associated in later international thought. The first, and most fundamental, was that the law of nations was simply the law of nature applied to commonwealths. The second, and currently the one identified as most characteristically Hobbesian, was that the international realm is a state of nature populated by fearful and competitive actors. These two conceptions were not be found in tandem in Hobbes's works before the composition of *De Cive* in 1641 nor did he elaborate or elucidate them after their appearance in *Leviathan* in 1651, save for their later translation into Latin in 1668. His failure to expound them systematically had three lasting consequences for his reputation and for the reception of his political philosophy. The first, arising initially in the seventeenth century, was to sharpen the division between naturalism and positivism in international law. The second, which emerged in the eighteenth and nineteenth centuries, was to distinguish his conception of the law of nations from his conception of the international state of nature. The third, arising from the previous two in the twentieth century, was to identify Hobbes as the classic theorist of international anarchy. This last is the most recent and the most contingent but remains the basis of Hobbes's reputation as a theorist of international relations.

The positivist response to Hobbes's naturalism originated even before the appearance of *Leviathan* with the publication in 1650 of the *Iuris et Iudicii Faecialis, sive, Iuris Inter Gentes* by the Royalist professor of civil law at Oxford, Richard Zouche. Zouche's later reputation as 'the first real positivist' in the history of international law rests on the distinction he made in that work between the *ius gentium* and the *ius inter gentes*.[36] The *ius gentium* comprised

---

[33] Thomas Hobbes, *A Dialogue Between a Philosopher and a Student of the Common Laws of England* (1666), ed. Joseph Cropsey (Chicago: University of Chicago Press, 1971), p. 57.

[34] Hobbes, *Leviathan*, p. 90.

[35] Heller, 'The Use and Abuse of Hobbes'; S. J. Hoekstra, *The Savage, the Citizen, and the Foole: the Compulsion for Civil Society in the Philosophy of Thomas Hobbes* (unpublished D.Phil., University of Oxford, 1998), pp. 69–84.

[36] Arthur Nussbaum, *A Concise History of the Law of Nations* (New York: Macmillan, 1947), p. 122.

all those elements common to the laws of various nations, such as the distinctions between freedom and slavery or private property and public property. This law of nations had to be distinguished from the law between nations, the *ius inter gentes*, which comprised the laws different peoples or nations observed in their dealings with one another, such as the laws of war and commerce.[37] According to this definition, the *ius inter gentes* was the product of convention and agreement and did not derive from any other source of law, natural or divine. Yet in an earlier manuscript version of his treatise, Zouche had originally defined the *ius inter gentes* as that which is common among diverse sovereigns or peoples and which is derived from the precepts of God, nature or nations, a definition derived from Gaius's in the *Digest*.[38] Zouche had clearly changed his mind about the definition of the *ius inter gentes* before 1650 and found it necessary to distinguish it from both the *ius gentium* and the *ius naturae*. The impulse for this shift seems to have been his reading of Hobbes on the law of nature and nations. There is no sign that Zouche had read any of Hobbes's works by the time he composed the manuscript version of the *Iuris Faecialis*, but *De Cive* did appear in the footnotes to the first chapter of the printed version.[39] Zouche may therefore have been the first legal theorist to resist Hobbes's conflation of the law of nations with the law of nature.

Within the later tradition of natural jurisprudence, from Pufendorf to Vattel and beyond, Hobbes would be acclaimed as a fundamental innovator on the basis of that conflation. By the late eighteenth century the relationship between the two forms of law appeared to be the primary question in determining the basis of obligation itself. As the first anglophone historian of the law of nations, Robert Ward, put it in 1795: 'Upon the whole the great points of difference concerning the mode of its structure, seem to turn upon this; Whether the Law of Nations is merely the Law of *nature* as it concerns man, *and nothing more*; or whether it is not composed of certain *positive Institutions* founded upon consent'. Ward took Hobbes, Pufendorf and Burlamaqui to be the key proponents of the first position; Suárez, Grotius, Huber, Bynkershoek, 'and in general the more recent authors, declare for the last'.[40] Pufendorf asked, 'Whether or no there be any such thing as a particular and positive *Law of Nations*, contradistinct to the *Law of Nature*?' and immediately answered his own question by quoting *De Cive*, XIV.4:

---

[37] Richard Zouche, *Iuris et Iudicii Faecialis, sive, Iuris Inter Gentes* (Oxford, 1650), p. 3.

[38] 'Ius inter Gentes est quod in Communione inter diversos Principis vel populos obtinet, et deducitur ab Institutis divinis, Naturae et Gentium': [Richard Zouche,] *Iuris Faecialis. Sive Juris et Judicii inter Gentes Explicatio*, BL, Add. MS 48190, fol. 14r.

[39] Zouche, *Iuris et Iudicii Faecialis*, p. 3.

[40] Robert Ward, *An Enquiry into the Foundation and History of the Law of Nations in Europe, From the Time of the Greeks and Romans, to the Age of Grotius*, 2 vols. (London, 1795), I, p. 4.

Thus Mr. *Hobbes* divides *natural Law, into the natural Law of Men, and the natural Law of States, commonly called the Law of Nations*. He observes, *That the precepts of both are the same . . .* This opinion we, for our Part, readily subscribe to.[41]

Burlamaqui concurred, after quoting the same passage from *De Cive*: 'There is no room to question the reality and certainty of such a law of nations obligatory of its own nature, and to which nations, or the sovereigns that rule them, ought to submit.'[42] By the time Emer de Vattel published his *Droit des gens* in 1758, Hobbes's contribution had become foundational but not incontrovertible:

Hobbes . . . was the first, to my knowledge, to give us a distinct though imperfect idea of the Law of Nations . . . His statement that the Law of Nations is the natural law applied to States or Nations is sound. But . . . he was mistaken in thinking that the natural law did not necessarily undergo any change in being thus applied.[43]

Before the twentieth century, Hobbes's conception of the international state of nature attracted much less comment and approval than his naturalist conception of the law of nations.[44] His early critics had attacked his conception of the interpersonal state of nature on the grounds that it made untenable assumptions about human motivation (as Grotius was the first to charge) or that it imported features of the civil state of humanity back into the pre-civil state (as Montesquieu contended, anticipating Rousseau).[45] However, they did not argue that his account of the relations between states was necessarily incorrect for the

---

[41] Samuel Pufendorf, *Of the Law of Nature and Nations* (1672), trans. Basil Kennett, 4th edn. (London, 1729), pp. 149–50 (*De Jure Naturae et Gentium*, II.3.23); cf. Robert Sharrock, *Hypothesis Ethike, De Officiis Secundum Naturae Ius* (Oxford, 1660), p. 229; Samuel Rachel, *De Jure Naturae et Gentium Dissertationes* (Kiel, 1676), p. 306; James Wilson, 'Lectures on Law' (1790–91), in *The Works of James Wilson*, ed. Robert Green McCloskey, 2 vols. (Cambridge, Mass.: Harvard University Press, 1967), I, p. 151 (quoting Pufendorf).

[42] Jean Jacques Burlamaqui, *The Principles of Natural Law* (1748), trans. Thomas Nugent (London, 1748), pp. 195–6 (*Les Principes du droit naturel*, VI.5).

[43] Emer de Vattel, *The Law of Nations or the Principles of Natural Law Applied to the Conduct and to the Affairs of Nations and of Sovereigns* (1758), trans. Charles G. Fenwick (Washington, DC: Carnegie Institution, 1916), 5a–6a (*Le Droit des gens*, 'Preface'); Emmanuelle Jouannet, *Emer de Vattel et l'Emergence doctrinale du droit international classique* (Paris: Pedone, 1998), pp. 39–52.

[44] A distinguished early exception was Leibniz, who commented favourably on Hobbes's image of interstate relations as gladiatorial: G. W. Leibniz, *Codex Iuris Gentium*, Praefatio (1693), in *Leibniz: Political Writings*, ed. Patrick Riley, 2nd edn. (Cambridge: Cambridge University Press, 1988), p. 166.

[45] 'Putat inter homines omnes a nature esse bellum et alia quaedam habet nostris non congruentia': Hugo Grotius to Willem de Groot, 11 April 1643, in *Briefwisseling van Hugo Grotius*, ed. P. C. Molhuysen, B. L. Meulenbroek and H. J. M. Nellen, 17 vols. (The Hague: Nijhoff, 1928–2001), XIV, p. 199; 'Hobbes demande *pourquoi, si les hommes ne sont pas naturellement en état de guerre, ils vont toujours armés? et pourquoi ils ont des clefs pours fermer leurs maisons?* Mais on ne sent pas que l'on attribue aux hommes avant cet établissement des sociétés, ce qui ne peut leur arriver qu'aprés cet établissement, qui leur fait trouver des motifs pour s'attaquer et pour se défendre . . .': Charles Secondat, baron de Montesquieu, *L'Esprit des Lois* (1748), ed. R. Derathé, 2 vols. (Paris: Garnier, 1973), I, p. 10.

same reasons that his account of the relations between atomised individuals was incorrect. In fact, the very exiguousness of Hobbes's empirical account of international relations helped to ensure almost two centuries of silence on the subject. Throughout the nineteenth century neither the first textbooks on international relations nor the first studies of Hobbes's thought found it necessary to treat him as an international theorist. For example, he did not appear alongside Grotius and Pufendorf in the most widely used American text on international relations of the nineteenth century, Theodore Woolsey's *Introduction to the Study of International Law* (1860), a work that would also be foundational for the emergent discipline of political science in the United States.[46] Similarly, none of Hobbes's nineteenth-century British students so much as mentioned his reflections on international relations or the law of nations,[47] while glancing allusions to his views on *Völkerrecht* appeared only in the second edition of Ferdinand Tönnies's study of Hobbes in 1912.[48]

Hobbes was only identified as a theorist of international anarchy once a consensus had emerged that the international realm was indeed anarchic. That consensus was the product of nineteenth- and early twentieth-century developments internal to the emerging modern disciplines of political science and international law.[49] It rested on a series of propositions, each of which had to be established before the 'discourse of anarchy' could be seen as plausible and coherent. First, it had to be accepted that the domestic and the international realms were analytically distinct. Then, the norms relevant to each realm had to be identified and distinguished. On that basis, it could be argued that states in their international capacity were unconstrained by any norms equivalent formally or obligatorily to those that applied to their own subjects. States were accordingly independent not just of one another but of any superior. Because they were atomistic they were agonistic: in the absence of any external authority, their relations were governed only by force. They therefore stood in relation to one another as competitive actors within an international state of nature. Hobbes's conflation of the law of nature with the law of nations would not support such a sharp analytical distinction between the internal and the external spheres. Though he admitted that the insecurity of individuals in the state

---

[46] Theodore D. Woolsey, *Introduction to the Study of International Law, Devised as an Aid in Teaching, and in Historical Studies* (Boston, 1860); Brian C. Schmidt, *The Political Discourse of Anarchy: a Disciplinary History of International Relations* (Albany: State University of New York Press, 1998), pp. 52–4.

[47] William Whewell, *Lectures on the History of Moral Philosophy in England* (London, 1852), pp. 14–35; F. D. Maurice, *Modern Philosophy* (London, 1862), pp. 235–90; George Croom Robertson, *Hobbes* (Edinburgh, 1886); James Fitzjames Stephen, *Horae Sabbaticae*, 2nd ser. (London, 1892), pp. 1–70; Leslie Stephen, *Hobbes* (London: Macmillan, 1904).

[48] Ferdinand Tönnies, *Hobbes, Leben und Lehre* (Stuttgart, 1896); Ferdinand Tönnies, *Thomas Hobbes, der Mann und der Denker* (Osterwieck: Zickfeldt 1912), pp. 165, 169.

[49] Schmidt, *The Political Discourse of Anarchy*, chs. 3, 5.

of nature was strictly incomparable to that created by the competition between sovereigns, Hobbes assumed an essential analogy between the relations between individuals and the relations between states as international persons.

Hobbes's conception of municipal law led to very different conclusions about the separation between the foreign and the domestic and about the nature of international relations. For the second generation of English utilitarians and their nineteenth-century heirs, Hobbes was not the founder of international legal naturalism; instead, he was the godfather of legal positivism, the theory of law as command 'set by political superiors to political inferiors', as his admirer the analytical jurisprude John Austin put it. Judged according to this strictly anti-naturalist definition of law, what had come to be called 'international law' could not be called law at all because it issued from no superior authority: it was therefore no more than what Austin notoriously described as '*positive* international *morality*'.[50] States in their relations with one another were unconstrained by any higher authority because the norms specific to the international and the domestic spheres were distinct and incommensurable. Within a tradition of juristic positivism that owed more to Hegel than to Austin, Hobbes similarly appeared as a denier of international law and as a proponent of the division between the external and the internal. In the words of Carl Schmitt, writing a century after Austin: 'The state has its order in, not outside, itself . . . Hobbes was the first to state precisely that in international law states face one another "in a state of nature" . . . Security exists only in the state. *Extra civitatem nulla securitas.*'[51]

Hobbes did not directly inspire the conception of the relations between states as fundamentally anarchic. It was instead the proponents of a 'discourse of anarchy' in international relations who co-opted Hobbes to support their theory and the opponents of that discourse who likewise invoked Hobbes to discredit it.[52] Juristic theorists of that state argued that 'theoretical isolation is the prime condition of its existence as a state, and its political independence is one of its essential attributes. This is what Hobbes meant in saying that, in regard to one another, separate states are to be viewed as in a "state of nature".'[53] In such a condition, 'every independent political community is, by virtue of its independence, in a State of Nature towards other communities'.[54] With states

---

[50] John Austin, *The Province of Jurisprudence Determined* [1832], ed. Wilfrid E. Rumble (Cambridge: Cambridge University Press, 1995), pp. 19, 112, 171, 229–33n.

[51] Carl Schmitt, *The Leviathan in the State Theory of Thomas Hobbes: Meaning and Failure of a Political Symbol* (1938), trans. George Schwab and Erna Hilfstein (Westport, CT: Greenwood Press, 1996), pp. 47–8.

[52] Schmidt, *The Political Discourse of Anarchy*, pp. 232–3.

[53] Stephen Leacock, *Elements of Political Science* (Boston: Houghton Mifflin, 1906), p. 89; compare Westel Woodbury Willoughby, 'The Juristic Conception of the State', *American Political Science Review* 12 (1918), p. 207.

[54] James Bryce, *International Relations* (New York: Macmillan, 1922), p. 5.

thus 'a law unto themselves', it followed that '[t]he condition of the world, from an international point of view, has long been one of polite anarchy'.[55] Pluralist critics of the juristic theory of the state contended that it not only described but in fact created a condition of international anarchy; they, too, invoked Hobbes in support of their contentions.[56] Conformity to the theory of sovereignty as independence ensured that 'the condition of international society would, indeed, be that which Hobbes in his day conceived it to be'.[57] 'The state is irresponsible', Harold Laski concluded, summing up this line of criticism: 'It owes no obligation save that which is made by itself to any other community or group of communities. In the hinterland between states man is to his neighbour what Hobbes says was true of him in the state of nature – nasty, mean, brutish.'[58]

Hobbes assumed his place among the founders of international thought as much in spite of as because of his own statements on the law of nations and the relations between states. Like many later critics of an allegedly 'Hobbesian' account of international relations, he recognised the limited analytical utility of the analogy between individuals and international persons in a state of nature.[59] He acknowledged that, though states could be just as fearful, vainglorious and competitive as individuals in their relations with one another, they were not vulnerable to the same degree nor was their existence as fragile. Agreements and exchanges were possible both in the interpersonal state of nature and the international state of nature. If the Hobbesian theory of international relations rests on a conception of international anarchy characterised by interstate com- petition without any possibility of cooperation, then Hobbes himself was no Hobbesian.

The standard account of Hobbes as an international theorist arose in condi- tions not of his own making. Positivists battled naturalists, pluralist theorists of the state criticised juristic theorists, and political scientists defined their disci- pline against international law and international relations theory. Hobbes could be invoked on both sides of each dispute. The naturalists pointed to his confla- tion of the law of nations with the law of nature as a foundational insight, while the positivists invoked Hobbes's command theory of law to deny the validity

[55] David Jayne Hill, *World Organization as Affected by the Nature of the Modern State* (New York: Columbia University Press, 1911), pp. 14, 15.

[56] Schmidt, *The Political Discourse of Anarchy*, pp. 164–87; on the pluralists and their debts to Hobbes see David Runciman, *Pluralism and the Personality of the State* (Cambridge: Cambridge University Press, 1997).

[57] James W. Garner, 'Limitations on National Sovereignty in International Relations', *American Political Science Review* 19 (1925), pp. 23–4.

[58] H. J. Laski, 'International Government and National Sovereignty', in *The Problems of Peace*, 1st ser. (London: Oxford University Press, 1927), p. 291.

[59] Edwin DeWitt Dickinson, 'The Analogy Between Natural Persons and International Persons in the Law of Nations', *Yale Law Journal* 26 (1916–17), pp. 564–91; Hedley Bull, *The Anarchical Society: a Study of Order in World Politics* (New York: Columbia University Press, 1977), pp. 46–51.

of international law as law. Anglo-American juristic theorists turned to Hobbes for their conception of legal personality much as their German counterparts turned to Hegel; critics of their monistic theory of sovereignty invoked Hobbes to warn against the consequences of invoking such a theory when describing the relations between states. Among political scientists, Hobbes's concept of the state would earn him a canonical place as one of the founders of modern political thought. Among international relations theorists, he would be baptised retrospectively as one of the founders of modern international thought, as he had once been hailed by the natural lawyers as a pivotal figure for their discipline.

Hobbes's successors identified him as the originator of the fundamental division between the domestic and the foreign, the inside and the outside of the state. That division rested on a further distinction, also endowed with a Hobbesian pedigree, between the internal realm of positive law and the external realm governed by the law of nature and nations. With the rise of international positivism in the era after the Vienna settlement of 1815, Hobbes came to be identified as one of the first theorists of what would later be called the 'Westphalian system' of sovereign states: after all, could it have been just a coincidence that *Leviathan* was published in 1651, only three years after the Peace of Westphalia in 1648?[60] It hardly mattered that Hobbes had first laid down the major elements of his conceptions of international relations and the law of nations in the *Elements of Law* and *De Cive*, well before 1648, or that he never displayed any knowledge of the terms or consequences of the Peace of Westphalia, unlike Pufendorf, for example.[61] Even if he had, he would hardly have inferred from them the emergence of a positive system of mutually recognising sovereign states: that would be the product of a much later 'myth of 1648', which preceded by almost a century the myth of Hobbes the theorist of international anarchy.[62]

Self-consciously *post*modern international thought has deconstructed the opposition of naturalism and positivism and has collapsed the distinction between the internal and the external dimensions of the state.[63] It has demolished

---

[60] For a recent example, see: Williams, *Kant's Critique of Hobbes*, 1: 'Hobbes's publication of the justification for the modern state coincided with what is often regarded as the birth of the "Westphalian system".'

[61] Samuel Pufendorf, *The Present State of Germany* (1667), trans. Edmund Bohun (London, 1690), pp. 135–96; Peter Schröder, 'The Constitution of the Holy Roman Empire after 1648: Samuel Pufendorf's Assessment in his Monzambano', *Historical Journal* 42 (1999), pp. 961–83.

[62] Stephen D. Krasner, 'Westphalia and All That', in Judith Goldstein and Robert O. Keohane (eds.), *Ideas and Foreign Policy: Beliefs, Institutions, and Political Change* (Ithaca: Cornell University Press, 1993), pp. 235–64; Andreas Osiander, 'Sovereignty, International Relations, and the Westphalian Myth', *International Organization* 55 (2001), pp. 251–88; Edward Keene, *Beyond the Anarchical Society: Grotius, Colonialism and Order in World Politics* (Cambridge: Cambridge University Press, 2002), pp. 20–2; Benno Teschke, *The Myth of 1648: Class, Geopolitics and the Making of Modern International Relations* (London: Verso, 2003).

[63] Martti Koskenniemi, *From Apology to Utopia: the Structure of International Legal Argument* (Helsinki: Lakimiesliiton Kustannus, 1989); R. B. J. Walker, *Inside/Outside: International Relations as Political Theory* (Cambridge: Cambridge University Press, 1993).

the historical and conceptual foundations of the Westphalian order and has proclaimed the advent of 'post-sovereignty'.[64] The contingent conditions and overdetermining theories that gave rise to the 'Hobbesian' theory of international relations have now either been unsettled theoretically or discredited historically. This has occurred in tandem with an expansion of the definition of political theory itself to include the international, the global and the cosmopolitan.[65] There are already signs that the boundaries of the history of political thought are being redefined to take account of that expansion.[66] This bodes well for the future study of the foundations of modern international thought.

[64] Jens Bartelson, *A Genealogy of Sovereignty* (Cambridge: Cambridge University Press, 1995); Stephen D. Krasner, *Sovereignty: Organized Hypocrisy* (Princeton: Princeton University Press, 1999).

[65] For example, Charles R. Beitz, *Political Theory and International Relations*, 2nd edn (Princeton: Princeton University Press, 1999); Howard Williams, *International Relations in Political Theory* (Basingstoke, 1990); Brian C. Schmidt, 'Together Again: Reuniting Political Theory and International Relations Theory', *British Journal of Politics and International Relations* 4 (2002), pp. 115–40.

[66] For example, Tuck, *The Rights of War and Peace;* Chris Brown, Terry Nardin and Nicholas Rengger (eds.), *International Relations in Political Thought: Texts from the Ancient Greeks to the First World War* (Cambridge: Cambridge University Press, 2002); Duncan S. A. Bell, 'International Relations: The Dawn of a Historiographical Turn?', *British Journal of Politics and International Relations* 3 (2001), pp. 115–26.

13   Surveying the *Foundations*: a retrospect and reassessment

Quentin Skinner

I

David Hume observes at the beginning of his autobiography that 'it is difficult for a man to speak long of himself without Vanity: Therefore I shall be short'.[1] I would go further and say that, in writing the kind of autobiographical essay on which I am embarking here, it is impossible to avoid some element of self-praise. Moreover, I cannot agree with Hume that the best means of coping with the problem is simply to speak as briefly as possible. The foregoing chapters about my work are of such an exceptionally high level of interest and originality that they demand to be examined at length. The only solution, as far as I can see, is to apologise at the outset for any crassness of tone and press on with the task in hand.

II

I am deeply indebted to Annabel Brett, James Tully and Holly Hamilton-Bleakley for editing this volume, and for giving me an opportunity to reflect anew on my intentions in writing *The Foundations of Modern Political Thought*. Re-reading the book, however, what chiefly strikes me is how far it falls short of the aspirations I originally had for it. My initial ambition – as I recorded in the acknowledgements – was to produce an historical survey encompassing the entire period from the Renaissance to the Enlightenment. While this was still a gleam in my eye, I delivered a course of lectures in Cambridge (as Mark Goldie recalls) under the title 'The Making of Modern Political Thought' in which, among other things, I vainly strove to understand the ideological origins of the French Revolution. I wish I could report that my decision to abandon my initial plan arose from recognising that there was something inherently questionable about the idea of tracing the rise of something called modernity in political thought. The more prosaic truth is that I despaired of acquiring sufficient learning to write with any confidence about such a long span of time.

---

[1] David Hume, 'My Own Life', in Ernest Campbell Mossner, *The Life of David Hume* (London: Nelson, 1954), Appendix A, p. 611.

I thereupon resolved to limit myself to investigating what I had come to regard as the central theme in early-modern political thought: the acquisition of the concept of the sovereign state, together with the corresponding idea that individual subjects are endowed with natural rights within and potentially against the state. I confess that I am less interested nowadays in writing this kind of history. The goal of tracing the origins of our current beliefs and arrangements admittedly remains fashionable, and there are always historians on hand to assure us that 'history is about continuities'.[2] But history is not about any one thing, and among the many things that historians can profitably investigate are discontinuities. As Marco Geuna notes, I have become more interested of late in the contrasts between our past and present systems of thought, and have even come to believe that this kind of history can have a practical significance.[3] To establish that some of our most cherished political concepts may have been wholly absent from earlier periods, or may have been understood in wholly different ways, strikes me as one of the most effective means of challenging the perpetual tendency of political philosophy to degenerate into merely serving the times.

This is not to imply that there is anything illegitimate about attempting to investigate the sources of our present beliefs, and the wish to engage in just such an investigation was undoubtedly what animated me in *The Foundations of Modern Political Thought* (to which I shall hereafter refer as *Foundations*). I am slightly shocked, however, to discover how unreflectively I felt able to equate the acquisition of the modern European concept of the nation state with the construction of the foundations of modern political thought. It is true that, in the intervening centuries, nation states have turned into a global phenomenon, so much so that we now have an institution – the United Nations – that ought properly to be called the United States, if it were not that one of its members has pre-empted that name. It is also true that the concomitant idea of natural rights has likewise been globalised, with the result that Western nations now like to speak of 'human' rights, and to urge them upon countries still too benighted to view the world through Western eyes. It is arguable, however, that an element of imperialism continues to underpin this rhetoric; and it is certain that, at the time when I was drafting *Foundations*, I was less attuned than I should have been to the parochialism of my perspective.

When I finally managed to sort out my lecture-notes and begin writing my book in 1972, I found it less difficult than I perhaps should have done to stake out

---

[2] For the most recent occurrence of this cliché, at the time of writing, see *The Times Literary Supplement*, 5 August 2005, p. 25.

[3] I announced this commitment in general terms in an article originally published in 1969. See Quentin Skinner, *Visions of Politics*, vol. I: *Regarding Method* (Cambridge: Cambridge University Press, 2002), pp. 86–9. But it is only more recently that I have made the commitment central to my research. See especially Quentin Skinner, *Liberty before Liberalism* (Cambridge: Cambridge University Press, 1998), pp. 101–20.

what seemed to me the appropriate boundaries of my narrative. I was clear that my story needed to begin with the humanism of the Italian *rinascimento*, and above all with an attempt to make sense of Machiavelli's political thought. As for my sense of an ending, I had no doubt (although this was another parochial insight) that my narrative ought to culminate with the English revolution of the mid-seventeenth century, and above all with the philosophy of Thomas Hobbes.

It is not difficult to remember why I originally hoped to end with Hobbes. Gierke was my Bible in those days, and I had it on his authority that with Hobbes the struggle to articulate the idea of the state as the bearer of sovereignty was finally brought to a triumphant close.[4] As I duly underlined in my conclusion, Hobbes himself declares in *De Cive* that the task of 'civil science' should now be that of making 'a more curious search into the rights of states and duties of subjects'.[5] My choice of starting point might appear more idiosyncratic, but I feel no inclination to echo Flaubert's wonderfully dismissive account in *L'éducation sentimentale* of why his anti-hero Frédéric embarked on his disconcertingly similar enterprise. Trying to forget a calamitous passion, Frédéric 'took up the first subject that came into his head, and resolved to write a *History of the Renaissance*'.[6] My own decision, by contrast, was heavily overdetermined.

One reason for my choice, as several contributors to the present volume recognise, was that I wanted to examine and criticise two prevailing views about the place of the Italian *rinascimento* in the history of modern political thought. I wanted in the first place to question a general assumption that had come to be associated with the name of Hans Baron and his classic study, *The Crisis of the Early Italian Renaissance*.[7] Geuna opens his chapter by recalling Baron's central argument: that medieval political theory can be distinguished by its adherence to an ideal of imperial monarchy, and that the birth of distinctively modern ideas about political liberty and self-government can be traced to the struggle between Florence and Visconti Milan at the beginning of the *quattrocento*. Baron drew the conclusion that the year 1400 accordingly marks a sharp and historic break between the medieval era and the modern world. These contentions came to be widely accepted, and I have always assumed that

---

[4] Otto von Gierke, *Natural Law and the Theory of Society, 1500 to 1800*, Ernest Barker (trans.), (Boston, Mass.: Beacon Press, 1957), p. 139.

[5] Quentin Skinner, *The Foundations of Modern Political Thought*, vol. II: *The Age of Reformation* (Cambridge: Cambridge University Press, 1978), p. 349.

[6] Gustav Flaubert, *L'éducation sentimentale*, ed. René Dumesnil, 2 vols. (Paris, 1942), p. 236.

[7] Hans Baron, *The Crisis of the Early Italian Renaissance*, 2nd edn (Princeton: Princeton University Press, 1966). I need to stress, however, that I owe a large debt to Baron's classic article on Machiavelli (Hans Baron, 'Machiavelli: the Republican Citizen and Author of *The Prince*', *English Historical Review* 76 (1961), pp. 217–53) and that there is a more general sense, as Eric Nelson, *The Greek Tradition in Republican Thought* (Cambridge: Cambridge University Press, 2004), pp. 8–9 points out, in which I am indebted to Baron's analysis of the uses of Roman history in the Renaissance.

John Pocock in his great work, *The Machiavellian Moment*, was among those who were influenced by Baron's line of thought, although Pocock informs us in his contribution to the present volume that this was never the case.

The other thesis I wanted to question was more specifically concerned with the interpretation of Machiavelli's thought. I was writing at a time when the German tradition – the tradition of Friedrich Meinecke, Ernst Cassirer and Leo Strauss – was still dominant in the historiography of Renaissance political philosophy. One of the leading tenets associated with these scholars was that Machiavelli was the first political theorist to organise his thinking around the concept of *lo stato*, the concept of an impersonal and sovereign state. To which they added that he was likewise the first to insist that states may have reasons for their actions – *ragioni di stato* – that would not necessarily count as good reasons in the mouths of their own subjects.

Against the first of these orthodoxies – that of Baron and his disciples – I argued that the ideals of *libertas* and self-government were articulated in the *Regnum Italicum* at a much earlier date than the magic year 1400. As Geuna observes, this claim had already been put forward by a number of historians who had associated these developments with the reception of Aristotle's *Politics* at the end of the thirteenth century. I was equally unhappy with this periodisation, however, for it seemed to me that the emergence of communal ideologies predated the availability of Aristotle's texts by several generations, and that the pioneering celebrations of republican government were indebted entirely to Roman rather than to Greek authorities. As for Machiavelli, I tried to show that each of his major works attempted in its own way to offer a critical commentary on these earlier and enduring patterns of neo-Roman thought. Although I called the first volume of my book *The Renaissance*, my title embodied an intentional irony: my emphasis was on the *longue durée*, not on any identifiable moment of rebirth.

It remains to explain what attracted me to the very idea of writing a history of early-modern political thought. It must be admitted that, at least at the outset, I was not primarily interested in making a contribution to the history or the historiography of the subject. As Goldie notes, I was much more concerned in those far-off days with questions about interpretation, explanation and historical method more generally. It is true that, during my first years of research (1963–6), I had published some mainly historical essays about the political theories of the English revolution, attending in particular to the figure of Hobbes. But the more I puzzled over the interpretative literature on *Leviathan*, the more I found myself worrying about the nature of interpretation itself, and in the following years (1966–71) I wrote a series of articles attempting to work out my own approach.[8] When I turned to writing *Foundations* in 1972, it was basically

---

[8] Some of the articles I wrote during this period were published several years later.

with the intention of using a broad canvas on which to illustrate some of the methodological and even philosophical conclusions at which I had by then arrived.

I was especially interested in challenging two widespread assumptions about the interpretation of political texts. One was that the most illuminating way of analysing the *œuvre* of any major political writer must be to extract from their various works the most coherent and systematic set of doctrines they can be made to yield. Among the 'classic' political theorists, Machiavelli had been subjected to this treatment with extreme severity. Federico Chabod, Gennaro Sasso and other Italian scholars had made it their business, as Geuna reminds us, to establish that Machiavelli's *Il principe* and *Discorsi* are best viewed as partial contributions to an overarching 'Machiavellian' whole, the underlying structure of which they attempted to lay bare.

By the time I began studying Machiavelli's texts for myself I had already become suspicious of this approach. I owed this suspicion in part to my reading of R. G. Collingwood, who had persuaded me that the most revealing way to interpret any philosophical text is to consider it as an answer to a specific set of questions, and to try to recover the questions being addressed. But I was no less influenced by a number of scholars who had not only developed a similar view of historical method in the 1960s but had gone on to put it to work. I am thinking here in particular of John Pocock and John Dunn. Pocock in his chapter in the present volume additionally singles out the name of Peter Laslett, whose editions of Filmer and Locke undoubtedly embodied a question-and-answer approach. But Laslett never supplied a theoretical account of his practice, whereas Dunn and Pocock both published pioneering methodological articles in the 1960s (Pocock in 1962, Dunn in 1968),[9] after which they proceeded to practise what they had preached. Dunn's classic monograph on John Locke appeared in 1969,[10] and in the same year Pocock permitted me to read a complete draft of his *Machiavellian Moment*, a masterpiece whose interpretation of Machiavelli's political theory exercised a profound influence on my own work.

We know how to speak *de mortuis*, but we are less adept at knowing how to speak *de viventibus*. W. H. Auden offers us an excellent guiding principle: 'Let us honour if we can the vertical man'. Among the vertical men to whom I remain most indebted is John Pocock, whose contribution to the present volume is a splendidly characteristic one. As always he is deeply generous, but as always he challenges us to re-examine our ingrained habits of thought. I demur only at his

---

[9] J. G. A. Pocock, 'The History of Political Thought: a Methodological Enquiry', in Peter Laslett and W. G. Runciman (eds.), *Philosophy, Politics and Society*, Second Series (Oxford: Oxford University Press, 1962), pp. 183–202; John Dunn, 'The Identity of the History of Ideas', *Philosophy* 43 (1968), pp. 85–104.

[10] John Dunn, *The Political Thought of John Locke: an Historical Account of the Argument of the 'Two Treatises of Government'* (Cambridge: Cambridge University Press, 1969).

referring to me as the leading exponent of the historical method I have described. His own leadership has been an inspiration to every intellectual historian of my generation and beyond.

The account I went on to give in *Foundations* of Machiavelli's political theory duly reflected my admiration both for Collingwood's philosophy and Pocock's scholarship. I assumed, that is, that each of Machiavelli's treatises was asking its own questions, and I looked for coherence only at the level of each individual text. Geuna objects that the outcome shows me too much a prisoner of my methodological commitments. I accept that I failed to do justice to the elements common to Machiavelli's leading works, and I agree with Geuna that Machiavelli's continual preoccupation with the role of time in politics – *i tempi, l'occasione* – offers one such example. But I am unrepentant in believing that my text-by-text approach is basically the right one to adopt, and I take comfort from the fact that no one would nowadays speak about Machiavelli as if the *Principe* and *Discorsi* were fragments of a more general treatise on politics that Machiavelli unaccountably failed to write.

I turn to the other prevailing assumption that I wanted to challenge and if possible discredit in *Foundations*. I had in my sights the view that historians of political theory should centre their attention on studying a canon of 'classic' texts. The value of this kind of history, we were told at the time, arises from the fact that these texts contain a 'dateless wisdom' in the form of 'universal ideas'. The best way to approach them must therefore be to concentrate on what each of them tells us about the 'fundamental concepts' and 'abiding questions' of political life. We must read them, in short, as if 'written by a contemporary' for our own edification and benefit.[11]

Among the classic theorists, it was generally agreed that Hobbes offers the best example of someone who devoted himself in a purely philosophical spirit to elucidating the key concepts in political theory, including the concepts of freedom, sovereignty, representation, natural rights, political obligation and so on and on. As a result of my researches in the early 1960s, however, I had come to feel that this basic assumption was questionable even in the case of Hobbes. As Hamilton-Bleakley rightly observes, the remark that most clearly encapsulated everything I had come to dislike about the 'canonist' approach was John Plamenatz's in his introduction to *Man and Society* in 1963. 'To understand Hobbes' he had declared, 'we need not know what his purpose was in writing *Leviathan* or how he felt about the rival claims of Royalists and Parliamentarians' in the English revolution.[12] This affirmation seemed to me as wrong as possible. I had come to believe that Hobbes's *Leviathan* was

---

[11] For the sources of the quotations in this paragraph see Skinner, *Visions*, I, p. 57.

[12] J. P. Plamenatz, *Man and Society: a Critical Examination of Some Important Social and Political Theories from Machiavelli to Marx* (London: Longmans 1963), vol. I, p. ix.

about the English revolution, and that there can be no prospect of understanding his interpretation of such concepts as freedom, sovereignty and representation without appreciating the specific character of the intervention he took himself to be making in the politics of his time.

It was this intuition, as Hamilton-Bleakley notes, that drew me to the work of Wittgenstein, Austin and Searle. Wittgenstein had enjoined us to ask not about the meanings but the uses of words. Austin and Searle had extended this insight into a general theory of speech acts, examining the multifarious ways in which we may be said to be doing something as well as saying something in the act of issuing any serious utterance. From their work I acquired the confidence to argue that textual interpretation should be concerned not merely with the recovery of the alleged meanings of texts, but also – and perhaps principally – with the range of things that texts may be said to be doing, and thus with the nature of the interventions they may be said to constitute.

With a giant leap of faith, this brought me to the principle on which *Foundations* is based. If, I recklessly put it to myself, the most illuminating way of writing even about Hobbes's political theory may be to treat it essentially as a political act, then perhaps this may be the most illuminating way of writing about political theory *tout court*. I used the preface of *Foundations* to summarise my scepticism about the rival view of the classic texts as timeless meditations on perennial themes. 'I take it', I replied, 'that political life itself sets the main problems for the political theorist, causing a certain range of issues to appear problematic, and a corresponding range of questions to become the leading subjects of debate'.[13] As Kari Palonen has recently stressed, my entire book was an attempt to substantiate that argument.[14]

My overriding aspiration in *Foundations* was thus to write the history of political theory essentially as a history of ideologies.[15] Goldie's chapter provides a highly perceptive analysis of the style of history to which this commitment gave rise, and I cannot hope to improve on it here. The one point I should like to underscore relates to the practical orientation of my approach. As Hamilton-Bleakley remarks, one of my aims was to give 'forms of life' priority over theories, and thus to challenge the assumption that intellectual history is separate from the history of institutions and behaviour.[16] I wanted, in other words, to undermine

---

[13] Quentin Skinner, *The Foundations of Modern Political Thought*, vol. I: *The Renaissance* (Cambridge: Cambridge University Press, 1978), p. xi.

[14] Kari Palonen, 'Political Theorizing as a Dimension of Political Life', *European Journal of Political Theory* 4 (2005), pp. 351–66.

[15] My references to 'ideologies' occasioned some confusion, so it is perhaps worth reiterating that I was employing the term not in a Marxist sense to refer to distortions of social reality, but rather in a Weberian sense to refer to discourses of legitimation.

[16] For a valuable elaboration of this point see Annabel Brett, 'What is Intellectual History Now?' in David Cannadine (ed.), *What is History Now?* (London: Palgrave, 2002), pp. 113–31, esp. p. 115.

the usual distinction between theory and practice. Writing in Weberian vein, I highlighted the fact that political practices normally require to be legitimised. As I argued, however, the ability to legitimise our behaviour while getting what we want depends in part on being able to show that our actions can be described by reference to some accepted value or principle. There is thus a sense in which the direction of political life will always be controlled by such principles, and will remain so even when the agents involved have no genuine attachment to the values for the sake of which they profess to act. This is how it comes about that, in Tully's pithy summary, the pen is a mighty sword.[17]

This account of my procedures – and especially of my desire to focus on legitimising discourses rather than classic texts – may suggest that I squarely accepted the claims that Michel Foucault was propagating at around the same time about the death of the author.[18] But as Hamilton-Bleakley rightly emphasises, I have always wanted to retain a place for the traditional figure of the author in the broader study of political 'languages'. One reason is that there is otherwise a danger (as Goldie notes) of slipping back into writing a disembodied history of 'isms' or 'unit ideas', a kind of history that readily loses sight of the varying purposes that different systems of belief can be made to serve. But my main reason for wanting to speak of authors and not merely of texts has always been to try to make sense of those moments when a prevailing *episteme* (to cite Foucault's terminology) is questioned or undermined. It seems to me a weakness of Foucault's more structuralist approach that he finds it so difficult to explain how such conceptual changes take place.

Consider, for example, the humanist vision of politics that I discuss in volume I of *Foundations*. According to this view of public life, the quality of *virtù* is at once the means to attain civic *gloria* and at the same time a summary of the moral virtues. These assumptions were subjected to an epoch-making challenge when Machiavelli proposed in *Il principe* that the quality of *virtù* must be the name of *whatever* range of attributes (moral or otherwise) conduce to the attainment of *gloria*. The outcome was a furious argument over whether there are any distinctive *ragioni di stato* that transcend ordinary moral rules. How can we hope to explain this development unless we are prepared to single Machiavelli out as the author of the work that sparked the argument off?

Apart from this traditional element in my narrative, however, it was certainly my aspiration in *Foundations* to focus as much as possible not on individual authors but on broader genealogies of discourse. I wanted to make it as clear as possible that even the most original authors are never the inventors of the language they speak, but are always the products of a pre-existing culture with

---

[17] James Tully (ed.), *Meaning and Context: Quentin Skinner and his Critics* (Cambridge: Polity Press, 1988), pp. 7–25.

[18] See especially Michel Foucault, 'What is an Author?' in Josué V. Harari (ed.), *Textual Strategies* (Ithaca, NY: Cornell University Press, 1979), pp. 141–60.

which they inevitably enter into dialogue.[19] As Goldie points out, my book was aggressively organised in such a way as to force the reader to confront this argument. If, for example, you consult the bibliography of primary texts in volume I, you encounter a list of nearly two hundred titles. But if you turn to the table of contents, you find only one political writer mentioned by name: the author (*sic*) of *Il principe*.

My attempt to show that political theory forms a part of political life initially occasioned much outrage. Michael Oakeshott was only the most distinguished of several hostile critics who berated me for failing to understand that 'genuine' political theory occupies an autonomous philosophical realm.[20] (Nor was he the only critic to make things easier for himself by inserting his preferred conclusion into his premises.) Since then, however, times have changed; and very much for the better, I think. None of the contributors to the present volume seems to find any difficulty with my cardinal assumption that, because in political argument there is nothing but the battle, the idea of being above the battle makes little sense. On the contrary, several of them explicitly align themselves with this essentially Nietzschean point of view.

Nevertheless, several contributors raise an interesting doubt about the scope of my argument. Goldie objects that it lacks what he describes as generic expansiveness.[21] Once we accept, he argues, that the characteristic activity of political theorists is that of legitimising or challenging existing institutions and beliefs, it becomes merely arbitrary to concentrate on self-confessedly 'political' texts as a means of illustrating the point. We ought instead to recognise that the poet, the painter and the musician may be no less skilled at mounting political arguments, and may even be capable of doing so with unmatchable force.

This strikes me as a justified criticism, and one that I would nowadays want to carry still further. Once we take Goldie's argument seriously, the notion of a distinct 'history of political theory' begins to melt into air. We need to replace it, I would now contend, with a more general form of intellectual history in which, even if we continue to centre on 'political' texts, we allow the principle of generic expansiveness the freest rein. If, for example, I were now to rewrite the chapters in volume I of *Foundations* about the early republicanism of the *Regnum Italicum*, I should certainly want to pay as much attention to the frescoes of Ambrogio Lorenzetti as to the treatises of Marsilius of Padua.[22] If, in the same vein, I were to write about the revival of *libertà* as a rallying cry in the

---

[19] For this formulation see Brett, 'What is Intellectual History Now?', p. 118.

[20] Michael Oakeshott, 'The Foundations of Modern Political Thought', *The Historical Journal* 23 (1980), pp. 449–53.

[21] Goldie, 'The context of *The Foundations*', in this volume, pp. 3–19.

[22] As I did when I returned to writing about *trecento* political theory in the 1980s. See Quentin Skinner, *Visions of Politics*, vol. II: *Renaissance Virtues* (Cambridge: Cambridge University Press), pp. 39–92.

risorgimento, I might well be inclined to attribute this development as much to the early operas of Verdi as to the writings of Mazzini or the speeches of Cavour. I agree, in short, that we need to cultivate a history of political theory in which a far broader range of sources can be integrated and put to work.

Warren Boutcher's chapter pursues a different complaint about the unduly narrow scope of my work. While he accepts that the basic aim should be that of recovering what texts are doing as well as what they are saying, he stresses that many agents besides their original authors may be doing things with texts, including those who copy them, sponsor their publication, recommend them to others or issue warnings against their influence. Furthermore, the interests of these later readers will inevitably differ from, and may often contradict, those of the *soi-disant* authors of the texts concerned. As a result, the meanings of such texts will come to depend in part on such processes of transmission, and may need to be recovered from examining much broader traditions of discourse than I allow.

This criticism undoubtedly scores a hit against my claim that we need to think of political texts essentially as interventions in some identifiable debate. But it hardly serves to invalidate my approach. Rather it calls for a supplementary form of enquiry into the *fortuna* of texts and the range of things that can be done with them. Pocock perfectly captures the point when he speaks of my predilection for trying 'to return the text, and the speech acts implied in writing it, to the language context existing at a particular time' in contrast to his own interest in asking 'what happens when a language of discourse persists and is redeployed in a historical situation, or context, other than that in which it was deployed previously'.[23] The latter idiom is not one in which I have ever aspired to write, but I certainly agree that it is capable of producing intensely illuminating effects. That this is so is evident from much of Pocock's own recent work,[24] and Boutcher's chapter furnishes some no less arresting examples. Writing, for instance, about La Boétie's *De la servitude volontaire*, Boutcher is able to demonstrate that it may sometimes be blankly impossible to identify the nature of the intervention that a text was originally intended to make; it may be possible to catch and examine it *only* in its post-authorial afterlife.

Of *Foundations* it would be true to say that it has a two-tiered structure. It offers a survey of the political literature produced in western Europe in the early-modern period, and especially in the sixteenth century. But at the same time it treats these materials as contributions to an emergent vision of the state as the bearer of sovereignty, and thereby views them as aspects of an over-arching and unifying theme. To offer this characterisation, however, is to suggest that the book is a *grand récit* in the very style so influentially excoriated by

---

[23] Pocock, 'Foundations and Moments', in this volume, p. 40.
[24] See especially J. G. A. Pocock, *Barbarism and Religion*, vol. III: *The First Decline and Fall* (Cambridge: Cambridge University Press, 2003).

Jean-François Lyotard in *La condition postmoderne*.[25] One question that accordingly arises, as several contributors to the present volume duly note, is how far my book is guilty of the crimes associated by Lyotard and other postmodern critics with the construction of meta-narratives.

The general objection to *grands récits* has always been that they present themselves as the only story to be told about their chosen theme. One reason why this is held to be objectionable is that, although there will always be a multiplicity of rival stories that could equally well be told, these will have to be suppressed in the name of safeguarding the meta-narrative. This is certainly an accusation that can fairly be brought against several sections of my book. Annabel Brett observes of my chapter on the second scholastic that, by concentrating on the views of the Dominicans about the *civitas* and *respublica*, I underestimate the extent to which they remained internationalist in their outlook, resisting the idea of individual commonwealths as juridically sealed off from each other. Martin van Gelderen similarly protests that my emphasis on national sovereignty ignores the fact that many republican writers of the early-modern period explicitly rejected the sovereign state in favour of defending rival models of localised and federated power.[26] The point on which these strictures converge is that, even at the end of the period with which I deal, the notion of the state as the most natural unit of political power was a subject of intense debate.

A second and related objection to *grands récits* is that, even when a particular body of texts can plausibly be presented as a contribution to some over-arching theme, the exigencies of the meta-narrative will cause the texts in question to be handled in an unduly procrustean style. Cathy Curtis suggests that this criticism can arguably be levelled against my treatment of humanist political theory, while Brett shows that it undoubtedly applies to my chapter on the second scholastic, in which I allow myself, as she puts it, to pick and choose.[27] Focusing on the undoubted contribution of the schoolmen to the theory of the modern state, I concentrate almost entirely on their views about law, justice and the nature of sovereign power. As a result, I pay too little attention to their equally systematic views about such issues as the legitimacy of private property, the ethics of empire and the laws of war. This complaint likewise strikes me as justified. I now see that there are several sections of my book in which, in order

---

[25] Jean-François Lyotard, *La condition postmoderne: Rapport sur le savoir*: (Paris: les Editions de Minuit, 1979), esp. pp. 7–9, 35–43.

[26] Martin van Gelderen, 'Aristotelians, Monarchomachs and Republicans: Sovereignty and *respublica mixta* in Dutch and German Political Thought, 1580–1650', in Martin van Gelderen and Quentin Skinner (eds.), *Republicanism: a Shared European Heritage*, vol. I: *Republicanism and Constitutionalism in Early Modern Europe* (Cambridge: Cambridge University Press, 2002), pp. 195–217.

[27] Annabel Brett, 'Scholastic political thought and the modern concept of the state', in this volume, p. 142.

to satisfy the demands of the meta-narrative, I pull the theories I am expounding out of shape.

Of all the objections to *grands récits*, the most damaging is that they force historical agents to feature in stories not of their own telling. It is the purpose of Harro Höpfl's chapter to mount exactly this attack on my analysis of scholastic political thought. None of the schoolmen, Höpfl insists, ever wrote about 'politics' or published treatises of 'political thought'. The term 'politics' in their vocabulary referred to a purely practical art, and hence to a subject about which no certitude can be acquired. But the schoolmen never occupied themselves with such arts; they were exclusively concerned with the acquisition of demonstrative knowledge, and hence with the study of the genuine sciences. To speak of a scholastic 'contribution' to 'political thought' is therefore to speak in woefully anachronistic terms.

Höpfl's indictment is presented with considerable force; so much so that one sometimes feels the machinery beginning to shake. Nor can it be denied that he is on to something. Nowadays I would see it as a sacred duty, when attempting to reproduce the contents of an argument, to make use of the exact terminology employed by the protagonists themselves. To fail to do so is inevitably to supply them with distinctions they did not make. But to supply someone with unfamiliar distinctions is to cease to report their beliefs. To this degree I share Höpfl's unease, and it is a source of surprise as well as distress to me to discover how relatively insouciant I was in *Foundations* about the observation of this vital rule.

None the less, I feel inclined to narrow my eyes a bit in the face of Höpfl's critique. The three highest faculties in the universities of early-modern Europe – the faculties in which the genuine sciences were taught – were law, theology and medicine. Yet medicine was also classified as a practical art. The schoolmen regarded it as possible, in other words, to study the practical arts in a genuinely scientific style. Brett in a fascinating section of her chapter explores the implications of this commitment for their analysis of political life. As she establishes, Aquinas was already prepared to argue that, because all communities have human beings as their constituent elements, we can hope to arrive at a scientific understanding of how they should be governed. According to Aquinas, the name of the science concerned with such questions is *scientia politica*, the science of politics. Following Aquinas's lead, a number of schoolmen went on to write at length about such 'political' themes, including the themes I single out in my chapters on scholastic thought: the nature of law, the requirements of justice, the powers of the secular state. This being so, there is I think nothing in the least anachronistic about the assertion that these writers were making a contribution to the history of political thought.

It seems to me, in short, that Höpfl's chapter goes too far. For a strongly contrasting and, I would argue, a more nuanced handling of the tricky question of nomenclature, I should like to refer him to the recent and path-breaking study, *Jesuit Political Thought: the Society of Jesus and the State, c.1540– 1630*. The introduction speaks without qualms about the 'political thinkers' of the second scholastic, about their views on 'political authority' and about their preoccupation with 'matters of state'. The ensuing survey goes on to evaluate their distinctive contribution to what is described, again without qualms, as 'the history of political thought'. There is a certain irony, however, in drawing Höpfl's attention to this important book, for he wrote it himself.[28]

III

I began by noting that I originally planned to bring *Foundations* to an end with the politics of the English revolution, and more specifically with the philosophy of Hobbes. However, far from encompassing the first half of the seventeenth century, as the fulfilment of this ambition would have required, I eventually drew to a close with the theorists of absolute sovereignty and their constitutionalist adversaries in the final decades of the sixteenth century. Pocock remarked at the time that, in view of my over-arching preoccupation with the idea of the state, this seemed a peculiar moment at which to sign off, and Goldie in the present volume roundly asserts that my book 'stops somewhat abruptly around 1600'.[29]

The accusation that I constructed a broken column is not I think justified. As I emphasised in my introduction, I was addressing an essentially Weberian theme. I was trying to recover the preconditions, material as well as intellectual, for the increasing acceptance in western Europe of the belief that the business of government should be placed in the hands of unitary authorities enjoying a monopoly of legitimate force. I took it that, with the statement of the theory of absolute legislative sovereignty in the work of Jean Bodin and his follow- ers, and with their articulation of the accompanying distinction between states and forms of government, my story was at an end. I still feel that this judg- ment was intellectually defensible, and it is worth recalling that even Julian Franklin, one of the most unsatisfied of my original critics, took it to be beyond dispute.[30]

I must admit, however, that I had a further reason for abandoning any attempt to cover the first half of the seventeenth century. I could not fathom the process by which, in the course of that period, the 'subject' of absolute sovereignty came to be identified in turn with the *persona ficta* of the state. I could see that this

---

[28] Harro Höpfl, *Jesuit Political Thought: The Society of Jesus and the State, c. 1540–1630* (Cam- bridge: Cambridge University Press), pp. 2, 4, 5.

[29] Goldie, in this volume, p. 13.

[30] Julian Franklin, 'Review of *The Foundations of Modern Political Thought*', *Political Theory* 7 (1979), pp. 552–8, at p. 553.

would need to be my guiding theme, and I could see that Hobbes's declaration in *Leviathan* that the state is 'One Person' would make an appropriate finale. But I could not see much more.[31] As a result, Hobbes is undoubtedly the most important missing person in my book. This being so, I feel especially grateful that no fewer than three chapters of the present volume are devoted to Hobbes's theory of the state. They provide me with a welcome opportunity to say something more about the evolution and orientation of his political thought.

David Armitage's chapter serves to remind me that, had I carried out my larger design in *Foundations*, I would have perpetuated a restriction of coverage observable throughout the book. As Armitage points out, I examine the state almost solely in relation to its internal organisation and capacities, and have almost nothing to say about its role as an international agent. This is undoubtedly a defect, but I am not sure how far it would have been exacerbated if I had written about Hobbes without examining this dimension of his thought. Why, after all, does Hobbes discuss the relations among states? Armitage does not raise the question, seemingly taking it for granted that Hobbes must have regarded the issue as an inescapable one. But it is I think arguable that the main reason why Hobbes introduces the topic is not because he is interested in the theory of international relations in itself, but rather because he wants to make a polemical point about the nature of the state.

One of the claims that Hobbes is most anxious to overturn in *Leviathan* is that we can only hope to preserve our liberty if we live as citizens of republics or 'free states'. He speaks with detestation of 'those Democraticall writers' who insist 'that the Subjects in a Popular Common-wealth enjoy Liberty; but that in a Monarchy they are all Slaves'.[32] To see how Hobbes's account of the relations between states enables him to discredit or at least to ridicule this line of thought, it will be helpful to begin with Armitage's careful anatomy of Hobbes's views about the international realm. As Armitage shows beyond doubt, Hobbes's basic contention in every mature version of his political theory is that the law of nations or *ius gentium* is straightforwardly identical with the law of nature or *ius naturale*. As Hobbes summarises in ch. 30 of *Leviathan*, they amount to 'the same thing'.[33]

To understand Hobbes's views about the relations among states, what we therefore need to grasp is what he means by the *ius naturale*. Hobbes supplies his most considered answer in ch. 14 of *Leviathan*, in which he enunciates two

---

[31] The attempt to make sense of the idea that the state is a represented *persona ficta* has in consequence been a theme of much of my recent research. See especially Skinner, *Visions*, II, pp. 386–413; *Visions of Politics*, vol. III: *Hobbes and Civil Science* (Cambridge: Cambridge University Press, 2002), pp. 177–208; Quentin Skinner, 'Hobbes on Representation', *European Journal of Philosophy* 13 (2005), pp. 155–84.

[32] Thomas Hobbes, *Leviathan, or The Matter, Forme, & Power of a Common-wealth Ecclesiasticall and Civill*, ed. Richard Tuck (Cambridge: Cambridge University Press, 1996), p. 226.

[33] Ibid., p. 244.

closely connected arguments. One is that the *ius naturale* can be equated with
the right of nature, the right possessed by everyone in the state of nature to
do whatever they deem necessary to protect themselves. The second argument
is that this right of nature can in turn be represented as a specific form of
freedom or natural liberty. As Hobbes summarises at the outset, 'the RIGHT
OF NATURE, which Writers commonly call *Jus Naturale*, is the Liberty each
man hath, to use his own power, as he will himselfe, for the preservation of his
own Nature; that is to say, of his own Life'.[34]

Armed with this analysis, Hobbes proceeds in ch. 21 of *Leviathan* to bring
off one of his most cunning rhetorical effects. *Now* we can see, he declares,
what the democratical writers must be talking about when they extol the liberty
of 'free states'. Given that the law of nations is nothing other than the liberty
of nature, they must simply be talking about the same kind of freedom that
every individual person may be said to possess in the state of nature. Just as
'every Particular man' in his natural condition has 'a full and absolute Libertie'
to protect himself, so 'every Common-wealth, (not every man) has an absolute
Libertie, to doe what it shall judge' to be 'most conducing to their benefit'.[35]
Hobbes's brilliantly deflationary move is thus to insist that the much-vaunted
liberty allegedly attainable only in 'free states' amounts to nothing more than the
liberty to defend themselves against other states. As he sardonically concludes,
'the *Athenians*, and *Romanes* were free; that is, free Common-wealths: not that
any particular man had the Libertie to resist their own Representative; but that
their Representative had the Libertie to resist, or invade other people'.[36]

Armitage rightly remarks that Hobbes's reflections on the relations among
states are noticeably 'cursory' and even 'meagre' in quality.[37] The reason, I
am postulating, is that it may be false to Hobbes's conception of his project to
suppose that he was attempting to make a 'contribution', as Armitage assumes,
'to international thought'.[38] Hobbes's sarcastic dismissal of the democratical
writers and their claims about the special merits of 'free states' is one of the
great rhetorical coups in *Leviathan*, and it is wholly dependent on his underlying
equation between the law of nations and the right of nature. But it is possible,
I am suggesting, that if he had not been so anxious to engineer this coup, he
might not have paid any attention to the law of nations at all.

I next want to examine the connections between the story I tell in *Foundations*
and the development of Hobbes's theory of the state. My own view of Hobbes,
as I have tried to show in my recent work, is that he deserves to be recognised as
the leading counter-revolutionary writer of his age.[39] To understand his stance,
we need to begin by considering the era of revolutionary politics in France and

---

[34] Ibid., p. 91.   [35] Ibid., p. 149.   [36] Ibid.
[37] David Armitage, 'Hobbes and the foundations of modern international thought', in this volume,
pp. 224, 221.
[38] Ibid., p. 221.   [39] See Skinner, *Visions*, II, p. 405.

the Netherlands at the end of the sixteenth century. Seeking to legitimise their protests against the Valois and Habsburg monarchies, the radical Calvinists in both these countries began to vindicate the lawfulness of resistance to heretical and tyrannical rule. I argued in *Foundations* that these 'monarchomach' or king-killing theorists, as William Barclay stigmatised them, made use in turn of Lutheran doctrines originally deployed against the Emperor Charles V. I now see that, as van Gelderen points out, this further argument may be questionable, since the Lutherans generally confined themselves to vindicating the right of self-defence. But there can be no doubt about my main contention: that among the leading Calvinist monarchomachs – such writers as Johannes Althusius in the Netherlands and the author of the *Vindiciae, contra tryrannos* in France – the general right of the people or their representatives to engage in forcible resistance to tyranny was unequivocally upheld.

Faced with this revolutionary challenge, a number of political writers responded by insisting on the need for absolute and irresistible sovereignty, among them Jean Bodin and William Barclay in France and Hugo Grotius in the Netherlands. Hobbes belongs, I would argue, essentially in the company of these counter-revolutionaries. With the outbreak of the English civil wars in 1642, such parliamentarians as Henry Parker, William Prynne and their followers succeeded in introducing the most radical arguments of the monarchomachs into anglophone political thought. The *Leviathan*, as I see it, is essentially Hobbes's response to these democratical writers and the blood-dimmed tide they loosed.[40]

Richard Tuck's main purpose in his scintillating chapter is to question this entire genealogy. Far from being a sworn enemy of the democratical writers, he retorts, Hobbes was 'a sophisticated and deep theorist of democracy'.[41] One of Hobbes's great achievements, especially in the earlier versions of his political theory – on which Tuck chiefly concentrates – was to provide a 'new theory of democracy'.[42] 'Hobbes's contribution to democratic theory', we are told, was 'perhaps one of his most important legacies.'[43]

According to Tuck, the form of democracy in which Hobbes was primarily interested was the one described by Aristotle in his *Politics* as 'radical' or 'extreme'. Aristotle is quoted as saying that, in the 'extreme' form, 'not the law, but the multitude, have supreme power, and supersede the law by their decrees'.[44] Tuck has two main claims to advance about this type of government, the first of which concerns the relationship between Aristotle's and Hobbes's accounts of it. There was a key intermediary, Tuck contends, in the form of Pietro Vettori's Latin translation of Aristotle's *Politics*, first published in 1576. When Vettori comments on the phrase *princeps enim populus fit*, 'the people becomes

---

[40] For a full statement of this case see Skinner, 'Hobbes on Representation'.
[41] Tuck, 'Hobbes and democracy', in this volume, p. 171.
[42] Ibid., p. 190.   [43] Ibid., p. 171.   [44] Ibid., p. 176.

a monarch', he explains that this transformation arises from the people's 'all coming together and making one man'. Fastening on Vettori's reference to the people as 'one man', Tuck declares that this 'must have been a source of Hobbes's thinking on the subject'.[45] This is certainly a possibility, but there is no independent evidence that Hobbes knew of Vettori's translation, so the affirmation that it 'must have been' in Hobbes's mind seems rather strong. Besides, a more likely source is surely John Dee's English version of the *Politics*, first published in 1598, in which we read in the relevant passage that 'the people becometh a monarch' when they rule 'altogither as one'.[46]

The question of transmission, however, is of less importance for Tuck than the second and pivotal claim he wishes to make about 'extreme' democracy. He argues that this form of government was 'special' for Hobbes, and in two distinct ways.[47] He first asserts that, when Hobbes discusses 'the formation of each kind of commonwealth', especially in *De Cive*, he maintains that 'extreme democracy is the paradigm commonwealth'.[48] One way, in other words, in which democracy is 'special' for Hobbes is that all other forms of government are said to arise out of it.

I agree that, when Hobbes considers how civil associations are 'instituted' – in *The Elements of Law* as well as in *De Cive* – he takes democracy to be, as he says in *The Elements*, 'first in order of time'.[49] Hobbes's clearest explanation of why this is so is given in ch. 7 of *De Cive*. When the members of a multitude come together to create a commonwealth, they must be assumed to agree that any decisions taken by the majority will be binding upon the rest. As soon as they begin to operate this principle, however, they will in effect be operating a democratic system of rule.[50] This is how it comes about that, as Hobbes puts it in *The Elements*, 'democracy precedeth all other institution of government'.[51]

Nevertheless, there are two doubts to be registered about this part of Tuck's argument. Kinch Hoekstra duly registers them in the course of his tenacious and overwhelmingly learned critique, and I am bound to say that both of them strike me as well-founded. First of all, it is an overstatement to claim that, in discussing the origins of government, Hobbes takes democracy to be 'paradigmatic' in every case.[52] Hobbes formulates two distinct paradigms in every version of his political theory, one of which he labels 'government by institution' and the other 'government by acquisition'. A government is said to be 'instituted' when the members of the multitude agree among themselves to establish a sovereign

[45] Ibid., p. 181.   [46] Aristotle, *Politiques, or Discourses of Government* (London, 1598), p. 192.
[47] Tuck, in this volume, pp. 183–4.   [48] Ibid.
[49] Thomas Hobbes, *The Elements of Law Natural and Politic*, ed. Ferdinand Tönnies, intro. M. M. Goldsmith, 2nd edn (London: Frank Cass, 1969), p. 118.
[50] Thomas Hobbes, *De Cive: the English Version*, ed. Howard Warrender (Oxford: Clarendon Press, 1983), p. 109.
[51] Hobbes, *The Elements of Law*, p. 118.   [52] Tuck, in this volume, p. 184.

power.[53] When a government is 'acquired', however, they simply submit their wills to the absolute power of a conqueror in return for being granted their life and bodily liberty.[54] In the latter case no democratic process of decision-making is involved at all.

It is likewise an overstatement to claim that Hobbes's understanding of these matters in *The Elements* and *De Cive* is 'broadly compatible' with his later accounts.[55] When Hobbes reissued his political theory in *Leviathan*, first in English and later in Latin, one of the arguments he took particular care to revise was his earlier suggestion that all instituted commonwealths begin life as democracies. In both versions of *Leviathan* he presents a new and strongly contrasting theory according to which 'government by institution' and 'government by acquisition' both arise when the individual members of a multitude authorise a sovereign representative to speak and act in their name.[56] His previous suggestion that, in the case of government by institution, we can trace a chronological sequence beginning with democracy is now completely suppressed.

I turn to the other respect in which, according to Tuck, Hobbes grants 'extreme' democracy 'a very special status' in his political theory, and does so in a 'quite unprecedented' way.[57] Tuck begins by conceding that Hobbes was admittedly no admirer of government by deliberative assemblies. None the less, he believed that, as long as democracies avoid committing themselves to this kind of administrative system, they are capable of being 'as effective and admirable as monarchies'.[58] He believed, in short, that a democracy need not be 'at all inferior to a monarchy', and it is even arguable that democracy may have been his preferred form of government.[59]

It seems to me that this interpretation rests on a failure to appreciate that the structure of Hobbes's argument about democracy is a profoundly ironic one.[60] Quintilian in his influential analysis of the figures and tropes had introduced a distinction between irony as a trope of speech and irony as a figure of thought. When we employ irony as a trope, we merely give a distinctive inflexion to some particular utterance. Seeking to introduce a tone of mockery, we 'say the contrary of what we want to be understood'.[61] When, by contrast, we employ irony as a figure of thought, we aim to produce a far more ambitious rhetorical

---

[53] Hobbes, *The Elements of Law*, p. 108; Hobbes, *De Cive*, p. 90; Hobbes, *Leviathan*, p. 121.

[54] Hobbes, *The Elements of Law*, p. 127; Hobbes, *De Cive*, 1983, p. 117; Hobbes, *Leviathan*, p. 121.

[55] Tuck, in this volume, p. 172.

[56] Hobbes, *Leviathan*, pp. 120, 138; Thomas Hobbes, *Leviathan, sive De Materia, Forma, & Potestate Civitatis Ecclesiasticae et Civilis* in *Opera philosophica*, ed. Sir William Molesworth, vol. III (London, 1841), pp. 123, 131–2, 150–1.

[57] Tuck, in this volume, p. 183.   [58] Ibid., p. 186.   [59] Ibid., p. 187.

[60] This may be what Kinch Hoekstra has in mind when he says in this volume that Hobbes speaks of democracy 'with serious irony' (p. 217).

[61] Quintilian, *Institutio oratoria*, ed. and trans. H. E. Butler, 4 vols. (London 1920–22), IX.VI.56, vol. III, p. 332: 'quodam contraria dicuntur iis quae intellegi volunt'.

effect. We seek in this case to present an entire chain of reasoning in such a way as to confound and thereby ridicule the expectations of our audience.[62] Quintilian gives the example of Socrates, whose ironic stance took the form of 'putting himself forward as an ignorant man intensely admiring of the wisdom of others'.[63] Socrates's eventual aim in doing so was to show his interlocutors that their premises can be made to yield conclusions of a completely unexpected and contradictory kind.

It is exactly this ironic strategy that Hobbes deploys in every version of his political theory against the democratical writers of his time. As we have seen, he fixes on their fundamental tenet that, unless we live in a 'popular common-wealth', we shall find ourselves condemned to living as slaves. Confronting this argument, he is careful to refrain from questioning the underlying assumption that the best form of civil association must be one in which the people rule. What he tries to show is that, if this is your idea of the best form of civil association, then you ought not to be a supporter of democracy. No democratic government can ever amount in practice to anything more than an aristocracy of orators absorbed in their own glory and factional ends.[64] If you genuinely want the people to rule, you ought instead to institute an absolute monarchy.

The key passage in which Hobbes springs this lethal trap is in ch. 12 of *De Cive*. I shall quote from the translation of 1651, since this is the version whose publication Hobbes permitted and perhaps even authorised:

> The *People* rules in all Governments, for even in *Monarchies* the *People* Commands; for the *People* wills by the will of *one man*; but the Multitude are Citizens, that is to say, Subjects. In a *Democraty*, and *Aristocraty*, the Citizens are the *Multitude*, but the *Court* is the *People*. And in a *Monarchy*, the Subjects are the *Multitude*, and (however it seeme a Paradox) the King is the *People*.[65]

Tuck treats this passage as the crucial one in support of his own argument. It is here, he maintains, that we encounter the suggestion that Vettori developed out of Aristotle's *Politics* and bequeathed to Hobbes. We are being told that there is a form of government – a form that Hobbes takes to be admirable – in which the people is one man and is at the same time the king. But it seems to me that this is precisely the opposite of what Hobbes is claiming here. He is not saying that it is possible for the people to be a king; he is saying that it is possible for a king to be the people. He is not claiming that there is an extreme form of democracy in which the people is king, and that this is an admirable form of government. He is not even talking about democracy, extreme or otherwise.

---

[62] Ibid., IX.II.48, vol. III, p. 402.

[63] Ibid., IX.II.46, vol. III, p. 400: 'agens imperitum et admirationem aliorum tanquam sapientium'.

[64] Hobbes, *The Elements of Law*, pp. 120–1; Hobbes, *De Cive*, p. 133; Hobbes, *Leviathan*, pp. 131–2.

[65] Hobbes, *De Cive*, p. 151.

He is talking about monarchy, and he is defending the avowedly paradoxical conclusion that, even under this form of government, the people may still be said to rule, because 'the King is the *People*'.

It remains for Hobbes to unpack his paradox and tell us what he means by saying that the king 'is' the people. In *The Elements* he explains, rather awkwardly, that what he has in mind is that the wills of the people can be said to be 'involved' or 'included' in the will of the king.[66] In *De Cive* he instead suggests, somewhat more perspicuously, that the will of the king may be said to 'stand for' the wills of all.[67] But it is only in *Leviathan* that he manages to turn his paradox into a recognisable argument. He does so by introducing the key concept of *authorisation* into his theory for the first time. This enables him to argue that, because each of us authorises our sovereign's conduct, we remain the authors and hence the 'owners' of whatever actions he may choose to perform in our names.[68] The actions of our sovereign, in other words, count as our own actions, for which we have to take complete responsibility.[69] But this is to say that, whenever an authorised sovereign acts, it is in fact the people who act, and this in turn is to say that the people rule at all times.

With this contention Hobbes arrives at his crowning irony. According to the democratical writers, the execution of King Charles I in 1649 served to liberate the people of England from an enslaving tyranny. With the abolition of the monarchy and the establishment of a 'free state', the people were at last able to rule themselves through the agency of the House of Commons as their authorised representative.[70] According to Hobbes's theory, however, the subjects of king Charles I, as the 'owners' of all his actions, had *already* been ruling themselves through the agency of an authorised representative.[71] The tragic irony is thus that the king was murdered and the constitution destroyed in the name of bringing about an outcome that, under the king himself, had already been fully achieved.

Tuck has one further argument to present, and it sometimes seems to be the one that interests him most of all. Hoekstra offers little comment on this aspect of Tuck's case, and their two brilliant chapters are complementary at this point. (If I were Tuck, I might well feel inclined to echo Buck Mulligan in *Ulysses*: 'God, Kinch, if you and I could only work together . . .'.)[72] Tuck's additional hypothesis is that it was basically from Hobbes's *De Cive* that the idea of 'extreme' democracy descended to the modern world. It was chiefly as the author of *De Cive* that Hobbes was known to Pufendorf, Leibniz, Spinoza

---

[66] Hobbes, *The Elements of Law*, pp. 63, 124.   [67] Hobbes, *De Cive*, p. 89.
[68] Hobbes, *Leviathan*, pp. 112, 114.   [69] Ibid., pp. 122–4.
[70] S. R. Gardiner, *The Constitutional Documents of the Puritan Revolution, 1625–1660*, 3rd edn (Oxford: Clarendon Press, 1906), pp. 386–7.
[71] Hobbes, *Leviathan*, p. 130.   [72] James Joyce, *Ulysses* (London: Bodley Head, 1960), p. 6.

and perhaps Rousseau, and it was in *De Cive* that his views about 'extreme' democracy were most fully laid out.

I can readily imagine an important book about the history of 'extreme' democracy, and it is devoutly to be hoped that Tuck will himself write it. The only cautionary note I would sound is one that echoes Boutcher's argument. Hobbes's *De Cive* may well have inspired later writers on popular sovereignty, and its possible influence on Rousseau would be especially worth investigating. While this may have been an important element in the afterlife of Hobbes's text, however, I remain convinced that Hobbes himself would have found it a deeply unwelcome example of the kind of irony he normally relished so much. He may have influenced the evolution of democratic theory, but the democratical writers of his own time were nevertheless the ones he feared and hated most of all.

IV

I should like to express a special word of thanks to those contributors who have recognised that one of my foremost aims in *Foundations* was to puncture an historical myth that enjoyed extensive vogue at the time. The myth centred around the alleged contribution of the Protestant reformation to the modern world. According to one part of the story, the modern theory of constitutionalism arose out of the monarchomach attack on tyranny and the subsequent 'revolution of the saints'. As Goldie and Brett both emphasise, however, one of my main ambitions in volume II of *Foundations* was to establish that the arguments deployed by the Protestant revolutionaries were almost entirely taken from their Catholic enemies. It was in late-medieval conciliarism and in the natural-law theories of the second scholastic that the fundamental concepts of modern constitutionalism were originally forged.

According to a second element in the myth, the growth of constitutionalism in the seventeenth century gave rise to a theory of liberty that proved to be among the most valuable items in our intellectual heritage. The concept of liberty came to be understood in negative terms as absence of interference, and it came to be accepted that one of the principal duties of the state is to protect and enlarge this area of non-interference as far as possible. However, as Geuna and van Gelderen both point out, volume I of *Foundations* was in part designed to suggest that the triumph of this vision of politics embodied a serious loss. The enthroning of the idea of freedom as non-interference involved the rejection of a far more exacting understanding of the concept that I associated with the humanism of the Renaissance. According to the humanist ideal of the *vivere libero*, the freedom of individual citizens is undermined not merely by active constraint but also, and more fundamentally, by background conditions of dependence and servitude. It was only with the rejection of this more democratic understanding of political liberty that the etiolated concept of freedom as non-interference conquered the modern world.

I cannot pretend that I succeeded in articulating the humanist vision of liberty with the philosophical sophistication it deserved. Although I wrote of *dependenza* and *servitù*, it was only with the help of Philip Pettit's path-finding work that I eventually managed to clarify to my own satisfaction the defining characteristics of the theory I had sketched.[73] I recognise too that I may have over-emphasised the extent to which the contrast between freedom and servitude was unambiguously endorsed by the humanists of the Renaissance. As Curtis's chapter shows, there were several important humanists, notably Sir Thomas More, whose view of the distinction remains at best unclear. Nevertheless, the chapters in *Foundations* about the ideal of the *vivere libero* remain the ones with which I feel least dissatisfied. They helped, I think, to open a window on to a world that liberalism had closed off, and they offered some grounds for thinking that the balance-sheet of gains and losses needed to be reassessed.

Before I lapse into self-entrancement, however, I need to acknowledge that Pocock registers some disquiet about this part of my argument. Pocock maintains that, when the defenders of the *vivere libero* speak about the *libertà* of citizens, they are invoking what he describes as 'the Aristotelian form' of 'the "republican" concept of active citizenship'. This is the form, he adds, that 'articulates at a high level the "positive" concept of liberty'.[74] Here he explicitly refers us to Isaiah Berlin's attempt to distinguish between what he called 'positive' and 'negative' liberty.[75] When Berlin speaks of 'negative' liberty he defines it, with a fair degree of consistency, as the view that we are free if and only if we are not subjected to physical or coercive interference.[76] When he turns to 'positive' liberty he speaks much less coherently,[77] but he generally defines it as the view that we are fully free if and only if we act in such a way as to realise our true nature.[78] It is this 'positive' understanding of liberty that Pocock attributes to the protagonists of the *vivere libero*. They believe, he claims, that what distinguishes a free citizen is that the pattern of his actions reveals him to be 'the political creature it is said one is, and ought to be, by nature'. They

---

[73] Philip Pettit, *Republicanism: a Theory of Freedom and Government* (Oxford: Oxford University Press, 1997).

[74] Pocock, 'Foundations and moments', in this volume, p. 43.

[75] Isaiah Berlin, 'Two Concepts of Liberty', in Henry Hardy (ed.), *Liberty* (Oxford: Oxford University Press, 2002), pp. 166–217.

[76] Berlin, 'Two Concepts', p. 170.

[77] For Berlin's different formulations of the concept see Berlin, 'Two Concepts', pp. 178–80; on the incompatibility between them see Quentin Skinner, 'A Third Concept of Liberty', *Proceedings of the British Academy* 117 (2002), pp. 237–68, at pp. 238–40.

[78] See Berlin, 'Two Concepts', p. 180, where 'positive' freedom is equated with self-realisation, and above all with the idea (as Berlin expresses it) of my self at its best. His most considered view of the positive concept is that, as he finally summarises (p. 180), 'whatever is the true goal of man . . . must be identical with his freedom'.

consequently believe that the enjoyment of freedom is not a 'negative' matter of being able to act without interference; it is a 'positive' matter of engaging, as Pocock puts it, in the exercise of virtue in the public realm.[79]

I see little evidence, however, that Machiavelli, Guicciardini and the other leading protagonists of the *vivere libero* adopted this view of what it means to be a free citizen. It seems to me that, as their repeated contrasts between *libertà* and *servitù* suggest, they cleave to the essentially Roman conception of freedom I have already mentioned, the conception that Cicero celebrated, that Tacitus commemorated, and that Justinian's *Digest* eventually defined in formal legal terms.[80] According to the *Digest*, the basic distinction we need to draw is between the independence that characterises free citizens and the dependence that characterises slaves. 'Slavery', as the *Digest* tells us, 'is an institution of the *ius gentium* by which someone is, contrary to nature, subjected to the dominion of someone else'.[81] It follows that, since everyone in a *civitas* is either bond or free, a *civis* or free citizen must be someone who is not under the dominion of anyone else, but is *sui iuris*, capable of acting in their own right.[82] It likewise follows that what it means for someone to lack the status of a free citizen must be for that person not to be *sui iuris* but instead to be *sub potestate*, under the power and hence dependent on the will of someone else.

This is the view of freedom that I hear echoing through such texts as Guicciardini's *Dialogo* and Machiavelli's *Discorsi*. Consequently, when these and other defenders of the *vivere libero* add that the exercise of *virtù* is indispensable to the preservation of *libertà*, I do not take them to be claiming that freedom is in some way to be equated with the exercise of virtue. I take them to be claiming that, unless we are prepared to take part in the public realm, and hence to cultivate the qualities needed for effective participation, we shall find ourselves dependent on the wills and decisions of others, thereby forfeiting our status as free citizens and descending into the condition of servitude.

Pocock goes on to distinguish the freedom of the *vivere libero* from the freedom demanded by the crown's opponents in early seventeenth-century England. 'The Italian citizen affirming his virtue', he declares, 'and the English subject defending his rights may without distortion be made to stand for [the]

---

[79] Pocock, in this volume, p. 43.

[80] For this story see Quentin Skinner, 'Classical Liberty and the Coming of the English Civil War', in Martin van Gelderen and Quentin Skinner (eds.), *Republicanism: a Shared European Heritage*, vol. II: *The Values of Republicanism in Early Modern Europe* (Cambridge: Cambridge University Press, 2002), pp. 9–28.

[81] Theodor Mommsen and Paul Krueger (eds.), *The Digest of Justinian*. trans. Alan Watson, 4 vols. (Philadelphia: University of Pennsylvania Press, 1985) I.V.4.35: 'Servitus est constitutio iuris gentium, qua quis dominio alieno contra naturam subicitur'.

[82] Mommsen and Kruger (eds.), *The Digest of Justinian*, I.VI.1.36: 'Some persons are in their own power, some are subject to the power of others, such as slaves, who are in the power of their masters'. ['quaedam personae sui iuris sunt, quaedam alieno iuri subiectae sunt . . . in potestate sunt servi dominorum . . .'].

"positive" and "negative" poles of Isaiah Berlin's "two concepts of liberty".'[83] This is to say, however, that in England the equation between freedom and virtue was replaced by a view of freedom as non-interference, and this interpretation does not seem to me tenable. It is true that critics of the crown in early Stuart England feared an increase of interference with established rights, as the Petition of Right makes plain when it charges that the people are being subjected to vexatious compulsion and otherwise 'molested and disquieted' in the exercise of their liberties.[84] But this is not the sole or even the primary sense in which the Parliamentarians complain about a loss of liberty. The basic accusation they level against the crown is that the people of England are being made to forfeit their standing as *liberi homines* or free-men.[85] The very existence of the royal prerogative, they insist, has the effect of making everyone dependent for the maintenance of their liberties upon the goodwill of the king, and this condition of dependence lowers their status from free-men to that of slaves.

This neo-Roman way of thinking is already evident in the parliamentary debates leading up to the Petition of Right in 1628, and it resurfaced with a vengeance as soon as Parliament reconvened in 1640.[86] Thereafter the argument was taken up by most of the leading Parliamentarian spokesmen at the beginning of the Civil War. We encounter it in Henry Parker's *Observations* of July 1642,[87] in John Marsh's *Debate in Law* of September 1642,[88] and in such anonymous tracts of early 1643 as *A Soveraigne Salve*,[89] *An Honest Broker*[90] and *Touching the Fundamentall Lawes*.[91] But perhaps the clearest summary can be found in John Goodwin's *Anti-Cavalierisme* of October 1642. What it means to be 'free men and women', Goodwin affirms, is to have 'the disposall of your selves and of all your wayes' according to your own will, rather than being subject to the will of anyone else. If your rulers are in possession of discretionary powers, you will be obliged to live 'by the lawes of their lusts and pleasures' and 'to be at their arbitterments and wills in all things.' But if they are able to 'make themselves Lords over you' in this fashion, then your birthright of 'civill or politick libertie' will thereby be cancelled, and you will instead be reduced to 'a miserable slavery and bondage'.[92]

I see no categorical difference, in short, between the freedom celebrated by the republican theorists of the Renaissance and the freedom demanded by the

---

[83] Pocock, in this volume, p. 46.   [84] Gardiner, *The Constitutional Documents*, pp. 66–70.
[85] The term is sometimes printed as two words, sometimes as one, but is generally hyphenated.
[86] See Skinner, 'A Third Concept of Liberty', pp. 250–3.
[87] Henry Parker, *Observations upon some of his Majesties late Answers and Expresses* (London, 1642), pp. 9–10, 17, 43–4.
[88] John Marsh, *An Argument Or, Debate in Law* (London, 1642), pp. 13, 24.
[89] *A Soveraigne Salve to Cure the Blind* (London, 1643), pp. 16–17, 36–8.
[90] *An Honest Broker* (London, 1643), Sig. C, 2ᵛ–3ʳ, Sig. E, 3ᵛ–4ᵛ.
[91] *Touching the Fundamentall Lawes* (London, 1643), pp. 10, 12 (*recte* 14).
[92] John Goodwin, *Anti-Cavalierisme* (London, 1642), pp. 38–9.

crown's opponents in early Stuart England. The basic contrast on which they all insist is between liberty and dependence, and hence between free-men and slaves. This is not a contrast that Berlin's distinction between 'positive' liberty and liberty as non-interference is capable of accommodating, and it may be because Pocock continues to follow Berlin's analysis that he remains, as he puts it, 'a little suspicious' of my references to neo-Roman freedom.[93] My own view is that Berlin's distinctions are best forgotten: when applied to the early-modern period they are not only anachronistic but completely fail to capture the range of categories in use at the time.

Despite these differences, I agree with Pocock that there is something 'oddly incomplete' about the discussion of freedom and citizenship in early Stuart England by comparison with Renaissance Italy.[94] As I see it, the incompleteness stems from the fact that almost nothing is said about the need for the body of the people to cultivate the civic virtues. The reason, I would argue, is that the English writers are no longer taking the *polis* or *civitas* as their model of civil association; they are thinking instead about the government of large-scale territorial states. Within such communities, as Henry Parker explains, the body of the people is prevented by 'the vastnesse of its owne bulke' from being able to act for itself. As a result, it is necessary 'to regulate the motions' of 'so cumbersome a body', and the best method of regulation, as most countries have discovered, is to institute representative assemblies to which the people hand over their political rights to be exercised in their name.[95] The people of England are being told, in other words, that there is no longer any need for them to exercise the qualities of active citizenship. They remain free-men, they are assured, because the House of Commons 'is' (by the alchemy of representation) the body of the people, so that the people may still be said to rule.[96] Nevertheless, they are now assigned a politically passive role all too familiar to us from our own frustrating experience of living under modern democratic regimes.

Pocock ends by generously asking about the direction of my current research. As will by now be clear, I have come to feel that among the key concepts in early-modern political theory that need to be further explored are those of freedom and representation, especially in relation to the ideal of popular sovereignty. These were the topics on which I focused in my Ford Lectures, about which Pocock enquires at the end of his chapter. I now hope to deepen my understanding of the process by which the Renaissance ideals of civic liberty and self-government came to be supplanted by the oxymoronic concept of representative democracy throughout so much of the modern world.

---

[93] Pocock, in this volume, p. 44.   [94] Ibid., p. 46.
[95] Parker, *Observations*, pp. 14–15.   [96] Ibid., pp. 28, 45.

V

While writing this reply to my critics, I have more than once found myself thinking about Turner's famous painting of the *Téméraire*. Against a setting sun we see a steam tug towing the old sailing-ship away. The image is an embarrassingly hackneyed one, but it is hardly surprising to find it flitting through my mind. There is no denying that *Foundations* is a very ancient vessel by the standards of contemporary scholarship. And although it is still afloat, it is undoubtedly holed beneath the waterline in a number of places, as the contributors to the present volume have all too clearly pointed out. But this makes me all the more grateful to them for their willingness to write about my book, and for their generosity in reconsidering and commenting on its arguments. I thank them all, in Hobbes's fine phrase, for thinking my studies something.

Bibliography

Acciaiuoli, Donato. *In Aristotelis Libros Octo Politicorum Commentarii* (Venice, 1566).

Airaksinen, Timo and Martin A. Bertman (eds.). *Hobbes: War Among Nations* (Aldershot: Avebury, 1989).

Akashi, Kinji. 'Hobbes's Relevance to the Modern Law of Nations', *Journal of the History of International Law* 2 (2000), pp. 199–216.

Albertus Magnus. *Ethicorum libri X*, in *Opera omnia* (Lyons, 1651).

Alexander, James. 'An Essay on Historical, Philosophical, and Theological Attitudes to Modern Political Thought', *History of Political Thought* 25 (2004), pp. 116–48.

Allen, J. W. *A History of Political Thought in the Sixteenth Century* (London: Methuen, 1957).

Althusius, J. *Politice methodice digesta* (3rd edn 1614), ed. Carl Joachim Friedrich (Cambridge, Mass.: Harvard University Press, 1932).

Anon. 'Discourse upon the beginning of Tacitus', in *Horae Subsecivae: Observations and Discovrses* London, 1620. *See also* [Cavendish, William]

An Honest Broker (London, 1643)

A Soveraigne Salve (London, 1643)

The Proceedings of the Present Parliament Justified by the Opinion of the most Judicious and Learned Hugo Grotius (London, 1689).

Touching the Fundamentall Lawes (London, 1643).

Aquinas, Thomas. *Summa theologiae*, in *Opera omnia iussu Leonis XIII edita*, t. 4–12 (Rome, 1888).

Octo Libros Politicorum Aristotelis Expositio, ed. Raymund M. Spiazzi (Turin: Marietti, 1966).

Sententia libri Ethicorum, in Opera omnia, t. 47 (Rome, 1969).

Sententia libri Politicorum, in Opera omnia, t. 48 (Rome, 1971).

Sententia libri Ethicorum, ed. Enrique Alarcón (Sociedad CAEL: *Corpus Thomisticum*, www.unav.es/filosofia/alarcon).

Sententia libri Metaphysicae, ed. Enrique Alarcón (Sociedad CAEL: *Corpus Thomisticum*, www.unav.es/filosofia/alarcon).

Sententia libri Politicorum, ed. Enrique Alarcón (Sociedad CAEL: *Corpus Thomisticum*, www.unav.es/filosofia/alarcon).

Arendt, Hannah. *The Human Condition* (Chicago: University of Chicago Press, 1958).

Aristotle. *Politiques, or Discourses of Government* (London, 1598).

Politics, ed. F. Susemihl (Leipzig, 1872).

Armitage, David, A. Himy and Quentin Skinner (eds.). *Milton and Republicanism* (Cambridge: Cambridge University Press, 1995).

Artifoni, E. 'Sull eloquenza politica nel Duecento italiano', *Quaderni medievali* 35 (1993), pp. 57–78.

'Retorica e organizzazione del linguaggio politico nel Duecento italiano', in P. Cammarosano (ed.), *Le forme della propaganda politica nel Due e nel Trecento* (Rome: École française de Rome, 1994).

Ashcraft, Richard. 'The Foundations of Modern Political Thought', *Journal of the History of Philosophy* 19 (1981), pp. 388–92.

Revolutionary Politics and Locke's Two Treatises of Government (Princeton: Princeton University Press, 1986).

Astell, Mary. 'An Impartial Enquiry into the Causes of Rebellion and Civil War', in Patricia Springborg (ed.), *Political Writings* (Cambridge: Cambridge University Press, 1996).

Austin, J. L. *How to Do Things with Words* (Oxford: Oxford University Press, 1962).

Austin, John. *The Province of Jurisprudence Determined* [1832], ed. Wilfrid E. Rumble (Cambridge: Cambridge University Press, 1995).

Baker-Smith, Dominic. *More's Utopia* (New York: Harper Collins, 1991).

Baron, Hans. 'Calvinist Republicanism and its Historical Roots', *Church History* 8 (1939), pp. 30–42.

The Crisis of the Early Italian Renaissance, 2 vols. (Princeton: Princeton University Press, 1955).

'Machiavelli: the Republican Citizen and the Author of the Prince', *The English Historical Review* 76 (1961), pp. 217–53.

The Crisis of the Early Italian Renaissance, 2nd edn (Princeton: Princeton University Press, 1966).

'Leonardo Bruni: "Professional Rhetorician" or "Civic Humanist"?', *Past and Present* 36 (1967), pp. 21–37.

Bartelson, Jens. *A Genealogy of Sovereignty* (Cambridge: Cambridge University Press, 1995).

Baumgold, Deborah. 'The Composition of Hobbes's *Elements of Law*', *History of Political Thought* 25 (2004), pp. 16–43.

Bayle, Pierre. *Dictionaire Historique et Critique* (Rotterdam, 1697).

Beitz, Charles R. *Political Theory and International Relations*, 2nd edn (Princeton: Princeton University Press, 1999).

Bell, Duncan S. A. 'International Relations: the Dawn of a Historiographical Turn?', *British Journal of Politics and International Relations* 3 (2001), pp. 115–26.

Beltrán de Heredia, V. (ed.). *Francisco de Vitoria. Comentario al tratado de la ley* (Madrid: CSIC, 1952).

Bergsma, Wiebe. *Aggaeus van Albada (c. 1525–1587), schwenckfeldiaan, staatsman en strijder voor verdraagzaamheid* (Groningen: Meppel, 1985).

Berlin, Isaiah. 'The Originality of Machiavelli', in Myron P. Gilmore (ed.), *Studies on Machiavelli* (Florence: Sansoni, 1972).

'Two Concepts of Liberty', in Henry Hardy (ed.), *Liberty* (Oxford: Oxford University Press, 2002).

Berten, A., P. Da Silveira and H. Pourtois. 'Introduction générale', in A. Berten, P. Da Silveira and H. Pourtois (eds.), *Libéraux et communautariens* (Paris: PUF, 1997).

Besold, Christoph. *Operis Politici Editio Nova* (Strasbourg, 1626).

Black, Antony. *Monarchy and Community: Political Ideas in the Later Conciliar Controversy 1430–1450* (Cambridge: Cambridge University Press, 1970).

Political Thought in Europe, 1250–1450 (Cambridge: Cambridge University Press, 1992).

'Christianity and Republicanism: from St Cyprian to Rousseau', *American Political Science Review* 9 (1997), pp. 647–56.

Bock, G., Quentin Skinner and M. Viroli (eds.), *Machiavelli and Republicanism* (Cambridge: Cambridge University Press, 1990).

Bodin, Jean. *The Six Bookes of a Common-weale*, trans. Richard Knolles (London, 1606).

Method for the Easy Comprehension of History, trans. Beatrice Reynolds (New York: W. W. Norton, 1969).

la Boétie, Étienne de. *De la servitude volontaire ou contr'un*, ed. Malcolm Smith (Geneva: Droz, 1987).

De la Servitude Volontaire ou Contr'un, ed. Nadia Gontarbert (Paris: Gallimard, 1993).

Œuvres complètes, ed. Louis Desgraves, 2 vols. (Bordeaux: William Blake, 1991).

Borrelli, Gianfranco. 'Hobbes e la teoria moderna della democrazia. Rappresentanza assoluta e scambio politico', *Trimestre* 24 (1991), pp. 243–63.

Boswell, J. C. *Sir Thomas More in the English Renaissance: an Annotated Catalogue* (Tempe: Arizona University Press, 1994).

Böttcher, Diethelm. *Ungehorsam oder Widerstand? Zum Fortleben der mittelalterlichen Widerstandsrechtes in der Reformationszeit (1529–1530)* (Berlin: Duncker & Humblot, 1991).

Boucher, David. 'On Shklar's and Franklin's Reviews of Skinner, *The Foundations of Modern Political Thought*', *Political Theory* 8 (1980), pp. 406–8.

Political Theories of International Relations: from Thucydides to the Present (Oxford: Oxford University Press, 1998).

Boutcher, W. 'The Making of the Humane Philosopher: Paul Oskar Kristeller and Twentieth-Century Intellectual History', in John Monfasani (ed.), *Kristeller Reconsidered: Essays on his Life and Scholarship* (New York: Italica Press, 2006), pp. 39–70.

Bouwsma, W. J. 'Reformation and Counter-Reformation', *Catholic Historical Review* 67 (1981), pp. 84–5.

Brett, Annabel. *Liberty, Right and Nature: Individual Rights in Later Scholastic Thought* (Cambridge: Cambridge University Press, 1997).

'What is Intellectual History Now?', in David Cannadine (ed.), *What is History Now?* (London: Palgrave, 2002).

la Brosse, Olivier de. *Le Pape et Le Concile. La comparaison de leurs pouvoirs à la veille de la Réforme* (Paris: Editions du Cerf, 1965).

Brown, Alison. 'De-masking Renaissance Republicanism', in James Hankins (ed.), *Renaissance Civic Humanism: Reappraisals and Reflections* (Cambridge: Cambridge University Press, 2000).

Brown, Chris, Terry Nardin and Nicholas Rengger (eds.). *International Relations in Political Thought: Texts from the Ancient Greeks to the First World War* (Cambridge: Cambridge University Press, 2002).

Brutus, Stephanus Junius. *Vindiciae contra Tyrannos*, ed. and trans. George Garnett (Cambridge: Cambridge University Press, 1994).

Bryce, James. *International Relations* (New York: Macmillan, 1922).

Buchanan, George. *De Iure Regni apud Scotos, Dialogus* (Edinburgh, 1579).

Bull, Hedley. *The Anarchical Society: a Study of Order in World Politics* (New York: Columbia University Press, 1977).

'Hobbes and the International Anarchy', *Social Research* 48 (1981), pp. 717–38.

Burlamaqui, Jean Jacques. *The Principles of Natural Law*, trans. Thomas Nugent (London, 1748).

Burns, J. H. 'Conciliarism, Papalism and Power, 1511–1518', in D. Wood (ed.), *The Church and Sovereignty c.590–1918: Essays in Honour of Michael Wilks* (Oxford: Oxford University Press 1991).

'Scholasticism: Survival and Revival', in J. H. Burns (ed.), *The Cambridge History of Political Thought 1450–1700* (Cambridge: Cambridge University Press, 1991).

'George Buchanan and the Anti-Monarchomachs', in Nicholas Phillipson and Quentin Skinner (eds.), *Political Discourse in Early Modern Britain* (Cambridge: Cambridge University Press, 1993).

The True Law of Kingship: Concepts of Monarchy in Early Modern Scotland (Oxford: Oxford University Press, 1996).

Burns, J. H. and Thomas M. Izbicki (eds.). *Conciliarism and Papalism* (Cambridge: Cambridge University Press, 1997).

Burtt, S. 'The Politics of Virtue Today: a Critique and a Proposal', *American Political Science Review* 87 (1993), pp. 360–8.

Butterfield, Herbert. *The Whig Interpretation of History* (London: G. Bell and Sons, 1931).

Canning, J. *The Political Thought of Baldus de Ubaldis* (Cambridge: Cambridge University Press, 1987).

Cano, Melchor. *De dominio indorum*, in L. Pereña et al. (eds.), *Juan de la Peña. De bello contra insulanos* (Madrid: CSIC, 1982).

Carta, P. 'Les exilés italiens et l'anti-machiavélisme français au XVIe siècle', in P. Carta and L. De Los Santos (eds.), *La République en exile (XVe – XVIe siècles)* (Lyons: ENS Editions, 2002).

Case, John. *Sphaera Civitatis* (Oxford, 1588).

Cavallar, Georg. *The Rights of Strangers: Theories of International Hospitality, the Global Community, and Political Justice since Vitoria* (Aldershot: Ashgate, 2002).

Caws, Peter (ed.). *The Causes of Quarrel: Essays on Peace, War, and Thomas Hobbes* (Boston: Beacon Press, 1989).

[Cavendish, William]. *Horae Subsecivae: Observations and Discovrses* (London, 1620)

Cicero, Marcus Tullius. *De Re Publica*, trans. C. W. Keyes (Cambridge, Mass.: Harvard University Press, 1928).

Coleman, Frank M. *Hobbes and America: Exploring the Constitutional Foundations* (Toronto: University of Toronto Press, 1977).

Collingwood, R. G. *An Autobiography* (Oxford: Oxford University Press, 1939).

Collini, Stefan. 'A Place in the Syllabus: Political Science at Cambridge', in S. Collini, D. Winch and J. Burrow (eds.), *That Noble Science of Politics: a Study in Nineteenth-Century Intellectual History* (Cambridge: Cambridge University Press, 1983).

'Disciplines, Canons, and Publics: the History of "The History of Political Thought" in Comparative Perspective', in Dario Castiglione and Iain Hampsher-Monk (eds.), *The History of Political Thought in National Context* (Cambridge: Cambridge University Press, 2001).

Collinson, Patrick. *De Republica Anglorum Or, History with the Politics Put Back: Inaugural Lecture delivered 9 November 1989* (Cambridge: Cambridge University Press, 1990).

Condren, Conal. 'Liberty of Office and its Defence in Seventeenth-Century Political Argument', *History of Political Thought* 17 (1997), pp. 460–82.

Argument and Authority in Early Modern England: The Presupposition of Oaths and Offices (Cambridge: Cambridge University Press, 2006).

Cornford, Francis Macdonald. *Thucydides Mythistoricus* (London: Edward Arnold, 1907).

Courtine, J.-F. *Nature et empire de la loi. Études suaréziennes* (Paris: Editions Vrin, 1999).

Creppell, Ingrid. 'The Democratic Element in Hobbes's *Behemoth*', *Filozofski vestnik* 24 (2003), pp. 7–35.

Crimmins, James E. 'Bentham and Hobbes: an Issue of Influence', *Journal of the History of Ideas* 63 (2002), pp. 677–96.

Curtis, Cathy. 'Richard Pace on Pedagogy, Counsel and Satire' (University of Cambridge PhD dissertation, 1996).

'Richard Pace's *De fructu* and Early Tudor Pedagogy', in J. Woolfson (ed.), *Reassessing Tudor Humanism* (Basingstoke: Palgrave Macmillan, 2002).

Davis, J. C. 'Political Thought during the English Revolution', in B. Coward (ed.), *A Companion to Stuart Britain* (Oxford: Oxford University Press 2003).

Delgado, M. 'Die Zustimmung des Volkes in der politischen Theorie von Francisco de Vitoria, Bartolomé de las Casas und Francisco Suárez', in F. Grünert and K. Seelmann (eds.), *Die Ordnung der Praxis. Neue Studien zur spanischen Spätscholastik* (Tübingen: Niemeyer, 2001).

Demerson, G. 'Les exempla dans le *Discours de la servitude volontaire*: une rhétorique datée?, in M. Tétel (ed.), *Etienne de La Boétie. Sage révolutionnaire et poète périgourdin*, Actes du Colloque International, Duke University, 26–28 mars 1999. *Colloques, Congrès et Conférences sur la Renaissance Européenne no.* 30 (Paris: Honoré Champion, 2004), pp. 195–224.

Dickinson, Edwin DeWitt. 'The Analogy Between Natural Persons and International Persons in the Law of Nations', *Yale Law Journal* 26 (1916–17), pp. 564–91.

The Digest of Justinian, ed. Theodor Mommsen and Paul Krueger, trans. Alan Watson, 4 vols. (Philadelphia, University of Pennsylvania Press, 1985).

[Digges, Dudley]. *The Vnlavvfulnesse of Subjects taking up Armes against their Soveraigne, in what case soever* ([Oxford], 1643).

Dionisotti, C. *Machiavelli letterato*, in Myron P. Gilmore (ed.), *Studies on Machiavelli* (Florence: Sansoni, 1972).

Machiavellerie. Storia e fortuna di Machiavelli (Turin: Einaudi, 1980).

Donato, M. M. 'Testo, contesto, immagini politiche nel tardo Medioevo. Esempi toscani', *Annali dell'Istituto storico italogermanico in Trento* 19 (1993), pp. 305–55.

Doyle, Michael W. *Ways of War and Peace: Realism, Liberalism, and Socialism* (New York: Norton, 1997).

Dunn, John. 'The Identity of the History of Ideas', *Philosophy* 43 (1968), pp. 85–104.

　The Political Thought of John Locke: an Historical Account of the Argument of the 'Two Treatises of Government' (Cambridge: Cambridge University Press, 1969).

Dzelzainis, Martin. 'Introduction' in John Milton, *Political Writings*, ed. Martin Dzelzainis (Cambridge: Cambridge University Press, 1991).

　'Milton's Politics', in Dennis Danielson (ed.), *The Cambridge Companion to Milton*, 2nd edn (Cambridge: Cambridge University Press, 1999).

Edling, M. and U. Mörkenstam. 'Quentin Skinner: from Historian of Ideas to Political Scientist', *Scandinavian Political Studies* 18 (1995), pp. 119–32.

Elton, G. R. *Return to Essentials* (Cambridge: Cambridge University Press, 1991).

Erasmus (of Rotterdam). *The Complete Works of Erasmus* (Toronto: University of Toronto Press, 1974).

　Erasmi Opuscula: A Supplement to the opera omnia, ed. W. K. Ferguson (The Hague: M. Nijhoff, 1933).

Farneti, Roberto. *Il canone moderno. Filosofia politica e genealogia* (Turin: Bollati Boringhieri, 2002).

Fasolt, Constantin. *Council and Hierarchy: the Political Thought of William Durant the Younger* (Cambridge: Cambridge University Press, 1991).

Ferguson, W. K. (ed.). *Erasmi Opuscula: a Supplement to the Opera Omnia* (The Hague: Nijhoff, 1933).

Fernández-Santamaría, J. A. *The State, War and Peace: Spanish Political Thought in the Renaissance, 1516–1559* (Cambridge: Cambridge University Press, 1977).

Ferraro, D. *Itinerari del volontarismo. Teologia e politica al tempo di Luis de León* (Milan: FrancoAngeli, 1995).

Figgis, J. N. 'On Some Political Theories of the Early Jesuits', *Transactions of the Royal Historical Society* 11 (1897), pp. 89–112.

　Studies of Political Thought from Gerson to Grotius, 1414–1625 [1907] (Cambridge: Cambridge University Press, 1923; Bristol: Thoemmes, 1998).

Filmer, Robert. *Patriarcha and Other Political Works of Sir Robert Filmer*, ed. Peter Laslett (Oxford: Basil Blackwell, 1949).

　Patriarcha and Other Writings, ed. Johann P. Sommerville (Cambridge: Cambridge University Press, 1991).

Fitzherbert, Thomas. *Treatise Concerning Policy and Religion* (London, 1616, 1610).

Flaubert, Gustav. *L'éducation sentimentale*, ed. René Dumesnil, 2 vols. (Paris, 1942).

Flüeler, C. *Rezeption und Interpretation der Aristotelischen Politica im späten Mittelalter*, 2 vols. (Amsterdam: B. Grüner, 1992).

Fontana, Biancamaria. 'In the Gardens of the Republic', *Times Literary Supplement*, 11 July 2003.

Forsyth, Murray. 'Thomas Hobbes and the External Relations of States', *British Journal of International Studies* 5 (1979), pp. 196–209.

Foucault, Michel. 'What is an Author?', in Josué V. Harari (ed.), *Textual Strategies* (Ithaca, N.Y.: Cornell University Press, 1979).

Franklin, Julian. 'Review of The Foundations of Modern Political Thought', *Political Theory* 11 (1980), pp. 552–8.

von Friedeburg, Robert. *Self-defence and Religious Strife in Early Modern Europe. England and Germany, 1530–1680* (London: Ashgate, 2002).

Gadamer, Hans-Georg. *Truth and Method*, 2nd rev. edn (London: Continuum, 2004).

Gallie, W. B. *Philosophers of Peace and War: Kant, Clausewitz, Marx, Engels and Tolstoy* (Cambridge: Cambridge University Press, 1978).

Gardiner, S. R. *The Constitutional Documents of the Puritan Revolution, 1625–1660*, 3rd edn (Oxford: Oxford University Press, 1906).

Garner, James W. 'Limitations on National Sovereignty in International Relations', *American Political Science Review* 19 (1925), pp. 1–24.

Garvie, A. F. *Aeschylus' Supplices: Play and Trilogy* (Cambridge: Cambridge University Press, 1969).

Gauthier, David. *The Logic of Leviathan: the Moral and Political Theory of Thomas Hobbes* (Oxford: Clarendon Press, 1969).

van Gelderen, Martin. *The Political Thought of the Dutch Revolt 1555–1590* (Cambridge: Cambridge University Press, 1992).

'Aristotelians, Monarchomachs and Republicans: Sovereignty and *respublica mixta* in Dutch and German Political Thought, 1580–1650', in Martin van Gelderen and Quentin Skinner (eds.), *Republicanism: a Shared European Heritage, I: Republicanism and Constitutionalism in Early Modern Europe* (Cambridge: Cambridge University Press, 2002).

van Gelderen, Martin and Quentin Skinner, (eds.), *Republicanism: a Shared European Heritage*, 2 vols. (Cambridge: Cambridge University Press, 2002).

Gerson, Jean. *Oeuvres Complètes*, vol. VI., ed. Mgr. Glorieux. (Tournai: Desclée, 1965).

Geuna, M. 'La libertà esigente di Quentin Skinner', in Quentin Skinner, *La libertà prima del liberalismo* (Turin: Einaudi, 2001).

Geuss, R. *History and Illusion in Politics* (Cambridge: Cambridge University Press, 2001).

Giddens, Anthony. *Politics and Sociology in the Thought of Max Weber* (London: Macmillan, 1972).

von Gierke, Otto. *Political Theories of the Middle Ages*, trans. F. W. Maitland (Cambridge: Cambridge University Press, 1900).

The Development of Political Theory, trans. Bernard Freyd (New York: H. Fertig, 1939).

Natural Law and the Theory of Society, 1500 to 1800, trans. E. Barker (Cambridge: Cambridge University Press, 1934; Boston, Mass.: Beacon Press, 1957).

Gilbert, Felix. *Machiavelli and Guicciardini: Politics and History in Sixteenth-century Florence* (Princeton: Princeton University Press, 1965).

Girot, J.-E. 'Une version inconnue du *Discours de la Servitude Volontaire* de La Boétie', *Bibliothèque d'Humanisme et Renaissance* 53 (2001), pp. 551–65.

Glaziou, Yves. *Hobbes en France au XVIIIe siècle* (Paris: PUF, 1993).

Goldie, Mark. 'J. N. Figgis and the History of Political Thought in Cambridge', in Richard Mason (ed.), *Cambridge Minds* (Cambridge: Cambridge University Press, 1994), pp. 177–92.

'The Unacknowledged Republic: Officeholding in Early Modern England', in Tim Harris (ed.), *The Politics of the Excluded, c.1500–1850* (New York: Palgrave, 2001).

'The English System of Liberty', in Mark Goldie and Robert Wokler (eds.), *The Cambridge History of Eighteenth-Century Political Thought* (Cambridge: Cambridge University Press, 2006).

Goodwin, John. *Anti-Cavalierisme* (London, 1642).

Grotius, Hugo. *De iure belli ac pacis libri tres* (Paris, 1625).

The Rights of War and Peace, ed. Jean Barbeyrac (London, 1738).

De Iure Praedae Commentarius, ed. H. G. Hamaker (The Hague, 1868).

Briefwisseling van Hugo Grotius, ed. P. C. Molhuysen, B. L. Meulenbroek and H. J. M. Nellen, 17 vols. (The Hague: Nijhoff, 1928–2001).

De Iure Praedae Commentarius: Commentary on the Law of Prize and Booty, vol. I, ed. Gwladys L. Williams and Walther H. Zeydel (London: Clarendon Press, 1950).

[Hugo Grotius]. *Mare Liberum* (Leiden, 1609).

Grouchy, Nicholas. *De Comitiis Romanorum Libri Tres* (Paris, 1555).

Grubb, James S. 'Elite Citizens', in John Martin and Dennis Romano (eds.), *Venice Reconsidered* (Baltimore: Johns Hopkins University Press, 2000).

Guy, John. 'The Monarchical Republic of Queen Elizabeth I', in J. Guy (ed.), *The Tudor Monarchy* (London: St Martin's Press, 1997).

'Tudor Monarchy and its Critiques', in J. Guy (ed.), *The Tudor Monarchy* (London: St Martin's Press, 1997).

Hacker, A. '*Capital* and Carbuncles: the "Great Books" Reappraised', *American Political Science Review* 48 (1954), pp. 775–86.

Hacker, P. M. S. *Wittgenstein's Place in Twentieth-Century Analytic Philosophy* (Oxford: Oxford University Press, 1996).

Hammond, Henry. *A Second Defence of the Learned Hugo Grotius* (London, 1655).

A Continuation of the Defence of Hugo Grotius in an Answer to the Review of his Annotations (London, 1657).

Hampsher-Monk, Iain. 'The History of Political Thought and the Political History of Thought', in Dario Castiglione and Iain Hampsher-Monk (eds.), *The History of Poltical Thought in National Context* (Cambridge: Cambridge University Press, 2001).

'Edmund Burke's Changing Justification for Intervention', *Historical Journal* 48 (2005), pp. 65–100.

Hankins, James (ed.). *Renaissance Civic Humanism: Reappraisals and Reflections* (Cambridge: Cambridge University Press, 2000).

Hansen, Mogens Herman. 'The Sovereignty of the People's Court in Athens in the Fourth Century BC and The Public Action Against Unconstitutional Proposals', *Odense University Classical Studies 4* (Odense: Odense University Press, 1974).

Hanson, Donald W. 'Thomas Hobbes's "Highway to Peace"', *International Organization* 38 (1984), pp. 329–54.

Harrington, James. *Politicaster* [1659] in *The Political Works of James Harrington*, ed. J. G. A. Pocock (Cambridge: Cambridge University Press, 1977).

The Art of Lawgiving [1659] in *The Political Works of James Harrington*, ed. J. G. A. Pocock (Cambridge: Cambridge University Press, 1977).

The Prerogative of Popular Government [1658] in *The Political Works of James Harrington*, ed. J. G. A. Pocock (Cambridge: Cambridge University Press, 1977).

Haug-Moritz, Gabriele. 'Widerstand als "Gegenwehr". Die schmalkaldische Konzeption der "Gegenwehr" und der "gegenwehrliche Krieg" des Jahres 1542', in Robert von Friedeburg (ed.), *Widerstandsrecht in der frühen Neuzeit. Erträge und Perspektiven der Forschung im deutsch-britischen Vergleich* (Berlin: Duncker & Humblot, 2001).

Hay, Denys. 'Review of Quentin Skinner's *"The Foundations of Modern Political Thought"*', *Journal of Ecclesiastical History* 31 (1980), pp. 223–6.

Heller, Mark A. 'The Use and Abuse of Hobbes: the State of Nature in International Relations', *Polity* 13 (1980), pp. 21–32.

Hill, Christopher. *Puritanism and Revolution* (London: Secker & Warburg, 1958).
Society and Puritanism in Pre-Revolutionary England (London: Secker & Warburg, 1964).
Intellectual Origins of the English Revolution (Oxford: Clarendon Press, 1965).

Hill, David Jayne. *World Organization as Affected by the Nature of the Modern State* (New York: Columbia University Press, 1911).

Hinsley, F. H. *Power and the Pursuit of Peace: Theory and Practice in the Relations Between States* (Cambridge: Cambridge University Press, 1963).

Hirst, Paul (ed.), *The Pluralist Theory of the State* (London: Routledge 1993).

Hitchcock E. V. (ed.), *The Life and Death of Sir Thomas More* (London: Early English Text Society, 1932).

Hobbes, Thomas. *Leviathan, Or the Matter, Forme, and Power of a Common-wealth Ecclesiasticall and Civil* (The 'Head' edition) (London, 1651).
Leviathan: Of van De Stoffe, Gedaente, ende Magt van de Kerckelyce Ende Wereltlycke Regeeringe (Amsterdam, 1667).
Thomae Hobbes Malmesburiensis Opera Philosophica Quae Latine Scripsit Omnia, ed. Sir William Molesworth, 5 vols. (London, 1839–45).
Elementorum philosophiae sectio prima de corpore, in Molesworth, *Opera Philosophica*, I (1839).
Leviathan, sive De Materia, Forma, & Potestate Civitatis Ecclesiasticae et Civilis, in Molesworth, *Opera Philosophica*, III (1841).
The Questions Concerning Liberty, Necessity, and Chance, ed. William Molesworth, *The English Works of Thomas Hobbes*, V (London, 1841).
Leviathan, ed. Michael Oakeshatt (Oxford: Basil Blackwell, 1946).
The Elements of Law Natural and Politic [1640], ed. Ferdinand Tönnies, intr. M. M. Goldsmith, 2nd edn (London: Frank Cass, 1969).
A Dialogue Between a Philosopher and a Student of the Common-Laws of England [1666], ed. Joseph Cropsey (Chicago: University of Chicago Press, 1971).
De cive ou Les fondements de la politique, trans. Samuel Sorbière (Paris: Sirey, 1981).
De Cive: the English Version, ed. Howard Warrender (Oxford: Clarendon Press, 1983).
De Cive: The Latin Version [1642], ed. Howard Warrender (Oxford: Clarendon Press, 1983).
Behemoth; or, the Long Parliament, ed. Ferdinand Tönnies (Chicago: University of Chicago Press, 1990).
Leviathan with selected variants from the Latin edition of 1668, ed. Edwin Curley (Indianapolis: Hackett, 1994).
Leviathan [1651], ed. Richard Tuck (Cambridge: Cambridge University Press, 1996).

On the Citizen, eds. Richard Tuck and Michael Silverthorne (Cambridge: Cambridge University Press, 1998).

Hoekstra, Kinch. 'Review of Quentin Skinner's *Reason and Rhetoric in the Philosophy of Hobbes*', *Filosofia Politica*, 11 (1997), pp. 139–43.

The Savage, the Citizen, and the Foole: the Compulsion for Civil Society in the Philosophy of Thomas Hobbes (unpublished D Phil., University of Oxford, 1998).

'The *De Facto* Turn in Hobbes's Political Philosophy', in Tom Sorell and Luc Foisneau (eds.), *Leviathan after 350 Years* (Oxford: Oxford University Press, 2004), pp. 33–73.

Hoffmann, George. 'The Montaigne Monopoly: Revising Montaigne's *Essais* under France's Privilege System', *Publications of the Modern Language Association* 108 (1993), pp. 308–19.

Höffner, J. *Kolonialismus und Evangelium. Spanische Kolonialethik im goldenen Zeitalter* (Trier: Paulinus Verlag, 1969).

Holmes, S. T. '*The Foundations of Modern Political Thought*: Vol. I, The Renaissance; Vol. II, The Age of Reformation', *American Political Science Review* 73 (1979), pp. 1133–5.

Hood, F. C. *The Divine Politics of Thomas Hobbes: an Interpretation of Leviathan* (Oxford: Clarendon Press, 1964).

Hooker, Richard. *Laws of Ecclesiastical Polity* (1593–7).

Höpfl, H. M. 'Orthodoxy and Reason of State', *History of Political Thought*, 23 (2002), pp. 211–37.

Jesuit Political Thought: the Society of Jesus and the State, c. 1540–1630 (Cambridge: Cambridge University Press, 2004).

Hornblower, Simon. *A Commentary on Thucydides*, I (Oxford: Clarendon Press, 1991).

Houston, Alan Craig. *Algernon Sidney and the Republican Heritage in England and America* (Princeton: Princeton University Press, 1991).

Hume, David. 'My Own Life', in Ernest Campbell Mossner (ed.), *The Life of David Hume* (London: Nelson, 1954).

Hüning, Dieter. '"Inter arma silent leges". Naturrecht, Staat und Völkerrecht bei Thomas Hobbes', in Rüdiger Voigt (ed.), *Der Leviathan* (Baden-Baden: Nomos, 2000).

Huxley, Andrew. 'The *Aphorismi* and *A Discourse of Laws*: Bacon, Cavendish, and Hobbes 1615–1620', *Historical Journal* 47 (2004), pp. 399–412.

Hyde, Edward. *A Brief View and Survey of the Dangerous and pernicious Errors to Church and State, in Mr. Hobbes's Book, Entitled Leviathan* (Oxford, 1676).

Israel, Jonathan. 'The Dutch Role in the Glorious Revolution', in Jonathan Israel (ed.), *The Anglo-Dutch Moment: Essays on the Glorious Revolution and its World Impact* (Cambridge: Cambridge University Press, 1991).

The Dutch Republic: its Rise, Greatness, and Fall 1477–1806 (Oxford: Oxford University Press, 1995).

James I. *Political Writings*, ed. Johann P. Sommerville (Cambridge: Cambridge University Press, 1994).

Janssen, D. 'Die Theorie des gerechten Krieges im Denken des Francisco de Vitoria', in F. Grünert and K. Seelmann (eds.), *Die Ordnung der Praxis. Neue Studien zur spanische Spätscholastik* (Tübingen: Niemeyer, 2001).

Jardine, Lisa. 'Before Clarissa: Erasmus, "Letters of Obscure Men", and epistolary fictions', in T. Van Houdt, J. Papy, G. Tournoy and C. Matheeussen (eds.), *Self-Presentation and Social Identification: the Rhetoric and Pragmatics of Letter Writing in Early Modern Times. Proceedings of the International Colloquium Leuven-Brussels, 24–28 May 2000*, Supplementa Humanistica Lovaniensia, 18 (Leuven: Brill, 2002), pp. 385–403.

Jedin, H. *A History of the Council of Trent*, trans. Ernest Graf, 2 vols. (London 1957–61).

Johnson, Laurie M. *Thucydides, Hobbes, and the Interpretation of Realism* (DeKalb: Northern Illinois University Press, 1993).

Jouannet, Emmanuelle. *Emer de Vattel et l'Emergence doctrinale du droit international classique* (Paris: Pedone, 1998).

Joyce, James. *Ulysses* (London: Bodley Head, 1960).

Kantorowicz, Ernst. *The King's Two Bodies: a Study in Medieval Political Theology* (Princeton: Princeton University Press, 1966).

Kaser, Max. *Ius Gentium* (Cologne: Böhlau, 1993).

Keene, Edward. *Beyond the Anarchical Society: Grotius, Colonialism and Order in World Politics* (Cambridge: Cambridge University Press, 2002).

Kelley, Donald R. *The Beginning of Ideology: Consciousness and Society in the French Reformation* (Cambridge: Cambridge University Press, 1981).

Kempshall, M. *The Common Good in Late Medieval Political Thought* (Oxford: Clarendon Press, 1999).

King, M. L. *Venetian Humanism in an Age of Patrician Dominance* (Princeton: Princeton University Press, 1986).

Kjellstrom, Peter. 'The Narrator and the Archaeologist: Modes of Meaning and Discourse in Quentin Skinner and Michel Foucault', *Statsventenskaplig Tidskrift* 98 (1995), pp. 21–41.

Koikkalainen, P. and Syrjämäki, S. 'On Encountering the Past: an Interview with Quentin Skinner', *Finnish Yearbook of Political Thought* 6 (2002) pp. 34–6.

Koskenniemi, Martti. *From Apology to Utopia: the Structure of International Legal Argument* (Helsinki: Lakimiesliiton Kustannus, 1989).

Krasner, Stephen D. 'Westphalia and All That', in Judith Goldstein and Robert O. Keohane (eds.), *Ideas and Foreign Policy: Beliefs, Institutions, and Political Change* (Ithaca: Cornell University Press, 1993).

Sovereignty: Organized Hypocrisy (Princeton: Princeton University Press, 1999).

Kretzmann, J. N., A. Kenny and J. Pinborg (eds.). *The Cambridge History of Later Medieval Philosophy* (Cambridge: Cambridge University Press, 1982).

Kristeller, P. O. 'Humanism and Scholasticism in the Italian Renaissance', *Byzantion: International Journal of Byzantine Studies*, American Series III, 17 (1944–5), pp. 346–74.

Studies in Renaissance Thought and Letters (Rome: Edizioni di Storia e Letteratura, 1956).

Renaissance Thought: the Classic, Scholastic and Humanistic Strains (New York: Harper and Row, 1961).

Lagarde, Georges de. *La naissance de l'esprit laïque au déclin du moyen âge*, 5 vols. (Paris: PUF, 1948).

Lamont, William. 'Arminianism: the Controversy that Never Was', in Nicholas Phillip-
    son and Quentin Skinner (eds.), *Political Discourse in Early Modern Britain*
    (Cambridge: Cambridge University Press, 1993), pp. 45–66.
van Langeraad, L. A. *Guido de Bray, zijn leven en werken* (Zierikzee, 1884).
Laski, H. J. 'International Government and National Sovereignty', in Geneva Institute
    of International Relations (ed.), *The Problems of Peace*, 1st ser. (London: Oxford
    University Press, 1927).
Leacock, Stephen. *Elements of Political Science* (Boston: Houghton, Mifflin, 1906).
Lefort, C. *Le travail de l'oeuvre. Machiavel* (Paris: Gallimard, 1972).
Lehmann, Hartmut and Günther Roth (eds.). *Weber's 'Protestant Ethic': Origins, Evi-
    dence, Contexts* (Cambridge: Cambridge University Press, 1993).
Leibniz, G. W. *Codex Iuris Gentium*, 'Praefatio' (1693), in *Leibniz: Political Writings*,
    ed. Patrick Riley 2nd edn (Cambridge: Cambridge University Press, 1988).
Leiser, Polycarp. *Regenten Spiegel, Gepredigt aus dem C i. Psalm, des königlichen
    Propheten Davids, auff gehaltenem Landtage zu Torgau dieses 1605. Jahres im
    Iunio* (Leipzig, 1605).
Leppin, Volker. *Antichrist und Jüngster Tag. Das Profil apokalyptischer Flugschriften-
    publizistik im deutschen Luthertum 1548–1618* (Gütersloh: Gütersloher Ver-
    lagshaus, 1999).
Lettinga, Neil. 'Covenant Theology Turned Upside Down: Henry Hammond and Car-
    oline Anglican Moralism: 1643–1660', *Sixteenth Century Journal* 24 (1993),
    pp. 653–69.
Limbrick, E. 'Métamorphose d'un philosophe en théologien', in Claude Blum (ed.),
    Montaigne, 'Apologie de Raimond Sebond'. De la 'Theologia' à la 'Théologie'
    (Paris: Honoré Champion, 1990).
Lintott, Andrew. *The Constitution of the Roman Republic* (Oxford: Oxford University
    Press, 1999).
Lipsius, Justus. *Saturnalium Sermonum libri duo, Qui de Gladiatoribus* (Antwerp,
    1585).
Lloyd, H. A. 'Constitutionalism', in J. H. Burns (ed.), *The Cambridge History of Political
    Thought* (Cambridge: Cambridge University Press, 1991).
Locke, John. *Two Treatises of Government*, ed. Peter Laslett (Cambridge: Cambridge
    University Press, 1988 [1960]).
Logan, George. *The Meaning of More's Utopia* (Princeton: Princeton University Press
    1983).
    'Interpreting *Utopia*', *Moreana* 31 (1994), pp. 203–58.
Lohr, C. 'The New Aristotle and "Science" in the Paris Arts Faculty (1255)', in O. M.
    Weijers and L. Holtz (eds.), *L'enseignement des disciplines à la Faculté des arts
    (Paris et Oxford, XIII–XV siècles)* (Turnhout: Brepols, 1997).
Lovejoy, A. O. *The Great Chain of Being: a Study in the History of an Idea* (Cambridge,
    Mass.: Harvard University Press, 1970).
Lupton, J. H. *The Utopia of Sir Thomas More* (Oxford: Clarendon Press, 1895).
Luther, Martin. *Martin Luther's sämmtliche Werke*, ed. E. L. Enders (Frankfurt:
    1883).
Lyotard, Jean-François. *La condition postmoderne. Rapport sur le savoir* (Paris: Editions
    de Minuit, 1979).

Mace, George. *Locke, Hobbes, and the Federalist Papers: an Essay on the Genesis of the American Political Heritage* (Carbondale and Edwardsville: Southern Illinois University Press, 1979).

Macpherson, C. B. *The Political Theory of Possessive Individualism* (Oxford: Oxford University Press, 1962).

Maddox, Graham. 'The Limits of neo-Roman Liberty', *History of Political Thought* 23 (2002), pp. 418–31.

Magnien, Catherine. 'Etienne Pasquier "familier" de Montaigne?', *Montaigne Studies* 13 (2001), pp. 277–313.

Malcolm, Noel. 'Hobbes and the European Republic of Letters', in Noel Malcolm, *Aspects of Hobbes* (Oxford: Oxford University Press, 2002).
    'Hobbes's Theory of International Relations', in Noel Malcolm, *Aspects of Hobbes* (Oxford: Oxford University Press, 2002).

Malnes, Raino. *The Hobbesian Theory of International Conflict* (Oslo: Scandinavian University Press, 1993).

Manent, P. 'Vers l'oeuvre et le monde: le Machiavel de Claude Lefort', in C. Habib and C. Mouchard (eds.), *La démocratie à l'oeuvre. Autour de Claude Lefort* (Paris: Editions Esprit, 1993).

Mariana, Juan de. *De Rege et Regis Institutione* (Toledo, 1599).

Marsh, John. *An Argument Or, Debate in Law* (London, 1642).

Marshall, John. *John Locke: Resistance, Religion and Responsibility* (Cambridge: Cambridge University Press, 1994).

Massingham, K. R. 'Skinner is as Skinner Does', *Politics* 16 (1981), pp. 124–9.

Mastnak, Tomaž. '*Behemoth*: Democratical and Religious Fanatics', *Filozofski vestnik* 24 (2003), pp. 139–68.

Mason, Roger. 'People Power? George Buchanan on Resistance and the Common Man', in Robert von Friedeburg (ed.), *Widerstandsrecht in der frühen Neuzeit. Erträge und Perspektiven der Forschung im deutsch-britischen Vergleich* (Berlin: Duncker & Humblot, 2001).

Matheron, Alexandre. 'The Theoretical Function of Democracy in Spinoza and Hobbes', in Warren Montag and Ted Stolze (eds.), *The New Spinoza* (Minneapolis: University of Minnesota Press, 1998).

Maurice, F. D. *Modern Philosophy* (London, 1862).

Maxwell, John. *Sacro-Sancta Regum Maiestas* (Oxford, 1644).

Mayer, T. *Thomas Starkey and the Commonwealth* (Cambridge: Cambridge University Press, 1989).

McCuaig, William. *Carlo Sigonio: the Changing World of the Late Renaissance* (Princeton: Princeton University Press, 1989).

McGrade, A. S. and J. Kilcullen (eds.). *William of Ockham: a Letter to the Friars Minor and other Writings* (Cambridge: Cambridge University Press, 1995).

Mendle, Michael. *Henry Parker and the English Civil War: the Political Thought of the Public's 'privado'* (Cambridge: Cambridge University Press, 1995).

Merula, Paulus. *Opera Posthuma* (Leiden, 1684).

Mesnard, Pierre. *L'essor de la Philosophie Politique au XVIe siècle*, 3rd edn (Paris: Editions Vrin, 1969).

Miethke, J. 'Die mittelalterlichen Universitäten und das geschriebene Wort', *Historische Zeitschrift* 251 (1990), pp. 1–44.

De potestate papae. Die päpstliche Amstcompetenz im Widerstreit der politischen Theorie von Thomas von Aquin bis Wilhelm von Ockham (Tübingen: Mohr Siebeck, 2000).

Millar, Fergus. *The Roman Republic in Political Thought* (Hanover, NH: University Press of New England, 2002).

Milton, John. *The Tenure of Kings and Magistrates*, in John Milton, *Political Writings*, ed. Martin Dzelzainis (Cambridge: Cambridge University Press, 1991).

Molina, Luis de. 'De bello', in *Luis de Molina y el derecho de la guerra*, ed. M. Fraga Iribarne (Madrid: CSIC, 1947).

Montaigne, Michel de. *The Complete Essays*, trans. M. A. Screech (Harmondsworth: Penguin, 1991).

Montesquieu, baron de (Charles Secondat). *L'Esprit des Lois*, ed. R. Derathé, 2 vols. (Paris: Garnier, 1973).

More, Thomas. *Utopia*, in *The Yale Edition of the Complete Works of St Thomas More*, ed. Edward Surtz and J. H. Hexter, 15 vols. (New Haven: Yale University Press, 1965), vol. IV.

Translations of Lucian, ed. C. R. Thompson, in *The Complete Works of St. Thomas More*, vol. III, part I (New Haven: Yale University Press, 1974).

The Latin Poems, eds. Clarence Miller et al., in *The Complete Works of St. Thomas More*, vol. III, part I (New Haven: Yale University Press, 1984).

Mulhall, S. and A. Swift. *Liberals and Communitarians*, 2nd edn (Oxford: Blackwell, 1996).

Najemy, John M. 'Baron's Machiavelli and Renaissance Republicanism', *American Historical Review* 113 (1996), pp. 119–29.

'Civic humanism and Florentine politics', in James Hankins (ed.), *Renaissance Civic Humanism: Reappraisals and Reflections* (Cambridge: Cambridge University Press, 2000).

Namier, L. B. *England in the Age of the American Revolution* (London: Macmillan, 1930).

Personalities and Power (London: Macmillan, 1955).

Navari, Cornelia. 'Hobbes and the "Hobbesian Tradition" in International Thought', *Millennium: Journal of International Studies* 11 (1982), pp. 203–22.

Nederman, C. J. 'Nature, Sin and the Origins of Society: the Ciceronian Tradition in Medieval Political Thought', *Journal of the History of Ideas* 49 (1988), pp. 3–26.

'Conciliarism and Constitutionalism: Jean Gerson and Medieval Political Thought', *History of European Ideas* 12 (1990), pp. 189–209.

'The Union of Wisdom and Eloquence Before the Renaissance: the Ciceronian Orator in Medieval Thought', *Journal of Medieval History* 18 (1992), pp. 75–95.

'Constitutionalism – Medieval and Modern: Against Neo-Figgisite Orthodoxy', *History of Political Thought* 17 (1996), pp. 179–94.

'The Meaning of "Aristotelianism" in Medieval Moral and Political Thought', *Journal of the History of Ideas* 57 (1996), pp. 563–85.

Nelson, Eric. 'Greek Nonsense in More's *Utopia*', *Historical Journal* 44 (2001), pp. 889–917.

The Greek Tradition in Republican Thought (Cambridge: Cambridge University Press, 2004).

Newman, W. L. *The Politics of Aristotle*, 4 vols. (Oxford: Clarendon Press, 1887–1902).

Noodt, Gerard. *Du Pouvoir des Souverains et de la Liberté de Conscience*, ed. Jean Barbeyrac (Amsterdam, 1714).

Norbrook, David. *Poetry and Politics in the English Renaissance* (London: Routledge, 1984).

'Lucan, Thomas May, and the Creation of a Republican Literary Culture', in Kevin Sharpe and Peter Lake (eds.), *Culture and Politics in Early Stuart England* (Stanford: Stanford University Press, 1993).

Writing the English Republic: Poetry, Rhetoric and Politics, 1627–1660 (Cambridge: Cambridge University Press, 1999).

Norton, Glyn P. *The Ideology and Language of Translation in Renaissance France and their Humanist Antecedents* (Geneva: Droz, 1984).

Nussbaum, Arthur. *A Concise History of the Law of Nations* (New York: Macmillan, 1947).

Oakeshott, Michael. 'The Foundations of Modern Political Thought', *Historical Journal* 23 (1980), pp. 449–53.

Oakley, Francis. 'On the Road from Constance to 1688', *Journal of British Studies* 2 (1962), pp. 1–31.

'Almain and Major: Conciliar Theory on the Eve of the Reformation', *American Historical Review* 70 (1965), pp. 673–90.

'Conciliarism at the Fifth Lateran Council?', *Church History* 41 (1972), pp. 452–63.

'Conciliarism in the Sixteenth Century: Jacques Almain Again', *Archiv für Reformationsgeschichte* 68 (1977), pp. 111–32.

'Nederman, Gerson, Conciliar Theory and Constitutionalism: *Sed contra*', *History of Political Thought* 16 (1995), pp. 1–19.

'"Anxieties of Influence": Skinner, Figgis, Conciliarism and Early Modern Constitutionalism', *Past and Present* 151 (1996), pp. 60–110.

The Conciliarist Tradition: Constitutionalism in the Catholic Church, 1300–1870 (Oxford: Oxford University Press, 2004).

Ockham, William of. *Ockham: Opera Politica*, vol. IV, ed. H. S. Offler (Oxford: Oxford University Press, 1997).

Olsen, Oliver K. *Matthias Flacius and the Survival of Luther's Reform* (Wiesbaden: Harrassowitz, 2002).

Osborne, Robin. *Demos: the Discovery of Classical Attica* (Cambridge: Cambridge University Press, 1985).

Osiander, Andreas. 'Sovereignty, International Relations, and the Westphalian Myth', *International Organization* 55 (2001), pp. 251–88.

Pace, Richard. *De fructu qui ex doctrina percipitur*, ed. and trans. F. Manley and R. S. Sylvester (New York: The Renaissance Society of America, 1967).

Packer, John W. *The Transformation of Anglicanism, 1643–1660, with Special Reference to Henry Hammond* (Manchester: Manchester University Press, 1969).

Pagden, A. R. D. *Lords of All the World: Ideologies of Empire in Spain, Britain and France c.1500–c.1800* (New Haven: Yale University Press, 1995).

Pallares-Burke, Maria Lucia. *The New History: Confessions and Conversations* (Cambridge: Polity Press, 2002).

Palonen, Kari. 'Liberty is too Precious a Concept to be Left to the Liberals', *Finnish Yearbook of Political Thought* 2 (1998), pp. 243–60.

Quentin Skinner: History, Politics, Rhetoric (Cambridge: Polity Press, 2003).

Die Entzauberung der Begriffe. Das Umschreiben der politischen Begriffe bei Quentin Skinner und Reinhart Koselleck (Münster: Lit Verlag, 2004).

'Political Theorizing as a Dimension of Political Life', *European Journal of Political Theory* 4 (2004), pp. 351–66.

Panichi, N. *Plutarchus Redivivus? La Boétie e i suoi interpreti* (Naples: Vivarium, 1999).

Panvinio, Onofrio. *Reipublicae Romanae Commentariorum libri III* (Venice, 1558).

Parker, Henry. *Observations upon Some of His Majesties Late Answers and Expresses* (London, 1642).

Jus Populi. Or, a Discourse Wherein Clear Satisfaction is Given, as well Concerning the Right of Subiects, as the Right of Princes (London, 1644).

Parry, Adam Milman. *Logos and Ergon in Thucydides* (New York: Arno Press, 1981).

Patten, Alan. 'The Republican Critique of Liberalism', *British Journal of Political Science* 26 (1996), pp. 25–44.

Peltonen, M. *Classical Humanism and Republicanism in English Political Thought, 1570–1640* (Cambridge: Cambridge University Press, 1995).

Périon, Joachim. *De Romanorum et Graecorum Magistratibus Libri Tres* (Paris, 1559; Strasbourg, 1607).

Persons, Robert. *A Conference concerning the Next Succession* (London, 1594/5).

A Treatise Tending to Mitigation Towardes Catholicke Subjectes in England (London, 1607).

Pettit, P. 'The Freedom of the City: a Republican Ideal', in A. Hamlin and P. Pettit (eds.), *The Good Polity* (Oxford: Blackwell, 1989).

'Liberalism and Republicanism', *Australian Journal of Political Science* 28 (1993), pp. 162–89.

'Negative Liberty, Liberal and Republican', *European Journal of Philosophy* 1 (1993), pp. 15–38.

Republicanism: a Theory of Freedom and Government (Oxford: Clarendon Press, 1997).

Petty, William. *The Petty Papers*, ed. Marquis of Lansdowne, II (London: Constable, 1927).

Plamenatz, J. *Man and Society: a Critical Examination of Some Important Social and Political Theories from Machiavelli to Marx*, 2 vols. (London: Longman, 1963).

Plumb, J. H. *The Growth of Political Stability in England, 1675–1725* (London: Macmillan, 1967).

Pocock, J. G. A. *The Ancient Constitution and the Feudal Law: A Study of English Historical Thought in the Seventeenth Century* (Cambridge: Cambridge University Press, 1957); reissued with a retrospect (Cambridge: Cambridge University Press, 1987).

'The History of Political Thought: a Methodological Enquiry', in Peter Laslett and W. G. Runciman (eds.), *Philosophy, Politics and Society, Second Series* (Oxford: Basil Blackwell, 1962).

'Time, Institutions and Action: an Essay on Traditions and their Understanding', in Preston King and B. C. Parekh (eds.), *Politics and Experience: Essays presented to Michael Oakeshott* (Cambridge: Cambridge University Press, 1968).

Politics, Language, and Time: Essays in Political Thought and History (New York: Atheneum, 1971).

'Verbalising a Political Act: towards a Politics of Language', *Political Theory* 1 (1973), pp. 3–17.

'Political Ideas as Historical Events: Political Philosophers as Historical Actors', in Melvin Richter (ed.), *Political Theory and Political Education* (Princeton: Princeton University Press, 1980).

'The Reconstruction of Discourse: towards the Historiography of Political Thought', *Modern Language Notes* 96 (1981), pp. 959–80.

Virtue, Commerce and History: Essays on Political Thought and History, Chiefly in the Eighteenth Century (Cambridge: Cambridge University Press, 1985).

'Virtues, Rights and Manners: a Model for Historians of Political Thought', in J. G. A. Pocock, *Virtue, Commerce and History* (Cambridge: Cambridge University Press, 1985).

'The Concept of a Language and the *métier d'historien*: some Considerations on Practice', in A. Pagden (ed.), *The Languages of Political Theory in Early Modern Europe* (Cambridge: Cambridge University Press, 1987).

'Texts as Events: Reflections on the History of Political Thought', in Kevin Sharpe and Steven N. Zwicker (eds.), *Politics of Discourse: the Literature and History of Seventeenth-Century England* (Los Angeles: University of California Press, 1987).

'Foundations of Modernity in Early Modern Historical Thinking', forthcoming in *Intellectual History Review* 19 (2007).

Barbarism and Religion, vol. III: *The First Decline and Fall* (Cambridge: Cambridge University Press, 2003).

The Machiavellian Moment: Florentine Political Thought and the Atlantic Republican Tradition: With a New Afterword by the Author [1975]. (Princeton: Princeton University Press, 2003).

Pocock, J. G. A. (ed.). *The Political Works of James Harrington* (Cambridge: Cambridge University Press, 1977).

Harrington: Oceana and a System of Politics (Cambridge: Cambridge University Press, 1992).

Ponet, John. *A shorte Treatise of Politike Power* (Menston: Scholor Press, 1967).

Preger, Wilhelm. *Matthias Flacius Illyricus und seine Zeit* (Erlangen, 1859–1861).

Pufendorf, Samuel. *The Present State of Germany* [1667], trans. Edmund Bohun (London, 1690).

Of the Law of Nature and Nations [1672], trans. Basil Kennett (Oxford, 1703); 4th edn (London, 1729).

Quintilian, *Institutio oratoria*, ed. and trans. H. E. Butter, 4 vols. (London, 1920–22).

Rachel, Samuel. *De Jure Naturae et Gentium Dissertationes* (Kiel, 1676).

Rahe, Paul. 'Situating Machiavelli', in James Hankins (ed.), *Renaissance Civic Humanism: Reappraisals and Reflections* (Cambridge: Cambridge University Press, 2000).

Raitere, M. N. 'More's *Utopia* and *The City of God*', *Studies in the Renaissance* 20 (1973), pp. 144–68.

Rawls, J. *Political Liberalism* (New York: Columbia University Press, 1993).

'The Priority of Right and Ideas of the Good', *Philosophy and Public Affairs* 17 (1988), pp. 151–76.

Renaudet, Augustin. *Préréforme et Humanisme à Paris pendant les premières guerres d'Italie: 1496–1517* (Paris, 1953).

Reynolds, Noel B. and John L. Hilton. 'Thomas Hobbes and the Authorship of the *Horae Subsecivae*', in *Thomas Hobbes, Three Discourses: a Critical Modern Edition of a Newly Identified Work of the Young Hobbes*, ed. Noel B. Reynolds and Arlene W. Saxonhouse (Chicago: University of Chicago Press, 1995).

Richter, M. *The History of Political and Social Concepts* (Oxford: Oxford University Press, 1995).

Rigolot, F. 'D'une Théologie "pour les dames" à une Apologie "per le donne"', in Claude Blum (ed.), *Montaigne, 'Apologie de Raimond Sebond'. De la 'Theologia' à la 'Théologie'* (Paris: Honoré Champion, 1990).

Robertson, George Croom. *Hobbes* (Edinburgh, 1886).

Rodgers, D. T. 'Republicanism: the Career of a Concept', *The Journal of American History* 79 (1992), pp. 11–38.

Rogers, E. *The Correspondence of Thomas More* (Princeton: Princeton University Press, 1947).

van Roosbroeck, R. 'Wunderjahr oder Hungerjahr? -Antwerpen 1566', in Franz Petri (ed.), *Kirche und gesellschaftlicher Wandel in Deutschen und Niederländischen Städten der werdenden Neuzeit* (Cologne/Vienna: Böhlau, 1980).

Rosemann, P. W. *Understanding Scholastic Thought with Foucault* (New York: St Martin's Press, 1999).

Rousseau, Jean–Jacques. *Du Contrat social*, in *Œuvres completes*, ed. Bernard Gagnebin and Marcel Raymond, vol. III (Paris: Gallimard, 1964).

Rubinstein, N. 'Le allegorie di Ambrogio Lorenzetti nella Sala della Pace e il pensiero politico del suo tempo', *Rivista Storica Italiana* 120 (1997), pp. 781–99.

Rudolph, Julia. *Revolution by Degrees: James Tyrrell and Whig Political Thought in the Late Seventeenth Century* (New York: Palgrave Macmillan, 2002).

Rummel, Erika. *The Humanist-Scholastic Debate in the Renaissance and Reformation* (Cambridge, MA.: Harvard University Press, 1995).

Runciman, David. *Pluralism and the Personality of the State* (Cambridge: Cambridge University Press, 1997).

Salmon, J. H. M. *The French Religious Wars in English Political Thought* (Oxford: Oxford University Press, 1959).

'The Beginning of Ideology: Consciousness and Society in the French Reformation: D. R. Kelley', *History of European Ideas* 4 (1983), pp. 325–30.

'An Alternative Theory of Popular Resistance: Buchanan, Rossaeus, and Locke', in John Salmon, *Renaissance and Revolt: Essays in the Intellectual and Social History of Early Modern France* (Cambridge: Cambridge University Press, 1987).

'Catholic Resistance Theory', in J. H. Burns (ed.), *The Cambridge History of Political Thought* (Cambridge: Cambridge University Press, 1991).

Salomonio, Mario. *De Principatu* (Rome, 1544).

Samuel, Raphael. 'British Marxist Historians, 1880–1980', *New Left Review* 120 (1980), pp. 21–96.

Sasso, G. *Niccolò Machiavelli*, 2 vols. (Bologna: Il Mulino, 1993).

Scattola, Merio. 'Before and After Natural Law: Models of Natural Law in Ancient and Modern Times', in T. J. Hochstrasser and Peter Schröder (eds.), *Early Modern Natural Law Theories: Contexts and Strategies in the Early Enlightenment* (Dordrecht: Kluwer, 2003).

Schmidt, Brian C. *The Political Discourse of Anarchy: a Disciplinary History of International Relations* (Albany: State University of New York Press, 1998).

'Together Again: Reuniting Political Theory and International Relations Theory', *British Journal of Politics and International Relations* 4 (2002), pp. 115–40.

Schmitt, Carl. *The Leviathan in the State Theory of Thomas Hobbes: Meaning and Failure of a Political Symbol* [1938], trans. George Schwab and Erna Hilfstein (Westport, CT: Greenwood Press 1996).

Schoek, R. J. 'More, Plutarch and King Agis', *Philological Quarterly* 35 (1956), pp. 366–75.

Schorn-Schütte, Luise. 'Obrigkeitskritik im Luthertum? Anlässe und Rechtfertigungsmuster im ausgehenden 16. und 17. Jahrhundert', in Michael Erbe et al. (eds.), *Querdenken. Dissens und Toleranz im Wandel der Geschichte* (Mannheim: Palatium Verlag in J & J, 1995).

Evangelische Geistlichkeit in der Frühneuzeit. Deren Anteil an der Entfaltung frühmoderner Staatlichkeit und Gesellschaft (Gütersloh: Gütersloher Verlagshaus, 1996).

'Die Drei-Stände-Lehre im reformatorischen Umbruch', in Bernd Moeller, *Die frühe Reformation in Deutschland als Umbruch* (Gütersloh: Gütersloher Verlagshaus, 1998).

'Obrigkeitskritik und Widerstandsrecht. Die *politica christiana* als Legitimitätsgrundlage', in Luise Schorn-Schütte (ed.), *Aspekte der politischen Kommunikation im Europa des 16. und 17. Jahrhunderts, Historische Zeitschrift*, Beiheft 39 (Munich: R. Oldenbourg Verlag, 2004).

Schröder, Peter. 'The Constitution of the Holy Roman Empire after 1648: Samuel Pufendorf's Assessment in his Monzambano', *The Historical Journal* 42 (1999), pp. 961–83.

'Natural Law, Sovereignty and International Law: a Comparative Perspective', in Ian Hunter and David Saunders (eds.), *Natural Law and Civil Sovereignty: Moral Right and State Authority in Early Modern Political Thought* (New York: Palgrave, 2002).

Scott, Jonathan. 'The Law of War: Grotius, Sidney, Locke and the Political Theory of Rebellion', *History of Political Thought* 13 (1992), pp. 565–85.

England's Troubles: Seventeenth-Century English Political Instability in European Context (Cambridge: Cambridge University Press, 2000).

Algernon Sidney and the Restoration Crisis, 1677–1683 (Cambridge: Cambridge University Press, 2002).

Seigel, J. E. '"Civic Humanism" or Ciceronian Rhetoric? the Culture of Petrarch and Bruni', *Past and Present* 34 (1966), pp. 3–48.

Sellers, M. N. S. *American Republicanism: Roman Ideology in the United States Constitution* (London: Macmillan, 1994).

The Sacred Fire of Liberty: Republicanism, Liberalism and the Law (London: Macmillan, 1998).

Seneca. *Epistulae Morales*, trans. Richard Gummere, *Loeb Classical Library*, vol. LXXVII (Cambridge, Mass.: Harvard University Press).

Senellart, M. 'Républicanisme, bien commun et liberté individuelle: le modèle machiavélien selon Quentin Skinner', *Revue d'éthique et de théologie morale, 'Le Supplément'* 193 (1995), pp. 27–64.

Sfez, G. *Leo Strauss, lecteur de Machiavel. La modernité du mal* (Paris: Ellipses, 2003).

Sharrock, Robert. *Hypothesis Ethike, De Officiis Secundum Naturae Ius* (Oxford, 1660).

Shklar, Judith. '*The Foundations of Modern Political Thought*. Volume I. The Renaissance. Volume II: The Age of the Reformation', *Political Theory* 7 (1979), pp. 549–58.

Sidney, Algernon. *Discourses Concerning Government* (London, 1699).

Sidney, Philip. *Miscellaneous prose*, ed. Katherine Duncan-Jones and Jan van Dorsten (Oxford: Clarendon Press, 1973).

The Countess of Pembroke's Arcadia (The Old Arcadia), ed. Jean Robertson (Oxford: Clarendon Press, 1973).

The Countess of Pembroke's Arcadia (The New Arcadia), ed. Victor Skretkowicz (Oxford: Clarendon Press, 1987).

Simon, Yves. *Philosophy of Democratic Government* (Chicago: University of Chicago Press, 1951).

Simpson, Peter L. Phillips. *A Philosophical Commentary on the Politics of Aristotle* (Chapel Hill, NC: University of North Carolina Press, 1998).

Skinner, Quentin. 'More's *Utopia*', *Past and Present* 38 (1967), pp. 153–68.

'Conventions and the Understanding of Speech Acts', *The Philosophical Quarterly* 20 (1970), pp. 118–38.

'Some Problems in the Analysis of Political Thought and Action', *Political Theory* 2 (1974), pp. 277–303.

The Foundations of Modern Political Thought, 2 vols. (Cambridge: Cambridge University Press, 1978).

Machiavelli (Oxford: Oxford University Press, 1981).

'Machiavelli on the Maintenance of Liberty', *Politics* 18 (1983), pp. 3–15.

'The Idea of Negative Liberty: Philosophical and Historical Perspectives' in R. Rorty, J. B. Schneewind and Quentin Skinner (eds.), *Philosophy in History* (Cambridge: Cambridge University Press, 1984).

'The Paradoxes of Political Liberty' in S. McMurrin (ed.), *The Tanner Lectures on Human Values*, 7 (Salt Lake City: University of Utah Press, 1986).

'Sir Thomas More's *Utopia* and the Language of Renaissance Humanism', in A. Pagden (ed.). *The Languages of Political Theory in Early-Modern Europe* (Cambridge: Cambridge University Press, 1987).

'Meaning and Understanding in the History of Ideas', in James Tully (ed.), *Meaning and Context: Quentin Skinner and His Critics* (Cambridge: Polity Press, 1988).

'Motives, Intentions and the Interpretation of Texts', in James Tully (ed.), *Meaning and Context: Quentin Skinner and His Critics* (Cambridge: Polity Press, 1988).

'Political Philosophy', in C. B. Schmitt (ed.), *The Cambridge History of Renaissance Philosophy* (Cambridge: Cambridge University Press, 1988).

'A Reply to my Critics', in James Tully (ed.), *Meaning and Context: Quentin Skinner and his Critics* (Cambridge: Polity Press, 1988).

'Il concetto inglese di libertà', *Filosofia politica* 3 (1989), pp. 77–102.

'The State', in T. Ball, J. Farr and R. L. Hanson (eds.), *Political Innovation and Conceptual Change* (Cambridge: Cambridge University Press, 1989).

'Machiavelli's Discorsi and the Pre-Humanist Origins of Republican Ideas', in G. Bock, Quentin Skinner and M. Viroli (eds.), *Machiavelli and Republicanism* (Cambridge: Cambridge University Press, 1990).

'The Republican Ideal of Political Liberty', in G. Bock, Quentin Skinner and M. Viroli (eds.), *Machiavelli and Republicanism* (Cambridge: Cambridge University Press, 1990).

'Who are "We"?: Ambiguities of the Modern Self', *Inquiry* 34 (1991), pp. 133–53.

'On Justice, the Common Good and the Priority of Liberty', in C. Mouffe (ed.), *Dimensions of Radical Democracy* (London: Verso, 1992).

'Two Concepts of Citizenship', *Tijdschrift voor Filosofie* 55 (1993), pp. 403–19.

Reason and Rhetoric in the Philosophy of Hobbes (Cambridge: Cambridge University Press, 1996).

Liberty before Liberalism (Cambridge: Cambridge University Press, 1998).

'Machiavelli's Political Morality', *European Review* 6 (1998), pp. 321–5.

'Hobbes and the Purely Artificial Person of the State', *The Journal of Political Philosophy* 7 (1999), pp. 1–29.

'The Rise of, Challenge to, and Prospects for a Collingwoodian Approach to the History of Political Thought', in Dario Castiglione and Iain Hampsher-Monk (eds.), *The History of Political Thought in National Context* (Cambridge: Cambridge University Press, 2001).

Visions of Politics, 3 vols. (Cambridge: Cambridge University Press, 2002).

'Ambrogio Lorenzetti: the Artist as Political Philosopher', in Quentin Skinner, *Visions of Politics*, II (Cambridge: Cambridge University Press, 2002).

'A Third Concept of Liberty', *Proceedings of the British Academy* 117 (2002), pp. 237–68.

'Classical Liberty and the Coming of the English Civil War', in Martin van Gelderen and Quentin Skinner (eds.), *Republicanism: a Shared European Heritage*, II (Cambridge: Cambridge University Press, 2002).

'From the State of Princes to the Person of the State', in Quentin Skinner, *Visions of Politics*, II (Cambridge: Cambridge University Press, 2002).

'History and Ideology in the English Revolution' in Quentin Skinner, *Visions of Politics*, III (Cambridge: Cambridge University Press, 2002).

'Hobbes and the Purely Artificial Person of the State', in Quentin Skinner, *Visions of Politics*, III (Cambridge: Cambridge University Press, 2002).

'Humanism, Scholasticism and Popular Sovereignty' in Quentin Skinner, *Visions of Politics*, II (Cambridge: Cambridge University Press, 2002).

'Interpretation and the Understanding of Speech Acts', in Quentin Skinner, *Visions of Politics*, I (Cambridge: Cambridge University Press, 2002).

'John Milton and the politics of slavery', in Quentin Skinner, *Visions of Politics*, II (Cambridge: Cambridge University Press, 2002).

'Liberty and the English Civil War', in Quentin Skinner, *Visions of Politics*, II (Cambridge: Cambridge University Press, 2002).

'Machiavelli on Virtù and the Maintenance of Liberty', in Quentin Skinner, *Visions of Politics*, II (Cambridge: Cambridge University Press, 2002).

'Meaning and Understanding in the History of Ideas', in Quentin Skinner, *Visions of Politics*, I (Cambridge: Cambridge University Press, 2002).

'Retrospect: Studying Rhetorical and Conceptual Change', in Quentin Skinner, *Visions of Politics*, I (Cambridge: Cambridge University Press, 2002).

'The Idea of a Cultural Lexicon', in Quentin Skinner, *Visions of Politics*, I (Cambridge: Cambridge University Press, 2002).

'The Idea of Negative Liberty: Machiavellian and Modern Perspectives', in Quentin Skinner, *Visions of Politics*, II (Cambridge: Cambridge University Press, 2002).

'The Practice of History and the Cult of the Fact', in Quentin Skinner, *Visions of Politics*, I (Cambridge: Cambridge University Press, 2002).

'The Principles and Practices of Opposition: the Case of Bolingbroke versus Walpole', in Quentin Skinner, *Visions of Politics*, III (Cambridge: Cambridge University Press, 2002).

'The Rediscovery of Republican Values', in Quentin Skinner, *Visions of Politics*, II (Cambridge: Cambridge University Press, 2002).

'Thomas More's *Utopia* and the Virtue of True Nobility', in Quentin Skinner, *Visions of Politics*, II (Cambridge: Cambridge University Press, 2002).

'"Social Meaning" and the Explanation of Social Action', in Quentin Skinner, *Visions of Politics*, I (Cambridge: Cambridge University Press, 2002).

'States and the Freedom of Citizens', in Quentin Skinner and Bo Stråth (eds.), *States and Citizens* (Cambridge: Cambridge University Press, 2003).

'Hobbes on Representation', *European Journal of Philosophy* 13 (2005), pp. 155–84.

Smith, Sir Thomas. *De republica Anglorum* (Menston: Scholar Press, 1970).

Sommer, Wolfgang. *Gottesfurcht und Fürstenherrschaft* (Göttingen: Vandenhoeck & Ruprecht, 1988).

'Obrigkeitskritik und die politische Funktion der Frömmigkeit im deutschen Luthertum des konfessionellen Zeitalters', in Robert von Friedeburg (ed.), *Widerstandsrecht in der frühen Neuzeit. Erträge und Perspektiven der Forschung im deutsch-britischen Vergleich* (Berlin: Duncker & Humblot, 2001).

Sorgi, Giuseppe. *Quale Hobbes? Dalla paura alla rappresentanza* (Milan: Franco Angeli, 1989).

Soto, Domingo de. *In causa pauperum deliberatio* (ed. together with his *Relectio de ratione tegendi et detegendi secretum* (Salamanca, 1566)).

'Deliberación en la causa de los pobres' in *El gran debate sobre los pobres en el siglo XVI. Domingo de Soto y Juan de Robles 1545*, ed. Felix Santolaria Sierra (Barcelona: Ariel, 2003).

De justitia et iure. De la justicia y del derecho (bilingual Latin-Spanish edition, Madrid: Instituto de Estudios Politicos, 1967).

Specht, R. 'Spanisches Naturrecht. Klassik und Gegenwart', *Zeitschrift für philosophische Forschung* 41 (1987), pp. 169–82.

Spinoza, Benedict de. *Tractatus Politicus*, in Spinoza, *Opera Posthuma* (n. p., 1677).

Spitz, J.-F. *La liberté politique. Essai de généalogie conceptuelle* (Paris: PUF, 1995).

'Le républicanisme, une troisième voie entre libéralisme et communautarisme?', *Le Banquet* 2 (1995), pp. 215–38.

Stapleton, Julia. *Englishness and the Study of Politics: the Social and Political Thought of Ernest Barker* (Cambridge: Cambridge University Press, 1994).

Stephen, James Fitzjames. *Horae Sabbaticae*, 2nd ser. (London, 1892).

Stephen, Leslie. *Hobbes* (London: Macmillan, 1904).

Stewart, Alan. *Philip Sidney: A Double Life* (London: Chatto & Windus, 2000).

Stone, Norman. 'The Religious Background to Max Weber', in W. J. Sheils (ed.), *Persecution and Toleration* (Oxford: Blackwell, 1984).

Starkey, Thomas. *A Dialogue between Pole and Lupset*, ed. T. F. Mayer (London: Royal Historical Society, 1989), vol. 37.

Strauss, Leo. *Thoughts on Machiavelli* (Glencoe: The Free Press, 1958).

Suárez, Francisco. *De legibus ac Deo legislatore* (Coimbra, 1612).

Sullivan, Vickie B. *Machiavelli, Hobbes, and the Formation of a Liberal Republicanism in England* (Cambridge: Cambridge University Press, 2004).

Talamo, R. 'Quentin Skinner interprete di Machiavelli', *CroceVia* 3 (1997), pp. 80–101.

Tarcov, Nathan. 'Quentin Skinner's Method and Machiavelli's *Prince*', in James Tully (ed.), *Meaning and Context: Quentin Skinner and His Critics* (Cambridge: Polity Press, 1988).

Tarlton, C. D. 'Historicity, Meaning and Revisionism in the Study of Political Thought', *History and Theory* 12 (1973), pp. 307–28.

Teschke, Benno. *The Myth of 1648: Class, Geopolitics and the Making of Modern International Relations* (London: Verso, 2003).

Thomas, Keith. *New York Review of Books*, 17 May 1979, p. 27.

Thucydides. *Eight Bookes of the Peloponnesian Warre*, trans. Thomas Hobbes (London, 1629).

Tierney, Brian. *Foundations of the Conciliar Theory: The Contribution of the Medieval Canonists from Gratian to the Great Schism* (Cambridge: Cambridge University Press, 1955).

Religion, Law, and the Growth of Constitutional Thought, 1150–1650 (Cambridge: Cambridge University Press, 1982).

Todd, M. *Christian Humanism and the Puritan Social Order* (Cambridge: Cambridge University Press, 1987).

Tönnies, Ferdinand. *Hobbes, Leben und Lehre* (Stuttgart, 1896).

Thomas Hobbes, der Man und der Denker (Osterwieck: Zickfeldt, 1912).

Trevor-Roper, Hugh. 'The Great Tew Circle', in Hugh Trevor-Roper (ed.), *Catholics, Anglicans and Puritans: Seventeenth Century Essays* (London: Fontana, 1989).

Tricaud, Francois. '"Homo homini Deus", "Homo homini Lupus": Recherche des Sources des deux Formules de Hobbes', in Reinhart Koselleck and Roman Schnur (eds.), *Hobbes-Forschungen* (Berlin: Duncker and Humblot, 1969).

Trinkaus, C. 'Review of *The Foundations of Modern Political Thought*' *American Historical Review* 85 (1980), pp. 79–80.

Trinquet, Roger. 'Montaigne et la divulgation du *Contr'un*', *Revue d'Histoire littéraire de la France* 64 (1964), pp. 1–12.

Troeltsch, Ernst. *The Social Teaching of the Christian Churches* (London: Macmillan, 1931).

Tuck, Richard. *Hobbes* (Oxford: Oxford University Press, 1989).

Philosophy and Government, 1572–1651 (Cambridge: Cambridge University Press, 1993).

The Rights of War and Peace: Political Thought and the International Order from Grotius to Kant (Oxford: Oxford University Press, 1999).

'The Utopianism of Leviathan', in Tom Sorell and Luc Foisneau (eds.), *Leviathan after 350 Years* (Oxford: Oxford University Press, 2004).

Tully, James. 'The Pen is a Mighty Sword: Quentin Skinner's Analysis of Politics', in James Tully (ed.), *Meaning and Context: Quentin Skinner and his Critics* (Cambridge: Polity Press, 1988).

An Approach to Political Philosophy: Locke in Contexts (Cambridge: Cambridge University Press, 1993).

Strange Multiplicity: Constitutionalism in an Age of Diversity (Cambridge: Cambridge University Press, 1999).

Understanding Imperialism Today (Cambridge: Cambridge University Press, forthcoming).

(ed.) *Meaning and Context: Quentin Skinner and His Critics* (Cambridge: Polity Press, 1988).

Tuplin, Christopher. 'Imperial Tyranny: some Reflections on a Classical Greek Political Metaphor', in P. A. Cartledge and F. D. Harvey (eds.), *Crux: Essays Presented to G. E. M. de Ste. Croix* (Exeter: Imprint Academic, 1985), pp. 348–75.

Übl, K. *Engelbert von Admont: Ein Gelehrter im Spannungsfeld zwischen Aristotelismus und christliche Überlieferung* (Vienna: Oldenbourg, 2000).

Ullmann, W. *A Short History of the Papacy in the Middle Ages* (London: Methuen, 1972).

Van Kley, Dale. 'Piety and Politics in the Century of Lights', in Mark Goldie and Robert Wokler (eds.), *The Cambridge History of Eighteenth-Century Political Thought* (Cambridge: Cambridge University Press, 2006), pp. 110–46.

Vattel, Emer de. *The Law of Nations or the Principles of Natural Law Applied to the Conduct and to the Affairs of Nations and of Sovereigns* [1758], trans. Charles G. Fenwick (Washington, DC: Carnegie Institution, 1916).

Vatter, M. E. *Between Form and Event: Machiavelli's Theory of Political Freedom* (Dordrecht: Kluwer, 2000).

Vázquez de Menchaca, Fernando. *Controversiarum Illustrium aliarumque usu frequentium libri tres* [1564], ed. Fidel Rodriguez Alcalde (Valladolid: Valverde, 1931).

Vettori, Pietro. *Politicorum libri octo ex Dion. Lambini & P. Victoriii interpretationibus* (Basle, 1582).

Vickers, Brian. *In Defence of Rhetoric* (Oxford: Clarendon Press, 1988).

Viroli, M. *From Politics to Reason of State* (Cambridge: Cambridge University Press, 1992).

Vitoria, Francisco de. 'On Civil Power', in *Vitoria: Political Writings*, ed. A. Pagden and J. Lawrance (Cambridge: Cambridge University Press, 1991).

'On Dietary Laws, or Self-Restraint', in *Vitoria: Political Writings*, ed. A. Pagden and J. Lawrance (Cambridge: Cambridge University Press, 1991).

'On the American Indians', in *Vitoria: Political Writings*, ed. A. Pagden and J. Lawrance (Cambridge: Cambridge University Press, 1991).

'On the Power of the Church', in *Vitoria: Political Writings*, ed. A. Pagden and J. Lawrance (Cambridge: Cambridge University Press, 1991).

Walker, R. B. J. *Inside/Outside: International Relations as Political Theory* (Cambridge: Cambridge University Press, 1993).

Walker, William. '*Paradise Lost* and the Forms of Government', *History of Political Thought* 22 (2001), pp. 270–91.

Walther, M. 'Potestas multitudinis bei Suárez und potentia multitudinis bei Spinoza', in F. Grünert and K. Seelmann (eds.), *Die Ordnung der Praxis. Neue Studien zur spanische Spätscholastik* (Tübingen: Niemeyer, 2001).

Walzer, Michael. *The Revolution of the Saints* (London: Weidenfeld and Nicolson, 1966).

Ward, Robert. *An Enquiry into the Foundation and History of the Law of Nations in Europe, From the Time of the Greeks and Romans, to the Age of Grotius*, 2 vols. (London, 1795).

Weber, Max. *Economy and Society: an Outline of Interpretive Sociology*, ed. Guenther Roth and Claus Wittich, 2 vols. (Berkeley: University of California Press, 1978).

  The Protestant Ethic and the 'Spirit' of Capitalism and Other Writings [1904] (New York: Penguin Books, 2002).

Weijers, O. M. *Le maniement du savoir. Pratiques intellectuelles à l'époque des premières universités* (Turnhout: Brepols, 1996).

Weijers, O. M., and L. Holtz (eds.). *L'enseignement des disciplines à la Faculté des arts (Paris et Oxford, XIII–XV siècles)* (Turnhout: Brepols, 1997).

Weiss, Matthias. *Die Politica Christiana. Grundzüge einer chrisltichen Staatslehre im Alten Reich* (Frankfurt: Ph.D. Dissertation, 2005).

Whewell, William. *Lectures on the History of Moral Philosophy in England* (London, 1852).

Wieland, G. *Ethica – scientia practica. Die Anfänge der philosophischen Ethik im 13. Jahrhundert* (Münster: Aschendorff, 1981).

Wight, Martin. 'An Anatomy of International Thought', *Review of International Studies* 13 (1987), pp. 221–7.

  International Theory: the Three Traditions, eds. Gabriele Wight and Brian Porter (Leicester: Continuum 1991).

Williams, Howard. *International Relations in Political Theory* (Basingstoke: Macmillan, 1990).

  Kant's Critique of Hobbes: Sovereignty and Cosmopolitanism (Cardiff: University of Wales Press, 2003).

Willoughby, Westel Woodbury. 'The Juristic Conception of the State', *American Political Science Review* 12 (1918), pp. 192–208.

Wilson, James. 'Lectures on Law' (1790–91), in *The Works of James Wilson*, ed. Robert Green McCloskey, 2 vols. (Cambridge, MA: Harvard University Press, 1967).

Wittgenstein, Ludwig. *Philosophical Investigations*, trans. G. E. M. Anscombe (Oxford: Oxford University Press, 1968).

Wokler, Robert. 'The Professoriate of Political Thought in England since 1914', in Dario Castiglione and Iain Hampsher-Monk (eds.), *History of Political Thought in National Context* (New York: Cambridge University Press, 2001).

Woolfson, J. *Padua and the Tudors: English Students in Italy, 1485–1603* (Cambridge: James Clarke and Co., 1998).

  'Between Bruni and Hobbes: Aristotle's Politics in Tudor Intellectual Culture', in J. Woolfson (ed.), *Reassessing Tudor Humanism* (Basingstoke: Palgrave Macmillan, 2002).

  (ed.) *Reassessing Tudor Humanism* (Basingstoke: Palgrave Macmillan, 2002).

Woolsey, Theodore D. *Introduction to the Study of International Law, Devised as an Aid in Teaching, and in Historical Studies* (Boston, 1860).

Worden, Blair. 'The Commonwealth Kidney of Algernon Sidney', *The Journal of British Studies* 24 (1985), pp. 1–40.

'English Republicanism', in J. H. Burns (ed.), *The Cambridge History of Political Thought* (Cambridge: Cambridge University Press, 1991).

'Republicanism and the Restoration, 1660–1683', in David Wootton (ed.), *Republicanism, Liberty, and Commercial Society, 1649–1776* (Stanford: Stanford University Press, 1994).

The Sound of Virtue: Philip Sidney's Arcadia and Elizabethan Politics (New Haven: Yale University Press, 1996).

'Factory of the Revolution', *London Review of Books*, 5 February 1998, pp. 13–15.

'Republicanism, Regicide and Republic: the English Experience', in Martin van Gelderen and Quentin Skinner (eds.), *Republicanism: a Shared European Heritage*, I (Cambridge: Cambridge University Press, 2002).

Woudhuysen, H. R. *Sir Philip Sidney and the Circulation of Manuscripts 1558–1640* (Oxford: Clarendon Press, 1996).

Zagorin, Perez. 'Hobbes without Grotius', *History of Political Thought* 21 (2000), pp. 16–40.

Zaller, Robert. 'The Figure of the Tyrant in English Revolutionary Thought', *Journal of the History of Ideas* 54 (1993), pp. 585–610.

Zamoscus, Johannes. *De Senatu Romano* (Strasbourg, 1607).

Zouche, Richard. *Iuris et Iudicii Faecialis, sive, Iuris Inter Gentes* (Oxford, 1650).

Zuckert, Michael P. 'Appropriation and Understanding in the History of Political Philosophy: on Quentin Skinner's Method', *Interpretation* 13 (1985), pp. 403–24.

Index

www.ingramcontent.com/pod-product-compliance
Ingram Content Group UK Ltd.
Pitfield, Milton Keynes, MK11 3LW, UK
UKHW020451010325
455719UK00015B/527